THE SCHOLARSHIP OF
TEACHING AND LEARNING
IN HIGHER EDUCATION
Contributions of Research Universities

The Scholarship of Teaching and Learning in Higher Education

Contributions of Research Universities

Edited by
William E. Becker
and
Moya L. Andrews

INDIANA UNIVERSITY PRESS

Bloomington and Indianapolis

This book is a publication of

Indiana University Press
601 North Morton Street
Bloomington, IN 47404-3797 USA

http://iupress.indiana.edu

Telephone orders   800-842-6796
Fax orders   812-855-7931
Orders by e-mail   iuporder@indiana.edu

Library of Congress Cataloging-in-Publication Data

The scholarship of teaching and learning in higher education : contributions of research universities / edited by William E. Becker and Moya L. Andrews.
    p. cm.
Includes bibliographical references and index.
ISBN 0-253-34424-7 (cloth : alk. paper)
1. Education, Higher—Research—United States. 2. Indiana University. Scholarship of Teaching and Learning Program. I. Becker, William E. II. Andrews, Moya L.
LB2326.3.S37 2004
378.1'2—dc22

2003021671

1 2 3 4 5   09 08 07 06 05 04

Contents

Contents

vi

Figures and Tables

Figures

vii

Tables

Figures and Tables

Contributors

Moya L. Andrews, Professor of Speech and Hearing Sciences; Vice Chancellor for Academic Affairs; and Dean of the Faculties, Indiana University

Lei Bao, Assistant Professor of Physics, The Ohio State University

William E. Becker, Professor of Economics, Indiana University; Editor, *Journal of Economic Education;* Editor, *Economic Research Network Educator;* and Adjunct Professor, School of International Business, University of South Australia

Claude Cookman, Associate Professor of Journalism, Indiana University

Laura Fingerson, Assistant Professor of Sociology, University of Wisconsin, Milwaukee

Marc Frantz, Research Associate in Mathematics, Indiana University

William H. Greene, Professor of Economics; and Faculty Fellow in Entertainment, Media and Technology, Stern School of Business, New York University

Kathryn Gold Hadley, Advanced Graduate Student in Sociology, Indiana University

George D. Kuh, Chancellor's Professor of Higher Education, School of Education, Indiana University; and Director, National Survey of Student Engagement, Center for Postsecondary Research

Jeni Loftus, Advanced Graduate Student in Sociology, Indiana University

Janice McCabe, Advanced Graduate Student in Sociology, Indiana University

Daniel P. Maki, Professor of Mathematics; and Chairperson, Department of Mathematics, Indiana University

Paul Ruggerio Namaste, Advanced Graduate Student in Sociology, Indiana University

Craig E. Nelson, Professor of Biology; and Adjunct Professor, Public and Environmental Affairs, Indiana University

Contributors

Bart S. Ng, Professor of Mathematical Sciences, Indiana University–Purdue University Indianapolis

Bernice Ann Pescosolido, Chancellor's Professor of Sociology; and Co-Director of the Preparing Future Faculty Program, Indiana University

Brian Powell, Allen D. and Polly S. Grimshaw Professor of Sociology, Indiana University

Edward F. Redish, Professor of Physics, University of Maryland

Stacy Scherr, Advanced Graduate Student in Sociology, Indiana University

Jeanne Sept, Professor of Anthropology; and Chairperson, Department of Anthropology, Indiana University

Lee S. Shulman, Charles E. Ducommun Professor Emeritus of Education, Stanford University; and President, The Carnegie Foundation for the Advancement of Teaching

Jenny Stuber, Advanced Graduate Student in Sociology, Indiana University

Acknowledgments

The topics covered in the twelve chapters of this volume were drawn from the wider diversity of topics discussed in seminars, workshops and colloquia conducted as part of the Scholarship of Teaching and Learning program at Indiana University Bloomington between 1999 and 2003. These chapter authors are mostly tenured faculty members at Indiana University but many others are from similar types of institutions that emphasize both research and teaching. We are indebted to these scholars who prepared original manuscripts for this volume. In addition to the contribution of these chapter authors, this book was made possible through the combined efforts of many others whom we gratefully acknowledge.

First, and most important, is Suzanne Becker. Sue is assistant editor of the *Journal of Economic Education*, which has its editorial office in the Department of Economics, College of Arts and Sciences, at Indiana University Bloomington. The authors of each of the chapters in this book have benefited from Sue's eye for detail and editorial forte. From the start to the completion of this project, Sue has been our editorial overseer. Reading behind Sue at Indiana University Press was Marvin Keenan, who together with the other production staff at IU Press ensured that this volume was of the highest quality. We are most appreciative.

In the offices of the *Journal of Economic Education*, the Dean of Faculties and IU Press respectively, Janet Tippin, Cyndi Connelley, and Linda Oblack deserve thanks for skilfully managing the flow of manuscripts, reviews, and chapters. Ray Smith, Mike Nelson, and the staff in

Acknowledgments

IUB's graphic art group also deserve thanks for arranging and providing the final camera-ready figures in this book. Kate Whitsett, IU Department of Economics, and Kate Moscrop, University of South Australia, are also thanked for providing word processing assistance.

Finally, we thank the scholars who reviewed each of the chapters in this book:

Larry A. Braskamp	Loyola University Chicago
Margaret W. Conkey	University of California Berkeley
Lee Gass	University of British Columbia
Ken Kobre	San Francisco State University
Joe Law	Wright State University
Robert Mislevy	University of Maryland
Helen A. Moore	University of Nebraska–Lincoln
Jeffrey S. Simonoff	New York University
Frances King Stage	New York University
Myra Strober	Stanford University
Robert Toutkoushian	University System of New Hampshire
Brian J. Winkel	United States Military Academy

Their insightful feedback on chapter drafts strengthened the book in significant ways.

William E. Becker
Moya L. Andrews

THE SCHOLARSHIP OF
TEACHING AND LEARNING
IN HIGHER EDUCATION

Contributions of Research Universities

Introduction

William E. Becker

Moya L. Andrews

This book illustrates the often-overlooked contributions that research universities make to pedagogical advances in higher education. It provides examples of a few of the many ways in which full-time, tenured or tenure-track faculty members at research universities advance teaching and learning of undergraduates by applying their research skills in their classrooms, laboratories and individualized work with students. The various chapters highlight: 1) a variety of models of the scholarship of teaching and learning at research universities; 2) the influence of discipline-based research on teaching, leading to more meaningful student activities; 3) advancements in the assessment of student outcomes through research; and 4) the dissemination of ideas about teaching and learning across disciplines and institutions. This book itself is a testament to the role of research universities in disseminating ideas about teaching through their own presses.

The material compiled in the book is the result of a four-year program at Indiana University in which faculty members from Indiana University as well as from several other research universities presented their work on the IU Bloomington campus in seminars and colloquia on the scholarship of teaching and learning. The authors contributing to this book were selected as a subset of the many scholars who made presentations on the Bloomington campus between 1999 and 2003.

This book is in part intended as a response to the assertions that both personal and institutional rewards for tenure-track and tenured faculty at research universities favor research at the expense of teaching. After all, the argument goes, every additional minute spent on teaching is one less minute available for research, which is critical to institutional prestige. But this assertion, as we show in this book, misses the complementarities in the production of academic outcomes that are inherent in scholarly pursuits. Reallocating a minute from research to teaching (or teaching to research) can actually often improve the teaching (research) product and be a transforming experience for researcher/teachers and learners as well. The assertion also involves a misunderstanding of what constitutes prestige in higher education.

The Carnegie Foundation for the Advancement of Teaching began classifying postsecondary institutions of education according to their primary functions in the early 1970s (Table I.1). Until 2000, it differentiated research universities from other doctoral degree-granting universities in the United States on the basis of their faculties' abilities to fund scholarly inquiry with government grants. The student orientation of baccalaureate degree-granting liberal arts colleges was eschewed by those who saw the Carnegie Foundation's classification as a prestige ladder rather than a functional classification method. Competition for funds led other doctoral degree-granting institutions to use their own resources to subsidize research. Between 1970 and 2000, for example, the proportion of research and development expenditures financed by individual-institution resources increased from 10 percent to 20 percent while external state and federal support fell (Table I.2).

Research is expensive. Thus, public community colleges with no research mission have thrived under the belief that a faculty devoted to research is not essential to performing the less expensive teaching function. The number of publicly supported community colleges (which offer a 2-year associate degree) increased dramatically from 1,063 in 1970 to 1,669 in 2000 while the number of liberal arts colleges fell from 721 in 1970 to 606 in 2000 (Table I.1). Today, over 50 percent of postsecondary institutions are community colleges. They carry the weight of entry-level tertiary education with faculties that are 76 percent part-time or full-time with nontenure-track appointments (Table I.3).

In recognition of the changing structure of the postsecondary education environment in the United States, the Carnegie Foundation set in motion a plan for changing its method of classifying institutions. The first step was the elimination of the sought-after "research university" label in the 2000 listing; the second phase involves the reworking of all categories by 2005. Unspoken in this reorganization of postsecondary education is the effect on innovations in teaching, educational assessment, and dissemination of ideas on the forefront of knowledge that emanate from faculties of the traditional research universities. A type of Gresham's law (inferior currency drives out superior currency) might

Table I.1. Classification of Postsecondary Educational Institutions

	1970		1976		1987		1994		2000	
	No.	Percent of Total	No.	Percent of Total	No.	Percent of Total	No.	Percent of Total	No.	Percent of Total
Doctoral/Research	173	7.2	184	7.3	213	7.8	236	8.2	261	8.3
Research	92	3.8	98	3.9	104	3.8	125	4.4	n.r.	n.r.
Doctorate	81	3.4	86	3.4	109	4.0	111	3.9	n.r.	n.r.
Masters	456	18.9	594	23.7	595	21.7	529	18.4	611	19.4
Baccalaureate	721	29.9	583	23.3	572	20.8	637	22.2	606	19.3
Associate (2–year)	1063	44.1	1146	45.7	1367	49.8	1471	51.2	1669	53.0
Total	2413		2507		2747		2873		3147	

Note: n.r. is not relevant because of a change in category definitions in 2000.

Data sources: Carnegie Foundation for the Advancement of Teaching, *A Classification of Institutions of Higher Education*. Various editions.

Table I.2. R&D Expenditures at Universities and Colleges, by Source of Funds

Fiscal Year	Total in Millions of Dollars	Federal Government	State and Local Government	Private Industry	Institutional Funds	All Other Sources
1970	2,335	1,647	219	61	243	165
Percent of Total		70.5	9.4	2.6	10.4	7.1
1980	6,063	4,098	491	236	835	403
Percent of Total		67.6	8.1	3.9	13.8	6.6
1990	16,286	9,638	1,324	1,127	3,006	1,191
Percent of Total		59.2	8.1	6.9	18.5	7.3
1999	27,505	16,071	2,019	2,028	5,395	1,992
Percent of Total		58.4	7.3	7.4	19.6	7.2
2000	30,042	17,508	2,196	2,152	5,933	2,253
Percent of Total		58.3	7.3	7.2	19.7	7.5
2001	32,723	19,191	2,315	2,234	6,553	2,430
Percent of Total		58.6	7.1	6.8	20.0	7.4

Data source: National Science Foundation, *Survey of Scientific and Engineering Expenditures at Universities and Colleges*. Selected years.

Table I.3. Faculty Academic Rank by Type of Institution

	Percentage Full-Time Tenured or Tenure-Track		Percentage Part-Time or Nontenure-Track Full-Time	
	1992	1998	1992	1998
Public Research	63.5	57.6	36.4	42.5
Public Doctoral*	53.9	49.6	46.1	50.5
Public Masters	56.1	51.8	43.9	48.1
Public Associate (2-yr.)	26.3	24.3	73.8	75.7
Private Research	40.5	45.6	59.6	54.4
Private Doctoral*	42.9	31.9	57.1	68.1
Private Masters	39.8	33.9	60.1	66.1
Private Baccalaureate	46.8	37.8	53.2	62.2
All institutions	41.0	38.0	59	62

* Includes medical schools.
Data source: American Council on Education and U.S. Department of Education, *National Study of Postsecondary Faculty*, 1993 and 1999.

suggest that the less expensive educational practices of public community colleges will force out the more expensive full-time, tenured faculty members teaching at the research universities. In fact, there is evidence of this happening. Between 1992 and 1998, both public research and doctoral institutions increased the proportions of both part-time and full-time faculty members with nontenure-track appointments (Table I.3). Following the community college model, universities are increasingly looking to part-time and nontenure-track docent-type appointments to teach in undergraduate baccalaureate programs.

The range of activities included in the chapters in this book demonstrates that full-time, tenured or tenure-track faculty members at research universities are deeply concerned about teaching. Their programs of discipline-based inquiry enhance undergraduate student learning in ways that are highly unlikely without an up-to-date research agenda. In Chapter 1, for example, Carnegie Foundation president and former Stanford University professor Lee Shulman discusses his vision of a university that places investigation at the center of its purpose and existence, and that supports its faculties not only in traditional disciplinary research, but also in research-based teaching and student learning activities within their disciplines. Shulman presents several models of how a research-oriented university can support, preserve, and enhance its faculties' work in the scholarship of teaching and learning. He describes four different models: interdisciplinary centers (similar to Women's Studies or Area Study Centers), graduate-level academies in the scholarship of teaching and learning (focusing heavily on doctoral students and their mentors), technology-based centers for instruction, and department-level units supported by central university funding.

The next six chapters demonstrate how the discipline-based research of faculty members influences their teaching and results in more meaningful student activities. Photographic historian Claude Cookman describes how he uses his own research in the Paris archives of the renowned photographer Henri Cartier-Bresson as a model to teach his History of 20th Century Photography course at Indiana University Bloomington. Drawing on the IUB research libraries' and museums' extensive photography collections, his students learn to situate their topics in historical and biographical contexts that enrich the images' meanings. Archaeologist Jeanne Sept discusses the strengths and weaknesses of three different approaches she has employed to engage undergraduates in interpreting the Stone Age of Africa using the tools of the Information Age: independent student research projects using a case study developed on a CD-ROM; collaborative student research projects using an original database and digital learning environment developed for the Internet; and a multimedia-authoring class focused on the presentation of alternative archaeological interpretations developed through student research projects. In contrast to the popular image of the research university's large lecture halls, Moya Andrews focuses attention on the individualized clinical teaching and learning activities in the allied health discipline of Speech and Hearing Sciences. William Becker and William Greene describe how they advance the use of computer technology in the teaching of quantitative methods aimed at the analyses of social science issues found in the news media and research literature. Biologist Craig Nelson reports on how his inquiry into an environmental issue led him to a refined understanding of how to advance the learning of his undergraduate students. At the close of this section, Bernice Pescosolido and her collaborators in sociology describe a university-wide effort to provide at-risk, entering first-year undergraduates with an intellectually exciting and socially engaging introduction to college life.

Chapters 8 through 11 provide examples of how university researchers are advancing the assessment of student outcomes. George Kuh describes how measurement instruments developed at research universities are being used, from community colleges to the most elite research universities, to assess institutional efforts with undergraduates. He provides explicit examples of the ways in which data from the Indiana University-based National Survey of Student Engagement (NSSE) are now used by all types of postsecondary institutions to gain an understanding of their students' performance vis-à-vis peer institutions. Janice McCabe and Brian Powell address grades, which provide the most basic of student outcomes. Their qualitative research demonstrates the difficulty in trying to change perceived or actual grade inflation because instructors attribute the problem to others but not to themselves or their own grading practices. Lei Bao and Edward Redish look at exams as a measure of student attainment. They ask: "What can we learn and what should we do when we find students giving inconsistent responses on test questions?" To answer these questions, they introduce a new quantitative method based on the principles of physics that works with multiple-choice questions, gives insight into students' conceptual states, and provides direction for instructional interventions. William Becker closes this section by calling attention to the difference between statistical inference and theoretical conjecture about student outcomes associated with alternative teaching strategies aimed at engaging students actively in the learning process. He draws on his own research to advance specific criteria for both conducting and exploring the strength of quantitative research into the teaching and learning process. Examples from the education literature on the teaching and learning process are also used to identify strategies that appear to increase student learning.

The final chapter in this book demonstrates how the research university's size and diversity may enhance the dissemination of ideas about teaching and learning across disciplines and among institutions. Daniel Maki, Marc Frantz and Bart Ng describe the goals, methods, and materials of their "Mathematics Throughout the Curriculum" project that has been supported by a large grant from the National Science Foundation to Indiana University. They provide specific examples of how faculty members from a wide array of disciplines and across multiple campuses have instilled mathematics into their courses and disseminated their efforts as part of an orchestrated effort to increase undergraduate skills in mathematical reasoning.

Our ability to illustrate the scope and diversity of the ways in which research universities contribute to the scholarship of teaching and learning was limited by page constraints. We hope, however, that the examples we provide are sufficient to show that higher education involves much more than the teaching of accepted doctrine. It is the academic inquiry that elevates higher education above mere training. At a research university teaching is actually enhanced because it can be made a part of an integrated and aggressive campaign of inquiry and scholarship.

Active researchers can engage students in the challenging ideas, questions and methods of inquiry at the forefront of their disciplines, whereas docents can be expected only to teach that which they have been taught or learned from textbooks. Teaching and learning are contextually based activities and in the context of a research university, where scholarship and not only teaching dominates, researchers teaching undergraduates can contribute markedly to activities such as student engagement, assessment of learning outcomes, the development of critical thinking and the testing of conceptual organizational schema. Our experiences in the early years of the Scholarship of Teaching and Learning (SOTL) program at Indiana University convinced us that academic researchers are especially adept at applying their discipline-based skills to pedagogical issues. We trust that the examples in this book will likewise convince the reader.

One

Visions of the Possible
Models for Campus Support of the
Scholarship of Teaching and Learning

Lee S. Shulman

Higher education confronts a venerable problem. In 1906—the same year the Carnegie Foundation for the Advancement of Teaching received its congressional charter—the Association of American Universities (then a simple group of fifteen public and private institutions) met in the San Francisco Bay Area, devoting one whole day of its discussions to the question: Should professors at research universities be required to teach? Just one month later, San Francisco experienced its legendary earthquake. Although it's unlikely that the two events were related, institutions of higher learning are today still trying to put the pieces of teaching and research back together, and continue to ask how teaching can find a right and dignified place in the research university setting.

In response to this question, I was inspired to spin out several visions of how things might look in higher education if campuses created organizational entities to support, preserve and enhance the scholarly work of teaching and learning. I will refer to these campus entities as "teaching academies," and I think of them as a combination of support structures and sanctuaries, that is, places where faculty whose scholarly interests include teaching and learning can find safety, support and even colleagueship for doing good work on the pedagogies of their fields. Within this general vision, I propose four possible models: the interdisciplinary center, the graduate education academy, the center for technology, and the distributed academy.

9

Model I: The Teaching Academy as an
Interdisciplinary Center

The first model is an interdisciplinary one. It draws together faculty members whose scholarly interests include teaching and learning but who may not find a sufficient group of colleagues for this work within their own academic departments or professional schools. The idea behind this model is to overcome faculty intellectual isolation by creating a new, multidisciplinary community of shared interests and work.

Think, in this regard, of women's studies centers, and how such centers provide an intellectual home for scholars from a variety of fields—history, economics, literature, among others—and make possible important new work and the development of a new field. Historically, such centers enabled scholars to engage with important issues, to build knowledge and to create new outlets for their work. *Signs: Journal of Women in Culture and Society,* for instance, developed out of the women's studies center at Stanford University and has become the primary scholarly journal in the field. At first, these centers had a shaky existence (publication in *Signs* was not held in high regard in its early days), but over time more stable, secure interdisciplinary entities evolved. Stanford now houses and fully supports the Institute for Research on Women and Gender, in part because the work done in centers such as this became more and more legitimate in the same departmental and professional school homes from which pioneering scholars had originally migrated in order to find more hospitable settings.

This kind of evolution is desirable for centers dedicated to the scholarship of teaching and learning, as well. In the best cases, scholars retain dual citizenship in both the disciplinary department and the interdisciplinary center—and I hope this would also be the case for faculty members affiliated with centers for the scholarship of teaching and learning in addition to their disciplinary units. Indeed, there may well come a time when the centers themselves disappear as their work becomes so fully integrated within the discipline or interdiscipline that a separate unit is no longer needed.

I am reminded of area studies and their centers for, say, African or Asian studies, which emerged a couple of decades ago. Philanthropic organizations, by the way, such as the Ford Foundation and the Carnegie Corporation of New York, played an extremely important role in helping to develop area studies. Here, again, was a phenomenon where in any given department there was likely to be only a single Africanist or East Asia specialist. But if these solitary scholars could develop an appropriate Area Studies Center, they could gather together a dozen or more faculty members on the campus from departments as diverse as English and Genetics, along with graduate students, and establish a certain intellectual critical mass for their work. A person remained both an historian (or geologist) and an Africa scholar. Happily, universities and foundations found reasons jointly to support these efforts, which have in turn influenced the work and shape of many fields.

It should be said in reference to this first model that interdisciplinary structures entail both strengths and potential weaknesses. Cuban (1999) completed a study, entitled *How Scholars Trumped Teachers*, about teaching and research over the last 100 years at Stanford University, and one theme is that, at Stanford, interdisciplinary entities were far more likely to innovate in their teaching and curriculum than were the entities located in a single disciplinary department. Why does this happen? Many departments treat teaching the same way they treat research; no one would dream of telling a departmental colleague what she should investigate in her research, and neither would one dream of telling her what or how she should teach. Most departments in most research universities support a conception of academic freedom in which all aspects of a faculty member's intellectual work are fully under her or his control. Curricula thus reflect the tastes of faculty members, rather than a more superordinate conception of what and how students in the field might best learn. But, as Cuban shows, when faculty members move to an interdisciplinary center, they leave behind some of these predispositions; in making an active choice to join such a center, they are choosing to do something new. At Stanford one such example is the human biology curriculum, which cuts across several schools and many departments, and which allows new and different work, both in the research that faculty members conduct and in their teaching and curriculum development. I would infer that the same kind of increased openness and flexibility would pertain to matters of scholarship, as well.

The handicap of such interdisciplinary programs is that the traditional department remains the structure for faculty reward—one can't get tenure in women's studies or area studies or human biology, but only in economics or history or biology. I'm not unhappy about that; centers and institutes are intended to be more flexible and adaptive than their more conservative departmental godparents. But we must recognize that an essential tension exists between these two structures, between the program of a center and the disciplinary focus of a department, a tension that would have to be explored if teaching academies were modeled after such centers. The advantages of flexibility and adventurousness of mission are clear. Nevertheless, it is a serious source of worry that the department's research emphasis would always trump the center's action-oriented investigations whenever crises—whether of budget or of political mission—are encountered. It is worrisome because the university must find ways to balance and trade off the legitimate competing demands of teaching and research in the life of the institution and its faculty members. Absent more creative approaches, departments will always be reactionary bodies in the world of higher education, ultimately stifling not only teaching innovations but also more adventurous research initiatives.

On the other hand, as interdisciplinary inquiry of all kinds increasingly becomes the norm for many fields in the Humanities and Sciences (as is already the case in many professional schools), the structural tensions between the disciplinary home and the research workplace will not be unique to the scholarship of teaching and learning. In any event, the notion of an interdisciplinary teaching academy somewhat patterned after earlier models in women's studies, or area studies, or other such entities, is one model for the teaching academy. And if this model makes sense, it might also make sense for someone to ask, "What in my university setting are the two best examples of new entities that were invented in this fashion and had a certain persistence over time, that have gained credibility and support both internally and externally, and that remain viable centers for important scholarly work? And why have these entities survived, when a dozen others have come and gone?" The answer to that question should reveal something about the most promising form for an interdisciplinary teaching academy for a particular campus.

Model II: The Teaching Academy as an Aspect of Graduate Education

My thoughts about this second model were stimulated by a visit to Princeton University in early 2001, where a deliberate decision was made to locate the teaching academy within the graduate school. The idea was to focus any first efforts on an aspect of work that is already central to the research university culture: preparing doctoral students for their responsibilities as scholars. This model of joining the work of a teaching academy with the mission of the graduate school can build on developments in the Preparing Future Faculty project (sponsored by the Association of American Colleges and Universities and the Council of Graduate Schools and funded by The Pew Charitable Trusts). The emphasis of a teaching academy would build especially on the notion that institutions need to go beyond "TA training" to address in a much more proactive way the need to prepare graduate students for the full range of academic activities associated with each discipline or professional field, including the scholarship of teaching and learning. An assumption behind this model—and some will find this an odd way to put it—is that the Ph.D. is, after all, a professional degree.

Those at the Carnegie Foundation for the Advancement of Teaching think of Ph.D. students as future "stewards" of their disciplines. That phrase implies that doctoral students are expected to assume several roles: 1) generating new knowledge in the discipline, or the more traditionally conceived role of researcher; 2) critiquing and conserving the knowledge that already exists through processes of review, publication, and selective doctoral education, as well as by deeply understanding the history and foundation of the discipline; and 3) transforming their own knowledge into communication and representation that will bring new understandings to their colleagues, to students of the discipline, to students in general, and to the greater society. The latter role can be seen as the teaching component of the doctorate, and it is there that the most natural connection with the goals of a teaching academy occurs. What better way to integrate teaching and scholarship than at this level, where Ph.D. students are already experimenting and innovating with their knowledge, where they are already creating ways of sharing their work with others, where new work is already being done, and all under the guidance of faculty? By involving doctoral students more directly with the scholarship of teaching and learning at the very beginning of their understanding of what it means to be a faculty member, we may create scholars who learn early on how to elegantly integrate their teaching with their research. And we also affect and involve in the process those faculty members who mentor and advise these doctoral students.

This brings me to the idea that another benefit of linking the teaching academy to graduate education is that the focus is not directly on faculty as the target population. Some might see this as a limitation, but campuses that move in the direction of this second model understand that one cannot reshape graduate education without involving faculty as mentors and models. Indeed, engaging faculty through work with graduate students might be seen as part of the "theory of action" behind this second model. It's a very useful way to think about how to start work on the scholarship of teaching, especially in institutions where research and scholarship of traditional kinds have taken precedence over teaching.

From an historical perspective, it's interesting to recall that this kind of connection between graduate and undergraduate education was explicitly advocated by such university leaders as Robert Maynard Hutchins of the University of Chicago. He took a rather extreme view of this connection, arguing that the undergraduate college should be viewed as a combination of pedagogical research laboratory and laboratory school for doctoral education, which was, after all, primarily teacher education for the postsecondary sector (McNeill 1991). Although I would certainly take a different view of the proper relationship between the missions of undergraduate and graduate education, his insight is worth preserving. Much like the teaching hospital of a medical school, whose dual purpose is both to heal and to educate the next generation of professionals, so undergraduate education must serve as both a setting for responsible innovation and experimentation, as well as a site for the carefully mentored and scaffolded professional education of professors. Such a commitment by graduate education would go a long way toward alleviating the justifiable complaints of doctoral students that their future vocations as educators receive far less attention from their mentors than do their future vocations as investigators. Moreover, it would also extend the proper venues of research from their traditional domains to the field of teaching and learning in one's discipline or profession.

Model III: The Teaching Academy
Organized around Technology

The impetus for this third model is much in evidence on many campuses today and will surely grow in the next decade. My vision is of a teaching academy whose reason for existence is connected to rapid developments in the use of technology in higher education. Whether you like it or hate it, technology presents a remarkable opening for the scholarship of teaching and learning. Many faculty members are asking serious questions about the role of technology in teaching and learning, such as how one knows whether these new technologies are effective in fostering student learning, and under what conditions. Furthermore, faculty members wonder what the difference is between the kind of learning that occurs in traditional venues and the kind that occurs in technologically mediated settings. So, the first advantage of this technology-oriented model of the teaching academy is that it builds on the fact that just about everybody agrees that teaching, learning and technology pose serious research questions that need to be addressed. Most universities have already committed significant resources to the uses of technology, and because technology is not something one simply plugs into the curriculum, such research questions spawn a much larger set of inquiries about curriculum, design of instruction, and assessment, thereby encouraging a more general spirit of inquiry about teaching and learning.

There is a second advantage, as well. As noted in much of the literature related to the Carnegie Academy for the Scholarship of Teaching and Learning, to call something "scholarship" is to claim that it is public rather than private, that it is susceptible to peer review and criticism, and that it is something that can be built upon by others. Technology, in much of pedagogy, has made the private public—through course websites, postings of syllabi online, and electronic resources such as the Crossroads Project. Randy Bass, a faculty member from Georgetown University, developed the Crossroads Project for the American Studies Association (and American Studies is, perhaps not coincidentally, an interdisciplinary field). On Randy's site, one can see syllabi from American Studies courses around the country and also read annotations of these syllabi, both by the people who created them and by others who bring relevant experience as reviewers. One can read case studies by faculty members whose syllabi are posted, in which they report on challenges in using technology to redesign courses they had been teaching for years (Bass 2003). My point is that resources such as Crossroads have moved faculties a good distance toward a public and exchangeable discourse about teaching and learning—which is a key ingredient in transforming *conversations* about teaching and learning into a *scholarship* of teaching and learning, which occupies a central role in a discipline or interdiscipline.

The other healthy, albeit frightening, thing about technology is that it represents a substantial investment for institutions. Therefore, asking about teaching in these new ways without asking about evidence for learning becomes increasingly difficult, though onlookers rarely make this demand of more conventional teaching. Those involved in the *scholarship of teaching* are at least as concerned about the *scholarship of learning*. It's hard for me to imagine a viable scholarship of teaching that does not ask about learning in general, and about the particular kind and quality of learning that occurs in the presence of, say, a new technology.

A serious legal and ethical problem develops when the distinctions between teaching and research are intentionally blurred, and this problem has already begun to vex the current generation of scholars of teaching. As long as teachers collected and examined data on student learning solely to evaluate and grade their students and to guide their own teaching, there was no question that teachers were fully entitled to gather and analyze that information. However, once teachers make the claim that they have an obligation to investigate the character of their own teaching and their students' learning, some would argue that the activity shifts from the category of instruction to that of research. Moreover, when teachers argue that the results of such investigations— like any other scholarly endeavor—must be made public, reviewed and built upon by professional peers, the concern over "the study of human subjects" increases.

I strongly propose that institutions must make a clear distinction between the kinds of scholarly work that are embedded in acts of teaching and learning and those that are engaged for purely research purposes. As long as students are clearly placed at no greater risk by the research than they would be in a teaching situation alone, there should be no need for engaging with the kinds of serious human subjects reviews designed for medical or basic social science research. These and other ethical issues associated with the scholarship of teaching and learning are discussed extensively in Hutchings (2002).

I would also point out that it is perfectly possible—as those of us in the field of psychology can attest—to spend generations studying learning without making any reference to teaching at all. A few years ago, I gave the Howard Bowen Lecture at Claremont Graduate University. Bowen (1977) was an eminent economist of higher education who wrote a wonderful book, *Investment in Learning.* In preparing my talk, I looked up "learning" in the index of this book and found scores of entries; when I looked up "teaching," I found a single entry saying "*see* learning." And so I argue that there is a reason to keep both teaching *and* learning explicitly in the picture, because a focus on teaching will necessarily include learning, but the reverse is not always true. Adding technology as the third component and creating teaching academies at the intersection of teaching, learning and technology may be just the right strategy at this point in time. I see lots of evidence that technology in this next decade may turn out to be the hardest-hitting and fastest-developing context for the creation and work of teaching academies.

Model IV: The Distributed
Teaching Academy

My fourth example is what I call a distributed academy. I met with Rebecca Chopp, now president of Colgate University, just after she had been appointed provost at Emory. Rebecca had previously chaired Emory's all-university committee on teaching, and her punishment was to be named provost. She told me that on her campus (and no doubt on many others), centralized offices are distrusted, and that the challenge was, therefore, to figure out how the provost's office could provide centralized support for teaching while locating the efforts in programs, schools, or departments. It's a bit like the environmental movement's old mantra of "think globally and act locally," but in this case it's "fund and support institutionally but act departmentally." The insight I gained is that one possibility for a teaching academy is that the university doesn't create an entity; rather, it builds capacity in various quarters where the work can best be done. These more local efforts, in turn, support initiatives that may grow into sources of strength for the whole institution.

This distributed model reflects the reality that on many campuses we find some departments or schools that already have extraordinary potential for doing the scholarly work of teaching and learning. People at Stanford, for instance, ask me where they can find the best examples of research in education, and I will (although education is my field) often direct them to the department of mechanical engineering, where Sheri Sheppard, Larry Leifer and their colleagues have been doing excellent research on the teaching and learning of design in engineering—research that meets all the standards of traditional forms of scholarship.

Similarly, when I was a professor of educational psychology and medical education at Michigan State University, one of my homes was an academic department called the Office of Medical Education, Research, and Development (OMERAD). My colleagues and I, who were drawn from medicine, education, sociology, nursing, and other fields, did what might be considered clinical or applied work as we invented a new medical school: curriculum development, evaluation design, the preparation of faculty to teach in the program, etc. But at the same time, Arthur Elstein and I were doing fundamental research on the psychology of medical decision-making and diagnosis, work that had an impact on cognitive psychology as well as on medical education. The departmental unit thus served other units of the university and the field as it developed capacity.

I note these examples to make two points. First, we need critical mass. The kind of work I'm pointing to could not be done by just one person in engineering or in medical education; the program must have the resources to establish a *community* of scholars. My second point is sort of the flip side of this argument: it's legitimate to undertake this kind of work in selected programs rather than across the board institutionally. I say this because scholars often feel that whatever they initiate has to be available equally to everybody. On the contrary, I would claim that insisting from the outset that the scholarship of teaching and learning must be done across the board is a formula for failure. Especially in these early years of the movement, it may make perfectly good sense to shape an approach that does not presume to be "institutionalized" in the usual sense of the word, but that takes advantage of generative pockets of interest and potential. There is, after all, good reason why "panacea," the word for a universal cure, has become a term of derision. These local centers of strength in the scholarship of teaching and learning should be supported institutionally, for they can contribute both to building the field and ultimately can seed a broader set of initiatives within the institution.

Other Possibilities

These, then, are four "visions of the possible" for supporting and advancing the scholarship of teaching and learning: the interdisciplinary academy for teaching and learning, the academy focused on preparing graduate students, the technology-centered academy, and the distributed academy. I'm sure there are many more. Indeed, one can easily imagine useful cross-fertilizations among the four. At Brown, for instance, the Harriet Sheridan Center might on the one hand be seen as an example of the first model—an academy that brings together faculty across fields to do work in common. But the Sheridan Center also works extensively with graduate students. Indeed, when I was at Brown for the Center's inauguration (it had been around for some time but was being rededicated in the name of the late and much-beloved dean, Harriet Sheridan), I saw Randy Bass, who had just established the new center at Georgetown based on the third model mentioned above. When I asked Randy what brought him to the event, he told me that he had been a graduate student at Brown and had developed his interests by working extensively through the Center on issues of teaching and learning in his field.

The point here is that the Carnegie Foundation and the American Association for Higher Education (the Carnegie Academy for the Scholarship of Teaching and Learning's partner in working with campuses) have absolutely no desire to propose a single canonical form for teaching academies. Indeed, when we imagine a network of CASTL teaching academies, we don't want them to look like identical siblings. Higher education will be much better off with lots of Darwinian variation, with the academies (and whatever other names these entities adopt) responding in different ways to local contingencies and circumstances, with them representing different theories of how this work might go forward.

One question about local circumstances is the extent to which the teaching academy (perhaps especially the interdisciplinary model) should be a broadening and elaboration of the functions of a center for teaching and learning that might already exist on campus. Opinions on this differ greatly. Some say that linking a teaching academy to such a center won't work because too many centers are seen as emergency rooms for teachers in pedagogic arrest, as it were—whereas the core idea of a proper teaching academy is as a place for scholarly work. But others say that their center for teaching is already moving in the direction of fostering inquiry and intellectual colleagueship around teaching and learning, and that the teaching academy is a further embodiment of an existing vision. What I would say is that these are local questions requiring local judgments, and that where a center's central purposes are technical assistance and faculty development—important as those are—that center is not a teaching academy in the sense I am here describing.

Teaching Academies as Foundations for Scholarly Communities

The importance of work that has the capacity to be more than local must be emphasized. Indeed, scholarship is by definition more than local, and if teaching academies are to contribute to a real scholarship of teaching and learning, then they cannot work in isolation; they must be connected, in communication, building on one another's work. How might this happen?

One answer is faculty exchanges. Tom Banchoff, who is a Brown University faculty member in mathematics, CASTL Carnegie Scholar, and former president of the Mathematical Association of America, recently spent a semester at Yale University to pursue his scholarship of teaching in a new venue. He later devoted a semester to work at the University of Notre Dame. Might not research universities with teaching academies develop a system of faculty exchanges of this kind?

Another possibility is the residential fellowship. I think here of the Stanford Humanities Center, where half the fellowships go to faculty on the campus, and the other half to those from elsewhere, with both groups selected through a competitive process. The Stanford center only invites fellows who do traditional scholarship, but this is just the kind of arrangement that teaching academies might sponsor. Indeed, fundraising to make this sort of thing possible would be a great task for presidents and provosts committed to the scholarship of teaching and learning.

And the last possibility I'll mention for connecting and broadening efforts entails documentation. The work done in and through teaching academies will be truly useful and consequential if it leaves behind an artifact or product that others can learn from and build on. Now, it happens that higher education is very good at preserving what we learn; think of libraries, museums, and laboratories, and the conventions established over decades whereby scholars learn (in different ways in different fields) to document, compress, organize and display their work to one another. (I say "compress" because although a study may take several years, it cannot take as long for others to understand and learn from that study.) The Carnegie Foundation has created the Knowledge Media Laboratory (KML) to facilitate these same kinds of knowledge-preserving artifacts for the scholarship of teaching and learning. We see the KML as an interactive museum or laboratory, as a library collection, or even as an investment bank where Carnegie Scholars doing the scholarship of teaching under our auspices will leave a "deposit" of their work, so that others can make "withdrawals." What I increasingly imagine is that campus-based teaching academies establish their own knowledge media laboratories, their own mechanisms for preserving, making available, and exchanging the scholarship of teaching and learning—and that these mechanisms would be linked in ways that maximize the impact of work being done in varied settings.

Other ways to link and connect campus-based activities and entities and teaching academies do, of course, exist and will, of course, be invented. Meanwhile, the next levels of work in the Carnegie Foundation's CASTL Campus Program are explicitly dedicated to promoting such links and networking, to ensure that teaching and scholarly work on teaching are not purely local activities. To that end, my colleagues are working with scholars across disciplines, institutions and educational sectors (e.g., community colleges, professional schools, K–12) to invent forms of documentation and communication that will do for the scholarship of teaching what the article, the monograph and the "letter" (as used in physics) have done for the traditional fields of study.

This is not to deny the importance and quality of the discipline-specific educational research journals that already exist and are already advancing the scholarly study of teaching and learning in their fields. Nevertheless, it is hard to deny that too often mainstream scholars in their disciplines marginalize these journals, however well they perform their functions. I envision a time when we witness the incorporation of scholarly contributions on the teaching and learning of the disciplines in general periodicals in those fields, as well as in the specialized education journals. These would then serve as a bridge between generalists (or specialists in other branches of a discipline) and specialists in teaching and learning.

Conclusion: The Intellectual and Moral Imperative

I want to conclude with a point that Pat Hutchings and I raised in a 1999 article in *Change:* Campuses need to reframe the demand for accountability in ways that meet their responsibilities as educational institutions (Hutchings and Shulman 1999). As things now stand, higher education's response to the increasing policy demand for accountability is mostly defensive and often cast in terms of efficiencies such as how many student credit hours to squeeze out of faculty members. But the institutions should be concerned with quality—particularly, the quality of what students come to understand, believe, and do. That is the kind of accountability to insist on, and scholars need to be able to conduct the scholarship that can help answer such questions in every discipline, as well as institutionally across programs. What do students who studied history at an institution now understand that they might not have understood without learning at that institution? What about those students in chemistry, management, or French? And what can an institution claim more generally about the skills, wisdom, and character of those whom it has educated?

These questions are not (and should not be) crisis-driven, no more than are those of traditional research. Scholars don't engage in traditional research because they failed when doing it before; they do it because they have done it well and now want to learn even more. Nor are they questions that can be taken up by offices of institutional research as they typically function; they cannot be asked from the top down. They can be facilitated, funded, encouraged, reported, and rewarded by the top, but the investigations must be conducted at the level of the individual school or program.

Teachers cannot be inhibited from designing their courses courageously and experimenting with their teaching creatively. Once those innovations are undertaken, there is a professional and ethical obligation to study their character, their efficacy, and both their intended and unintended consequences. Students in such situations are not human *subjects* in the traditional sense; they are partners and collaborators in the pedagogical enterprise. Instead of seeking more reasons for impeding such efforts, university and college administrators should be developing new mechanisms for facilitating and encouraging the scholarship of teaching while affording assurances that no serious excesses will be tolerated.

Here I propose a vision of the research university as an institution that puts investigation at the very center of its existence. (My inspiration is William Rainey Harper, the first president of the University of Chicago, though, no doubt, others have said similar things.) Being a research university means that everything is a proper subject of investigation, and that there can be no political correctness that designates certain questions out of bounds, least of all questions pertaining to the work of the institution itself. Harper held a vision of the research university as an institution that did not limit the objects of investigation to those matters outside of itself. Indeed, it was critical that a research university treat itself as a proper subject for investigation and its own work as an ongoing experiment for such investigation. The university must be constantly and critically asking about its own work, its own efficacy, its own role—vis-à-vis its students, its community and its society.

After Harper's tragic death at the age of 49, his Chicago colleague, the pioneering sociologist Albion Small, described Harper's image of the new university:

> His imagination had pictured the most important contribution that could be made to American education—a university which would be distinctive in its combination and emphasis of three things. The first was investigation. Every important subject within the possible realm of knowledge should be regarded as a field for research, so far as it presented scientific problems. Not least among the problems which the University should investigate was itself. It should never so far take itself for granted as to presume that its methods were final. Education, from nursery to laboratory, should be treated as a perpetual experiment, and methods should be changed to meet either new conditions or better insight into the conditions. The second trait of the University should be its active ambition for human service. Knowledge for general use, not for the culture of scholars, was the ideal. Scholarship should be promoted as zealously as though it were an end unto itself, but the final appraisal of scholarship should be, not its prestige with scholars, but its value to human life. The University should be, not a retreat from the world, but a base of operations in the world. The third distinctive trait should be accessibility. The University should have more ways of entrance than older institutions had provided, and it should have more direct channels of communicating the best it could give to the world. Besides attempting to reach these special ends, it should do its share of the conventional work of imparting knowledge by the best methods that had been discovered . . . (Wegener 1978, pp. 59–60)

This vision of the university is also the vision behind the scholarship of teaching and learning. The higher education community can hardly be a moral community with mission statements that talk about the central place of teaching and learning, if it is not also a place to investigate those processes and place them at the center of the scholarship in which it properly takes such pride. Doing so will require a true sea change in how university educators and administrators do their work—and I'm more optimistic than ever that it just might happen.

References

Bass, R. 2003. The electronic archives for teaching the American literatures. Retrieved April 25, 2003. http://www.georgetown.edu/tamlit/tamlit-home.html

Bowen, H. R. 1977. *Investment in learning: The individual and social value of American higher education.* San Francisco: Jossey-Bass.

Cuban, L. 1999. *How scholars trumped teachers: Change without reform in university curriculum, teaching, and research, 1890–1990.* New York: Teachers College Press.

Hutchings, P. 2002. *Ethics of inquiry: Issues in the scholarship of teaching and learning.* Menlo Park, CA: The Carnegie Foundation for the Advancement of Teaching.

Hutchings, P., and L. S. Shulman. 1999. The scholarship of teaching: New elaborations, new developments. *Change* 31 (September/October): 10–15.

McNeill, W. H. 1991. *Hutchins' university: A memoir of the University of Chicago, 1929–1959.* Chicago: University of Chicago Press.

Wegener, C. 1978. *Liberal education and the modern university.* Chicago: University of Chicago Press.

Two

Transforming Students into Historical Researchers
A Photographic Historian's Perspective

Claude Cookman

Education is what you have left after you've forgotten all you learned.

For many years I smiled knowingly at this anonymous witticism. I could certainly identify with the latter part of the sentence. My college major was classical Greek, but when I graduated in 1965, the draft and a year in Vietnam quickly diverted me from reading the classics. Soon I had forgotten the grammar, syntax, and much of the vocabulary learned in 36 hours of studying Homer, Sophocles, Herodotus, and Plato. About a decade ago, I started to take the what-you-have-left part of the statement seriously. Even though I could no longer read Greek, I always believed some residue remained, that my study of this beautifully precise language had made my thinking sharper and my writing clearer. As a teacher, I began to wonder what the students in the history of photography courses that I offer at Indiana University's Bloomington campus would have left after they forgot the ostensible content of my courses. What residue would I contribute to their education? As a scholar at a major research university, I decided to teach them not only the standard survey of content, but also the methodology that I use as an historian of photography. I wanted my students to master the critical and creative thinking skills practiced in my discipline. I wanted them to learn to find primary and secondary sources, subject them to rigorous analysis, and synthesize them into a convincing paper.

In this chapter I describe how I integrate my academic research with my teaching by presenting the discipline of the history of photography not merely as a domain of knowledge but also as a methodology of practice. I argue that when students learn methodology, they retain knowledge longer, are motivated to continue learning after the semester ends, and acquire valuable analytical and creative skills that they can transfer to other intellectual endeavors and to their personal lives. I also point out how teaching methodology is especially well suited to a research university that is rich in resources for students to use for their projects. The ideas and examples presented grow out of my reading of pedagogical literature and out of courses that I have taught since coming to Indiana University in the fall of 1990. They include undergraduate seminars on 20th-century French photography taught in Paris through Indiana University's Overseas Studies Program; graduate seminars on such topics as French street photography, the social documentary tradition, and war photography; and a course surveying the entire medium. Primarily, the chapter draws on my History of 20th Century Photography course, a large-lecture survey course taught in alternate spring semesters. Cross-listed in the School of Journalism and the School of Fine Arts and targeted to upper-class and graduate students, it enrolled 90 students in the spring of 2002. Most of these students anticipated careers as art photographers or photojournalists; a few planned to be art historians, and a few took the course for personal enrichment.

Course Content and Objectives

The students and I surveyed photography as a medium of art and communication from the Pictorialist movement, which began in the 1890s, through the postmodern currents of the 1990s. We examined such art genres as portraiture, landscape, still life, the nude, and conceptual photography and studied such communication categories as war photography, the social documentary tradition, the magazine picture story, fashion, and advertising. We explored how developments in optical, chemical, and mechanical technologies created new aesthetic possibilities. We situated photographers and their work within biographical, historical, economic, and social contexts, and we considered the impact of postmodern theory on the understanding of how photography functions in society. We did this while examining the work of more than 125 major photographers.

The ambitious content is matched by an equally ambitious set of course objectives. I tell my students in the syllabus and during the first class that I want them to:

- acquire a broad knowledge of the history of 20th-century photography through readings, lectures, discussions, and other active-learning experiences;

- acquire a deep knowledge of a specific photographer, movement, critical issue, or other aspect of 20th-century photography through a research project;
- develop the ability to articulate, in oral speech and writing, their intellectual, aesthetic and emotional responses to photographs;
- develop a historical consciousness;
- develop the motivation and the methodological skills to continue studying the history of photography after the course ends.

The last objective raises an important pedagogical question: Why teach research methodology to students who are professionally oriented? My response concerns my personal motivation for research, which I hope to imbue in my students. One of higher education's cherished ideals is that teaching and research should support each other in a symbiotic relationship. Many people, in and outside of the university, understand this to mean that faculty members lecture about their research findings. Rarely is it that simple. Most scholars research narrowly defined problems. Most courses survey broad fields. In my case, for example, much of my research has focused on the French photographer Henri Cartier-Bresson. Beginning in the early 1930s, he was one of the first to show the potential of the then new 35mm camera to capture spontaneity. His picture stories—published in such magazines as *Life, Look, Harper's Bazaar, Holiday, Paris Match, Stern, Du,* and *The Queen*—and his one-person exhibitions at such museums as the Louvre in Paris, the Museum of Modern Art in New York, and the Victoria and Albert in London, ranked him among the most important 20th-century photographers. Notwithstanding his stature, I can incorporate my research on Cartier-Bresson as only a part of one lecture. That leaves 29 other class sessions where the contents of my research specialization do not apply.

Instead of lecturing on my research findings, I share my research methodology. Although I do not tell "war stories" from my professional career or gossip about the important photographers I have worked with and interviewed, I do relate my personal beginning in photographic history as a way to motivate my students to embrace research. It goes like this: In the late 1970s, while picture editor of the *Louisville Times,* I took a course in the history of photography at the University of Louisville. A research paper on social documentarian Russell Lee was my first opportunity to practice the history of photography. My topic led me to the University's photographic archives which included the photographic collection, correspondence, and memorabilia of Lee's boss, Roy W. Stryker. (Stryker and Wood 1973; Hurley 1978) A former economics instructor at Columbia University, Stryker directed the U.S. Farm Security Administration's historical section, which documented the Great Depression in photographs. My discovery of this turbulent era through original prints, memoranda, letters, and newspaper clippings was an enticing first encounter with practicing history through primary sources.

This personal engagement, among other causes, prompted me to pursue a doctorate in the history of photography at Princeton University, where I was fortunate to study in a large collection of original prints and other primary documents at Princeton's Art Museum. I could, for example, read the actual letters and manuscripts of Minor White, who championed the photograph as metaphor, and apply them to my interpretation of his sequences of photographs. I could study those sequences not as reproductions in books but as original prints.

By the time I began my dissertation research, I had acquired the methodological tools to study Cartier-Bresson's prints, contact sheets, field captions, and manuscripts at Magnum Photos, his agency in Paris, and to reconstruct the historical context of his work at such libraries as the Bibliothèque Nationale, the Pompidou Center, the Maison Européenne de la Photographie and the Bibliothèque historique de la Ville de Paris. Immersed in primary and secondary materials, I relived the liberation of Paris in 1944, the funeral of Mohandas Gandhi in 1948, the fall of Beijing to Mao Tse-Tung's forces in 1948, the student rebellion in Paris in 1968, and numerous other events that Cartier-Bresson photographed during the middle decades of the 20th century. Far from being an academic chore, these archival studies enriched me by giving me access to eras, events, and personalities that I could never encounter personally. As a scholar who teaches, I try to infect students with my enthusiasm for such enrichment as a tangible benefit of historical research. I liken it to that staple of science fiction, the time machine. Supplemented by knowledge and imagination, a musty document or a dog-eared print can transport the researcher into the past. Because Indiana University is a major research institution with extensive photographic collections and with faculty and curatorial staff members who offer expertise on the holdings, students can experience a similar engagement with primary sources here on the Bloomington campus.

Those who see the world in either-or dualities may object that emphasizing methodology necessarily results in a corresponding loss in students' knowledge. The number of classroom hours are fixed, and time spent on methodology cannot be spent on transmitting content. If instructors are interested in more than short-lived retention, this is a false dichotomy. To learn at the higher cognitive levels, students must actively process knowledge through critical thinking. In addition, no academic discipline consists solely of declarative knowledge. All scholars creatively search their fields for fresh, important questions to explore or problems to solve. All scholars use the methodologies of their field to answer these problems. If they only transmit existing knowledge, they deny students the chance to participate in the creation of new knowledge, a major objective of the research university. Scholars cannot claim to have taught their disciplines if they have not included problem finding, problem solving, and other procedural knowledge of their disciplines. Nor can they say they have prepared their students for future learning.

Another pedagogical reason for teaching methodology is that students cannot understand history completely without practicing it. Historical analysis is a complex and varied human activity that has been practiced for at least two and a half millennia. Yet students and adults alike are often unclear about what history is and what historians do. Among the morass of misconceptions they harbor about history, three stereotypes surface frequently: history is everything that happened in the past, history is all about memorizing dates, and history is boring. Nobody who has practiced history harbors such misconceptions. The solution to such limiting stereotypes is to transform students into historical researchers. In the context of the 20th-century photography course, acquiring a research methodology requires students to build a repertoire of critical and creative thinking skills, and a set of mental operations that will prepare them to gather information and write a paper of 15 to 20 pages on a topic of their choice. To neglect such methodology would be like chemistry professors' requiring their students to memorize the periodic table without introducing them to the scientific method.

My students and I begin the practice of critical thinking by examining the idea of history itself. On the first day of class, I challenge the stereotype that history is everything that happened in the past by asking: "If we could assemble every photograph ever taken since the announcement of photography's invention in 1839, and if we had unlimited time to look at them all, would that constitute a history of photography?" Most students find this prospect of history by denotation unsatisfying, because they expect meaning from history. They want connotation.

Some students seem surprised at my intentionally provocative definition: "History is what I do for a living." But I use it to make the point that historical analysis is a human activity, not an immense, amorphous past. I point out that history involves seeing the past through the filters of contemporary thought. As a methodological definition, I explain that history is the result of both creative and critical thought by individuals who select art objects, events, printed documents, oral statements, and other evidence; who structure these materials, often in a narrative form; and who construct meaning from them. History is not a one-to-one transcription of the past, but a representation and interpretation of that past. It is necessarily selective and constrained by the perspective of the historical researcher and by the limitations of available data, language, and time. The intent of all these definitions is to help students understand that they can practice history, not just read other people's versions of it.

There are other pedagogical justifications for emphasizing research methodology. Much of higher education still concerns itself with transmitting knowledge and testing its acquisition by students. Now, almost 50 years after the educational psychologist Bloom (1956) theorized that the retention of knowledge is the lowest level of students' cognitive operations, some professors still employ only the lecture, expecting that students will retain the transferred knowledge. The perceived obligation to cover a prescribed content—sometimes to survey an entire discipline —in one semester emphasizes professors' teaching, to the neglect of students' deep learning. (Barr and Tagg 1995) Whatever they might profess, the classroom practices of some faculty members show they expect little more from their students than parroting back lecture notes on multiple-choice examinations. After the tests, students soon forget much of what they retained during the short term. This transmission-of-knowledge approach assumes that students' minds are empty containers. By attending enough lectures, reading enough textbooks, and passing enough examinations, students fill their empty minds and qualify for a diploma that certifies they are educated.

Lecturing fails to help students achieve the higher cognitive levels that Bloom identified: comprehension, application, analysis, synthesis, and evaluation. Moreover, lecturing cannot transfer all the important knowledge. In most disciplines the traditional canon has eroded and new knowledge is increasing exponentially. Even if students retain everything they hear during lectures, it might not be the knowledge they need, or it might become outdated by newer knowledge. Outdating applies to skills as well. As a newspaper copy editor in the mid-1970s, I could read lead type upside down and backwards. In today's era of electronic printing, such a skill might qualify as an oddity, but hardly as useful. In short, the rapid transformation toward information- and technology-based systems demands that workers continue to learn the latest knowledge and skills.

Because students cannot learn enough in four years to last them throughout their careers, the alternative approach is to prepare them to engage in lifelong learning. At a minimum this preparation must result in students' mastering the tools to acquire new knowledge and to evaluate it critically. At Indiana University, former President Myles Brand (1997, pp. 17–18) urged incoming freshmen to learn to think critically, delivering this challenge:

> You are in college not just to study literature and language, or music and medicine; you are in college to learn how to think about these subjects—and many more. You are in college to learn how to be critical. At a time when vast data are literally at your fingertips, I urge you—I implore you—be critical. Assume the mantle of the skeptic. Analyze what you read. Question what you hear. Never give up your search for the truth.

Critical Thinking

Of course, critical thinking can become empty jargon, one more buzz phrase that everybody supports and nobody takes responsibility for. A few years ago, Bob Orsi, then associate dean for undergraduate education in Indiana University's College of Arts and Sciences, observed this happening in proposals for topics courses. He wrote to his COAS colleagues:

> Critical thinking has become the dingus of the Topics curriculum —the oft-named but obscure object of desire and pursuit. I've thought about banning the term from all discussions of Topics, and particularly from proposals. The regular invocation of "critical thinking" functions as a gesture of good intention, but the challenge now—in this period of refining the objectives and methods of the curriculum—is to specify with more precision what we mean by "critical thinking." (1998, p. 1)

Instead of banning the term, Orsi proposed a two-part challenge to faculty members proposing topics courses: first, to explain clearly and explicitly what they meant by the term "critical thinking" within the context of their courses, then to develop specific exercises and assignments to "give students practice" at the various discipline-specific operations involved.

As part of the methodology of practicing the history of photography,

I offer my students a two-part definition of "critical thinking." The syllabi for my courses include the following:

> Here is how I define critical thinking for this course: First, we will learn to read critically; that is, to identify an author's thesis and arguments, and to evaluate whether those arguments convincingly support his or her conclusions. The larger objective is to apply similar critical analysis to your own writing in order to improve it.

> Second, we will engage in several mental operations that are essential to studying a visual art and to practicing history. They include observing and describing, comparing and contrasting, summarizing, classifying, analyzing, synthesizing, interpreting, formulating a thesis, testing a thesis, and constructing concept maps.

In my observation, most students read for information, highlighting facts with yellow markers. Helping them learn to read critically begins with my modeling the reading of a challenging passage, exposing its hidden assumptions, analyzing its arguments, and evaluating its use of evidence. A second step involves asking reading and discussion questions that prompt students to search for theses and analyze arguments. A third step is helping students learn to rank the quality of various kinds of texts. The course reading packet includes criticism, interviews, autobiography, artistic statements, academic research, critical theory, and other genres. I want students to extract useful information from criticism in the popular photographic press, to evaluate how much credence they can put in a photographer's autobiography, and to appreciate the peer-review process that undergirds articles and books written by academic researchers. In addition, the readings range in difficulty from those with ideas that are easily accessible to some texts whose dense expression and esoteric theory make them very challenging.

To help students become better critical readers, I used an approach called Just in Time Teaching (JiTT) during the spring semester of 2002. Gregor Novak and his colleagues in physics and other sciences developed JiTT at Indiana University Purdue University Indianapolis during the 1990s. Under this method, shortly before class students respond electronically to questions about the day's assigned readings, or about lab problems or other academic content. As the professor reads the students' responses, she or he gains insights about their thinking, including misconceptions, which help shape the day's lecture, discussion, and other classroom activities. As Novak et al. (1999, p. 3) explain:

> We have built the JiTT system around Web-based preparatory assignments that are due a few hours before class. The students com-

plete these assignments individually, at their own pace, and submit them electronically. In turn, we adjust and organize the classroom lessons in response to the student submissions "Just-in-Time." Thus, a feedback loop between the classroom and the Web is established. Each lecture is preceded and informed by an assignment on the Web.

None of my questions concerned the retention of facts such as names, titles, dates, etc. By asking questions at the levels of Bloom's higher cognitive skills, I used JiTT to advance my objective of making my students better critical readers. Early in the semester, I used comprehension questions, asking students to summarize the readings in their own words. After a few weeks, I moved on to questions of analysis. For example, I might ask whether a writer engaged in hagiography of the photographer under discussion and, if so, how. As we advanced through the readings, I added synthesis, asking students to compare a current writer's perspectives with that of a previous author. Almost always, I asked evaluation questions that required students to take a position on the issues and defend it. Typically, there were three open-ended essay questions for each daily reading. One example will suggest the flavor: For a reading from Bolton's *The Contest of Meaning* (1996), an anthology of postmodern writings, I asked students to identify the unstated assumptions and attitudes that shape his introduction:

> To help you read between the lines, discuss at least three of the following five questions. Don't feel limited to them, however. If you like, feel welcome to pose and discuss other questions that deconstruct Bolton and his position. What is the tone of Bolton's introduction? What do you think his attitude toward photographers might be? How does he position himself and his writers in relation to photography? What do you think he would most like to change in ordinary people's understanding of photography? What is his ultimate objective?

Students reacted positively to the JiTT method, which I referred to as pre-assignments, short for pre-class assignments. Several complained about the extra work involved. But at the end of the semester in response to the question: "Did the pre-assignment questions help you process the readings at a deeper level?"—92.3 percent responded "yes." A sample of responses to the open-ended question: "Please say anything you would like about the pre-assignments."—included: "Writing forces you to learn in a way that is different from reading alone." "They were a lot of work, but I thought they were a great way to process the readings." "They prepared me for class. I felt like contributing more after answering the questions."

From my perspective, JiTT was a great success. Students were more engaged in the course as we discussed the pre-assignment questions. Based on my review of their answers before class, I was able to improve my lectures by addressing misconceptions and spending more time on concepts the students found difficult. It was clear that more students were doing the readings than in any previous course that I have taught.

Mental Operations

Although critical reading prepares students to deal with secondary sources, the mental operations itemized in the syllabus are essential to studying photographs as primary sources, to organizing research findings, and to writing a convincing paper. Those operations include:

Observing and Describing

Art historians are fortunate to work with concrete objects. The common assumption is that art objects speak for themselves, that anybody with a pair of eyes can look at them—even at a photographic reproduction of them—and absorb everything they offer. This assumption collapses when we acknowledge how very little time most of us spend looking at anything in a concentrated, purposeful way. Even in art museums, people typically glance at a painting or sculpture for only a few seconds before moving on to the next object.

Because photographs are so ubiquitous, they are especially susceptible to receiving only a cursory glance. Students need to be taught to see photographs at a deep level. Asking them to describe a photograph—to translate their perceptions into oral or written expression—requires deep, sustained observation. This is the first step in building a set of tools for practicing photographic history. What makes observation and description challenging is that art is never merely about content. Artists have always used form to distinguish themselves. Thousands of paintings share the Madonna and child motif, for example, but it is the individual artist's formal invention that makes his or her treatment of such a motif interesting. Students must learn a specialized vocabulary in order to make a formal description of a photograph. It includes visual elements such as texture, tonality, and directional forces; design principles such as balance, emphasis, simplicity, unity, and variety; and perceptual concepts such as how the illusion of spatial depth is created on a flat surface. They must also master a technical vocabulary to describe the effects of the numerous kinds of cameras, lenses, and chemical processes. The ultimate objective is for them to be able to articulate what the form adds to the viewer's response to the content. That is, to move beyond the image's denotative content to its connotative meaning.

Comparing and Contrasting

A second basic operation, comparing and contrasting, is integral to art historical pedagogy. From lectures to discussions, from examinations to papers, instructors and students alike frequently compare and contrast two works of art instead of examining just one. The objective is to see a single work more deeply by considering it against how a second artist handled a similar motif or theme. The alternate version shows that the first work of art is not inevitable, but the result of an artist's decisions. Of all the operations listed, the ability to compare and contrast effectively may be the skill most transferrable to students' other intellectual endeavors and to their daily lives.

Summarizing

Description may work for a single photograph, and comparing and contrasting may work for two, but how should students deal with a large body of photographs presented in an exhibition or a book? Indeed, how should they handle an oeuvre generated over a lifetime? They must learn to summarize large groups of photographs that will form the basis for discussing a few images in depth. This requires identifying and generalizing about an artist's photographic vision, craft, genres, and recurring themes that unify her or his entire body of work.

Classifying

Yet another essential operation is classifying. Perhaps the first response a professional art historian has when engaging a previously unknown work is to classify it. Although it's not always possible with reproductions, when looking at original photographic prints students need to learn to distinguish a pictorialist print from a straight-photography print, a social-documentary image from a surrealist or a conceptual one. Classifying depends on students' mastering the domain knowledge of photographic history. They must construct a network of categories based on chemical processes, periods, movements, schools, chronologies, and major artists.

Analysis

Analyzing involves breaking complex entities into their constituent parts. With photographs, it works at the level of describing all the elements of content and form. Students must also analyze primary verbal documents, secondary texts, and causes and effects.

Synthesis

Analysis, by itself, does not create new knowledge. The research paper allows students to synthesize, or recombine the results of analyzing many images and texts into a fresh combination. This is one aspect of the creativity required to practice photographic history; others will be discussed below.

Concept Maps

As the researcher makes connections among the acquired data, synthesis requires organizational skills. Like many in my generation, I learned the outline as a tool of organization in junior high school. Several years ago, I discovered a better tool, the concept map (Angelo and Cross 1993; Pace and Pugh 1996). Concept maps let scholars connect information, ideas, images, etc., in a graphic format. With magic markers and large pads of paper, mappers brainstorm their accumulated contents onto the pages, drawing circles and boxes around some items, connecting others with arrows. Invariably, the first drafts are messy, because they match the inchoate state of knowledge and thought in the mapper's mind. The point is not to make a pretty map for other people to admire, but instead, from a welter of information, to excavate relationships, antitheses, and chains of causes and effects. Concept maps benefit both the instructor and the students. "Concepts maps allow the teacher to discover the web of relationships that learners bring to the task at hand—the students' starting points. . . . By literally drawing the connections they make among concepts, students gain more control over their connection making." (Angelo and Cross 1993, p. 197) Because the concept map is in a graphic form, it can be held in the mind as a visual gestalt in a way that a verbal outline cannot. I show my students concept maps that I have created as models (Figure 2.1) and require them to create their

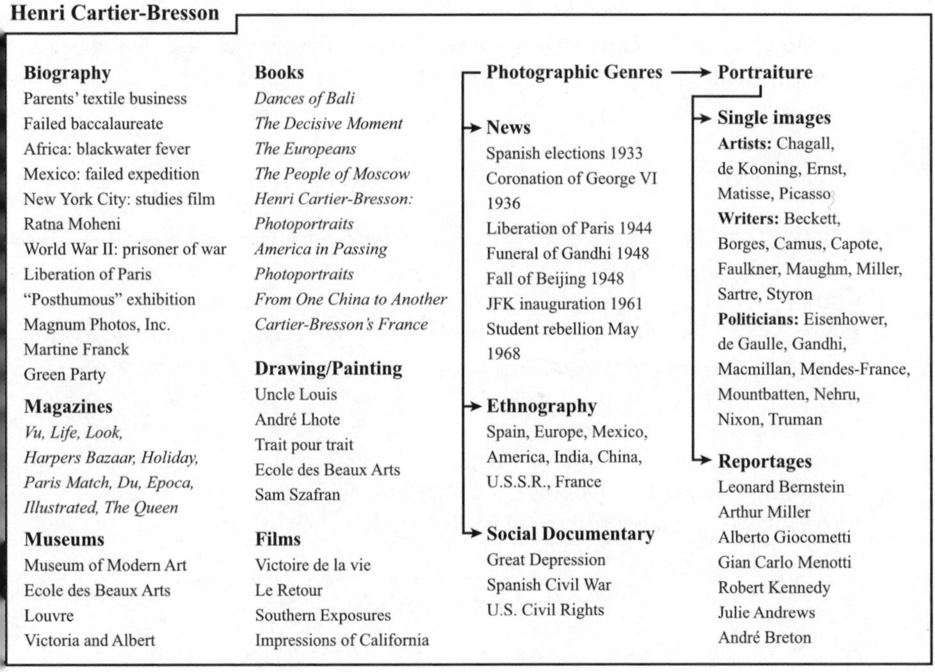

Henri Cartier-Bresson

Biography
Parents' textile business
Failed baccalaureate
Africa: blackwater fever
Mexico: failed expedition
New York City: studies film
Ratna Moheni
World War II: prisoner of war
Liberation of Paris
"Posthumous" exhibition
Magnum Photos, Inc.
Martine Franck
Green Party

Magazines
Vu, Life, Look,
Harpers Bazaar, Holiday,
Paris Match, Du, Epoca,
Illustrated, The Queen

Museums
Museum of Modern Art
Ecole des Beaux Arts
Louvre
Victoria and Albert

Books
Dances of Bali
The Decisive Moment
The Europeans
The People of Moscow
Henri Cartier-Bresson:
Photoportraits
America in Passing
Photoportraits
From One China to Another
Cartier-Bresson's France

Drawing/Painting
Uncle Louis
André Lhote
Trait pour trait
Ecole des Beaux Arts
Sam Szafran

Films
Victoire de la vie
Le Retour
Southern Exposures
Impressions of California

Photographic Genres → **Portraiture**

→ **News**
Spanish elections 1933
Coronation of George VI
1936
Liberation of Paris 1944
Funeral of Gandhi 1948
Fall of Beijing 1948
JFK inauguration 1961
Student rebellion May
1968

→ **Ethnography**
Spain, Europe, Mexico,
America, India, China,
U.S.S.R., France

→ **Social Documentary**
Great Depression
Spanish Civil War
U.S. Civil Rights

→ **Single images**
Artists: Chagall,
de Kooning, Ernst,
Matisse, Picasso
Writers: Beckett,
Borges, Camus, Capote,
Faulkner, Maughm, Miller,
Sartre, Styron
Politicians: Eisenhower,
de Gaulle, Gandhi,
Macmillan, Mendes-France,
Mountbatten, Nehru,
Nixon, Truman

→ **Reportages**
Leonard Bernstein
Arthur Miller
Alberto Giocometti
Gian Carlo Menotti
Robert Kennedy
Julie Andrews
André Breton

Figure 2.1 Model of a concept map

own. I have even included drawing a concept map as an optional question on the final exam.

Formulating Theses

Just as I train my students to identify an author's thesis in their readings, I require them to formulate their own theses in their writing. It is never enough to assemble and regurgitate information; students must take a point of view on their research findings and express it as a thesis. I explain that a thesis statement will serve the readers by telling them what they can expect to find in the paper. I also emphasize that a well-crafted thesis will serve the students as they write. If the research has been thorough, there is always much more information than can be used. No matter how interesting, materials that do not contribute to the argument should be cut. I urge students to use their theses to determine what must be kept and what can be eliminated. For many students, even at the upper-class and graduate levels, this is still a difficult task. I encourage those having trouble to visit a website on constructing theses, created by Indiana University's Instructional Support Services.[1] With clear explanations and examples, it shows students how to refine a vague thesis into an effective one.

Testing Theses

Finally, I encourage my students to test their theses. This process helps them divide their research into two phases. During the first phase, students read and look widely, often with a vague purpose and an unformed topic. After this initial prospecting phase, I push them to formulate a working thesis that makes a claim about the information they have gathered. Then I ask them to test it with the question: "What information do I still need to gather in order to argue my thesis convincingly?" This question considerably narrows the second phase of their research. At this point, students are looking for specifics—no longer rambling across broad swaths of data that may never be used in their papers.

Presenting Creativity

Analysis is not enough to practice history. Creativity is also required, but creativity cannot be left to chance. I explicitly make students aware of the creative aspects of their research project, including the following:

Problem Finding

If traditional academics feel comfortable with creativity, it is usually when couched in a phrase like "creative problem solving." Few think or talk about creative problem finding, but most practice it in their own research. For knowledge to advance, researchers must identify new problems to solve. For beginners in a discipline, problem finding is much harder than problem solving. At the level of transforming students into photographic historians, problem finding means: "What topic will I choose for my research project?" A topic is not just picking a photographer whose work the student likes, but identifying a problem or an issue that the work poses or seeing it in a fresh way through a theoretical perspective.

Fluency and Flexibility

To pick a good topic, students must generate several possible topics. This leads to discussing and applying two key measures of creativity:

fluency and flexibility. Fluency refers to how many ideas a person can generate. Flexibility refers to how varied those ideas are. Brainstorming is the most basic tool for generating ideas. Students are familiar with brainstorming, but may not use it unless they are specifically encouraged to do so. Many students are victims of the mistaken notions that creativity strikes as a flash of inspiration and there is nothing they can do except wait and hope. When I introduce the course project assignment, I show students an overhead slide of some of my brainstorming lists. Then we take class time for them to brainstorm about photographers, images and issues that intrigue them. As they approach the writing phase, I talk about verbal fluency as a component of good writing. The ability to conceive of several ways to express a thought and then to choose the best is one mark of a mature writer.

Imagination

Imagination is another dimension of creativity required to practice history. There is a long-standing debate about whether history is an art or a science. During the middle decades of the 20th century, the rise of quantitative methods in history seemed to tip the scale toward scientific methodologies. But numbers, by themselves, mean nothing. At some point quantitative researchers must interpret those numbers. Using them to reconstruct the past requires a creative act of imagination. For the photographic historian working in the humanist tradition, imagination may take the form of empathizing with the subject of a photograph, thus relocating oneself in another time, place, and situation. Yet another major dimension of creativity is synthesis, discussed above in the section on mental operations.

The bifurcation of critical from creative thinking may be useful for discussing them, but most professional and student historians alike practice them simultaneously. Perkins (1994) offers a fresh perspective that subsumes both kinds of thinking under cognitive schema. He makes a strong argument that studying art helps people develop strategies for thinking in "broad and adventurous, clear and organized ways." Perkins, who is not an art historian but a cognitive psychologist at Harvard University, lists several features of art that make it especially effective for developing thinking. Art involves a concrete object that anchors discussion and thought; the work of art is always there as a reference point. Art is accessible, which promotes personal engagement, motivation and sustained reflection. Art also promotes wide-spectrum cognition. "Although we tend to think of art as primarily a visual phenomenon," Perkins maintains, "looking at art thoughtfully recruits many kinds and styles of cognition—visual processing, analytical thinking, posing questions, testing hypotheses, verbal reasoning, and more." (1994, p. 5) Finally, he points out that art encourages making rich connections "with social themes, philosophical conundrums, features of formal structure, personal anxieties and insights, and historical patterns." (1994, p. 5) Some of these cognitive developments may happen in a traditional lecture course, but an active-learning approach that requires students to practice a research methodology increases their occurrence.

Resources for Historical Research

Art history instructors typically show slides during class and assign textbooks that include reproductions; they may also post images on a World Wide Web site. None of these types of images achieves the level of engagement that Perkins claims for a work of art. For that, actual paintings, sculptures, photographic prints, etc., are required. Although many people do not differentiate between a reproduction and a photograph, there are important differences including scale, color values, tactile surface qualities, the effects of aging, and aspects of presentation such as matting, framing, the artist's signature, other surface writing, etc. To engage students with actual works of art, I require them to study original photographic prints as part of their research. Although some students choose to travel to collections in Indianapolis, Louisville, St. Louis, Chicago, and elsewhere, Indiana University's Bloomington campus is richly endowed with primary photographic sources. Its five major collections cover a wide range of photographic artists, styles, movements, periods, and issues. The five collections are:

- **The Art Museum.** The Art Museum began its photography collection in the 1970s, before the market boom put the work of many photographic artists out of its budget range, notes Nanette Esseck Brewer, the museum's Lucienne M. Glaubinger Curator of Works on Paper. The collection now numbers about 2,000 works, excluding the archives. Numerous major photographers are represented in the collection, including such 20th-century masters as Ansel Adams, Berenice Abbott, Ruth Bernhard, Brassaï, Henri Cartier-Bresson, Laszlo Moholy-Nagy, Lucas Samaras, Paul Strand, Jerry Uelsmann, Edward Weston, and Minor White. The museum also holds the archives of Art Sinsabaugh, who photographed the midwestern landscape, and Henry Holmes Smith, who launched the studio photography program at Indiana University Bloomington, and made innovations in abstract color imagery using camera-less photography. The two archives, which comprise about 8,000 items, constitute the largest public holdings of materials by these artists.

I guide students in small groups as they visit the museum's study room to see original prints. These visits form a prelude for their own independent research in museum collections.

- **The Kinsey Institute.** The Kinsey Institute's photography collection contains approximately 48,000 inventoried images dating from the 1870s to the present, from the United States and Europe (primarily Britain, France, Germany and Italy), according to curator Catherine Johnson. Many of these images, which deal with human sexuality, are made by amateurs, but there are major photographic artists represented as well, including Wihelm von Gloeden, George Platt Lynes, and Joel Peter Witkin.[2]
- **The Lilly Library.** The Hohenberger collection, dating from 1917 to 1960 and housed in the Lilly Library, consists primarily of photographs by Frank M. Hohenberger, 1876–1963, a Brown County photographer and newspaper journalist. The collection includes 8,300 prints, 9,400 negatives, correspondence, a lengthy diary by Hohenberger describing many of his photographic tours and processes, and copies of his "Down in the Hills o' Brown County" articles. The total collection comprises more than 18,700 items.[3]
- **The Mathers Museum.** Mathers, which houses artifacts and collections related to anthropology, has about 16,000 photographic images, reports curator Thomas Kavanagh. The largest group is the Wanamaker Collection, comprising about 8,000 images of Native Americans, taken between 1908 and 1922. The Charles Shaw–Charles Starks Collection includes photographs taken in and around Bloomington, and the Bridgwaters Collection documents the black community in Bloomington. Students can explore these holdings on a Mathers Web page[4] and can work in the collection by appointment.
- **University Archives.** The University Archives' collection of photographs dates from about 1850 to the present, and includes prints, negatives, slides, films, and videotapes. Major categories of photographic subjects include: individual faculty, staff, students, and alumni; groups of faculty, staff, students, and alumni participating in various activities including sports, commencement, departments,

and organizations; buildings and campus scenes; and aerial photos of the city of Bloomington.

Also maintained by the University Archives is the Charles Weever Cushman collection of 18,000 Kodachrome slides taken between 1938 and 1969. It is currently being digitized by IU's library under a $147,000 National Leadership Grant.[5]

In addition to their contents, the five collections are maintained by curators with expertise in the holdings who can help students with their research projects.

As important as primary sources are, they need to be complemented with secondary sources. Indiana University's library system is rich in holdings in the history of photography. A search of the electronic catalog generated more than 12,000 titles on the Bloomington campus.

Dimensions of Historical Consciousness

The research in primary documents, the emphasis on critical and creative thinking, and the inculcation of mental operations all contribute to the fourth course objective, that students develop a historical consciousness. We become aware of ourselves as living in a historical moment by reconstructing the lives and work of other people living in earlier periods. In my syllabus, I point out five dimensions of historical consciousness; all involve critical or creative thinking, or both. They are:

Understanding Change

Discerning which experiences, attitudes, ideas, and practices are continuous with the past, and which represent significant breaks is essential to practicing history. Beneath such superficials as clothing fashions, hair styles, and speech patterns, students want to believe there are constants in human nature, but they cannot let this obscure their recognition of genuine discontinuities.

Eliminating an Egocentric Point of View

One of the values in studying history is the opportunity to get outside one's limited perspective, but this is difficult. I want my students to learn when not to project their ideas, feelings, and experiences onto the past so they can understand real differences across time and place. This is accomplished through studying original prints, reading extensively, and recreating contexts.

Understanding Historical Cause and Effect

The past is a welter of events, an ongoing chain of causes and effects. I want my students to learn to identify significant chains of causes and effects. I want them to recognize how individuals are affected by events, yet also able to affect events.

Contextualization

Gestalt psychology has made the term "closure" commonplace in our contemporary vocabulary. We are impelled to find, or impose, meaning in photographs, biographical details, statements, etc. Learning to contextualize—that is, situating a photograph in the time and location in which it was produced and understanding how that time and place shaped its form and content—helps students delay jumping to a hasty closure that prevents deeper understandings.

Acquiring Models

This practical dimension of historical consciousness holds great appeal for professionally oriented students. They enthusiastically mine the past for motifs, insights, practices, and ways of seeing that they can adapt to their own photographing.

No doubt there are other aspects of creative and critical thinking, other mental operations, and other research methods that historians of art and photography practice. This itemization represents my own methodology, developed during graduate school and subsequent research. It constitutes the added value that I want my students to receive from the History of 20th Century Photography course. It is the residue I hope they carry with them through a life of learning. I have always believed that studying photographic history enriches the lives of my students, but I want it to be valuable to their careers as well. Most of these research skills can be applied to gathering information in any of the humanistic disciplines. More importantly, the creative and critical thinking skills can apply to most domains of knowledge, to students' careers, and to their personal lives.

So far, I have presented only the methodology that I practice, a traditional approach to finding, analyzing, and contextualizing information about the past, then organizing and presenting it in a thesis-argument-conclusion structure. But I want my students to be aware of other ways to understand the medium, and, if they choose, to use them in their course projects. Typically, these other methodologies are subsumed under postmodernism, an amorphous term for an array of theories—including Marxism, feminism, semiotics, structuralism, and post-structuralism—that have gained currency, even ascendency, in several academic disciplines. If these theories share anything in common, it is supplanting the meta-narratives that have shaped western culture since the Enlightenment period began in the 18th century.

One of the advantages of studying at a major research university, such as Indiana University, is that the faculty and professional staff is large enough and diverse enough that students can access experts with diverse methodologies. I can refer students interested in alternate methodologies to colleagues on the Bloomington campus who practice, and can advise them about, such approaches. So, for example, I would send students interested in discussing photography from the perspective of post-colonial theory to Professor Radhika Parameswaran in the School of Journalism, who publishes extensively in that field. I would send students interested in a cultural theory to Professor John Lucaites of the Department of Communications and Culture, who researches iconic photographs from the perspective of visual rhetoric. Also on the Bloomington campus are numerous other faculty members who can provide contextual guidance in such fields as women's studies, African-American studies, sexual identity, etc.

Conclusion

For assumed reasons of efficiency, many university courses can still be characterized as experts lecturing to novices. If nothing else happens in a course, this approach is a false efficiency. Transmission of content is never enough, because students rarely remember what is transmitted after the exam, because there is never time to cover all the important existing knowledge, and because new knowledge is constantly generated. To oppose domain knowledge to methodology in an either-or duality is a false dichotomy. To learn at the higher cognitive levels, students must actively process knowledge. The critical thinking and mental operations required by a research methodology engage students in such processing. Moreover, no academic discipline consists solely of declarative knowledge. All scholars search their fields for fresh problems to solve and use the methodologies of their field to answer these problems. Scholars cannot claim to have taught their disciplines if they have not included problem finding, problem solving, and other procedural knowledge. Nor can they claim they have prepared their students for future learning.

In this chapter, I have shared my personal aspiration to transform my history of photography students into historical researchers and to provide active-learning experiences to help them process content at levels deeper than mere retention. As an added benefit, students who are applying, analyzing, synthesizing and evaluating knowledge do increase their retention. Practicing historical research gives students the skills and increases the motivation to continue learning the history of photography after the semester ends.

If my perspective is valid, there is no competition between domain knowledge and research methodology. Separating the two is as false a bifurcation in the classroom as it is in a professional historian's work. For me, teaching the methodology of my discipline is the best way to engage students with the contents of the history of photography, to help them process those contents at deeper cognitive levels, to help them acquire new content after graduation, and to foster such career and life skills as critical and creative thinking. As an added benefit, it helps students lose some of the negative stereotypes about history that limit their access to the rich legacy of the past.

Acknowledgments

I am indebted to David Pace, professor of history at Indiana University, for showing me how to operationalize course objectives to enhance student learning, and to Craig Nelson, professor of biology at IU, and Joan Middendorf, former director of the Teaching Resources Center, for showing me how to use collaboration and discussion as active-learning strategies.

Notes

1. How to write a thesis statement. http://www.indiana.edu/~wts/wts/thesis.html
2. The Kinsey Institute for Research in Sex, Gender and Reproduction: Art, artifacts and photography. http://www.indiana.edu/~kinsey/library/artifacts.html
3. The Lilly Library: The collections. http://www.indiana.edu/~liblilly/collections.shtml
4. Mathers Museum of World Cultures: Photographic collections. http://www.indiana.edu/~mathers/new/collections/photos/index.html

5. Pleasantville and beyond in Kodachrome. http://www.indiana.edu/~libadmin/cushman.html

References

Angelo, T. A., and K. P. Cross. 1993. *Classroom assessment techniques: A handbook for college teachers*, 2nd ed. San Francisco: Jossey-Bass.

Barr, R., and J. Tagg. 1995. From teaching to learning—a new paradigm for undergraduate education. *Change* 27 (Nov./Dec.): 12–25.

Bloom, B. S., ed., 1956. *Taxonomy of educational objectives; the classification of educational goals, by a committee of college and university examiners. Handbook 1. Cognitive domain.* New York: Longmans, Green.

Bolton, R., ed. 1996. *The contest of meaning: Critical histories of photography.* Cambridge: MIT Press.

Brand, M. Freshman induction ceremony. August 27, 1997, unpublished speech in the Indiana University archives.

Hurley, F. J. 1978. *Russell Lee: Photographer.* Dobbs Ferry, NY: Morgan & Morgan.

Novak, G. M., et al. 1993. *Just in time teaching: Blending active learning with web technology.* Upper Saddle River, NJ: Prentice Hall.

Orsi, R. 1998. "Critical thinking: What's it to ya?" Topics of conversation: A forum on the College of Arts and Sciences topics curriculum. Bloomington: Indiana University COAS. Spring.

Pace, D., and S. L. Pugh. 1996. *Studying for history.* New York: Harper Collins.

Perkins, D. N. 1994. *The intelligent eye: Learning to think by looking at art.* Santa Monica, CA: The J. Paul Getty Trust.

Stryker, R. E., and N. Wood. 1973. *In this proud land: America 1935–1943 as seen in the FSA photographs.* Boston: New York Graphic Society.

Three

The Stone Age in the Information Age
Helping Undergraduates Think like Archaeologists

Jeanne Sept

I had the opportunity in 2002 to return to teach archaeology classes at the research university where I sharpened my academic trowel as a student. The lecture halls and classrooms had not changed much in the 30 years since I had taken my first freshman prehistory course, and as I flipped through the fading lecture notes kept from those days, I could still hear the voices of my favorite professors echoing through the halls. Yet, I was preparing to teach a class on African prehistory that bore little resemblance to the undergraduate course I had taken years before. In this chapter, I reflect on what has changed and why. After all, students of the Stone Age are now living in a public Information Age—how does this affect our ability to teach and learn about our ancient past?

Although some of the instructional challenges discussed here are unique to archaeology, they illustrate more fundamental pedagogical issues that are widely shared by faculty teaching survey courses in the social sciences. How can we give students a broad overview of the fundamental issues in a field and simultaneously engage them in real-world problem-solving, using the analytical methods of our disciplines? Professors develop their own, cumulative understanding of a field and want to share their perspective with students. Yet students learn best if the subject comes alive—if they can participate directly in the process of building knowledge in the classroom, and also practice how to apply new perspectives and skills in their own lives.

Questions of Teaching and Learning
in Archaeology

If it is difficult for students to imagine life in ancient times, it is often harder for them to understand how archaeologists use disparate fragments of evidence to reconstruct those remote images. Archaeology is less a process of discovery than a science of interpretation and multidisciplinary collaboration. Yet few students in an archaeology classroom experience the rich empirical detail, the integrative teamwork, or the analytical debates that are so central to archaeological inquiry.

In many archaeology classrooms university students are told a story of the human past—a narrative that weaves together the names and dates of different sites and prehistoric cultures. The goal of this approach is to give students a broad overview of the record of the human past without overwhelming them with detail, or confusing them with too much controversy. The best teachers illustrate this narrative well, with slides, multimedia, museum exhibits or artifact replicas; they have "electric story-telling skills, the ability to explain eloquently how archaeology works" (Fagan 2000, p. 125). Such survey courses can cover fascinating material, and have been the mainstay of undergraduate archaeology curricula for the last 50 years (Krass 2000). Consequently, the structure of textbooks generally supports this traditional model of instruction.[1] However, the clear weakness of this "culture change" approach to teaching archaeology is that students are encouraged to memorize the story but often gain little understanding of how it was constructed. The facts they learn—names of sites, dates, artifact types —can be relatively superficial and often de-contextualized. If a student's only exposure to archaeology is through an elective class that takes this approach, whatever "content" is learned may be quickly forgotten.

Alternatively, some professors prefer to organize their survey courses methodologically, using case studies of important sites to illustrate the process of archaeological interpretation. Students study examples of techniques used to investigate particular questions about the human past, such as evidence for ancient diet. Some textbooks facilitate this approach,[2] and teachers can use slides or materials from their own research to supplement published materials. Increasingly, site reports published on CD-ROM or the World Wide Web (WWW) provide rich, visual raw materials to use as examples. However, there are two disadvantages to such methodologically based surveys: (a) undergraduates have little opportunity to do more than memorize a different type of content, in this case a list of methodologies and featured sites; and (b) they rarely learn how to compare or generalize from individual studies to build an integrated understanding of the human past. Even in archaeology courses organized around methodological themes, students are more likely to learn passively about the ideas of others than to engage in the process of interpretation for themselves. Why? In part this is a byproduct of the unwieldy volume and multivariate dimensions of real archaeological data. It is much easier for professors to present a summary description of a site than to give students access to excavated data in a way that lets students explore it and learn to analyze it as evidence. If instructors provide problem-solving exercises[3] for their students, these often are based on simplified data sets that reinforce students' views that there are right answers to dig for, rather than tantalizing problems with ambiguous, long-buried clues that are difficult to solve. And rather than emphasizing teamwork, all too often such class assignments demand that students work and write independently.

Regardless of which type of traditional course organization is followed, the risk is that undergraduates will leave their content- or method-focused archaeology course with a head full of memorized facts merely juxtaposed with their professor's summarized script, having learned very few skills that transfer to other learning contexts. This is a pedagogical problem all too common in college classrooms today (e.g., Laurillard 1993; Bostock 1997). It is ironic that in the so-called Information Age we are still graduating passive, solitary learners poorly equipped to cope with the explosion of information resources competing for their attention.

A Case Study: African Prehistory

The example of a regional survey course can be a useful case study with which to evaluate different strategies for teaching archaeology. In this case, the region is Africa, a continent with the longest sequence of human achievements on earth, an archaeological record over 2.5 million years old. With its great time depth, African prehistory can serve as a comparative yardstick for the archaeological records of other areas. Analogously, strategies for teaching and learning about African prehistory can form an effective model for almost any survey course in archaeology.

For the average undergraduate, Africa is remote, both in time and space. Any archaeology student must confront the conceptual challenge of imagining time, but to come to grips with millions of years of prehistory is a particularly daunting task. Moreover, the continent is vast, and many of our students are poorly informed about Africa. Students are most likely to have thought about Africa in the context of popular media, where news stories tend to focus on past and present slavery, famine, disease or conflict; at the same time the public image of the continent is driven largely by the safari tourist industry and Hollywood, emphasizing a romantic image of Africa as wild or timeless (Hall 1998). The result is that many undergraduates do not see Africa's past as relevant to their own lives. Yet a key professional organization, the Society for American Archaeology, has charged archaeologists with the responsibility of teaching about stewardship, ethics, and issues of diverse heritage and social relevance, as well as fundamental skills (Bender and Smith 2000). Thus, to teach American students about African archaeology is first, and foremost, to confront our cultural stereotypes, and secondly to help students see themselves through a kaleidoscope of human experience across immense regions and through imponderable depths of time.

A survey course of African prehistory also highlights the intellectual challenge archaeology students face learning to analyze and integrate patterns of evidence at different spatial and temporal scales. At a fine scale, archaeological evidence is rarely preserved and is, at best, an uneven sample of ancient times. The job of the prehistorian is to not only discover and recover rare traces of evidence, but to develop interpretations, one fragment, one site, at a time. For students to understand archaeology, they must confront the scientific details and biases of multidisciplinary evidence at individual sites, everything from the mechanics of stone tool manufacture to the sedimentary context of fossil pollen samples. Collaborative, multidisciplinary teamwork is an important part of archaeological investigation, and, ideally, student experiences should capture this process. Micro-level questions students should be able to address, individually or in groups, in an African prehistory course could include:

- Are the damage patterns preserved on the fossil bones at a site likely to be the result of carnivore feeding behavior or proto-human scavenging, or both?
- How did the types of grave goods differ between individuals of different age and sex buried at the site, and what might this mean about the social organization of the people who lived there?
- Can phytoliths (micro-botanical remains) in soil samples demonstrate that domestic stock were kept at the site?

At a larger scale, to understand Africa's place in the human past, students must also be able to compare sites in a broader context, and learn how and why they can be integrated. Examples of macro-level questions students should be able to grapple with in an African prehistory course could be:

- Which proto-human species were likely responsible for making the first stone tools, and why?
- Can archaeological evidence for symbolic expression in Africa support the evolutionary argument that modern humans originated in Africa?
- What impact did climate change seem to have on the spread and diversification of agricultural economies in different parts of the African continent?

At the same time, as in any social science, interpretations differ, sources of evidence carry different weights, research questions shift with the history of science and the perspectives of different researchers. So, for students to understand African prehistory, they must learn to cope both with fine-grained and coarse-grained ambiguity in evidence, and learn how to evaluate competing hypotheses at different scales.

Is this all too much to ask of undergraduates? Not necessarily. The classroom experiments described below illustrate the strengths and weaknesses of several different approaches to achieving such pedagogical goals. These classroom strategies vary in the conceptual demands they place on students in three dimensions distinguished by Boyer (1990) in the broader context of scholarly activity in higher education: discovery (research investigation), integration (synthesis, interdisciplinary analysis) and application (real-world problem-solving, public engagement) (Figure 3.1). One could imagine a student as a hypothetical novice, starting with low levels of experience and skill in these three dimensions of African archaeology, then being coaxed to discover, interpret and apply knowledge and skills at higher and higher levels, moving closer to the position of an experienced expert in the field through the teaching and learning process. Students are individuals, and the pace and degree of each student's learning experience within a single course will be dependent on many variables the professor has no control over. However, some instructional strategies provide more opportunity for growth along different dimensions than others. It is the responsibility of professors to design opportunities, and set expectations that facilitate such learning. As scholars of teaching and learning, we must also decide how to evaluate results, and judge the impact of our instructional choices.

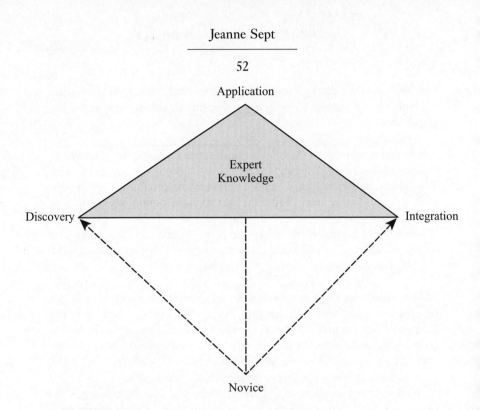

Figure 3.1 Model of learning

A Traditional Approach to Teaching
African Prehistory

I had the opportunity to study at a research university with two of the leading archaeologists doing research in Africa, Glynn Isaac and J. Desmond Clark. Each of them taught a 10-week undergraduate survey course in African prehistory as a comprehensive overview, treating the prehistoric record chronologically, and including descriptions of important individual sites, demonstrations of artifacts, and assignments of voluminous readings. The summarizing lectures were entertaining, and had a sense of fun that derived from the personalities and rich field experiences of both instructors. Examining the structure of these courses in retrospect, Clark, the preeminent authority on African archaeology for most of the 20th century, required students to know the details of over 125 different archaeological sites for his exams in the African prehistory class, as he taught it between 1977 and 1982. The version of the class that Isaac taught in 1975 spent more time in depth on fewer sites (75 overall), and focused more on describing the methods archaeologists used to evaluate the large-scale patterns for students. Both professors set exams that required the description of important features of key sites, as well as a selection of essays that asked for a review of major themes that had been emphasized in the lectures and readings. Clark's classes are still held by many of my colleagues as *tours de force* of survey courses. As archaeologist Rob Blumenschine remarked, "I do not believe there is anybody in the world who can competently teach such a broad range, broad sweep, of prehistory over such a huge area of the world" (Clark 2002, p. 459). It was our responsibility as students to remember as much of this detail as we could, and make sense of it in a broader scheme.

When I began teaching my own African prehistory course, I believed it was my responsibility as a professor to recreate such learning experiences for my students, to teach as I had been taught. But my lectures about African sites often became secondhand accounts, lacking the charming anecdotes my mentors could tell from decades of field research. Students were attentive, even interested; but few got excited. To engage students more effectively, I began to experiment with case study exercises using real data from different sites.

Three Strategies for Problem-Based Learning in an African Prehistory Course

Discovering the Details of a Single Site

Instructional challenge. Archaeologists commonly advocate "hands-on" or inquiry-based learning. The challenge in an archaeology survey course has been how to help students get access to the necessary resources—students can often only experience archaeological lab work or fieldwork in small classes, separate from their larger survey courses. And many professors, especially at nonresearch universities, have access only to limited teaching collections. This has prompted creative everyday teaching solutions, such as the "participant archaeology" advocated by Rice (1997), or the material culture field school of Wilk and Schiffer (1981), where students learn archaeological method and theory by interpreting the world around them through an archaeologist's eyes. A common option has been to develop data analysis exercises, with paper handouts, or use published workbooks (e.g., Daniels and David 1982; David, Driver and Daniels 1989). But such paper-based exercises are heavily text-based and generally limited in interpretive scope. They cannot do justice to the complex, multidisciplinary data with which archaeologists normally work.

The advent of computers helped alleviate the constraints of paper-based exercises. Digital media made it possible for students easily to examine images and manipulate data sets. Despite this, many instructional programs, whether on CD-ROM or the network, still use simplified data sets for their archaeological exercises (e.g., Price and Gebauer 1997; Michaels and Fagan 1997; Kappelman 2003; Dibble, McPherron and Roth 1999). Such assignments can backfire by reinforcing students' suspicions that there are right answers to dig for, rather than hypotheses to test.

The solution. As previously described (Sept 1998, 2000), in 1991 I decided to develop an alternative approach to using computers for archaeological instruction. Because Indiana University is a large research institution, I had no trouble securing the help of staff from our campus Instructional Support Services (ISS) in the design of a program that would take advantage of the emerging multimedia capacity of personal computers to improve the realism of the case-study type of exercises that I wanted to use for my African prehistory course. It took several years to develop the *Investigating Olduvai* software; at first students could access it only in computer classrooms through the campus network, but later ISS and I were able to reprogram it and shift it to a CD-ROM format for improved stability, accessibility and multimedia quality, and eventual publication (Sept 1997).

I designed the program to help students explore, and learn to interpret, the rich, multivariate data available from a single, important archaeological site, the type of fine-grained analysis critical to one of my instructional goals—helping students learn to "think like archaeologists." The site I chose was a famous African site that was central to my research specialty, and that could also serve as a case study in method and theory for a wide range of classes. The program did not lead students through material, as many instructional programs are designed to do. Instead, we created an interface that was simple to navigate, with an open structure that allowed students to explore and connect a wide range of materials in a nonlinear way. The program had a three-part structure. First, it challenged students with authentic research questions at different levels of complexity. Second, it established theoretical background with an analytical framework and toolkit. Third, it gave students access to rich, multivariate data from the site that they could investigate.

Implementation and evaluation. The first working test of the program,

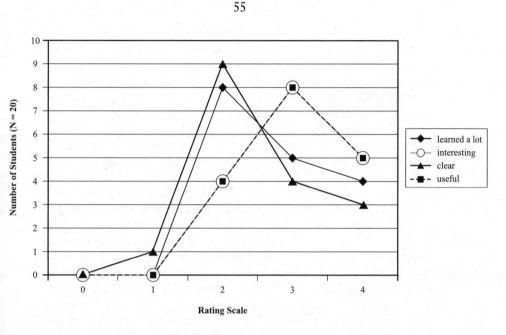

Figure 3.2 First classroom evaluation of *Investigating Olduvai* CD-ROM, 1992

one week in a class with 20 students in 1992, provided encouraging formative assessment information (Figure 3.2),[4] with volunteered comments such as:

- "I liked drawing my own conclusions about evidence."
- "Computer program was great. Different approach to studying prehistory of Africa. A nice change of pace. Encouraged us to think about information and decide for ourselves. Definite change from other classes."
- "I learned a lot from the computer assignment and feel that, with a little improvement, it could be a great teaching tool."

The program subsequently went through many cycles of student testing and evaluation during development, and we tried to incorporate as many student suggestions as possible into the final, published CD-ROM. Since its publication, *Investigating Olduvai* became technologically dated in only five years, but still remains pedagogically valuable. No other program gives students the open-ended responsibility and tools to pursue research questions with an authentic data set the way *Investigating Olduvai* does.

Over the years, for my African prehistory course I used the program for both in-class group exercises, and individual take-home essay assignments, and collected some basic feedback from students that suggested it was a successful instructional approach (Sept 2000). For example, 90 percent or more of the students responding to in-class surveys (N = 85, response rate of 82 percent) thought that using the *Investigating Olduvai* program required them to use higher level thinking skills than other assignments (90 percent), allowed them to apply concepts they had learned in class (96 percent), and made class material seem more relevant to them (93 percent).

Olduvai assignments accounted for about 20 percent of graded work in the course. However, I never tried to formally assess exactly what the program helped students learn, or how different students used the program in different ways. It seemed clear from their essays that students plunged into real data in a way I had rarely had the opportunity to do as an undergraduate; the best students were able to get involved in data analyses comparable to what graduate students were doing, and all students engaged the materials critically, and learned to build arguments from archaeological evidence. They made progress in learning about the process of research and discovery, but probably less about integration and application (Figure 3.3a). Still, as a professor I wondered about the instructional tradeoffs of asking students to spend so much time with one fine-grained case study in what was supposed to be a survey course of the continent. Compared to the hundred sites I had learned about as a student in African prehistory, my students were studying a few dozen. Once again it was a question of scale: how well could students understand the forest if they were mainly asked to study the leaves of a few trees?

Integrating Patterns of the Past

Instructional challenge. The Internet emerged as a new avenue for instructional development at about the same time that I was finishing *Investigating Olduvai*. In contrast to a CD-ROM, the World Wide Web promised to be a digital learning environment without limits, open to the world.[5] Because there are (and were) extensive student computing facilities across the campus, the Internet had the potential to help IUB students learn how to pull information together from different sites to address the sorts of large-scale questions important for archaeological synthesis. Instead of giving students comprehensive lectures on the big patterns of African prehistory, I wanted to create a set of multimedia data resources and tools that would allow me to ask students to work

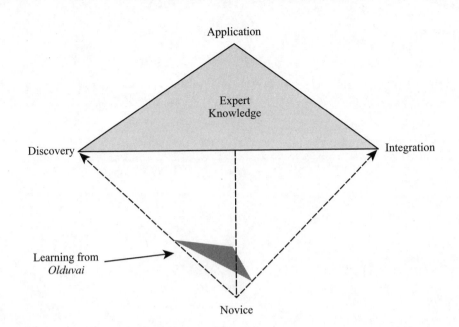

Figure 3.3a Model of learning from *Investigating Olduvai*

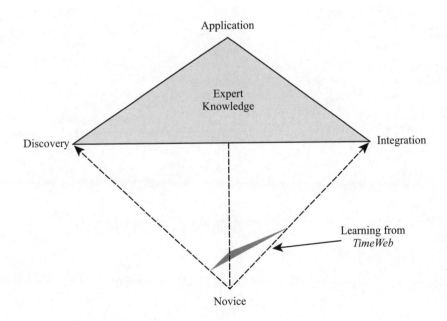

Figure 3.3b Model of learning from *TimeWeb*

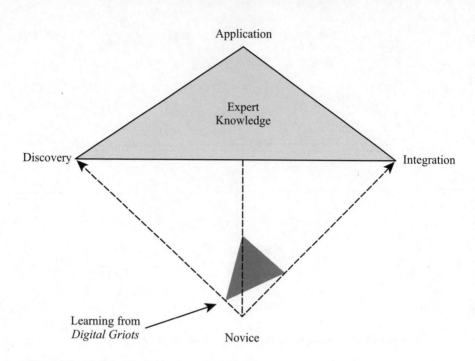

Figure 3.3c Model of learning from *Digital Griots*

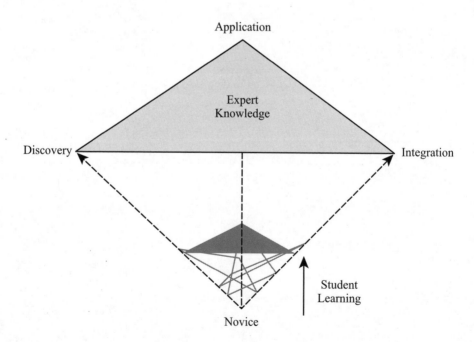

Figure 3.3d Model of cumulative learning from three different approaches

together, in teams, to research large-scale questions for themselves, to use the multimedia power of personal computers to help them learn to visualize and analyze evidence for the human past in space and time.

The challenge, however, was how to do this in a way that would not simply overwhelm students with volumes of information, confound them with what Wurman (1996) described as "a tsunami of data." For example, one of the oldest, extensive archaeological digital databases, designed for research and instruction in the classics, is *Perseus*.[6] This distinguished collection of artifact images, hypertexts, and maps related to ancient Greece is available on CD-ROM and the WWW. It has been used at many universities as a multimedia archive for lecture presentations and student assignments. Students can navigate through the online materials, examine images, look up lexical links, and do word counts. Designed primarily as a virtual library, however, the program does not attempt to mediate the process of teaching or learning how to organize, analyze and interpret these data. Introductory students, in particular, reported feeling overwhelmed by the volume of content in the *Perseus* archive and frustrated by their inability to find what they were looking for.[7]

Access to information is not enough. Students need tools to help them learn to evaluate and integrate the ever-expanding ocean of digital data, to learn to do more than surf the waves of our Information Age. As Roszak (1986, p. 162) reminded us before the WWW existed, "If anything, we suffer from a glut of unrefined, undigested information . . . so much that the forest gets lost among the trees." Students need teaching and learning tools that clarify the complexity of archaeological information without oversimplifying it, tools to help them build their own knowledge of the human past from bits and pieces of ancient evidence. *The solution.* To create a new type of teaching and learning resource for archaeology students focused on African prehistory, I collaborated with an Indiana University colleague specializing in human computer interface design, Martin Siegel. We set out to design a digital learning environment (Siegel and Sousa, 1994; Siegel and Kirkley 1997) for archaeology students that could bridge the gap between current efforts to amass digital archives of multimedia data, and efforts to use such virtual libraries for classroom instruction. The project developed over five years,[8] and has three main components.

The first component is the *African Archaeology Database*. Using Oracle software we created a complex relational database containing multimedia data from African archaeological sites, organized for instructional use. It was important to design a new type of flexible, instructional database that could eventually accommodate a large amount of detailed information about many different types of archaeological site (e.g., from fossil hominid localities, to rock art sites, to Iron Age villages) with different types of data classified in many different ways (e.g., from the decorative motifs on ceramics, to the species and the body part of different wild and domestic animal bones).

The second component of the project is *TimeWeb*. Using Java software we designed and built a web-based environment that students could use to search and explore the *African Archaeology Database* and visualize archaeological patterns in space and time across the African continent. It was important to create a tool that would allow students to ask realistic, complex questions about sites in our database without getting lost in the complexity of the data structure. The query interface we designed allowed students to visually explore the data hierarchy, and select logical criteria for their database searches from different categories simultaneously. For example, I asked a class to form teams to research the question "What is the earliest evidence for food production in different parts of Africa?" In response, the teams searched for evidence in different regions of the continent. More importantly, each team had to decide on what type of data to look for that would be considered evidence of food production, and each type of evidence had different potential archaeological biases they needed to take into account. Some teams began with searches for sites where seeds of specific domestic plant species were preserved. Other teams decided to look for sites with bones of domestic animal species, or focused on finding sites with particular farming implements and/or specific settlement patterns. Each query yielded a different sample of sites, and the student teams then had to compare results from different regions and evaluate different possible answers to the question.

It was also important to encourage students with different learning styles to explore the bold patterns of their query results in different ways. The *TimeWeb* interface allowed students to generate lists or simple graphs of their query results, or to plot the data on zoom-able maps or on a dynamic timeline that could be stretched to show a time-slice of five years or five million years. For informed comparisons and visual analysis, students could easily display the "big picture" or "forest view" of their query results, showing the large scale map or timeline patterns of archaeological sites, or quickly zoom down to a finer-grained site chronology at the "tree view," just one click away from the details of individual site data in a "leaf view."

The third component of the project is *Prehistoric Puzzles*. I designed new curricular strategies and instructional materials using *TimeWeb* and the *African Archaeology Database,* and used them in several different archaeology classes, including African prehistory. Each lesson targeted different types of individual and team-based learning. It was important to create a model series of nested exercises and related pedagogical resources that would both introduce students to the use of the *TimeWeb* program and allow them to investigate important questions linked to the pedagogical goals of the course. The *Prehistoric Puzzles* website was created to house these materials for students and to allow easy dissemination to colleagues.

The project was designed to enhance the opportunities for archaeological faculty to be mentors, rather than lecturers, helping students learn to piece together the puzzles of prehistory for themselves, with tools to help develop a community of learners and teachers (Harasim 1993). Rather than encourage passive learning, I tried to help the students become researchers and constructors of knowledge. The software facilitated student access to rich, authentic multimedia data in a context that engaged them in the discovery of evidence of the past, and encouraged them to develop integrative, problem-solving skills. In a learner-centered and problem-based instructional support system, learning is organized around a series of complex, real-world issues rather than memorization of facts and principles (Brown, Collins, and Duguid 1989; Duffy and Jonassen 1992; von Glasersfeld 1995). Students were given the role of active researchers, learning to systematically investigate problems, question interpretations, and build their own understanding from specific details to general patterns. A digital toolkit was designed to help students organize and analyze interdisciplinary archaeological information, distill patterns of evidence across dimensions of space and time, and build their own sense of prehistoric patterns.

Finally, I wanted students to be able to work together in this process, and easily share and present results of their analyses to their peers, for discussion and suggestions for revision and further inquiry—to become both collaborators and critics. Students can learn to think like archaeologists, not only individually, but in the context of team research, so that they experience the power and debate intrinsic to collaborative efforts, and learn to generate insightful comparisons of alternative (peer or expert) theories through teamwork. I wanted to engage students in a process of peer review and evaluation to motivate their investigations and encourage the development of their rhetorical and critical thinking skills. The ultimate goal was to give students the opportunity to take on the role of interpreters of the past—both internally, with known classmates as their audience, and externally, through asynchronous, digital discussions with students in other classes and other schools.

Implementation and evaluation. *TimeWeb* has been used in five different archaeology classes, and there is survey evaluation data, and classroom observation data samples and interviews from a total of 192 users from 1999–2002. Overall the students found many positive aspects to the program. They thought it was a valuable educational resource and gave them access to, in one student's words, "vast amounts of data." They found it to be a new and interesting way to learn, enjoyed the different presentations of the material, and thought that the program did, indeed, help them visualize patterns of prehistoric data. However, they also found many bugs in the program, had many suggestions for interface design revision, felt they needed more time to learn how to use this new type of computer tool for research, and felt they needed more systematic help in class learning to compare their research findings with the results of other students. Ultimately, despite the normal trials and tribulations of a software development process, our pedagogical approach has value, but it is a work in progress.

TimeWeb has been used in two of my African prehistory survey classes. The first time, early in the fall semester of 1998, the 21 students used *Investigating Olduvai* for an exercise, and later in the semester used a prototype of *TimeWeb* for in-class exercises during three class periods, when the class met in a computer lab. Although this was before the database had been developed, students gave us informal feedback on the interface design, and on how effective they thought the exercises were. At the end of the semester, 19 students responded to questions on a standard student evaluation form using a 5-part scale (4 = strongly agree, 0 = strongly disagree). All 19 agreed with the statements "I learned a lot in this class" (mean 3.8) and "Assignments in this class helped in learning" (mean 3.7). Ten mentioned either the use of the *Investigating Olduvai* CD-ROM, or the use of *TimeWeb*, or both, as things they liked most about the course, and three mentioned *TimeWeb* as the aspect of the course they liked the least.

The second time I used *TimeWeb* in the African prehistory course was fall semester 2000, with 38 students enrolled. Students used *TimeWeb* for two different exercises over four total class periods. We collected classroom observation data and responses to three different surveys: a questionnaire about background information and familiarity with computers taken at the beginning of the semester (n = 28); a pretest questionnaire about learning strategies and content knowledge administered mid-semester, just before *TimeWeb* was used in class (n = 35); and an identical posttest questionnaire (n = 22) given after use of *TimeWeb* had been completed several weeks later. Nineteen individuals returned both the pretest and posttest questionnaires, but only 14 completed all three surveys. There were no detectable differences in the response patterns

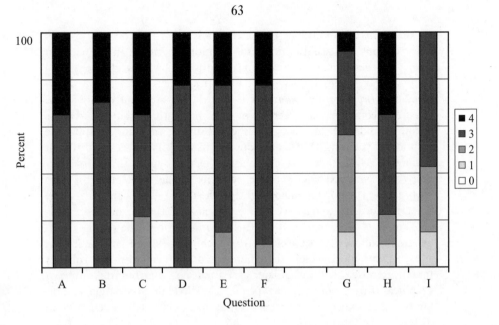

Figure 3.4 Student responses to learning in African prehistory course

between students who did or did not complete the different surveys. However, the sample of data from this one class is too small for reliable statistical comparisons, and I did not have access to data from the university registrar (e.g., student GPA or SAT scores) that could have been used as independent measures of student academic performance to help assess potential biases in our student samples (cf. Becker, this volume). Even so, the responses do provide an interesting profile of student attitudes about instructional strategies for an archaeology course, and suggest some hypotheses we could pursue in future studies of the use of *TimeWeb* in this type of survey class.

As summarized in Figure 3.4,[9] 35 of 38 students who completed the pretest survey in the middle of the semester seemed to enjoy attending class, found the course interesting and thought they were learning a lot about archaeology and a wide variety of African archaeological sites. They generally felt comfortable asking other students in the class questions, and agreed that it was important to discuss questions with each other. However, as a class they were less positive about working in groups and only a few students reported that they commonly discussed African prehistory with classmates outside of class.

Four exercises were run in class using *TimeWeb*. The first exercise introduced students to how to use the tool, and asked them to work in pairs to look for geographical and temporal patterns in the earliest known archaeological sites (e.g., those with "Oldowan" technology) and contemporary proto-human fossil localities because they had just finished the *Investigating Olduvai* CD-ROM case study of one of those sites. A second exercise asked them to compare the variety of artifacts found at Oldowan sites, and their distribution, to living chimpanzee technology patterns. (Different populations of chimpanzees in different regions of Africa today use distinct sets of tool types.) In a third exercise they compared Oldowan site patterns to the distribution of sites with a new type of technology, the "Acheulian" (e.g., handaxes). The objectives of this exercise were to get a sense of: the narrow geographical sample of sites that exist for earlier time periods, the temporal and geographical overlap between the two technologies, and how Acheulian sites become more widely distributed and abundant through time. A fourth exercise a few weeks later asked pairs of students to study geographical patterns of artifact types for the "Middle Stone Age," a later period when much more artifact variation is evident between sites in different regions.

Most students had trouble finishing the exercises in the class periods, for what seemed to be two main reasons.

1. They were not used to working in teams and classroom observations noted that they did not "divide the labor" to collaborate on their research, although they were encouraged to do so, and every student in the class had a separate computer workstation. Instead, for most pairs, one student ran the *TimeWeb* queries and the other student watched and discussed the results. The tasks may have been overly ambitious for students who were familiar with neither African archaeology nor *TimeWeb*.

2. They initially had a difficult time getting used to using the *TimeWeb* program; the program had bugs; and the program performed very slowly with that number of simultaneous users working on computers with relatively slow processor speeds. The usability tests of the program before class had suggested that it was working well. But the "real-world" tests of the programs revealed a number of weaknesses in the program's functionality that were not anticipated. Of course a number of the students missed the first "Introduction to *TimeWeb*" exercise in class, did not try to read or use the self-paced *TimeWeb* tutorial that was available on the class website, and then complained that they did not know how to use the program.

After the fourth exercise there was not time in class for the students to share the results of their *TimeWeb* research, and the results they turned in on worksheets were inconsistent. Therefore (after administering the posttest), I took the next few lecture periods to present my own synthesis of the same problems and clear up points of confusion— exactly what I was trying to avoid by having them do the exercises.

What effect did the *TimeWeb* exercises have on student understanding of the African prehistory course content, or their reactions to different instructional strategies? This can be evaluated by comparing answers to questions on different surveys administered before and after the use of *TimeWeb* in class, but the sample sizes are small. I gave students a pretest and posttest with seven generalized questions about their understanding of the interpretation of archaeological evidence (Figures 3.5a and b).[10] One of these questions asked about an archaeological principle, uniformitarianism, that was touched on in many ways during the course, but was not expected to improve through the use of *TimeWeb*. So responses to this question could theoretically serve as a comparative gauge for the specific effects of *TimeWeb* on student learning (Figure 3.6a). Eleven of the 19 students who took both tests (52 percent) reported no change in their familiarity with the principle of uniformitarianism after using *TimeWeb*, whereas five students (26 percent) felt more familiar—but three of these five also reported the largest improvements in understanding for all these questions (Figure 3.6b). In practice, seeking to isolate the effects of *TimeWeb* exercises on student learning in this type of class may be unrealistic, because, in an ideal world, the goal of such instructional technology is to stimulate student interest in the other resources in the class (such as readings) as well. Most (74 percent) of the students acknowledged some learning related to issues that *TimeWeb* was designed to help them with, but overall, these 19 class members reported a wide range of learning responses (Figure 3.6b).

As summarized in Figure 3.6a, student understanding of African archaeology did seem to have been positively influenced by the use of *TimeWeb* in several ways, but it was not a simple effect. First, as a group, their familiarity with African geography improved, with 12 of the 19 students (63 percent) reporting improved understanding after using *TimeWeb*. To put this in context, however, although the pretest was administered after the students had already been studying African prehistory for six weeks, over half of the students surveyed responded that they were only "a little" (1) or "kind of" (2) familiar with the geography of Africa on the pretest. After using the *TimeWeb* mapping tool, nine of

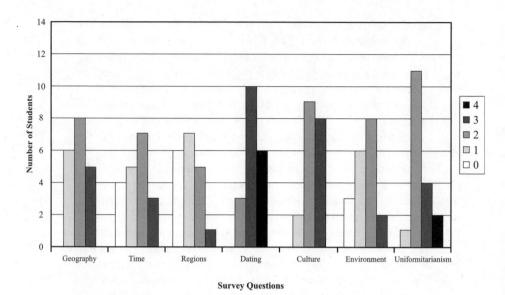

Figure 3.5a Student understanding of African archaeology before using *TimeWeb*

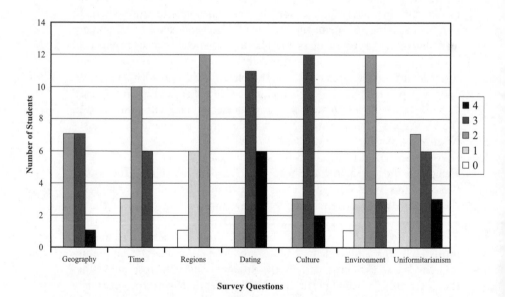

Figure 3.5b Student understanding of African archaeology after using *TimeWeb*

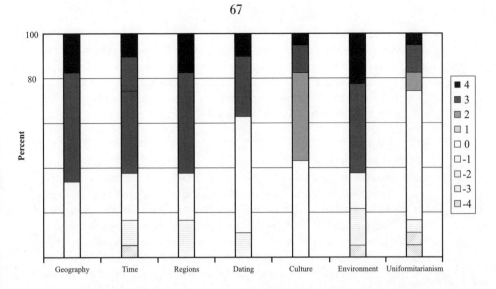

Figure 3.6a Change in student understanding of African archaeology after using *TimeWeb*

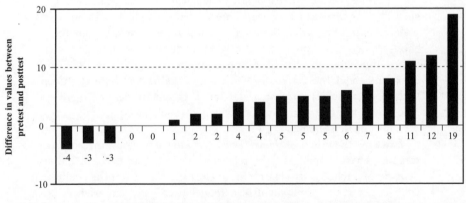

Each bar represents the cumulative change in one student's learning

Figure 3.6b Cumulative change in each student's learning about African archaeology

these 10 students reported improved familiarity. Yet only one of the five students who initially reported that they were "quite familiar" (3) with African geography reported an improvement to "very familiar" (4) after using the program. This pattern of change might suggest (a) that the *TimeWeb* mapping interface was difficult to understand, or (b) that the exercises they were assigned did not encourage in-depth study of the geography, only a general understanding, or (c) that students did not spend enough time on the exercise to learn a significant amount. Clearly these hypotheses are not mutually exclusive, so further evaluation of *TimeWeb* should try to tease apart these variables. In this class we did not attempt to compare the use of *TimeWeb* with the effects of mapping exercises using paper maps, for example (although this was done in another class).

Two other questions from this set also indicated some class improvement in understanding of the spatial distribution of archaeological evidence. When asked "How comfortable are you now in associating different types of artifacts with different regions in Africa?" the class as a whole began with little understanding and improved to modest levels, and 63 percent (12/19) of the students reported positive change. Responses to the question "How well do you now understand the different problems archaeologists face in reconstructing patterns of culture change within and between regions?" showed 11 of the 19 (58 percent) sampled reported individual improvement. When asked "How comfortable are you now in associating different types of artifacts with specific time periods?" student responses varied widely. As a group, the class showed improvement because all nine students who had had poor initial understanding improved between one and three intervals. But four of the five students who had initially been "quite comfortable" either stayed the same or actually dropped in their confidence. This raises questions about the extent to which our timeline tool helped students with different levels of prior understanding, gave students a more realistic concept of how complex the ancient chronological patterns were, or merely confused them.

To assess the effect of *TimeWeb* on learning strategies, my objectives targeted several aspects of the relationships between teachers and students in an archaeology classroom, to shift the class from the traditional content-centered, professor-driven model that I had experienced as a student to a more problem-based active learning approach, mediated through technology. Students were surveyed about their background in the use of technology and preferred learning styles early in the semester. Figure 3.7a illustrates the range of instructional technological experience and attitudes expressed initially by the subset of students who also responded to both the other *TimeWeb* surveys later in the semester (n = 14).[11] Figure 3.7b illustrates the same students' attitudes about different classroom learning strategies.[12] The students generally liked using computers for class, but acknowledged the value of traditional lectures and readings.

This group also reported some interesting reflections on their own learning styles that highlight the challenges faced by instructors in this type of elective survey class. For example, these were advanced undergraduates (juniors and seniors) and most considered themselves to be "critical thinkers" (13/14, 93 percent agreed or strongly agreed), and good at "collecting information and drawing conclusions from it" (10/14, 71 percent agreed or strongly agreed). Most enjoyed "learning by exploring" (12/14, 85 percent agreed or strongly agreed), and seemed generally receptive to the use of a program like *TimeWeb*. And yet these same students rejected the idea that they liked to "access information rather than have it presented" to them (half disagreed or strongly disagreed, and 5/14, 36 percent were unsure). They also preferred to have professors choose essay topics for them (9/14, 64 percent agreed or strongly agreed) rather than choose essay or research topics themselves (only 2 students agreed). This suggests that careful mentoring will be needed to wean students of passive learning habits. However, given the small size (n = 14) and unknown sampling bias of this comparative sample, no reliable statistical relationship (either Pearson r or Chi-square) could be demonstrated between students' preferred learning styles or use of technology on the one hand and either how they rated their understanding of geographical or chronological dimensions of African prehistory on the pretest and posttest questionnaires, or any change in their understanding of space/time patterns after using *TimeWeb*.

Students had widely varying opinions about the value of working in groups and discussing class issues with other students before the use of *TimeWeb* in class, and their reported attitudes did not improve after these group exercises. For example, their response to the question "Is it important for students to discuss course content with each other?" stayed about the same, as did the number of discussions they had outside of class with their classmates after using *TimeWeb*. In fact over half the students (8/14, 57 percent) expressed *less* willingness to ask classmates about course content after the *TimeWeb* experiences.

Overall, the experimentation with *TimeWeb* had a negative impact on student perceptions of the course, as captured by the standard student evaluation forms collected by the department and summarized by the university's Bureau of Evaluation Statistics and Testing (BEST) at the end of every course (Figure 3.8).[13] On the one hand, student BEST ratings of my performance as an instructor, which had improved steadily over the years since the *Investigating Olduvai* program was introduced, held steady through the use of *TimeWeb*. On the other hand, after *TimeWeb* was introduced, student impressions of the course as a whole dropped sharply and fell even more as the program was used more

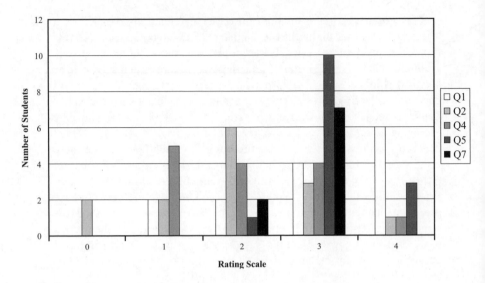

Figure 3.7a Student responses to the use of computers for learning

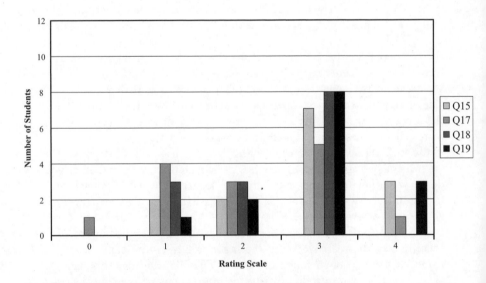

Figure 3.7b Student responses to collaborative learning strategies

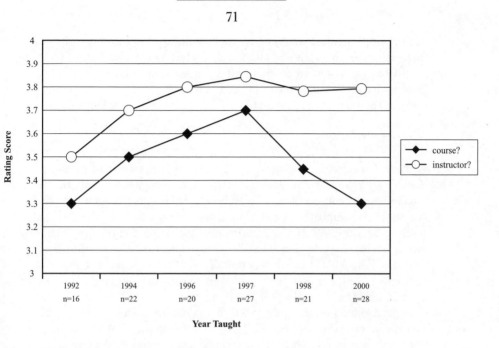

Figure 3.8 Student evaluations of African prehistory course and instructor

extensively in the subsequent course. Because few other attributes of the course had changed (e.g., similar topics, reading load, quizzes, written assignments), these results are likely due to the *TimeWeb* exercises. Although these are still good course evaluation scores (rating by BEST in the top 20 percent of all courses evaluated across the university in the year 2000), 15 of the students specifically mentioned their frustrations using *TimeWeb* as their least favorite part of the course. This is reflected in comments such as "I didn't really like the group computer activities. I didn't learn much from those sessions, even though I feel *TimeWeb* is a valuable program." and "The only aspect of the course I found frustrating was the use of *TimeWeb*. Although it was complicated, it was tolerable and a good source of info."

If the *TimeWeb* program had worked perfectly during these classroom trials, then I would question the strategy of trying to integrate such a tool into a survey course, because the overall results, at their best, show modest learning gains and, at their worst, show a negative impact. However, the fact that the program itself was in development, and did not function as it was supposed to during class, makes it difficult to evaluate the value of the pedagogical approach separately from its imperfect implementation. When it works well, students find it to be an interesting way to study the large-scale patterns of Africa's past. Thus it still has the potential to be an effective learning tool, especially for helping students learn how to build a "big picture" of African prehistory for themselves (Figure 3.3b).

Authoring Archaeology

Neither *Investigating Olduvai* nor *TimeWeb* was designed to meet the Society of American Archaeology's challenge to engage students in the broader, public context of applied archaeology. However, this was exactly the strategy behind the African prehistory class I had been invited to teach in spring 2002 at the Multimedia Authoring Center for Teaching in Archaeology[14] (MACTiA) lab of the University of California at Berkeley. The MACTiA lab was founded by Professor Ruth Tringham (Tringham 2001) with this very goal in mind—to engage students in actively learning about the past by asking them to author interpretations of archaeological evidence designed for public audiences. Through the process of creating multimedia "narratives" for the WWW, students not only learn to collaborate in teams and sift through real archaeology evidence, but they also engage in peer review and think explicitly about the different audiences their work could/should be designed for. One key element of the project was digital story telling. Traditional story tellers and guardians of oral tradition in many parts of west Africa are called "griots" or "griottes" (Hale 1998). Because students were learning to construct stories about the human past in Africa that revealed the strengths and weaknesses of archaeological evidence, our class project was called *Griots of African Archaeology.*

Instructional challenge. The challenge of teaching such a class is in simultaneously introducing students to how to create multimedia—both the method and theory of digital media—while also luring them into the archaeological record and public context of African archaeology. The class was designed as a small (13-student) studio class that met six hours a week, with the professor and a graduate student instructor/lab manager. Students met in seminar for two hours each week for the first half of the semester. First they reviewed and critiqued current digital resources about African archaeology (including the *Investigating Olduvai* CD-ROM and the *African Archaeology Database*) and subsequently they decided, as a group, how their class wanted to contribute to this on the WWW. They chose to design an interactive game, with each class member researching and authoring a particular topic related to African archaeology that would ultimately be integrated with the other students' work. Secondly, in seminar we reviewed six interpretive debates, illustrating different time periods and regions of Africa, to model for students the type of arguments they could pursue in their own research. During this same period students had four hours of programming tutorials and computer lab time each week, demonstrated by the MACTiA lab manager, to introduce them to a range of multimedia authoring tools, to create everything from interactive web pages to three-dimensional landscapes. Then, for the second half of the semester, students worked on developing their project, with a final public presentation and critique the last day of class.

Implementation and evaluation. Ultimately we had mixed success. All the students worked as a team and became literate in a variety of forms of multimedia expression, and each of them finished a good multimedia story. About half of them produced excellent, innovative and imaginative projects, and worked to integrate them well with other students' efforts. However, the excitement and challenge of mastering a variety of complex, new programming tools sapped everyone's time and energy, and half the students were unable to complete the equivalent of a high quality research paper on their chosen topic in African archaeology.

In principle, the students' work could have created a multimedia project on African prehistory that, collaboratively, could have had the same scope of coverage as a traditional survey course. The whole should have become more than the sum of its parts. In practice that did not happen that semester, as students sampled the time depth and geography of the continent unevenly, and some left the class with narrower views of African prehistory than had been anticipated. In retrospect they would have benefited from more specific direction. Still, our digital griots and griottes were all engaged in finding a personal connection to Africa's past, and explaining that pursuit to their peers and the public. It was an intense learning experience for everyone. As one student said at the end of the semester, "I had always felt comfortable with just a scientific perspective. This class challenged me to think about archaeology in new, creative ways, and I will never be the same." Compared to the survey course model using either *Investigating Olduvai* or *TimeWeb*, these students made real progress on the application of archaeological knowledge (Figure 3.3c) in a very important real-world context.

Conclusions

Our undergraduates are living in a public Information Age. They are *Growing Up Digital* (Tapscott 1998) in ways that transcend our different disciplines. In some ways these students are impatient with traditional

modes of instruction in college classrooms that rely on recursive reading, precise lectures, and slow discussion. They like hands-on and interactive exercises, and they want a fast, visual pace and quick feedback.
From an instructional perspective, I wonder if students' growing experiences with powerful commercial search engines and Internet portals at
home and in other classes have made many of them even more intellectually complacent, confident that they could easily find a web page with
the right answers to any question with the click of a mouse. Do students
seem more passive, more reluctant to recognize the ambiguity of evidence in digital form than had previous generations of students using
paper-based resources? Do we risk running faster and faster only to stay
in the same pedagogical place, an evolutionary phenomenon made famous by the Red Queen with Alice in Wonderland (Carroll 1872)?

Information technology gives instructors both an opportunity and a
responsibility. I have described three different approaches to this twin
challenge in the context of teaching survey courses in African prehistory. The approaches varied in focus: the detailed interpretation of evidence from a single site; the synthesis of evidence to address larger-scale
questions about the human past; and the explanation of archaeology to
engage different audiences. Ultimately, if students have the opportunity
to experience all three approaches to studying archaeology, they will find
themselves on a well-balanced intellectual platform that much closer to
expert knowledge in all three dimensions of learning (Figure 3.3d). All
three approaches take advantage of digital media to give students access
to the rich and varied data that are needed to address authentic archaeological problems. All three approaches also provide students the digital
tools and intellectual guidance they need, not only to navigate through
different sources of information, but also to begin to select, compare,
analyze and use this information in ways that will help them learn to
argue about the past. As researchers at leading research universities, we
have the responsibility to help develop new intellectual tools to help our
students and colleagues think about the future as well.

Clearly a number of practical challenges face any professor trying to
evaluate the use of such complex teaching and learning tools in class.
No two classes will ever be the same, and the ability to interpret student
performance measures in such classes is compromised without access to
independent measures of student aptitude and previous understanding.
Small class sizes enable flexible, powerful learning environments, but
make quantitative assessment of classroom strategies problematic. Experimenting with innovative approaches to teaching while developing
computer-based learning tools requires time, money, patience, a collabo-

rative spirit, and determination. However, if professors who are research experts in their fields do not take responsibility for innovation and evaluation of instructional strategies, who will? Chief financial officers? Commercial media enterprises? Politicians? A passive professoriate is no match for larger institutional or public pressures. One key message in Boyer's (1990) call to a scholarship of teaching and learning is public accountability, and this resonates with the Society of American Archaeology's call for new approaches to teaching archaeology in the 21st century (Bender and Smith 2000). As archaeologists privileged to teach at research universities, we owe it to our students, and ourselves, to study not only ancient human behavior, and archaeological epistemology, but also how students can learn most effectively about the meanings of the human past in the modern world. Just as we teach our students the importance of learning to cope with ambiguity in archaeological evidence, so we must learn to pursue and evaluate the gaps and ambiguities that emerge when our diverse instructional strategies intersect the common learning goals we set for our students.

Acknowledgments

Support for *Investigating Olduvai* was provided by a grant from Indiana University, Bloomington, Dean of Faculties, and the staff of Instructional Support Services and the Teaching and Learning Technology Lab. The *Prehistoric Puzzles/TimeWeb* project was supported by grants from the National Endowment for the Humanities and the U.S. Department of Education Fund for the Improvement of Post Secondary Education (FIPSE) to the author and Martin Siegel, as well as support from the IU School of Education, and *WisdomTools* inc. *Griots of African Archaeology* was supported by the University of California, Berkeley, Department of Anthropology, the UCB Archaeological Research Facility, their Multimedia Authoring Center for Teaching in Archaeology (MACTiA), and the Phoebe Acheson Hearst Museum of Anthropology.

Notes

1. There are few textbooks focused on African archaeology, but most of them are organized into temporal groupings: *The Prehistory of Africa* (Clark 1970) is still the gold standard, or classic textbook. A more recent textbook,

African Archaeology (Phillipson 1993), is organized the same way, but includes much less detail.

2. There is really only one textbook focused on African material that is methodologically organized: *Archaeology Africa* by Hall (1996), and it exemplifies a thematic treatment.

3. The two *Archaeology Workbooks* (Daniels and David 1982; David, Driver, and Daniels 1989) are excellent published examples of archaeological exercises in a traditional format; they are fairly open-ended, but still suffer from the limitations of the paper publishing medium, including limited graphics and small, simple data sets. Fugawiland (v. 2.0) (Price and Gebauer 1997) is a comparable set of computer exercises giving students a simple, artificial data set to interpret. More recently archaeologists have collaborated to develop interactive archaeology exercises. "Archaeology Africa" at http://www.archafrica.uct.ac.za/archhome.htm, a segment of Multimedia Education Group directed by Martin Hall at the University of Cape Town http://www.meg.uct.ac.za/ is a good example. These packages take advantage of the multimedia capabilities of the Internet and the power of networked resources, but still are designed according to the traditional model of simplified exercises.

4. Note that the distribution of ratings in Figure 3.2 is identical for the program rated as interesting and rated as useful, so these points and lines overlap completely.

5. One of my professional goals was to make information on African prehistory more accessible to Africans (cf. Hall 1997). Although it has taken a few years to grow, the comparative access to information now, compared to a decade ago, is astonishing (Hall 1998). Since 1997 I have had over 170,000 "hits" on the portal to the instructional web pages about Africa and African prehistory that I created, but only about 1 percent of these came from Africa itself. Given the statistics about Internet growth on the continent, there is amazing potential for growth and access. Africa Internet status report July 2000: http://www3.wn.apc.org/africa/afstat.htm

6. Perseus http://www.perseus.tufts.edu/; Crane (1998) http://www.dlib.org/dlib/january98/01crane.html

7. Perseus project 1993–1996 Evaluation report to FIPSE by Marchionini (1996) (http://www.perseus.tufts.edu/FIPSE/report_final.html)

8. Our project was funded by grants from the National Endowment for the Humanities and from the Department of Education Fund for the Improvement of Post Secondary Education (FIPSE). The evaluation of our project was done by ROCKMAN *ET AL*, an independent research and consulting firm. They studied the use of *TimeWeb* in several academic settings from the 1998–1999 to the 2001–2002 academic year. Their final report on our project is available on our Prehistoric Puzzles website: http://www.indiana.edu/~puzzles/eval/rockman.html

9. The proportions of responses of African prehistory students who took the

pretest questionnaire and answered the following questions in 2000. (5-point scale: 4 = strongly agree, 0 = strongly disagree) (n = 35)

A   I am interested in the subject matter of this course.
B   I am interested in African archaeological sites.
C   I am learning a lot about archaeology in this course.
D   I enjoy attending this class.
E   I enjoy researching questions related to the field of archaeology.
F   I am learning about a wide variety of archaeological sites in this course.
G   In general I enjoy working with other students on class assignments.
H   I am comfortable asking classmates questions about the course content.
I   I am very comfortable working in a group during class.

10. African prehistory students (n = 19) in 2000 who took a pretest survey, used *TimeWeb* in class, and took the same survey afterwards posttest, responded to these seven questions (using the 5-point scale in note 9):
Geography: How familiar are you now with African geography?
Time: How comfortable are you now in associating different types of artifacts with specific time periods?
Region: How comfortable are you now in associating different types of artifacts with different regions in Africa?
Dates: How complex a process do you think determining the age of ancient sites is?
Culture: How well do you now understand the different problems archaeologists face in reconstructing patterns of culture change within and between regions?
Environment: How comfortable are you now in associating different prehistoric culture groups with different ancient environmental zones in Africa?
Uniformitarianism: How comfortable are you now with the idea that information from the modern world can be used to interpret evidence from the past?

11. Distribution of student responses to the following questions, rated on a 5-point scale (4 = strongly agree; 0 = strongly disagree):
1: I am very comfortable using technology to access course material.
2: I am very comfortable using technology to make presentations.
4: Computers are impersonal tools.
5: I enjoy using the Internet as an educational resource.
7: Computers are valuable instructional tools.

12. Rated on a 5-point scale (4 = strongly agree; 0 = strongly disagree) to questions:
Q15: I learn very effectively when I work with my classmates in labs.
Q17: I like discussing research questions with my classmates.
Q18: I like working in the archaeology labs or on computers in groups.
Q19: I am learning a lot about how to do research in this course.

13. Student ratings of African prehistory course in different years, rated on a 5-point scale (4 = strongly agree; 0 = strongly disagree) to questions:
    1. I would rate the quality of this course as outstanding.
    2. I would rate this instructor as outstanding.
    Investigating Olduvai was introduced for the first time in 1992 as a network application, and was available for student purchase as a CD-ROM for the first time in 1997. *TimeWeb* was first tested as a course exercise in 1998, and was used extensively in 2000.

14. MACTiA is directed by Ruth Tringham and was managed by Michael Ashley Lopez during the semester this class was taught. More information can be found on their website http://www.mactia.berkeley.edu, and a showcase of the student work for our *Griots of African Archaeology* project can be viewed at http://www.mactia.berkeley.edu/134b_2002/P/P_Intro.html

References

Bender, S. J., and S. S. Smith, eds. 2000. *Teaching archaeology in the twenty-first century.* Washington, DC: Society for American Archaeology.

Bostock, S. J. 1997. Designing web-based instruction for active learning. In B. H. Khan, ed., *Web-based instruction,* pp. 225–30. Englewood Cliffs, NJ: Educational Technology Publications.

Boyer, E. 1990. *Scholarship reconsidered: Priorities of the professoriate.* Princeton, NJ: Carnegie Foundation for the Advancement of Teaching.

Brown, J. S., A. Collins, and P. Duguid. 1989. Situated cognition and the culture of learning. *Educational Researcher* 18 (1): 32–41.

Carroll, L. 1872. *Through the looking glass and what Alice found there.* London: MacMillan & Co.

Clark, J. D. 1970. *The prehistory of Africa.* London: Thames and Hudson.

———. 2002. *An archaeologist at work in African prehistory and early human studies: Teamwork and insight.* An oral history conducted in 2000–2001 by Timothy Troy, Regional Oral History Office, The Bancroft Library, University of California Berkeley.

Crane, G. 1998. The Perseus project and beyond. *D-Lib Magazine,* January, http://www.dlib.org/dlib/january98/01crane.html

Daniels, S., and N. David. 1982. *The archaeology workbook.* Philadelphia: University of Pennsylvania Press.

David N., J. Driver, and S. Daniels. 1989. *The next archaeology workbook.* Philadelphia: University of Pennsylvania Press.

Dibble, H. L., S. P. McPherron, and B. Roth. 1999. *VIRTUAL DIG: A simulated archaeological excavation of a middle paleolithic site in France.* Mayfield Publishing Company. Paperback workbook (128 pages); CD-ROM.

Duffy, T. M., and D. H. Jonassen, eds. 1992. *Constructivism and the technology of instruction: A conversation.* Hillsdale, NJ: Lawrence Erlbaum Associates.

Fagan, B. M. 2000. Strategies for change in teaching and learning. In S. J. Bender and G. S. Smith, eds., *Teaching archaeology in the twenty-first century*, pp. 125–32. Washington, DC: Society for American Archaeology.

Hale, T. 1998. *Griots and griottes*. Bloomington, IN: Indiana University Press.

Hall, M. 1996. *Archaeology Africa*. London: James Currey.

———. 1997. Virtual university/segregated highway? The politics of connectivity. Paper delivered at the convention *Education and Technology in the Commonwealth: Making the Transition*, Gaborone, Botswana, 28–30 July, 1997. http://www.uct.ac.za/depts/meg/virtual.htm

———. 1998. Africa connected. *f ¡ ® s ƒ--m ? ñ d @ ¥ y* 3 (11). (peer-reviewed Internet journal) http://www.firstmonday.dk/issues/issue3_11/hall/

Harasim, L. 1993. Collaborating in cyberspace: Using computer conferences as a group. *Interactive Learning Environments* 3 (2): 119–30.

Kappelman, J. 2003. Virtual laboratories for introductory physical anthropology CD-ROM, 3rd ed. Belmont CA: Thompson/Wadsworth.

Krass, D. S. 2000. What is the archaeology curriculum? In S. J. Bender and G. S. Smith, eds., *Teaching archaeology in the twenty-first century*, pp. 9–16. Washington, DC: Society for American Archaeology.

Laurillard, D. 1993. *Rethinking university teaching*. London: Routledge.

Marchionini, G. 1996. Final Report to FIPSE for the Perseus evaluation, 1993–1996. http://www.perseus.tufts.edu/FIPSE/report_final.html

Michaels, G. H., and B. M. Fagan. 1997. The past meets the future: New approaches to teaching archaeology. In C. P. Kottack, J. J. White, R. H. Furlow, and P. C. Rice, eds., *The teaching of anthropology: Problems, issues and decisions*, pp. 239–46. Mountain View, CA: Mayfield.

Phillipson, D. W. 1993. *African archaeology*. Cambridge, England: Cambridge University Press.

Price, D., and G. Gebauer. 1997. *Adventures in Fugawiland. A computer simulation in archaeology*, 2nd ed. Mountain View, CA: Mayfield.

Rice, P. C. 1997. Participant archaeology. In In C. P. Kottack, J. J. White, R. H. Furlow, and P. C. Rice, eds., *The teaching of anthropology: Problems, issues and decisions*, pp. 247–54. Mountain View, CA: Mayfield.

Roszak, T. 1986. *The cult of information: The folklore of computers and the true art of thinking*. New York: Pantheon Books.

Sept, J. M. 1997. *Investigating Olduvai: Archaeology of human origins* CD-ROM. Bloomington IN: Indiana University Press.

———. 1998. Engaging students in prehistoric problem-solving: The development of *Investigating Olduvai: Archaeology of human origins* CD-ROM. In N. Millichap, ed., *Enhancements: How using technology changes what faculty do*, pp. 108–12. Indianapolis: Indiana Higher Education Telecommunications System. (Full text online: http://www.ihets.org/learntech/distance_ed/fdpapers/1998/33.html)

———. 2000. Digital digging: A problem-based approach to undergraduate education in archaeology. In D. Brown, ed., *Interactive learning: Vignettes from America's most wired campuses*, pp. 113–15. Bolton, MA: Anker.

Siegel, M. A., and S. Kirkley. 1997. Moving toward the digital learning environment: The future of web-based instruction. In B. H. Khan, ed., *Web-based instruction,* pp. 263–70. Englewood Cliffs, NJ: Educational Technology Publications.

Siegel, M. A., and G. Sousa. 1994. Inventing the virtual textbook: Changing the nature of schooling. *Educational Technology* 34 (7): 49–54.

Tapscott, D. 1998. *Growing up digital.* New York: McGraw Hill.

Tringham, R. 2001. The democratization of multimedia technology: Multimedia authoring in the archaeology classroom. Presentation for the MATRIX 2001 workshop, November 7–11 2001. http://www.mactia.berkeley.edu/tringham/RET_SAACurriculum_web/RETSAACurric.htm

von Glasersfeld, E. 1995. *Radical constructivism: A way of knowing and learning.* Washington, DC: Falmer.

Wilk, R., and M. B. Schiffer. 1981. The modern material-culture field school: Teaching archaeology on the university campus. In M. B. Schiffer, ed., *Modern material culture, the archaeology of us,* pp. 15–30. Tucson: University of Arizona Press.

Wurman, R. S. 1996. *Information architects.* Zurich, Switzerland: Graphis Press Corp.

Four

Studies of Teaching and Learning in the Context of One-on-One Interactions
A Clinical Perspective

Moya L. Andrews

The public's perception of the importance given to one-on-one instruction in research universities appears to be quite negative. For example, the discussion by Hearn (1992) certainly confirms this impression. Yet research universities provide many opportunities for faculty to work with students on an individual basis. A great deal of teaching in the visual arts and in applied music involves one-on-one interactions in studio contexts, and these disciplines are usually represented on research university campuses. Additionally, by definition, research universities have large numbers of graduate programs, and the mentoring of students engaged in research for theses and dissertations involves intensive one-on-one teaching by faculty in their offices and laboratories. Despite the public's perception, one-on-one instruction occurs frequently in research institutions as undergraduates, as well as graduate students, are given opportunities to undertake research directed by faculty. Faculty appear to value the opportunities provided by research institutions to work with students on an individual basis, as can be seen by their willingness to offer readings courses and accept research direction assignments. It is not uncommon for the majority of prospective faculty who are being interviewed for positions to state that one of the reasons they would like to be employed at a research university is because of the opportunities it provides for having one's own students to work with individually.

Why then, when faculty seem to value the opportunities for one-on-one instruction that are afforded by research universities, and large numbers of students on such campuses are currently engaged in at least some individualized teaching experiences, does the negative public perception of its importance persist? Perhaps it can be explained by the minimal attention this type of teaching has been given in university promotional materials and news releases, and also because, in recent years, so much attention has been directed to the challenges of teaching large classes.

In medical schools and in allied health programs where patient care is taught, students learn both in classroom courses and in supervised practical experiences. It is not surprising, therefore, that the research on how faculty teach students to adapt to individual traits of patients, as well as how faculty themselves adapt to the individual traits of student learners, has provided information concerning both teaching and learning in one-on-one contexts. Some of this information, developed through the study of clinical interactions, may also provide insights that may be useful when other types of individualized instruction in research universities are considered.

In this chapter, I review some studies of certain aspects of one-on-one teaching within the framework of a graduate professional program at Indiana University. The program grants the master's degree (the entry degree for the professional) and a research Ph.D. in speech and hearing sciences. As well as completing the graduate school academic requirements, students enrolled in the master's program concurrently complete the clinical requirements for professional training.

So that students can complete the clinical component, the department provides an on-site clinic that offers services to the community as well as to students from the campus. Graduate student clinicians enrolled in practical experience courses provide supervised therapy to patients, and these practical experiences are meshed with the sequence of academic course work to provide the professional preparation leading to certification. I will focus in the subsequent discussion on the learning of concepts, attitudes and skills by graduate student clinicians in this clinical context. I will discuss students' learning as it applies specifically to the area of therapy for voice problems.

Interactions in the Speech Clinic:
Adaptive Behavior

Like most types of one-on-one instruction, voice therapy is interactive and when it works well, desired cognitive or behavioral changes occur in both participants. Effective voice therapy relies upon knowledge and skill on the part of the clinician and motivation and trust on the part of the patient. Both the clinician and the patient are partners in the therapeutic process (Andrews 2002), and it is the quality of the collaboration, rather than the procedural skill of the clinician alone (Andrews and Schmidt 1995) that predisposes a successful outcome. Students must learn to analyze therapy sessions; yet analyzing the factors contributing to a kaleidoscopic pattern of events is challenging. Some clinical researchers developed systems to document the type and frequency of behaviors sequentially (e.g., Boone and Prescott 1972), and others have used traditional content analysis methods but these systems have not been widely used by faculty members.

Many factors influence the structure of a treatment session. These include the nature and degree of the patient's communication disorder, clinician and patient characteristics and the clinician's theoretical orientation. The theoretical orientation of the clinician exerts a major, if not primary, influence on the way a therapy session is implemented. However, most voice clinicians, when asked to describe their approach to treatment say they have an eclectic approach and combine symptom modification and counseling techniques, matching their patient's needs with specific treatment strategies.

Matching each patient's needs implies that clinicians are highly variable in their behavioral adaptations to each patient and from session to session. It is interesting to speculate about this variability, flexibility or adaptability. Which specific clinician and patient attributes and behaviors change or do not change across therapy sessions? To what extent are behaviors stable or unstable within the clinician-patient dyad? To answer these questions, Schmidt and Andrews (1993) examined interactions between graduate student clinicians and patients in the Indiana University voice clinic. The specific purpose was to see how consistent student clinicians were across two therapy sessions when the student clinicians were observed working with two different patients. The reason for the study was to inform the faculty supervisor concerning how beginning student clinicians adapted, or didn't adapt to their patients. It was hypothesized that students may not be able to adapt their behaviors at all in response to different patients' needs and traits. Seven graduate student clinicians in their first clinical practice experience with patients with voice disorders participated in the study. Each student clinician worked with two different patients with a similar voice problem of mild severity. Materials used with all patients were similar. All of the therapy sessions were conducted in small, sound-treated therapy rooms typical of those in university voice clinics. Two video cameras were used to obtain 20-minute video-recorded samples of two therapy sessions for each of the seven clinicians. The taped segments were extracted from the middle portion of 30-minute sessions that occurred between the 4th and 9th weeks of a 15-week semester of a once-per-week therapy program. Because videotaping is routinely used in speech clinics, and releases had been signed, it was not believed to be intrusive to either clinicians or patients.

Ratings of Clinicians and Patients

Two experienced judges independently rated the videotapes of the clinician and patient pairs obtained during 14 20-minute therapy sessions. Ratings of clinicians and patients were determined by means of semantic differential scales and the Adjective Checklist (ACL) (Gough and Heilbrun 1980). Five-point semantic differential scales were used to rate (a) quality of interaction between clinician and patient (poor-excellent), (b) pace (slow-fast), (c) vocal variability of the clinician (low-high), (d) task involvement of the patient (low-high), (e) use of the counseling model of voice therapy (low-high), (f) use of behavior modification model (low-high), and (g) amount of clinician feedback to patient (low-high). The counseling model was defined as being in use when the clinician engaged in activities that focused on development of patient insights about voice problems. The behavior modification model was defined as being in use when the clinician engaged in specific symptom modification by means of drill, practice, and feedback to the patient.

The ACL is a standardized measure comprising 300 adjectives in which raters check as many or as few adjectives as apply to the person or object being rated. Three ACL scales were used: (a) number of favorable adjectives checked, (b) number of unfavorable adjectives checked, and (c) intraception. Intraception is defined by Gough and Heilbrun (1980) as the tendency to engage in attempts to understand one's own behavior or the behavior of others. The favorable and unfavorable scales were used to evaluate both patient and clinician in both sessions. The intraception scale was applied only to the clinician.

Interjudge reliability for each of the points of evaluation was determined through use of Spearman rank order correlation (Table 4.1). The degree of agreement across variables was generally high, with the best interjudge agreement for ratings of the amount of feedback given to the patient, and the favorable and unfavorable ACL scales used in evaluation of the patient (Table 4.1). Relatively modest agreement ($r = 0.63$) was found for pace and use of the behavioral model.

To examine the primary question of consistency, Spearman rank order correlations for ratings of two therapy sessions were determined (Table 4.2). As can be seen, moderately high positive correlations were found for negative ratings of the clinician and the clinician's scores for

Table 4.1. Interjudge Reliability for Ratings of Clinician and
Patient

Variable	r
Favorable adjectives—clinician	0.80
Unfavorable adjectives—clinician	0.81
Intraception—clinician	0.76
Quality of interaction	0.72
Pace	0.63
Vocal variability of clinician	0.81
Task involvement of patient	0.74
Use of behavioral model	0.63
Use of counseling model	0.72
Amount of feedback	0.90
Favorable adjectives—patient	0.87
Unfavorable adjectives—patient	0.85

intraception, indicating that these aspects of the clinician's behavior were relatively stable across two therapy sessions—despite the fact that the sessions involved different patients (Table 4.2). Favorable ratings of the clinician and use of the counseling model were moderately consistent across the two sessions.

In contrast, a moderately strong negative correlation was found for pace ($r = -0.60$), indicating that pace was the least consistent aspect of clinician behavior. Likewise, a moderately negative correlation was found for quality of clinician/patient interaction. These results show that there was wide intraclinician variability in pace and quality of interaction. This suggests that the pace of therapy and ratings of the quality of interaction may be linked to patient characteristics. It appears that clinicians were adapting to individual differences in their patients.

Several aspects of therapy were not related across two observations. These included vocal variability of the clinician, task involvement of the patient, use of the behavioral modification model, and amounts of feedback given to the patient. Again, this lack of stability with different patients seems to be indicative of clinician adaptation.

In further analysis, favorable and unfavorable ACL ratings of the patient were correlated with ratings of the clinician and the overall therapy session (Table 4.3). Favorable attributes of the patient were strongly correlated with perceived task involvement of the patient which would be expected. Moderately high positive correlations were observed between favorable patient ratings and quality of interaction, pace, and

Table 4.2. Spearman Rank Order Correlations for Ratings across Two Therapy Sessions

Variable	r
Favorable adjectives—clinician	0.39
Unfavorable adjectives—clinician	0.63
Intraception—clinician	0.63
Quality of interaction	−0.38
Pace	−0.60
Vocal variability of clinician	0.12
Task involvement of patient	−0.21
Use of counseling model	0.35
Use of behavioral modification model	−0.18
Amount of feedback to patient	−0.15
Favorable adjectives—patient	0.87
Unfavorable adjectives—patient	0.85

Table 4.3. Spearman Rank Order Correlations between Ratings of Patient and Clinician across Two Observations

	Patient Ratings	
Variable	Favorable	Unfavorable
Favorable—clinician	0.04	−0.22
Unfavorable—clinician	0.11	0.08
Intraception—clinician	−0.08	−0.08
Quality of interaction	0.49	−0.53
Pace	0.43	−0.37
Vocal variability—clinician	0.04	−0.13
Task involvement—patient	0.78	−0.77
Use of behavioral model	0.37	−0.38
Use of counseling model	−0.08	0.27
Amount of feedback	0.00	−0.10

use of the behavior modification model. Favorable ratings of the patient had near zero correlations with favorable and unfavorable ratings of the clinician, clinician's intraception, clinician's vocal variability, use of the counseling model, or amount of feedback given to the patient.

As might be expected, unfavorable ratings of the patient were strongly negatively correlated with perceived task involvement of the patient. Moderate negative correlations were found between unfavorable patient ratings and quality of the interaction, use of the behavioral model, and pace. Correlations between unfavorable patient ratings and all other variables were low. This suggests that unfavorable ratings of the patient do not seem to predict ratings of other aspects of therapy. Experienced judges (such as these certified professional clinicians) would be expected to separate the roles of the student clinicians and their patients in the therapy interactions.

The results of this study indicate that the degree of consistency of behavior displayed by a student clinician varies widely according to the aspect of therapy being evaluated. Six of 10 dimensions of therapy were found to be relatively inconsistent across two observations, with the pace of therapy being the least stable. Pace, the quality of interaction, vocal variability of the clinician, task involvement of patient, use of the behavior modification model, and amount of feedback seem to be patient-dependent aspects of therapy. In contrast, ratings of clinician traits (i.e., favorable, unfavorable, intraception) were the most stable across two observations. There was also some consistency in use (or lack of use) of the counseling model from session to session. This also suggests the student clinicians were responding to the perceived needs of their clients.

It should be noted that evaluations of the efficacy of the treatment were not included in this study, so it is not possible to link the consistency of clinician behaviors to outcomes of the treatment. However, findings like these help those faculty who train student clinicians and also help student clinicians themselves to discuss ways in which clinicians adapt to different patients. Results such as these, when compared across disciplines, could also provide insights relevant to emphases in different types of programs where one-on-one instruction occurs. It is not surprising, for example, that the pace of the session was the most likely aspect to change in response to different patients. In most teaching situations an instructor would be likely to adjust the pacing with respect to the learner's perceived level of comprehension or acquisition of skills. The way a teacher varies his or her voice is also related to the way a learner reacts. Teachers use pitch and loudness changes in their voices, as well as pauses and rate changes, in order to get and hold their listeners' attention. They also vary their voices to emphasize key points. Similarly the amount of feedback a teacher provides is certainly related to behaviors of the specific learner in a one-on-one interaction. The perceived quality of the engagement of teacher and learner also may change when different learners are working individually with the same teacher. This is affected by how much the learner is on-task, and how many behaviors must be modified. It would seem that all six of the 10 aspects of therapy which were inconsistent when the same student clinicians were rated while working with different patients could be relevant in other one-on-one interactions in cross-disciplinary contexts. It also seems possible that these aspects are related to the experience level of instructors generally.

Learning through Observation

In many teaching/learning situations observation of activities and interactions for the recording of data and for later analysis and discussion occurs. The American Speech-Language-Hearing Association, like many allied health professional organizations, specifies an exact number of hours of observation of varied clinical activities as part of its requirements for certification. The requirements include documentation of both the hours student clinicians must spend observing live and videotaped clinical sessions of patients with a range of disorders, as well as the hours that student clinicians must be observed by their faculty supervisors, as the students themselves work with patients. Additionally, even after a clinician is certified and employed in service delivery, formal evaluation of employees is usually based on a prescribed number of observations by a supervisor. Thus, it can be seen that both clinical teaching and learning in allied health fields rely heavily on the use of structured observations. Anderson (1988) stressed the importance of observation experiences as tools for learning and noted that although published Interaction Analysis Systems for recording observational data have been used extensively in education, counseling and psychotherapy, they have never been used consistently in speech and hearing training programs. Anderson believed that one reason for this is that analysis systems are likely to be misconstrued as evaluation systems rather than learning tools. Faculty in research universities have been trained in precise data collection and resist the notion that any one system can be seen as objective or can be used as a template. Rather, faculty in speech and hearing programs in research universities are more likely to apply their own individualized research methodologies to explore aspects of student learning through observational activities. An example of an approach to the study of the differences between inexperienced and experienced observers of therapy follows. The goal of this study was to compare the reliability of the perceptions of naive versus experienced observers of therapy sessions.

All graduate student clinicians in speech and hearing are required to observe therapeutic interactions between master clinicians and patients who exhibit a wide variety of communication disorders. Informed observation of specific behaviors has traditionally been recognized as a prerequisite to the development of clinical insight. As part of this observation experience beginning student clinicians need to be oriented to a variety of salient, yet often subtle, behavioral signs. Students seem to be most challenged by the need to select and focus on pertinent behavioral characteristics and to make inferential judgments. Presumably they cannot, at first, focus simultaneously on every aspect of complex therapeutic interactions. One could speculate that naive observers initially zero in on the more concrete behavioral changes in the patient (e.g., outcomes) that occur during treatment. Outcome measures are usually documented by comparisons of pretreatment and subsequent patient behaviors. Although change in patient behaviors is undoubtedly important, it is not a comprehensive measure of treatment efficacy. Frattali (1991) and Kamhi (1994) among others have argued that clinical effectiveness is defined not only by technical, procedural and knowledge-based qualities of the clinician or by specific symptom reduction by the patient but also by interpersonal engagement and attitudinal change.

Andrews and Schmidt (1999) examined new graduate student clinicians' observational data. The novice responses were also compared with those of experienced certified clinical observers. Novice raters' focus of attention was also examined by means of a free-response format in which the novices indicated positive and negative aspects they perceived while observing individual therapy sessions.

Results indicated that the novice observers demonstrated an acceptable degree of interrater reliability across all 12 items that were rated: quality of verbal interaction, quality of nonverbal interaction, task involvement of patient, task involvement of clinician, amount of explanation by clinician, clarity of clinician's explanation, amount of feedback to patient, clinician's initiative, clinician's attention to patient, patient's attention to clinician, quality of task sequence, use of counseling. Notably, the highest degree of interrater consistency was obtained for items pertaining to the behavior of the patient. This was confirmed by qualitative as well as quantitative analysis. Novices seem to focus on the learner, and rate learner (patient) behaviors in similar ways. The lowest interrater reliability was found for items pertaining to clinician behaviors (e.g., clarity of explanation, task involvement, amount of feedback, clinician's attention to patient, quality of task sequence, and quality of nonverbal interaction). A notable exception to this low reliability was the item "clinician's initiative," indicating greater agreement among raters. In qualitative analysis, the lowest rates of agreement were found for clinician's task sequence and clinician's interest and attitude.

The generally higher interrater reliability for patient behaviors could be a reflection of the rater's previous educational experience. It is typical in speech and hearing academic instruction for students' attention to be directed toward the description, analysis, and comparison of communication disorders exhibited by patients. Thus, novice raters' higher consistency in ratings of the patients may be linked to a focus on what the patient says and does, how the patient improves, and other overt manifestations of patient responsiveness. The raters' basic assumption may be that effective therapy is defined by an attentive patient who improves. Novice raters appear to be more heterogeneous in their perceptions of possible cause-effect relationships implicit in the treatment process and in the more subtle interactional variables, and this is probably related to their clinical inexperience. It may also be possible that there is a developmental aspect to the observation of salient characteristics of voice therapy interactions. That is to say, inexperienced raters may be able to describe or interpret the patient's behaviors more precisely at first and only later gain greater consistency in describing or interpreting clinician and interaction variables. This was borne out by the comparison with certified clinicians, who proved to be more reliable than inexperienced evaluators on ratings of clinician behaviors.

Inexperienced raters' comments about the strengths and weaknesses of therapy sessions emphasized overt behaviors on the part of the patient as well as the clinician (i.e., strategies, feedback, and explanation). Whereas the focus of attention on these factors was high, the novice raters indicated somewhat less agreement in their perceptions of some clinician behaviors, compared with perceptions of the patients' behaviors. It could be speculated that the somewhat lower degree of agreement concerning comments on clinician behaviors contrasted with patient behaviors may be caused by greater variation in role expectations (e.g., "ideal" clinicians versus "ideal" patients). Whereas most would agree that the range of appropriate patient behaviors is somewhat predictable (e.g., attentiveness variables), there is likely greater variability in novice raters' preconceptions of appropriate clinician behavior. Differences in and interactions among clinician personality, rater personality, therapeutic model, preferences for organizational structure, strategy selection, etc., may also have contributed to the somewhat lower reliability noted for ratings of clinicians.

Qualitative analysis of comments revealed some additional insights beyond the issue of reliability. For example, novice raters seemed to respond adversely if clinicians they were observing did not seem overtly in control of the sessions. The following comments document this point: "The patient kind of took control and repeated herself if she thought here was a hard onset [tension in the production of a vowel at the beginning of a word], while the clinician should have provided feedback." "It seemed like the clinician was taking the easy way out having the patient analyzing . . . " "Overall, the patient is the one figuring out her own problems." "The patient seems to know more than the clinician. The clinician expects the patient to monitor and self-correct. The clinician should do it herself." "The patient seems to be leading the therapy: The patient is analyzing her production a lot." These comments, intended to be negative, may indicate that naive raters were not able to recognize the benefits of self-monitoring by the patient in therapy. Rather, they appeared to view it as the clinician's abdication of responsibility and control.

In summary, the results of Andrews and Schmidt's (1999) study indicated that the reliability of observations of voice therapy by novice clinician observers seemed to be acceptable and was in some cases quite high. However, it seemed as if naive observers tended to focus primarily on patient performance and attentiveness variables and clinician strategies, feedback, and modeling. It is probably not surprising that the earliest focus of naive clinician observers' attention was on the clinical procedures. That is, they focused on stimulus and response but did not seem to assess the more abstract relational aspects. That is a helpful finding for clinical faculty members engaged in sequencing both observations and early clinical practicum experiences. In this study, the procedures for modifying hard onsets in the sessions observed were specific and easily identified. Hard onsets are demonstrated by many voice and fluency patients, and the procedures for modifying hard onsets appear to be easily grasped by inexperienced clinicians. The findings suggest that such overt behavior modifications, because they are concrete, may be particularly appropriate as clinical targets for beginning clinicians to observe. Baseline data and results of practice trials for such behaviors are also easily quantified and recorded.

Another result with implications for clinical training is the confirmation that novice observers do not focus on the more abstract, psychodynamic aspects of treatment. For example, intent, cause-effect, sequencing, and the quality of interaction do not appear to be salient to them, although these aspects were salient to the experienced, certified observers. Similarly, novice observers do not recognize the range of ways in which a clinician may reinforce or empower a patient. This seems to support Andrews' (1996, 2002) view that an awareness of the psychosocial dimensions of therapy has to be created, not merely assumed. Specifically, once students have mastered the procedural aspects of therapy, faculty members must then provide them with directed learning experiences to address the more abstract aspects of the interaction.

Most students' general consciousness can be raised as they progress through graduate-level courses and practical experiences. However, clinical educators should intentionally create additional opportunities for specific active learning of the psychosocial dimensions of treatment. The ability to decode and infer from relevant social cues is probably influenced most by directed practical experience and informed supervisory guidance.

The results of this investigation suggest there is likely a developmental process involved not only in students' learning of what to observe, but also in the subsequent application and integration of procedural and psychosocial skills. The study noted above provides some empirical data to support long-held intuitive views of how clinical insights and skills are acquired. In classroom instruction as well as in the supervisory conference, faculty members must help students conceptualize and identify specific attitudes and behaviors that are embedded in the therapeutic interaction.

These results may also be of value to faculty members engaged in one-on-one teaching in other clinical contexts as well as nonclinical settings in research universities. The reliability of the inexperienced observers' ratings suggests homogeneity in the way beginners analyze interactions they are observing. For instance, the attention to the more concrete aspects of the interactions versus the inattention to the more subtle abstract aspects adds credibility to an intuitive faculty assumption that behaviors that can be easily seen and heard should be analyzed and discussed first. The perceived roles of the clinician versus the patient and the way the inexperienced clinicians assumed that participation on the part of the patient threatened the clinician's control of the session are also interesting and may be able to be generalized. Students bring stereotypical role-related ideas to learning situations that are related to their past experience, cultural background and personality. Instructors in all one-on-one pedagogical contexts may need to address the probability of preconceived notions of prescribed roles that can obstruct awareness of the dynamics of teacher/learner engagement. In the next section we look at some ways to sensitize students to the individual traits demonstrated by participants in clinical interactions. This may also be relevant to other one-on-one teaching within research universities.

Teaching Clinicians about
Interactional Variables

There is not a great deal of literature to guide the faculty supervisor of speech and hearing clinicians who seeks to help students understand differences in patient responsiveness in therapy. Many beginning clinicians have the expectation that all patients will respond in a similar manner if the session is appropriately planned. In a research university clinic, where a large number of college-aged patients are available, it is possible to pair student clinicians, at first, with patients of their own age who have similar cognitive levels, interests and experiences. This allows them to practice the procedural aspects of planning and implementing therapy with patients who are more likely to be compliant. There is the added advantage that these patients, many of whom are self-referred, generally have relatively minor communication problems relative to pediatric or geriatric patients. The supervisor of clinical interactions has the responsibility to ensure best practices for the patient as well as positive learning experiences for the clinician. Thus a compliant patient allows a beginning clinician a greater chance of success. If therapeutic interactions do not proceed well, beginning clinicians lose confidence and feel guilty about the patient's lack of progress and also worry about the effect this will have on their own grade. One way in which a supervisor may depersonalize the failure of a session, or the perceived lack of rapport or patient compliance, is to use some framework to help the clinician to understand the factors influencing an interaction. The important aspect is to direct the student's attention to analysis of differences in personality or learning styles, rather than to frustration with self, or negativity towards the patient.

Although a number of formats may be used for this purpose, the Myers-Briggs Type Indicator (Carlyn 1977) has been used as a framework to heighten student clinicians' awareness of their own personality characteristics and how these may be different from those of their patients. With college-aged patients, a supervisor may suggest that both partners in the therapy complete the Myers-Briggs Type Indicator (MBTI-Form F) and compare scores on extraversion-introversion (EI), sensing-intuition (SN), thinking-feeling (TF), and judgment-perception (JP). Discussion of the differences between the patient and clinician may provide an avenue for the clinician to understand aspects of the therapeutic interaction and to adapt to the patient differently. Andrews and Schmidt (1995) studied 19 clinician-patient pairs while they were engaged in behavior modification tasks that were narrowly defined. All subjects were college-aged. The videotaped sessions were rated by certified clinicians as well as novice clinicians and clinician/patient eye contact was quantified using a durational recording procedure.

The results of this study provide three perspectives on personality issues pertinent to the therapeutic process: ratings of therapy in relation to patient personality, clinician personality, and differences in patient-clinician personality. When patient personality characteristics are considered alone, it is apparent that, among the Myers-Briggs variables, thinking-feeling (TF) and judgment-perception (JP) relate most strongly to ratings of therapy. The amount of feedback was greater in dyads involving thinking patients. The ratio of clinician-to-patient eye contact was greater when clinicians worked with feeling patients. Eye contact with clinicians was greater in sessions when the patients were classified as thinking patients. Sessions in which patients were relatively high on perception (P) tended to receive high ratings on items pertaining to amount and clarity of explanation. Likewise, sessions involving perceiving (P) patients tended to evidence more eye contact on the part of the patient.

The results for judgment-perception may be interpreted in light of descriptions of the perceiving personality type that is noted for characteristics of openness, flexibility, and adaptability—qualities that may make for a responsive patient in treatment. Conversely, the judging personality type, given its predilection for control, order, and closure, may be indicative of a patient who is perceived as somewhat less responsive or less attentive.

Regardless of clinician personality, clinicians are apparently more likely to provide greater amounts of feedback to thinking patients, and thinking patients are more likely to establish or maintain eye contact with the clinician. At the same time, however, the ratio of clinician-to-patient eye contact is more likely to be greater in sessions involving feeling patients—regardless of clinician personality. As with perception, the patient characteristic of thinking is apparently linked to the degree to which the patient appears to be "on-task." Results for patient characteristics of EI and SN suggest that these patient personality characteristics are not significant factors in ratings of therapy or clinician/patient eye contact behavior.

In contrast to what might be expected, clinician personality characteristics, when examined in isolation, were for the most part not correlated with ratings of therapy. Sessions that involved judging (J) clinicians evidenced higher quality of explanation to the patient and greater patient attentiveness to the clinician. It is interesting to note that, as stated already, sessions involving perceiving (P) patients evidenced higher amounts of clinician explanation. Thus, at least in some respects, perception (P) in the patient and judgment (J) in the clinician appear to be linked with perceptions of greater engagement. It may be that this is a natural outcome because the judging clinician and perceiving patient personality characteristics mesh with the traditional notion of appropriate clinician-patient roles (i.e., the well-organized clinician and the receptive patient).

A somewhat different picture emerged when the degree of similarity in clinician-patient personality characteristics was examined. For example, task involvement of the patient appears to be greater the more alike patient and clinician are on sensing-intuition. Interestingly, this SN relationship also holds for greater clinician attention and eye contact. However, the patient's attention and eye contact were not related to similarity on this variable. The opposite was found for clinician eye contact and thinking-feeling: Greater eye contact was associated with greater differences in thinking-feeling between patient and clinician. For judgment-perception, the greater the similarity between patient and clinician, the greater the tendency for use of counseling by the clinician. In contrast to the other Myers-Briggs variables, extraversion-introversion, whether studied solely as a patient or clinician characteristic or as a difference between patient and clinician, was not linked with any ratings of therapy or eye contact behavior. Faculty supervisors may expect an outgoing clinician to be more effective than a less animated one, but this and other studies do not substantiate this intuition.

In summary, there are a great many facets of the patient-clinician relationship and many permutations of personality factors that are operative in treatment. However, the Myers-Briggs variables of sensing-intuition, thinking-feeling, and judgment-perception appear to be particularly applicable in elucidating the nature of therapeutic dynamics. Moreover, these personality characteristics are relevant when considered either as an individual patient or clinician variable or as a patient-clinician difference variable. In previous research, cited earlier, clinicians were found to be flexible in that their behaviors in one therapy session did not predict their behaviors in another session involving a different patient. Thus, it seems clinicians can and do adapt behavior in response to their patients. It seems that the use of the Myers-Briggs variables can enhance clinicians' knowledge of their own and their patients' personality characteristics and associated behavioral tendencies, and that with the use of this or other similar frameworks, individualization can be targeted and adaptive behavior can be explored and taught.

Conclusion

I have discussed clinical studies undertaken for the purpose of enhancing the specialized one-on-one instruction that occurs in speech and hearing graduate programs. The environment in which the instruction occurs undoubtedly exerts a powerful influence on what occurs during the sessions in the voice clinic.

However, some of the factors which have been discussed in relation to clinical training have the potential for generalization to one-on-one instruction in other settings in the research university—for example, faculty members need to be aware of preconceived ideas about roles and responsibilities that learners bring to sessions, as well as inexperienced students' likelihood to attend to the more concrete aspects of behaviors when they first analyze an interaction they are observing. Associate instructors preparing for faculty careers could benefit not only from observations of experienced teachers working one-on-one with students, but also from an in-depth analysis and discussion of both the procedural and relational aspects of those interactions.

One-on-one instruction is pervasive in research universities. In all disciplines faculty are heavily engaged in the mentoring of both graduate and undergraduate research. Yet there has not been much attention given to preparing future faculty members for this specialized supervisory work, and few current faculty members have received training in this type of teaching. In lieu of training, most faculty seem merely to draw on their own past experiences as supervisees when they are supervising research projects, theses and dissertations. Those who have had positive experiences as students verbalize that they, in turn, try to treat their students the way they themselves were taught and mentored. Those who perceive that their research directors were less than optimal seem to make it a point not to act the same way with their own students. Most frequently, however, we hear comments only about the amount of time research directors take to return work to students. For example, "my major professor always got chapters back to me within a week and I appreciated it so much when I was writing my dissertation that I always try to do the same for my students." Or, at the other extreme, "my dissertation director kept my chapters for months and I vowed then never to be delinquent in returning my students' work when they are writing up their research."

Yet prompt attention to timelines is only one of the myriad of factors that contribute to successful learning within one-on-one teacher-student relationships. For example, the quality of one-on-one research direction probably may rely on the initial match of the personalities, work habits, and research/teaching preparation and interests of the participants involved. Another crucial aspect may be the amount of time it takes for both partners to learn to accommodate to each other's styles and to master the techniques that are necessary to produce an acceptable product. Part of the process of co-production of the end result of the learning experience (e.g., the thesis, dissertation, or paper) is the meshing of two individuals who often have very different expectations of what the product must finally be like to be acceptable. The context in which it will be presented, the institutional culture as well as the student's and professor's own personal standards and future ambitions may all contribute to the level and standard of acceptability. Additionally, there is often a dissonance in both parties' perceptions of goals and roles of partners in one-on-one learning. The professor may see the writing of a dissertation as a preparation for a career of writing similar research projects and strive for learning that can be generalized across that career. The student may see the exercise as a final sprint to the post, an end in itself, with learning subordinated to the goal of getting the degree and being finished in more ways than one.

Differences in the expectations of teachers and students are, of course, a problem that crosses all types of instruction. In recent years considerable energy has been expended on studying this as well as other aspects of teaching and learning in large classes. There has also been increased emphasis on the importance of small learning communities where students form closer relationships with each other and more importantly with their teachers. Although economic and cultural forces have dictated the exploration of efficiencies through other models of instruction, there has always been recognition of those individual relationships that knit together educational experiences. Our initiatives in the Scholarship of Teaching and Learning activities should be expanded to include increased emphasis on the study of individualized instruction, where relationships between students and faculty are formed and transformed. The research university is the ideal setting in which to pursue this type of inquiry.

References

Anderson, J. 1988. *The supervisory process in speech-language pathology and audiology.* Boston: Little, Brown and Company.

Andrews, M. L. 2002. *Voice treatment for children and adolescents.* San Diego, CA.: Singular.

———. 1996. Treatment of vocal hyperfunction in adolescents. *Language, Speech and Hearing Services in Schools* 27 (3): 251–56.

———. 1993. Professional speakers: Younger voice users. *Journal of Voice* 7 (2): 160.

Andrews, M. L., and C. P. Schmidt. 1995. Congruence in personality between clinician and client: Relationship to ratings of voice treatment. *Journal of Voice* 9 (3): 261–69.

———. 1999. Reliability of student evaluations of voice therapy: Implications for theory and training. *Journal of Voice* 13 (2): 227–33.

Boone, D., and T. Prescott. 1972. Content and sequence analysis of speech and hearing therapy. *American Speech–Language Hearing Association* 14 (2): 58–62.

Carlyn, M. 1977. An assessment of the Myers-Briggs type indicator. *Journal of Personality Assessment* 41 (5): 461–73.

Frattali, C. 1991. In pursuit of quality: Evaluating clinical outcomes. *National Student Speech Language Hearing Association Journal* 18 (90–91): 4–17.

Gough, H. G., and A. B. Heilbrun. 1980. *The adjective checklist manual.* Palo Alto: Consulting Psychologists Press.

Hearn, J. C. 1992. The teaching role of contemporary American higher education: Popular imagery and organizational reality. In W. E. Becker and D. R. Lewis, eds., *The economics of American higher education,* 17–68. Boston: Kluwer.

Kamhi, A. G. 1994. Toward a theory of clinical expertise in speech-language pathology. *Language, Speech and Hearing Services in Schools* 25 (2): 115–18.

Schmidt, C. P., and M. L. Andrews. 1993. Consistency in clinicians' and clients' behavior in voice therapy: An exploratory study. *Journal of Voice* 7 (4): 354–58.

Five

Bringing Contemporary Quantitative Methods into the Undergraduate Computer Classroom

William E. Becker

William H. Greene

Applications of quantitative methods to economics and the other social sciences are not universally viewed as distinctive. For example, in his influential statistics textbook, Sir Ronald Fisher (1970) bluntly stated:

> The science of statistics is essentially a branch of Applied Mathematics, and may be regarded as mathematics applied to observational data.
>
> Statistical methods are essential to social studies, and it is principally by the aid of such methods that these studies may be raised to the rank of sciences. This particular dependence of social studies upon statistical methods has led to the unfortunate misapprehension that statistics is to be regarded as a branch of economics, whereas in truth methods adequate to the treatment of economic data, in so far as these exist, have mostly been developed in biology and the other sciences. (pp. 1–2)

Fisher's dismissive view toward the contribution of the "social studies" to the development of quantitative methods is traceable to the first version of his classic 1925 treatise on statistics. Because his numerous and great contributions to statistics were in applications within biology, genetics, and agriculture, his view is understandable. Still, it was refuted by sociologist Clifford Clogg and the numerous commentaries on Clogg's (1992) article that posed a natural challenge to Fisher's view, namely: if there are special data characteristics in issues confronted by biologists and other researchers in the natural sciences that require in-

99

sights gleaned from the discipline, shouldn't this also be true for economics and the other social sciences?

There are indeed unique features of the problems, data and issues in the social sciences that suggest special methods of analysis. The undergraduate student in sociology, economics, political science, etc. can and should be confronted with these. We assert that the essential tasks for those who teach quantitative courses in the social sciences are to identify important issues that lend themselves to quantitative analyses and then to help students develop an understanding of the appropriate key concepts for those analyses. Moreover, mindful of current technology and methods, we advocate the use of computer technology in the teaching of these quantitative methods.

Relative to the amount written on the teaching of mathematics little has been written on the teaching of quantitative methods in the social sciences. An early exception is Sowey's (1983) commentary on the teaching of econometrics where the field is defined as "the discipline in which one studies theoretical and practical aspects of applying statistical methods to economic data for the purpose of testing economic theories (represented by carefully constructed models) and of forecasting and controlling the future path of economic variables." (p. 257) In Sowey's era, instructors and their students interested in "applying statistical methods to economic data" had to trek over to a university computing center with their punch cards in tow; data were typically provided by the instructor for hand entry by students; and machine calculations required knowledge of a complicated programming syntax, which was also keypunched on cards. It is not surprising that Sowey downplayed the "practical aspects of applying" and presented a highbrow (theoretical) view of what econometricians should teach, leaving the teaching of applications to others. Although Becker (1987) provided an alternative view involving the use of then innovative computer labs stocked with microcomputers, the "chalk and talk" mode of instruction continues to dominate the teaching of econometrics as well as business and economic statistics.

Sowey's discussion emphasizes a dichotomy between teaching aimed at "specialists" and "nonspecialists." Because proportionally almost none of the undergraduates who enroll in an entry level statistics or quantitative methods course (or even those who enroll in a second) will ever ultimately become "specialists" in the field, we submit that this dichotomy may not be the most helpful approach to take toward this subject, whether in sociology, politics, or any other field. We depart from a few propositions that might seem self-evident, but nonetheless, do bear repeating. For most students who enroll in the gateway course, this course will be their last formal exposure to the subject. As such, it seems more useful to design the course to focus on its ultimate purpose rather than on the appropriate level of rigor in the presentation. If the intent of the course is to provide the student with the skills to carry out informed and appropriate analysis of nonexperimental data—the hallmark of applications in the social sciences, as distinct from many of Fisher's applications—then we contend that theorems and proofs, which form the staples of many courses that we have observed, have relatively little utility. Of course, there is a balance to be struck. We do not feel that the role of the course is simply to teach students which buttons to push in commercial software and what numbers to harvest from the computer outputs. Our contention is that modern technology and actual situations and related real data provide ample opportunity to strike that balance between rote, dry theory and rank unstructured empiricism.[1]

How We Teach

Quantitative methods are often taught as branches of mathematics, even when taught in business schools. There is a vast supply of statistics textbooks available, most of which provide a common, familiar presentation of definitions, concepts, teaching resources, and so on. Rather than attempt to select a few from a large set, we have listed in Table 5.1 some of the compilations of concepts, definitions, and courses that can be found online.[2] A cursory review of the material in Table 5.1 suggests considerable agreement on the concepts and procedures to be presented across the social sciences in the introductory courses. It also suggests that the focus in the teaching materials is on presenting and explaining theory and technical details with secondary attention given to applications, which are often manufactured to fit the procedure at hand.[3] Little appears on cutting-edge issues being addressed by the established stars and rising stars in the social sciences. At the extreme, this renders quantitative methods dry and abstract to the novice and lends support to Fisher's outdated assertions about the sources of quantitative methods.

In two national surveys, Becker and Watts (1996, 2001) found that problem sets are used more heavily in statistics and econometrics courses than in other undergraduate economics courses. Surprisingly, however, those applications are rarely based on events reported in newspapers, magazines or scholarly journals in the social sciences. Instead, they appear to be contrived situations with made-up data, as in textbooks that are characteristic of the chalk and talk teaching methods predominant across the undergraduate curriculum in economics. Especially troubling are authors' comments such as "This numerical example is not

Table 5.1. Statistics Curriculum Websites

Glossaries of Statistics:
http://www.stats.gla.ac.uk/steps/glossary/index.html

HyperStat Online Contents (resources arranged by concepts):
http://davidmlane.com/hyperstat/index.html

Statistical Science Web Courses with Online Materials:
http://www.maths.uq.oz.au/~gks/webguide/courses.html

Statistics on the Web (resources arranged by teaching, research, other areas):
http://www.execpc.com/~helberg/statistics.html

General Educational Issues (resource arranged by areas, not all of which involve statistics):
http://www.merlot.org/artifact/BrowseArtifacts.po?catcode=486&browsecat=4

necessarily realistic." In reply, students likely are thinking, "So why do it?" Economist, sociologist and Nobel Laureate Gary Becker's (1996, p. 19) admonition that "students have unnecessary difficulties learning economics because textbooks generally do not have enough good examples of real-world applications" may be more troubling in econometrics than in other courses offered by departments of economics.

Descriptions of actual situations and easily retrievable data are abundant today. There are at least three sources for vivid examples to engage students: history, news, and the classroom itself. Stephen Stigler, in his work on the history of statistics, has pointed out a number of episodes that can make convincing classroom examples. For example, Stigler (1999, pp. 13–41) describes an exchange between statistician Karl Pearson and three renowned economists—Alfred Marshall, John M. Keynes, and Arthur C. Pigou—about a study Pearson did that suggested that alcoholism is not inherited and does not wreak havoc on offspring. The debate was widely covered by major newspapers in 1910, when then as now the reasons for and consequences of alcohol consumption were a hotly debated issue of general interest to god-fearing souls. In another vignette, Stigler (1996, pp. 355–357) related a disagreement between Pigou and statistician G. Udny Yule regarding the policy relevance of Yule's multiple regression analyses of the percentage of persons living in poverty. Pigou argued that statistical reasoning alone could not be used to establish a relationship between poverty and relief because even with multiple regression, the most important influences could not be measured quantitatively. Naturally, issues such as whether certain traits are heritable or whether anti-poverty policies are effective continue to have considerable relevance for many students today and continue to be cutting-edge research topics in anthropology, sociology, psychology and economics.

Headline-grabbing events in the news can often be used to engage students in applications that establish the importance of economics and statistics for use in real situations. During early work on this paragraph, for example, there were featured stories in *Business Week* (June 11, 2001) about the potential costs connected with the analyses of conflicting data on the rollover characteristics of Ford Explorers and tread separation of Firestone tires; on TV (June 5, 2001) Larry King asked guest James Randi (a critic of psychics) for the number of binary questions and number of correct answers that guest Rosemary Altea (a spiritual medium) would have to achieve to win the one million dollars Randi has pledged to anyone who can prove psychic powers; and a front-page article in the *Wall Street Journal* (June 8, 2001) begged for calculation of an implied mean and variance of family income from the information that 15 percent of Duke University students come from families making less than $50,000 per year and 60 percent come from families making more than $100,000. Many timely issues reported in the press can certainly be discussed, critiqued, and used for data at the undergraduate level.

There are resources available for teachers who want to consider including more historical and current newsworthy examples in their class. Becker (1998) provides numerous examples of how the news media can be used to teach quantitative methods. There is a course in "quantitative literacy" called Chance, which is available on the web at <http://www.dartmouth.edu/~chance>. The course material includes many examples drawn from the media, and one can even receive a web newsletter with recent examples. However, much of the analysis found at this website is focused broadly on quantitative literacy rather than on examples connected explicitly to the theoretical base found in the social sciences.

There are also ample examples of instructors who have found ways to teach statistics in more active ways in the classroom. The *Journal of Statistics Education*, available on the web at <http://www.amstat.org/publications/jse>, often has articles that suggest active learning techniques; for instance, Anderson-Cook (1999) offers "An In-Class Demonstration to Help Students Understand Confidence Intervals." Curiously, however, these active learning activities are seldom based on issues addressed by social scientists working at the frontiers of their sciences.

Key Concepts and Skills

The starting point for any course in statistics or quantitative methods is the calculation and use of descriptive statistics—mean, median, standard deviation, and such—and mastery of basic spreadsheet skills related to data management, computation and graphing. In addition to these fundamentals, what concepts and skills are essential for analyses of actual situations confronted by social scientists, which students have difficulty learning? We submit that a short list includes probability, sampling distribution of an estimator, bootstrapping, hypotheses testing, regression to the mean, the least-squares estimator, and alternatives to the least-squares estimator. We address these concepts and provide examples for teaching them in the remainder of our chapter.

Probability

Undergraduates are typically able to regurgitate basic rules and formulas for probability, as found in elementary statistics textbooks, but in applications the distinctions between marginal, joint and conditional probabilities continue to confuse students and their teachers alike.

The "Let's Make a Deal" problem offers a striking illustration of this confusion. As discussed by Nalebuff (1987) in *The Journal of Economic Perspectives* and popularized by Marilyn vos Savant (1990) in her *Parade* magazine column, the question involves a contestant on a game show who chooses one of three doors. Behind one door is a valuable car; behind the other two are goats. After the contestant picks a door, the host opens one of the other doors and reveals one of the goats. (The host never reveals the car, since that would spoil the suspense.) Then the host says to the contestant, "Do you want to stay with your original choice or pick the other door?" The immediate reaction of many players is that switching cannot matter, because after one of the goats is revealed there are still two doors and only one desirable prize, which seems to imply that it is a 50:50 chance whether to switch or not. But this is incorrect. To see the intuition behind the correct answer, recognize that the player's chance of being correct in the first choice is one in three. If the player is correct in the first choice, then switching will be wrong. However, if the player is incorrect with their first choice, which happens two times out of three, then switching will lead to winning the prize. Thus, two times out of three switching is a winning strategy. At a more subtle level, the key to the problem is to understand the nature of the information revealed in the second stage. As long as the game show host reveals one of the goats, switching in this sequential game is equivalent to a single-choice game in which the host says "do you want one door or a set of two?"[4]

Examples involving probability such as this abound. Marilyn vos Savant's weekly *Parade* magazine column is a great source of everyday problems people have with probabilities associated with state lotteries, insurance, genetics and the like. For those interested in results of a more systematic search, Paulos (1995) contains a collection of engrossing vignettes including discussions of voting schemes, the decline in SAT scores, and the alleged link between cellular phones and brain cancer.[5]

The awarding of the 2002 Nobel Prize in economics to psychologist Daniel Kahneman provides an ideal opportunity to call students' attention to the blind application of probability concepts to decision-making. Historically, statistics courses taught in mathematics departments have not emphasized the differences and similarities among objective and subjective probabilities, uncertainty, ambiguity, chance and risk; but yet, as the work of Amos Tversky, Kahneman and other social scientists makes clear, these distinctions are critical in the social sciences.

For example, the Ellsberg paradox makes apparent the distinction between risk, defined in terms of probability, and ambiguous uncertainty. Becker's (2003) version of the paradox has a player (student) facing two bins, each with 10 balls. The first bin contains 5 regular white golf balls and 5 Flying Lady pink golf balls, but the distribution of white and pink balls in the second bin is unknown. The objective probability of blindly drawing a white (or pink) from the first bin is 0.5, and in the absence of additional information (or an assumed probability distribution) even the subjective probability of a white (or pink) ball from the second bin is ambiguous. Players are not indifferent to a choice of bin when betting on the draw of a white (or pink) ball. They typically select the first bin, which is a choice in a decision-making situation that is inconsistent with the notion of a unique probability measure as used in expected utility theory—the backbone of economic and financial theory. Becker has been able to demonstrate, in both small classrooms and large auditoriums, the preference for a known probabilistic choice over ambiguity time and again by offering as little as $1.00 for the draw of a player's desired ball color and bin to a succession of three to five players.

This golf ball demonstration of the Ellsberg paradox is but one example that demonstrates that preferences in different types of situations involving uncertainty and ambiguity need not be the same. Following a short classroom experiment, students can appreciate that the schooling-versus-work decisions, whether to consume or save, and portfolio allocation choices are qualitatively different events than which bet to accept on the outcome of a coin flip or a dice roll. The former choices involve ambiguities but not well-defined probability distributions. The latter choices involve standard probability measures of risk.

As illustrated in a four-article series on "Robustness of Uncertainty" (*American Economic Review*, May 2001, pp. 45–66), economists are formulating models of decision-making that attempt to capture the sources of ambiguities without imposing explicit probability distributions on uncertainties. The mathematics of this approach are challenging for graduate students but via activities such as Becker's classroom simulation of the Ellsberg paradox even first-year undergraduates can be engaged in the paradoxes of human behavior on which leading economists are now working. Similarly, in classroom activities undergraduates can experience other examples of cutting-edge work being done by economists, psychologists, sociologists and political scientists.

Sampling and Sampling Distributions

Students have little trouble grasping randomness in sampling, that is, the notion that their data represent random draws and that other samples would yield somewhat different values. Thus, the "margin of error" that is commonly reported in the popular press with survey results on questions of general interest is a concept with which most observers are comfortable. Likewise, the public does not question why the number of people surveyed is usually reported with the margin of error. The idea that larger samples are better than small ones is intuitively appealing. The formalities of these notions, however, are less obvious.[6] Students have tremendous difficulty grasping the notion that statistics calculated from sample data and used to estimate corresponding population parameters are themselves random, with values that can be represented in a histogram known as the sampling distribution of the statistic. Students are typically asked to understand this concept purely through an exercise of imagination: "Imagine that we went back to the population and drew another sample of *n* items, calculated another sample mean . . . and another . . . " Given the importance of understanding the notion of a sampling distribution in the social sciences, it is unfortunate that many teachers leave its development to the imagination when modern-day computers (or old-fashioned dice throwing) could make real the development of a histogram of possible values of a sample statistic. In small groups students can quickly and easily discover the principles in experiments that they carry out (and modify) themselves in a computer laboratory.

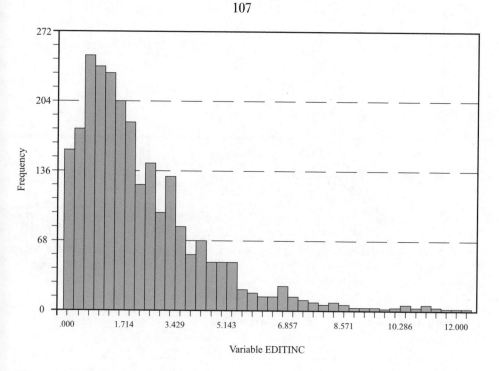

Figure 5.1 Histogram of raw income data

Contemporary software makes it easy for instructors to construct crystal-clear demonstrations of the sampling properties of estimators. To provide a present-day example that ties into the hundred-year-old debate between Pigou and Yule about alcoholism, we draw on a study of alcohol consumption by Donald Kenkel and Joseph Terza (2001). Their data set consists of a sample of 2,467 actual observations on alcohol consumption, monthly income, and a number of other sociodemographic variables.[7] A histogram of the raw (monthly) data is shown in Figure 5.1, where the positive skew that is characteristic of observed income is evident.[8]

For our experiments, we examine the behavior of means of sample of size 3, 25 and 500 observations that are repeatedly drawn from these data—500 different samples are drawn for each of these three sample sizes. The histograms of the observed 500 means associated with each of the three samples sizes are then constructed (Figures 5.2a, b and c). Looking from Figure 5.2a to 2b to 2c clearly shows the force of the law of large numbers. The essential ingredient that makes the point visually

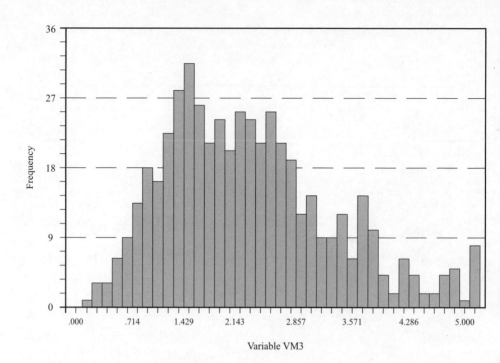

Figure 5.2a Histogram for means of three observations

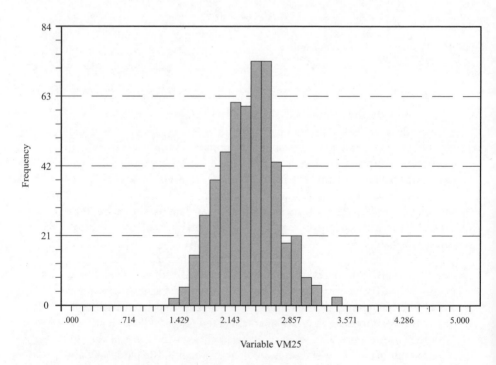

Figure 5.2b Histogram for means of 25 observations

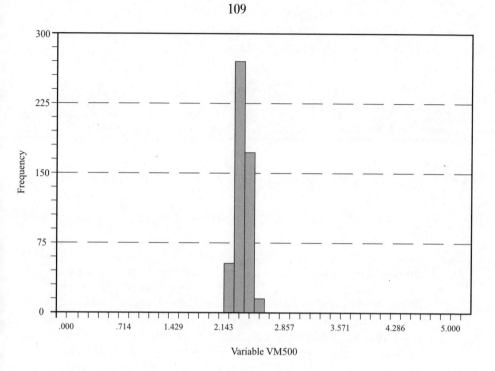

Figure 5.2c Histogram for means of 500 observations

is plotting the three histograms with the same bins (scales). Once again, this is an exercise that can be done easily with many modern econometrics and statistics packages.[9] The results of the experiment are shown in Figure 5.3.

Students can also be encouraged to tinker with the sample sizes. Alternatively, they might carry out the same exercise with one of the zero-one covariates (dummy variables) in this data set to simulate the exercise of surveying the public with a "yes or no" question. Or, they could use the random number generators in statistical programs to simulate sampling from populations with different distributions.

Some textbooks show what happens to the sampling distribution of the mean for increasing sample sizes for drawing samples from uniform and skewed populations (as was done nicely by Wonnacott and Wonnacott 1980), but none that we have seen go the full distance of actively pursuing an inquiry method of teaching it. Robert Wolf, for example, <http://archives.math.utk.edu/software/msdos/statistics/statutor/.html>, provides a computer-based tutorial on sampling distributions, estima-

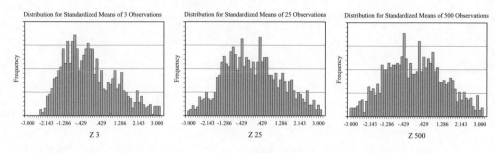

Figure 5.3 The force of the Central Limit Theorem in samples of 3, 25, and 500 observations

tors, and related topics that can be freely downloaded for individual student and classroom use.

One important lesson students can learn from their own inquiries into sampling and resampling data, and looking at means and variances of their distributions, is the difference between the law of large numbers and the central limit theorem. The law of large numbers, illustrated in the preceding example, holds that as the size of the sample increases, the sample mean will converge to the true mean (the sampling distribution of the mean collapses on or degenerates to a spike at the population mean). The central limit theorem, on the other hand, states that for many samples of like and sufficiently large size, the histogram of their sample means will appear to be a normal distribution.

Working in small groups at computers, students can quickly see how the distribution of the sample mean at first becomes normal (central limit theorem) but then degenerates to the population mean (law of large numbers) as the sample size increases. They can also see (as pictured in Goldberger 1991) how standardization of a sample mean creates a standard normal random variable (with mean of zero and standard deviation of one) that does not degenerate to a single value as the sample size goes to infinity.[10] They are able to compare histograms of the means (Figure 5.2) with histograms of the standardized values of these means (Figure 5.3).

Confusion on the difference between the law of large numbers and central limit theorem in the social sciences can be seen in the early work of Adolphe Quetelet (1797–1874). In addition to inventing the "average man" (*L'homme moyen*), Quetelet looked for "normality in nature," which he felt could always be found by drawing bigger samples. He missed, however, the connection between the mean of one sample and the distribution of means from all such samples. A modern-day example of this confusion, which a student should be able to recognize, can be seen in Peter Bernstein's (1996) *Against the Gods: The Remarkable Story of Risk*:

> Do 70 observations provide enough evidence for us to reach a judgment on whether the behavior of the stock market is a random walk? Probably not. We know that tosses of a die are independent of one another, but our trials of only six throws typically produced results that bore little resemblance to a normal distribution. Only after we increased the number of throws and trials substantially did theory and practice begin to come together. The 280 quarterly observations resemble a normal curve much more closely than do the (70) year-to-year observations. (p. 148)

By the law of large numbers, the mean of a sample of 280 observations will likely look like the mean of the population from which the sample is drawn, which need not be normal. The sampling distribution of the sample means for samples each of 280 observations will be approximately normal by the central limit theorem.

Examples of historical and current-day researchers confusing the law of large numbers with the central limit theorem can be used to drive home the importance of the distinction, and working at computers enables students to quickly see the distinction. With this hands-on experience, the notions of probability limits and limiting distributions become more than algebraic expressions. The computer exercise shown in the preceding example can be slightly modified to demonstrate this effect. The results of the experiment are shown in Figure 5.3. The computer instructions are shown in the appendix. Students engaged in this exercise might explore the question of how large a sample is needed to observe the force of the central limit theorem.

The above experiments are simple and quickly carried out in a computer lab. The simulations shown in our figures take only a few seconds each. The instructions needed are few in number, and can be tailored to interactive explanations ("in real time on one's feet"). Or, students can easily explore them on their own—the program syntax is "self-documenting." This is typical of modern software, and provides students with the ability to construct their own elaborate experiments with only a small amount of effort and a minimal amount of setup learning of the software itself.

Bootstrapping

With students working at computers, bootstrapping is a natural real-world extension of their work with sampling distributions and classical parameter estimation. In the bootstrapping approach, repeated samples of size $n - k$ are taken (with replacement) from the original sample of size n. The distribution of the desired descriptive statistic is then deduced from these samples. This sampling distribution is used to construct an interval estimate of the population parameters of interest, which requires no added assumptions about the underlying distribution of the population or the context of the real-world problem considered. Econometricians and psychometricians are making ever-greater use of bootstrapping approaches in their work. Thus, using the bootstrap as a teaching tool gives students early and hands-on exposure to a powerful research tool that is made possible through powerful and cheap computing power. As with previous examples, this exercise can be carried out easily with modern software to demonstrate the principle at work. Our income example is concluded by comparing the theoretically derived sampling standard deviation estimator with the empirical estimator based on bootstrapping. The sample mean is $\bar{x} = 2.22591$. The estimated standard error of the mean is $(s/\sqrt{n}) = 0.03626$. The histogram in Figure 5.4 shows the observed bootstrapped sample means, where the root mean squared deviation from the sample mean using 100 bootstrapped samples is 0.03955.

Hypothesis Testing

By the time students reach a course that aims at applying the theories of their field to observed data, instructors may wrongfully assume that knowledge of tradeoffs between Type I and Type II errors is fully understood and appreciated in all contexts. A Type I error occurs when a maintained hypothesis is rejected erroneously. A Type II error occurs when that hypothesis is not rejected when it is in fact false. What instructors ignore is the considerable controversy in the social sciences over the application of statistical significance versus the magnitude and practical importance of an effect.

From the time of the early work of Tversky and Kahneman (1971) in psychology to the later work in economics of McCloskey and Ziliak (1996), social scientists have been concerned about the three Ss (sign, size, and significance) when they point out that a fixation on whether test statistics are statistically significant can result in a situation where potentially large effects are neglected purely because statistical precision is low, not because the results are untrue. With the possible exception of psychology, social science textbooks emphasize statistical significance with minimal attention given to the size of the estimated effect. Confidence intervals (which provide a range of "plausible" values based

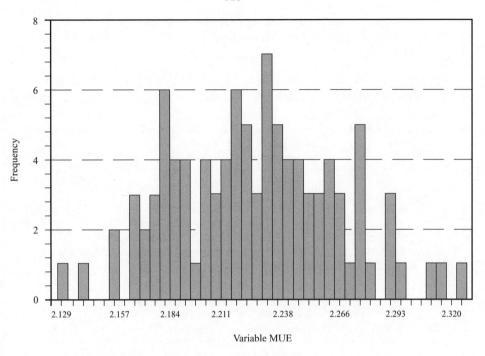

Figure 5.4 Histogram of 100 bootstrapped sample means from the full sample

on the sample information and classical techniques or the bootstrap) can be used to emphasize the importance of all three of the Ss without the need for formal null hypothesis, but this is seldom done in econometrics textbooks.

As an example for stimulating student discussion on significance versus effect size, consider the newspaper report on the collapse of a merger of Guidant Corp. and Cook Inc., two international medical supply companies that specialize in coronary stents (Werth 2003). According to the article, within the merger contract were two conditions that could void the merger. "The first was that a new drug-coated stent trial had to be 40 percent better than noncoated stents. The second was that legal issues . . . had to be solved in a timely manner." Although the deal fell apart because of the second condition, the statistics that could have arisen regarding the first of these conditions can drive home a misplaced reliance on significance. In particular, have the students assume a medical research team employed by one of the companies tests the following null and alternative hypotheses:

H_0: $p \le .4$, where rho is the probability a drug-coated stent is better than noncoated.

H_A: $p > .4$

This research team conducts two experiments, each with 100 independent and identical trials and gets the following results:

Drug-coated is better than nondrug (x*)	Number in Experiment (n)	E(X), if rho = .4 and n trials	Pr[X ≥ x* | E(X)]
53	100	40	0.0058
55	100	40	0.0017

An executive of the other company distrusts these results and hires a second research team to conduct new and independent experiments. This team gets the following results:

Drug-coated is better than nondrug (x*)	Number in experiment (n)	E(X), if rho = .4 and n trials	Pr[X ≥ x* | E(X)]
13	24	9.6	0.1143
10	18	7.2	0.1347
14	26	10.4	0.1082
12	22	8.8	0.1207
9	16	6.4	0.1423
8	14	5.6	0.1501
11	20	8	0.1275
12	22	8.8	0.1207
13	24	9.6	0.1143
8	14	5.6	0.1501

What conclusion and action should this executive of the second company take?

If the students are careful, they observe that in the first case of significant results for the aggregate of 200 there were 108 cases where drug-coated stents were superior to the uncoated ones but in the second case with 10 insignificant results there were 110 cases for which the drug-coated stents were superior in the 200 trials. The presentation of these data in class leads to lively classroom discussion on sample size, effect size, the meaning and importance of statistical significance, and the meaning of replication.[11] It provides a starting point for students to attempt their own meta-analyses to assess the effect of sample size and alternative methods of combining study results.

Students who understand the idea of a sampling distribution usually have little trouble grasping the idea of a Type I error. But the conditional nature of a Type II error is more difficult for students, because initial intuition suggests that the probability of a Type II error is one minus the probability of a Type I error. That the probability of a Type II error depends on the true value of the parameter being tested is a stretch unless it can be demonstrated. Here again, hands-on computer experience can be very useful. R. Todd Ogden, in the Department of Statistics at the University of South Carolina, provides a Java applet that gives students the opportunity to see the changing size of the Type II error as sample size is increased at <http://www.stat.sc.edu/~ogden/javahtml/power/power.html>.

Regression to the Mean

A common fallacy in statistical analysis involves the regression to the mean artifact; that is, the observation that relatively high values fall toward the average and relatively low values rise to the average is incorrectly taken as a sufficient condition to conclude convergence. Indeed, Nobel Laureate Milton Friedman (1992, p. 2131) wrote: "I suspect that the regression fallacy is the most common fallacy in the statistical analysis of economic data . . . " Similarly, psychologists Donald Campbell and David Kenny (1999, p. xiii) state: "Regression toward the mean is a artifact that as easily fools statistical experts as lay people."

The fallacy often arises when the analyst first splits the sample into high-value and low-value points, and then analyzes these points separately. In a classic example, Secrist (1933) argued that business enterprises were converging in size based on the observation that the group of the largest enterprises tended to decrease in size over time while the group of smaller enterprises tended to increase over time. Similarly, Sharpe (1985, p. 430) looked at the return on equity for firms that started in the top quintile and found that it tended to decline over time, while return on equity for firms that started in the bottom quintile tended to rise over time. The issue also arises in comparative studies of national economic growth, when the sample is divided into fast- and slow-growth countries. The discussion of growth patterns of various countries in Baumol, Blackman, and Wolff (1989) serves as an excellent vehicle for classroom explanations of the issues and shows the difficulty of rooting out appealing fallacies. (In another chapter of this book, Becker discusses the regression fallacy in the context of research aimed at the testing of students before and after engagement in an educational program.)

As Hotelling (1933) pointed out in a review of the work of Secrist (1933), Wainer (2000) points out in a discussion of Sharpe's (1985) book, and Friedman (1992) points out in a number of contexts including the Baumol, Blackman and Wolff analysis, if regression to the mean truly exists, then over time, the variance of the distribution as a whole should decline; that is, all the values should cluster ever-closer to the mean. Looking at subgroup averages does not show, one way or another, whether the variance of the entire distribution has declined. Based on these examples students can be charged with the task of finding other examples of the regression to the mean fallacy.

Motivating the Least-Squares Estimator

Scatter plots traditionally have provided the means for introducing linear least-squares regression, which introduces another problem for students. They must make a difficult leap of intellectual faith from the idea of estimating a mean value of the dependent variable, Y, conditional on the values of the independent variables, X, to understanding why minimizing the sum of the squares of the residuals should be the right tool to accomplish this goal.

There are several familiar approaches to motivating the least-squares estimator. Murray (1999) demonstrates how to get students to come up with them on their own. First, one can seek to draw best-fit lines through a scatter plot. As a second step, students can consider alternative ways of getting an equation for such a line. The instructor can lead the discussion to possibilities like the algebraic equation of the line drawn through extreme points, least absolute deviations from such a line, minimum sum of deviations, and so on. A third approach is to rely on the intellectual pedigree of the least-squares approach, whereas a fourth approach is to promise to show later that a least-squares approach has good properties. Unfortunately, it must be said that although these approaches can help students understand a variety of ways of looking at data, together with fallacies that may arise, it remains true that many students still perceive the least-squares estimator as essentially drawn out of thin air, with no obvious reason as to why it should produce an estimate of the population parameter of interest.

An approach to regression analysis that has not yet received adequate attention in undergraduate textbooks (with the notable exception of

Goldberger's books) is estimation based on the method of moments, which is now the norm in graduate education at the major research universities. In keeping with the history of thought and recent developments in the theory of estimation, the intuition for this approach rests on the insight that an estimator of a population parameter comes from the corresponding or analogous feature of the sample—that is, population parameter estimators must have sample properties that mimic similar properties in the population model. Instead of starting from the data, a method of moments analysis starts with the properties of the population. For example, the standard starting point for a population model calls for a linear deterministic relationship between Y and X, where deviations in the Y values from that expected from this linear relationship are assumed to be unrelated to the X value and have a zero mean at that value of X, regardless of the X value considered. That is, the expected deviations in Y from its expected value conditional on any X value must be zero. The method of moments says that sample data generated from this population model must have the same properties, which are forced on the data through the selection of the intercept and slope of the sample regression line.

When demonstrated in class in this fashion, method of moment estimates can be compared to the least-squares estimates. Multiple regression (an extension of the preceding to more than one explanatory variable) and instrumental variables regression (an intuitively appealing modification of the preceding least-squares procedure) can easily be motivated in the method of moments framework. (We note that good examples for least-squares estimation abound, but accessible and interesting examples for instrumental variables are less common. We suggest Ashenfelter and Krueger's [1994] study of twins and the returns to education as an intriguing candidate. An alternative is to set up a pre-post experiment in the classroom in which the post-treatment test is a function the pre-treatment test but measurement error in the pretest gives rise to the regression fallacy and an instrumental variable procedure is warranted.)

Alternatives to Least Squares

The conventional "blackboard" course in econometrics focuses on the algebra of least-squares estimation of parameters in highly structured models, with some discussion of applications requiring data transformations (logarithms, powers differencing, etc.), dummy variables, time trends, instrumental variables and so on. However, recent developments in computational procedures and the underlying theory place a greater variety of tools easily within students' reach. Nonlinear modeling of all sorts as well as nonparametric regression techniques are now available to undergraduates working in a computer lab and thus can be capitalized on by the up-to-date teachers at research universities.

As an example of what can be done in computer labs consider a widely circulated application in Spector and Mazzeo (1980). They estimate a model to shed light on how a student's performance in a principles of macroeconomics class relates to his/her grade in an intermediate macroeconomics class, after controlling for such things as grade point average (GPA) prior to the class. The effect of GPA on future performance is less obvious than it might appear at first. Certainly, it is possible that students with the highest GPA would get the most from the second course. On the other hand, perhaps the best students were already well equipped, and if the second course catered to the mediocre (who had more to gain and more room to improve) then a negative relationship between GPA and increase in grades (GRADE) might arise. A negative relationship might also arise if artificially high grades were given in the first course.

In Figure 5.5 we provide an analysis similar to that done by Spector and Mazzeo (using a subset of their data). The horizontal axis shows the initial grade point average of students in the study. The vertical axis shows the relative frequency of the incremental grades that increase from the first to the second course. The darker curve shows the estimated relative frequency of grades that improve in the second course using a probit model (the one used by Spector and Mazzeo). These estimates suggest a positive relationship between GPA and the probability of grade improvement in the second macroeconomics course throughout the GPA range. The lighter curve in Figure 5.5 provides the results using a much-less-structured nonparametric regression model.[12] The conclusion reached with this technique is qualitatively similar to that obtained with the probit model for GPAs above 2.6, where the positive relationship between GPA and the probability of grade improvement can be seen, but it is materially different for those with GPAs lower than 2.6, where a negative relationship between GPA and the probability of grade improvement is found. Possibly these poorer students received gift grades in the introductory macroeconomics course. Such a supposition can be used to stimulate classroom discussions.

We note that the social science literature now abounds with interesting, relevant applications that use the sorts of techniques mentioned here. To cite one example, Kenkel and Terza (2001), which provided the data for our earlier examples, apply this kind of analysis to the effect of physician advice on alcohol consumption, a perennial subject of the

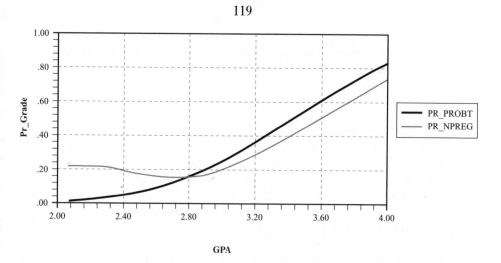

Figure 5.5 Predicted parametric and nonparametric probability of grade increase

popular press that is in keeping with our first example, on the debate about alcoholism between Karl Pearson and his early 20th-century counterparts.

There are other alternatives to least squares that undergraduates can work with in computer labs—for example, least absolute deviations. The least absolute deviations approach is a useful device for teaching students about the sensitivity of estimation to outliers. It is also a straight-forward process to find examples that show that even if least-squares estimation of the conditional mean is a better estimator in large samples, least absolute deviations estimation of the conditional median can some-times offer a better performance in small samples. The important point is that although students must master least squares, they also need to see alternatives to least squares. These alternatives have long been incorpo-rated in many computer programs used by researchers. What differs now is the ease with which these tools can be placed in students' hands within computer labs without first requiring them to master complex programming syntax and several mathematical specialties. Such devel-opments are allowing instructors at research universities to engage stu-dents in increasingly creative hands-on classroom activities.

Conclusion

The identification of real-life issues of the type familiar to undergradu-ates has been lacking in both classrooms and textbooks. Possibly because of the effort required on the part of the instructor to find those good examples and getting the necessary data for analysis, the emphasis has been on the concepts and methods and not the applications. Yet, at least conceptually, all faculty members engaged in empirical research should have the wherewithal to engage undergraduates in the identification of important issues that lend themselves to quantitative analyses, and they should be able to help students identify and employ the appropriate key statistical concepts for that analysis employing computer programs. After all, one of the rationales for students attending a research university is exposure to the most current thinking and practices in a discipline.

Unfortunately, the reward structure at research universities may be a deterrent to instructors' attempting alternatives to chalk and talk and theorem and proof teaching methods. As pointed out by Becker and Watts (1999), traditional end-of-semester student evaluations of instructors may actually deter innovation because they seldom include questions about the instructor's use of technology in real-world applications. Thus, the widespread adaptation of what we are proposing may require some institutional changes. Given those changes, teachers of quantitative methods at research universities would have no excuse for failing to incorporate into their undergraduate teaching the cutting-edge techniques they are using in their own research and that we are proposing for the undergraduate classroom.

We have demonstrated in this chapter how students can get hands-on experience in both the theoretical and practical aspects of applying statistical methods to social science data for the purpose of testing theories and of forecasting and controlling the future paths of variables. We demonstrated how the availability of inexpensive computer technology now provides the means for instructors to effectively exploit those applications for the benefit of students. We identify some of the electronic and hard copy sources for finding timely examples to engage students in applications involving probability, the sampling distribution of estimators, bootstrapping, hypotheses testing, regression fallacies, the least squares and alternatives to the least-squares estimation.

Appendix: Computer Instructions for Sampling Experiments and Models

/* This first experiment assumes that the Kenkel and Terza data have been read into the program. The data set contains 26 variables and 2434

observations. We use only the variable named EDITINC, which is the edited version of the INCOME variable. Using all the sample data, compute the mean and standard deviation.
*/ A histogram clearly reveals the skewed distribution of the income data.

```
        Sample   ; all $
        Calc     ; mue=xbr(editinc) ; sigmae = sdv(editinc) $
        Histogram ; rhs=editinc $
```

/* Procedure sets the overall sample then draws a random sample with the specified number of observations for each replication. VRES will collect the observations on means of random samples. VRESN will contain the replications on the standardized means. The master sample is restored before each replication.
*/

```
        Procedure = LLN_CLT(vres,vresn,ni)$
        Create   ; if (i = 1) | vres = 0 ; vresn = 0 $
        Sample   ; all $
        Draw     ; n = ni $
        Calc     ; xbar = xbr(editinc) ; z=sqr(ni) * (xbar—mue) /
        sigmae$
        Create   ; vres(i) = xbar $
        Create   ; vresn(i) = z $
        Endproc $
```

/* Experiment for a particular sample size. These draw 500 samples of 3 observations, then 25 observations, then 500. VMn is the column of sample means. VMNn is the sample of standardized means, sqr(ni)*
*/ (mean(i)-mu)/sigma.

```
        Execute  ; i=1,500;proc=lln_clt(vm3,vmn3,3) $
        Execute  ; i=1,500;proc=lln_clt(vm25,vmn25,25) $
        Execute  ; i=1,500;proc=lln_clt(vm500,vmn500,500) $
```

/* Now display the results for the sample means. This illustrates the law of large numbers. A bit of preparation, we set up a histogram with the same bins to be used for all three samples of means. This will show clearly the force of the law of large numbers. The three commands below just save some typing. The bin limits could just be
*/ specified as part of the histogram command.

```
        Sample   ; 1-40 $
        Create   ; limits = trn(0,.125) $ (This is 0, .125, .250, . . . ).
        Matrix   ; ai=limits $
        Sample   ; 1—500 $
        Histogram ; Rhs = vm3 ; Limits = ai $
        Histogram ; Rhs = vm25 ; Limits = ai $
        Histogram ; Rhs = vm500 ; Limits = ai $
```

```
/* Display the results for the standardized means.
*/ This illustrates the central limit theorem.
        Sample   ; 1—40 $
        Create   ; Limits = Trn(−3,.15)$
        Matrix   ; ai = limits $
        Sample   ; 1—500 $
        Histogram ; Rhs = vmn3 ; limits=ai $
        Histogram ; Rhs = vmn25 ; limits=ai $
        Histogram ; Rhs = vmn500 ; limits=ai $
/* Finally, we illustrate the use of bootstrapping to estimate the sam-
*/ pling standard deviation of the mean.
        Sample   ; All $
        Procedure
        Calc     ; mue = xbr(editinc) $
        EndProc
        Exec     ; Bootstrap = mue ; N = 100 ; Histogram $
        Calc     ; List ; s_mean = sdv(editinc)/sqr(n) $
```

/* The next set of instructions produces figure 5.5. This is based on the
    Spector and Mazzeo data set. There are 32 observations and 5
    variables named OBS, GPA, TUCE, PSI, GRADE. Only the
*/ GRADE and GPA data are used for this example.

```
        Probit   ; lhs = grade;rhs = one,gpa ; prob = pr_probt $
        Npreg    ; lhs = grade;rhs = gpa ; keep = pr_npreg $
        Plot     ; lhs = gpa ; rhs = pr_Probt,pr_npreg
                 ; fill ; limits = 0,1  ? limits for vertical axis
                     ; endpoints=2,4 ? limits for horizontal axis
                     ; grid
                 ; yaxis = Pr_Grade
                 ; Title=Predicted parametric and nonparametric
                 probability of grade increase $
```

Notes

This article is based in part on material presented by the authors at the 2001 Allied Social Sciences Association meetings (New Orleans, January 6, 2001) sponsored by the American Economic Association Committee on Economic Education; their subsequent article "Teaching Statistics and Econometrics to Undergraduates," *Journal of Economic Perspectives*, 15 (4), Fall 2001: pp. 169–182; and William Greene's presentation "New Developments in the Teaching of Metrics" to the Scholarship of Teaching and Learning Lecture Series at Indiana University (February 13, 2002).

1. Before departing this section, we do think it appropriate to raise a comment about the use of proofs in the econometrics course. Once again, it might seem self-evident, but we submit that it remains useful to subject the theorem/proof approach to teaching to a test itself. Proofs and derivations have little utility in their own right. They can serve two useful purposes. First, and probably the more important, a proof can serve as the foundation for further derivations on similar lines. Thus, proofs of the consistency and asymptotic normality of least squares in the multiple regression model, done in detail with close attention to all assumptions, are valuable tools because they form the platforms for subsequent derivations in other models. The first application needs only to be modified slightly to be extended to other situations, such as the generalized regression model. The second reason for doing a proof is to demonstrate how to do proofs. We submit that this latter exercise is the province of more advanced courses directed at "specialists." The practitioners or the "applied" econometricians are unlikely to do much theorem proving of their own, and may have little use for this skill. It seems to us that the instructor embarking on a theorem/proof teaching exercise can benefit from asking of the exercise at hand, "why do this?" This approach might well derail a lengthy derivation of the properties of some arcane test statistic.

2. There do not yet seem to be comparable websites for econometrics although a Glossary of Econometrics can be found at <http://www.oswego.edu/~kane/econometrics/glossaries.htm>.

3. Several of the econometrics textbooks listed, such as Lawler (2000), Ramanathan (2002), Studenmund (2001) and Wooldridge (2000), are oriented to theory but yet contain many applications. Although dated, Berndt (1991) is especially noteworthy for its emphasis on empirical applications and it contains a fair amount of theory. A comparison of the first and fourth editions of Gujarati (2003) shows a movement to the use of examples; however, those examples are not necessarily tied to the world that students see in the media. They tend to come from academic journal articles.

4. For a detailed discussion of how this problem depends on the details of the question asked and the situation, see the article in *American Statistician* by Morgan, Chagantry, Dahiya and Doviak (1991), the letter from vos Savant and the rejoinder from the authors. Students can find and play the "Let's Make a Deal" game at <http://www.stat.sc.edu/~west/javahtml/LetsMakeaDeal.htm>. There is a collection of similar Java applets written by several different authors at <http://www.stat.duke.edu/sites/java.html>.

5. Most of Paulos' (1995) examples draw on the multiplication of probabilities associated with independent events to show the very small likelihood of claims or allegations. Some of these, such as his analysis of a tennis match of Andre Agassi, produce intriguing and unintuitive results.

6. We note, for example, the inclination among some of our colleagues in

finance to estimate simple statistics using samples of several million observations, stretching both computing power and patience, apparently unaware of the marginal benefit of all but the first few tens of thousands of those observations.

7. These data may be downloaded from the data set archive of the *Journal of Applied Econometrics*, <http://qed.econ.queensu.ca/jae/2001-v16.2/kenkel-terza/ktdata.zip>. In addition to this archive of data, other collections of data for students to sample are readily available at many websites. Some good starting points for data are the sites maintained by Robin Lock, a statistician in the Department of Mathematics at St. Lawrence University, who provides links to data sources at <http://it.stlawu.edu/~rlock>, and the sites listed by the Econometrics Laboratory at the University of California provided at <http://elsa.berkeley.edu/eml/emldata.html>. For information and access to a wide variety of econometrics programs, the *Econometrics Journal* website has a sizeable collection of links at <http://www.econ.vu.nl/econometriclinks/software.html>. Links to information about a wide range of statistical software packages are available at <http://www.oswego.edu/~economic/econsoftware.htm>.

8. We draw random samples from this "population" of observations. Instructors using such a data set might digress briefly to discuss the idea of sampling from finite (albeit fairly large) populations. Also, 33 of the observations with negative or extremely high incomes have been removed from this sample, so our experiment is based on 2,434 observations with incomes ranging from zero to $12,000 per month. This edited sample may be downloaded from <http://www.stern.nyu.edu/~wgreene/kenkel-terza_short.dat> The variables in the file are identical to the original, save for the removal of the noted 33 observations, leaving a sample of 2,434 observations. The file with all the LIMDEP commands may be downloaded from <http://www.stern.nyu.edu/~wgreene/kenkel-terza_short.lim>

9. The computations done here were carried out with Version 8.0 of LIMDEP (Econometric Software, Inc., 2003). (The program instructions are given in the Appendix.) The data file with all the LIMDEP commands may be downloaded from <http://www.stern.nyu.edu/~wgreene/kenkel-terza short.lim>

10. Standardization of a random variable, X, maps values of X into a new random variable, Z, which has a mean of zero and standard deviation of one. Standardization begins by subtracting X's mean or expected value, $E(X) = \mu$ from each value of X; this creates a transformed random variable $(X - \mu)$, which has a mean of zero. Dividing this transformed random variable by X's standard deviation, σ, creates the standardized random variable $Z = (X - \mu)/\sigma$. In the case of the sample mean, $\overline{X}$, which also has an expected value of μ and standard deviation of $\sigma_{\overline{X}} = \sigma/\sqrt{n}$, standardization yields $Z = (X - \mu)/\sigma_{\overline{X}}$. Although the distribution of $\overline{X}$ collapses on μ, as n goes to infinity, its standardization Z (generally) converges to something normally distributed as n gets larger, a result students can see for themselves with a resampling program, as shown in our application. The effect of stan-

dardizing X, as well as other Java applications involving, $\overline{X}$ can be seen at http://www.umd.umich.edu/casl/socsci/econ/StudyAids/JavaStat/applet.htm.

11. Utts (1991) provides excellent alternative examples involving misconceptions and misuse of replication, effect size, and statistical significance.

12. The plot for the probability model was produced by first fitting a probit model of the binary variable GRADE, as a function of GPA. This produces a functional relationship of the form Prob(GRADE = 1) = $\Phi(\alpha + \beta\,\text{GPA})$, where estimates of α and β are produced by maximum likelihood techniques. The graph is produced by plotting the standard normal CDF, $\Phi(\alpha + \beta\,\text{GPA})$ for the values of GPA in the sample, which range between 2.0 and 4.0, then connecting the dots. The nonparametric regression, although intuitively appealing because it can be viewed as making use of weighted relative frequencies, is computationally more complicated. (Today the binomial probit model can be fit with just about any statistical package but software for nonparametric estimation is less common. LIMDEP version 8.0 [Econometric Software, Inc., 2003] was used for both the probit and nonparametric estimations.)

The nonparametric approach is based on the assumption that there is some as yet unknown functional relationship between the Prob(GRADE = 1) and the independent variable, GPA, say Prob(Grade = 1 | GPA) = $F(\text{GPA})$. The probit model based on the normal distribution is one functional candidate, but the normality assumption is more specific than we need at this point. We proceed to use the data to find an approximation to this function. The form of the "estimator" of this function is $F(\text{GPA*}) = \Sigma_{i=\text{all observations}}$ $w(\text{GPA*} - \text{GPA}_i)\text{GRADE}_i$. The weights, "$w(.)$," are positive weight functions that sum to 1.0, so for any specific value GPA*, the approximation is a weighted average of the values of GRADE. The weights in the function are based on the desired value of GPA, that is GPA*, as well as all the data. The nature of the computation is such that if there is a positive relationship between GPA and GRADE = 1, then as GPA* gets larger, the larger weights in the average shown above will tend to be associated with the larger values of GRADE. (Because GRADE is zeros and ones, this means that for larger values of GPA*, the weights associated with the observations on GRADE that equal one will generally be larger than those associated with the zeros.) The specific form of these weights is as follows: $w(\text{GPA*} - \text{GPA}_i) = (1/A)$ $\times (1/h)K[\text{GPA*} - \text{GPA}_i)/h]$. The "$h$" is called the smoothing parameter, or bandwidth, $K[.]$ is the "kernel density function" and A is the sum of the functions, ensuring that the entire expression sums to one. Discussion of nonparametric regression using a kernel density estimator is given in Greene (2003, pp. 706–708). The nonparametric regression of GRADE on GPA plotted in the figure was produced using a logistic distribution as the kernel function and the following computation of the bandwidth: let r equal one-third of the the sample range of GPA and let s equal the sample standard deviation of GPA. The bandwidth is then $h = .9 \times \text{Min}(r, s)/n^{1/5}$. (In spite of their apparent technical cache, bandwidths are found largely by experimentation. There is no general rule that dictates what one should use in a particular case, which is unfortunate because the shapes of kernel density plots are heavily dependent upon them.) The Spector and Mazzeo data used for the study may be downloaded from http://www.stern.nyu.edu/~wgreene/ spector-mazzeo.dat. The data file with the LIMDEP commands that produce Figure 5 may be downloaded from http://www.stern.nyu.edu/~wgreene/spector-mazzeo.lim. (We note that there are a number of alternatives to the simple nonparametric estimator suggested here that might, in some situations, provide greater precision or sidestep some statistical pitfalls such as boundary problems--the possibility of predicting a probability less than zero or more than one. We have chosen the particular approach used here purely for illustration and for convenience in the exposition.)

References

Anderson-Cook, C. M. 1999. An in-class demonstration to help students understand confidence intervals. *Journal of Statistics Education* (Fall), http://www.amstat.org/publications/jse.

Ashenfelter, O., and A. Krueger. 1994. Estimates of the return to schooling from a new sample of twins. *American Economic Review* 84 (December): 1157–73.

Baumol, W. J., S. A. B. Blackman, and E. N. Wolff. 1989. *Productivity and American leadership: The long view*. Cambridge: The MIT Press.

Becker, G. 1996. Not-so-dismal scientist. *Business Week*. October 21: 19.

Becker, W. E. 2003. Undergraduate choice: Sexy or non-sexy? *Southern Economic Journal* 70 (1): 219–25.

———. 1998. Engaging students in quantitative analysis with the academic and popular press. In W. Becker and M. Watts, eds. *Teaching economics to undergraduates: Alternatives to chalk and talk*. Cheltenham, UK: Edward Elgar, pp. 241–67.

———. 1987. Teaching statistical methods to undergraduate economics students. *American Economic Review* 77 (May): 18–24.

Becker, W. E., and M. Watts. 2001. Teaching economics at the start of the 21st century: Still chalk and talk. *American Economic Review* 91 (May): 440–46.

———. 1999. How departments of economics evaluate teaching. *American Economic Review* 89 (May): 344–50.

———. 1996. Chalk and talk: A national survey of teaching undergraduate economics. *American Economic Review* 86 (May): 448–54.

Berndt, E. R. 1991. *Practice of econometrics: Classic and contemporary*. Boston: Addison-Wesley.

Bernstein, P. 1996. *Against the gods: The remarkable story of risk*. New York: John Wiley & Sons, Inc.

Campbell, D., and D. Kenny. 1999. *A primer on regression artifacts*. New York: The Guilford Press.

Clogg, C. C. 1992. The impact of sociological methodology on statistical methodology. *Statistical Science* 7 (May): 183–96.

Econometric Software, Inc. 2003. LIMDEP, Version 8.0. Plainview, NY.

Fisher, R. A. 1970. *Statistical methods for research workers*, 14th ed. New York: Hafner.

Friedman, M. 1992. Communication: Do old fallacies ever die? *Journal of Economic Literature* 30 (December): 2129–32.

Goldberger, A. S. 1991. *A course in econometrics*. Cambridge: Harvard University Press.

Greene, W. H. 2003. *Econometric analysis*, 5th ed. Saddle River, NJ: Prentice Hall.

Gujarati, D. N. 2003. *Basic econometrics*, 4th ed. Boston: McGraw Hill.

Hotelling, H. 1933. Review of *The triumph of mediocrity in business*, by H. Secrist. *Journal of American Statistics Association* 28 (December): 463–65.

Kenkel, D., and J. Terza. 2001. The effect of physician advice on alcohol consumption: Count regression with an endogenous treatment effect. *Journal of Applied Econometrics* 16 (March): 165–84.

Lawler, K., et al. 2000. *Econometrics: A practical approach*. London: Routledge Press.

Mathews, P. H. 2001. Positive feedback and path dependence using the law of large numbers. *Journal of Economic Education* 32 (Spring): 124–36.

McCloskey, D., and S. Ziliak. 1996. The standard error of regression. *Journal of Economic Literature* 34 (March): 97–114.

Morgan, J. P., N. R. Chagantry, R. C. Dahiya, and M. J. Doviak. 1991. Let's make a deal: Player's dilemma. *American Statistician* 45 (November): 284–87.

Murray, M. 1999. Econometrics lectures in a computer classroom. *Journal of Economic Education* 20 (Summer): 308–21.

Nalebuff, B. 1987. Puzzles: Choose a curtain, duel-ity, two point conversions, and more. *Journal of Economic Perspectives* 1 (Fall): 157–63.

Paulos, J. 1995. *A mathematician reads the newspaper*. New York: Anchor Books.

Ramanathan, R. 2002. *Introductory econometrics with applications*, 5th ed. Fort Worth: Harcourt College Publishers.

Secrist, H. 1933. *The triumph of mediocrity in business*. Evanston, IL: Bureau of Business Research, Northwestern University.

Sharpe, W. F. 1985. *Investment*, 3rd ed. Englewood Cliffs, NJ: Prentice Hall.

Sowey, E. R. 1983. University teaching of econometrics: A personal view. *Econometrics Review* 2 (May): 255–89.

Spector, L. C., and M. Mazzeo. 1980. Probit analysis and economic education. *Journal of Economic Education* 11 (Spring): 37–44.

Stigler, S. 1999. *Statistics on the table*. Cambridge: Harvard University Press.

———. 1996. *The history of statistics: The measurement of uncertainty before 1900*. Cambridge: Harvard University Press.

Studenmund, A. H. 2001. *Using econometrics: A practical guide*. Boston: Addison Wesley.

Tversky, A., and D. Kahneman. 1971. Belief in the law of small numbers. *Psychological Bulletin* 76 (2): 105–10.

Utts, J. 1991. Replication and meta-analysis. *Statistical Science* 6 (4): 363–78.

vos Savant, M. 1990. Ask Marilyn. *Parade Magazine* 2 (December): 25.

Wainer, H. 2000. Visual revelations: Kelley's paradox. *Chance* 13 (Winter): 47–48.

Werth, B. 2003. Stent woes killed $3 billion sale. *Hoosier Times* (June 8): J4.

Wonnacott, R. J., and T. H. Wonnacott. 1980. *Econometrics*. New York: Wiley.

Wooldridge, J. 2000. *Introductory econometrics: A modern approach*. Cincinnati: Southwestern College Publishing.

Six

The Research-Teaching-Research Cycle
One Biologist's Experience

Craig E. Nelson

One theme question for this volume is clear: How does a heavy emphasis on research at institutions like Indiana University (IU) not only allow for good teaching, but sometimes even substantially enhance under-graduate education? My response to this question is probably idiosyn-cratic. It is certainly personal. It is the story of a new Ph.D. who came to IU in 1966, certain of many of the answers in science and certain that the exciting content of evolutionary biology would hold my classes in thrall just as it had me. And transparent enthusiasm, organization and fair tests did elicit good course evaluations almost from the start. This created the illusion of more teaching success than I now would retrospectively see as justified.

As the chapter develops, a couple of myths that I then agreed with will emerge. One of these is reflected in a remark by a colleague that, although undergraduate students at IU are often taught science in large sections, "at least they have the advantage of being taught by people who are on the cutting edge of doing the research." My colleague was then teaching introductory biology to 350 students. I asked: "How much of which lectures in your introductory course have been informed by any of your own research?" After a moment's reflection, he agreed that his work was not relevant to the vast majority of the sessions in this class. Indeed, he concluded, as little as parts of one or two lectures directly reflected his own research.

If asked about the connection between research and teaching, science faculty members in research universities, like my colleague, often state that their own research allows them to keep course content more up-to-date than is the textbook's treatment. This is transparently true for many graduate courses (in which texts are rarely used for this very reason), often true for some portions of upper-division undergraduate majors courses and dubious (at least in my mind) for many lower-division courses.

In contrast, my thesis here is going to be that, in at least some cases, the effects of our research on our teaching are much deeper and more important than simply keeping the course content current. In my case at least, as my research experience changed, I decided I had to radically modify the core topics I included in the courses I teach and, sometimes, even that I had to develop new courses that hadn't previously existed. Even more fundamentally, I changed my views of the central goals of teaching.

First, however, let me grant that my opening anecdote underrepresents the extent to which faculty members' research-related activities inform their undergraduate classes. In teaching an introductory biology course for a few years, I found that the biggest impact on content was not from my own research, but from the way teaching affected my reading. When I was teaching this course, and for some years afterward, as I read major journals I not only attended to the articles that were at the core of my intellectual interests or that represented really major breakthroughs (my usual reading strategy given limited time), I also examined a wider range of articles that related to any of the topics in the course. So reading for research expanded to reading for teaching. The same has been true for each of the courses I have taught. If many undergraduate science courses at research universities are indeed more cutting edge in content than parallel courses in other kinds of institutions, I suspect that a major part of the effect comes from the breadth of journal articles that most research university faculty encounter while doing the reading that is essential to the pursuit of their research.

However, I have worked intensively with faculty from a wide array of postsecondary institutions while leading "Chautauqua Short Courses for College Teachers" on various aspects of teaching science. I have found that colleagues from those nonresearch institutions that have moderate teaching assignments are often as current on content as my colleagues at IU. Some of them have suggested that where the teaching load is modest, extensive expectations for research may actually interfere with keeping up-to-date on course content. Meta-analyses have tended to find essentially no relationship between research productivity and instructional effectiveness, though most of the data appears to be from comparisons within institutions (Feldman 1987; Hattie and Marsh 1996).

Changing Goals: From Presenting Content
to Making a Bigger Difference

When I began teaching at IU, I knew nothing of the scholarship on pedagogy, and my own views of teaching and how to do it were very conventional. I was asked to teach evolution and vertebrate zoology for upper-class majors, alternating the latter with a graduate course of my own devising. I had repeatedly taught the lab for vertebrate zoology in graduate school and really liked a course where students could have extensive contact with whole animals. Evolution seemed the most exciting course in the entire undergraduate curriculum, not just the science curriculum, because it synthesizes so broadly across several sciences and addresses topics of such deep existential interest (including origins, deep time, immense change and the nature and limits of science). Like many professors elsewhere, faculty members in biology at IU had often taught the same courses for decades, changing the content as necessary to keep up-to-date and changing the pedagogy very little. I assumed that I would do the same. I was striving to become an outstanding lecturer and expected to reach retirement still teaching vertebrate zoology and evolution and teaching them in much the same way.

If I had been asked how my expectations were different from those in institutions with substantially heavier teaching assignments, I too would have focused on the ability to keep the content more current. The connections of my research to the content I was teaching could not have been clearer—I was studying various aspects of vertebrate evolution. My research, and especially the reading I did in conjunction with it, informed several class periods in each of these upper-division classes for majors.

Unanticipated changes in my teaching emerged as my research-related reading on vertebrate biology brought me to the new data on the effects of environmental degradation. For example, it had become clear that the use of DDT was leading to population collapse in bald eagles, peregrine falcons, and scores of other bird species worldwide. Moreover, in reaching this conclusion, researchers had established that it was the DDT that mattered, rather than the brake fluid and related compounds that were present in eggs at higher concentrations than the DDT. Thus, it also had become clear that DDT was a tiny bit of a very large problem. Clearly something had to be done.

So even before I was tenured, and decades before retirement, my research interests began to lead to changes in what I taught. Specifically, I began to coordinate and co-teach courses on environmental options and issues with other scientists, economists, political scientists and even an environmental engineer. To teach in this new area, I had to abandon my beloved course in vertebrate zoology, intermittently at first and then permanently.

My teaching goals began to change also. I was no longer satisfied with students just learning the science and then ignoring or forgetting it. I yearned to make a difference in how they subsequently thought about their own behavior and about our collective effects and governmental policies. I didn't feel that they had to agree with my decisions and goals, but it seemed that they should grapple with the issues. It was also clear that these nascent but more important goals were not nearly as easy to achieve as had been my earlier ones focused more closely on presenting current content.

My Initial Encounter with Deep Complexity

As I taught more about environment issues, I read more about them and became more deeply engrossed. This reading for teaching led to changes in my research. In the face of a public policy controversy about nuclear power plants in Indiana, a graduate assistant and I began what we envisioned as a "quick" research project on the assorted tradeoffs between coal and nuclear power. Which was cheaper? Which released less radiation? Which was otherwise environmentally safest? When we began I assumed that there would be a clear and simple answer to these questions (as the very form of the questions assumed) and that the controversy existed because no one had attempted a real synthesis. Instead, the tradeoffs between coal and nuclear power turned out to be the most complex issue I had yet grappled with in depth.

A conclusion was not secure on either the environmental or economic tradeoffs. For example, mining and burning coal can release significant amounts of radioactive pollutants. The actual environmental effects are strongly dependent on the particular coal seams and pollution control technology used. In addition, power plants that produce energy by burning coal are initially much less expensive than are those that use nuclear energy, but annual fuel costs are higher for coal. Consequently, which one is less expensive per unit energy over the life of the plant depends on the cost of the capital and, hence, on the anticipated rate of inflation and the interest rates. The point of expected equal cost lay near the middle of the range of then recent inflation rates. Further, in arriving at a decision on the economics, one had to try to anticipate the kinds of environmental regulations that would be put in place over the next 20 or 30 years and estimate their costs and relative benefits. In brief, no one actually knew with any certainty whether coal or nuclear power would actually be cheaper or which would be less environmentally harmful. More accurately, several experts claimed they knew, but they did not agree on the underlying economic, regulatory and environmental assumptions and, consequently, they disagreed on the conclusions.

This research into environmental issues helped me further refine my teaching goals. If I were going to make a difference in how my students thought about their own behavior and governmental policies in relation to environmental issues, I needed to find a way to help them rise above the morass of disagreeing experts. Indeed, I realized, showing that apparent experts disagreed was a major ploy used by vested interests to impede progress on environmental and public health issues. Cigarette smoking even then provided an especially clear example.

In class, when I presented a dilemma to my students, it was clear that the students could see the morass much more clearly than they could rise above it. The complexity of understanding that was emerging from my research on power sources was leading me to revise my teaching goals and also was making clear just how far my classes were from meeting those revised goals.

I was moving into apostasy. I had begun to see that just delivering up-to-date content was a fairly trivial goal next to fostering the complexity of understanding needed for environmental issues. I even began to question the importance of cutting-edge content. It seemed more important that students have the thinking and decision-making skills to use information that would emerge after my class was long over. A key question emerged: How could I most effectively teach these critical thinking skills?

Focusing Explicitly on Critical Thinking:
Applying Perry's Scheme

Serendipity intervened. At a teaching development session on a quite different topic, a faculty member from the humanities mentioned in passing a then new book by Perry (1970) on intellectual and ethical development in college. Perry clarified the various processes that make up critical thinking and the barriers students face in trying to master these processes. This transformed my ideas of what teaching should accomplish and how I might begin to approach it. And, in passing, it showed me that I would have to transform the ways I thought about complex issues.

Perry sketches a progression of ways that one can think about issues. Most basic is the expectation that for any issue there is a simple, clear, permanent answer that one can obtain by asking any appropriate expert. Nuclear power is either economic salvation or it is dangerous and should be banned. All competent experts will reach the same conclusion. Although it pains me to admit it, this is probably the basic stance that I initially brought to this controversy. I still remember both being puzzled as to why there was disagreement and harboring suspicions that some incompetent "experts" might need to be exposed. I ultimately came to see that my initial response to a complex problem mirrored the way many textbooks present science, even at the college level: Here is the truth as known to experts. Here is an illustrative bit of evidence. Memorize it all!

In Perry's analysis, the key factor that helps students move beyond this stance of simple dependence on experts is the recognition that important legitimate uncertainty lies at the heart of any complex issue. For me, in the nuclear power controversy, this understanding came when I finally understood that because of the uncertainty in projecting inflation, interest rates and changes in regulatory constraints over the next thirty years, it was impossible for anyone, no matter how expert, to know with certainty which power sources would be less expensive and which would be less disruptive environmentally.

Perry found that many students, when faced with such uncertainty, assume that all opinions are equally acceptable. When no one really knows the answer, then any answer is as good as any other answer. My students often feel initially that to question anyone's views is to fail to be appropriately open-minded.

This stance, held by a majority of graduating college students as well as much of the general public (e.g., King and Kitchner 1994), is a difficult one to dissuade. The remedy is to help students learn the tools and vocabulary of the discipline in which the problem resides. The goal is that they understand how experts (scientists, economists, etc.) choose better answers within the contexts of their disciplines. A key strategy is to teach students to formulate alternative answers to the problem and then to set those answers next to criteria for telling which alternatives are better and which worse. When students are first presented with such an exercise, they often seem to think they are simply playing some sort of silly "teachers' game." However, Perry found that what begins for students as an exercise for earning grades leads to a transformation as students begin reflexively to think in these more complex ways, the ways of the disciplines.

This disciplinary game approach to thinking runs into trouble for those issues in which different disciplines see different comparisons as appropriate, use different sets of criteria and come to partially or wholly

divergent answers. This was part of my problem in the nuclear controversy. Within an environmental science approach, it became clear that I
had to consider how to trade off uncertain but potentially catastrophic
risks from nuclear plant explosions against reasonably well-known and
moderately severe health and environmental effects from air pollution,
together with then quite uncertain effects from global warming, both
resulting from coal. Similarly, within a public policy approach, beyond
simple calculations of comparative costs, uncertain in themselves, I also
had to consider issues such as the extent to which a diverse energy base
protected the economy against price fluctuations and against external
manipulations by OPEC.

After much stewing, I gradually saw that experts could agree on all
or nearly all of the facts about tradeoffs between coal and nuclear power,
for example, and still quite legitimately disagree about what should be
done. One expert could emphasize the importance of a diverse energy
base and look for the most appropriate mix. Another could emphasize
the importance of slowing global climatic change and argue for minimizing the use of all fossil fuels. Yet a third could focus on the catastrophic level of disruption that is possible, though unlikely (at least
prior to the threat of terrorism), from nuclear plant accidents and argue
for minimizing or eliminating the use of nuclear power.

The most shocking thing for me was that facts, although central, left
both experts and students a long way from an appropriate decision. This
is not to say that facts are unimportant. Having the facts straight is
very helpful. But students also must understand how to include consequences, risks, and values in the decision sequence. I now understood
why Perry called his scheme "intellectual and ethical development."

Perry's book allowed me to reframe the way I taught. My understanding of how to foster cognitive development was further advanced by the
gradual appearance of a series of empirical studies that built on and
expanded Perry's work (Basseches 1984; Belenky et al. 1986; Baxter
Magolda 1992, 1999, 2001; King and Kitchner 1994; for a broader review and technical comparison see Hofer and Pintrich 1997). I still try
to help students understand the apparent facts and their sources but I
now focus more heavily on the uncertainties. For these, I ask what alternatives should be compared and help the students examine criteria for
comparing them within a decision-making framework that I call the
game of science. Then I turn to helping the students understand some
examples of the controversies that arise over the meaning or applications
of the results of the game of science. Here students must learn to examine consequences and risks and explore their own values and the values
of those who disagree with them. As they do so they can begin to make

the kinds of mature decisions that I was hoping for from my teaching of environmental issues.

An especially important challenge in teaching from this framework is providing concrete methods that the students can use, especially at the more complicated end of the scale. This led me to start teaching elementary risk assessment and decision theory. Conflicts become more manageable for students when risk is expressed concretely. For example, eating either a charbroiled steak or a tablespoon of peanut butter each has approximately the same effect on one's longevity as smoking one cigarette. Of course the equivalent of a two-pack-a-day (forty cigarettes) habit is hard to achieve with steaks or peanut butter. Similar help comes from explicit cases such as evolution/creation where two people can agree on the scientific date and emphatically disagree on the conclusion because they see radically different consequences (Nelson 1996, 2000; Nelson, Nickels and Beard 1998). Divergent views of consequences, much more than of data, underlie most public policy debates on the application and significance of scientific findings.

Interim Summary: Research to Teaching

The question at the beginning of this chapter was: "How does a heavy emphasis on research at institutions like Indiana University not only allow for good teaching, but sometimes even substantially enhance undergraduate education?" In my case, I started out simply following developments in ecological and evolutionary biology. These led me to an early awareness of the emerging environmental problems. I was able to pursue this awareness readily because the branch library in the biology building then received some 1200 journals and periodicals and many more were available elsewhere on campus. Note that this was in the years surrounding 1970. Accessing titles that were not available on campus still required the movement of physical copies by interlibrary loan, with the necessity of filling out forms and with delays of weeks between initiation and receipt. Having the resources of a research university's library in the same building allowed (and still allows) rapid scanning and evaluation of many more articles than would have otherwise been possible. Similarly, although most of the biologists, economists and political scientists on campus were not especially interested in interdisciplinary exploration of environmental problems and possibilities, departments at IU were large enough that each of these and several other departments contained one or two colleagues who either had environmental expertise or were willing to delve into environmental topics. Collectively, we developed an Environmental Studies major and, soon thereafter, a new

School of Public and Environmental Affairs. When I was appointed the first Director of Environmental Studies, it was assumed (without my input) that I naturally would require extra resources to also keep my research program going. Hence, as part of the normal operations of a research university, I was given university funds for two graduate research assistants each year. These funds allowed me to devote a graduate student's time to the question of the relative merits of alternative power sources. I would not have otherwise had the time to assemble the necessary literature base to allow me to pursue this topic. The funding for another graduate student, as well as for a secretary, also helped give me the time flexibility needed to pursue both this topic and the literature on college pedagogy, all in addition to continuing basic research in evolutionary biology. Thus, with no prior intention on my part, research on vertebrate biology, when coupled with these various resources and the attendant time flexibility, led me to literature research in new areas. Ultimately, this new exploration transformed my own ability to think about complex issues and also transformed what topics and courses I taught, and what I wanted my teaching to achieve and the ways I tried to achieve this. The journey thus far described is the research to teaching part of the cycle in my title. The teaching to research part has been even more important to my career, but can be described more briefly.

Teaching to Research and Back Again

In examining the teaching issues, especially in exploring how to apply Perry's ideas to teaching science, I moved, again without prior intent, into a new kind of research. My first efforts in the scholarship of teaching and learning (SOTL) asked how we could use Perry's framework to generate a series of teaching moves that help students learn the more sophisticated modes of critical thinking. My main examples were drawn directly from my teaching and included ways of understanding the controversies around evolution, nuclear power, and other environmental issues.

I successfully argued that these new activities should officially be regarded as scholarship within the department. This was important partly because individual research productivity is a central part of the department's formula for allocating raises. A key point in gaining this acceptance was that my publications in this field (Nelson 1986, 1989) had required mastering the literature in a new field of scholarship. Thus, these publications were not simply a reporting of teaching experience, but rather required a synthesis of my own experience with diverse theoretical and empirical studies of pedagogy. Similarly, the publications led fairly quickly to invitations to serve on editorial boards and on National Science Foundation and other federal grant review panels, most of which were for educational research (rather than for teaching improvement projects). It may also have been relevant that two colleagues and I also received a series of NSF grants spanning 10 years. Although these grants were for institutes for high school biology teachers, they totaled over $2,000,000 and led to a small series of additional publications (including Nickels, Nelson and Beard 1996; Nelson, Nickels and Beard 1998; Nelson and Nickels 2001). These standard accoutrements of research helped my work in the new field be accepted as research.

In my case, the movement of energy from teaching back into research (the second half of the cycle in my title) was further accelerated by yet another benefit of being in a research university, graduate courses centered on faculty interests. I first co-taught our departmental course for Ph.D. students on teaching college biology in 1975 and have co-taught or taught it a dozen times since. This, of course, required that I become familiar both with overall summaries of the research on college teaching (one of my perennial favorites has been the various editions of McKeachie, now 2002) and with pertinent individual studies and articles. Key topics addressed in the course have included: why do students find even elementary scientific ideas so hard (e.g., Herron 1975), alternative frameworks for developing critical thinking (e.g., Kurfiss 1989), learning styles and their use in designing instruction (e.g., Svinicki and Dixon 1987), and the dilemmas of content coverage (e.g., Russell, Hendricson and Herbert 1984; Sundberg and Dini 1993) and of traditional approaches to grading (e.g., Milton, Pollio and Eison 1986).

Building on the learning and insights from successive rounds of teaching this graduate course, I have been on a long journey of refining my understanding of what is known about college and university teaching and learning and of how that knowledge can be applied to improve teaching both in my own classes and more generally. I realized that the use of the structured student-student interactions that are at the heart of collaborative learning is an important, probably essential, tool for fostering the kinds of advanced critical thinking that are now at the core of my instructional goals. Ultimately this led to articles advocating this synthesis and proposing ways to achieve it (Nelson 1994, 1997). More troubling to me was a gradual recognition that traditional pedagogy, especially in science and math, that fails to use collaborative learning and fails to provide explicit structure to support complex thinking is unintentionally but quite effectively biased against students from nontraditional backgrounds (e.g., Adams 1992; Fullilove and Treisman 1990; Rose 1989; Rosser 1986; Steele 1997; Treisman 1992; and Tobias 1990). This recognition eventually led to an article summarizing some of the literature that supports this conclusion and some of the suggestions for ways to address it (Nelson 1996). I thus have become increasingly engaged in a cycle that includes teaching the graduate course on pedagogy, applying ideas developed in the graduate course in teaching undergraduate courses, and further scholarship of teaching and learning that is both built on this teaching and further informs it.

Institutionalization

In retrospect, including SOTL as one of my fields of research seems to have been an almost inevitable, albeit unplanned, development. The major breakthrough was finding very helpful prior scholarship by Perry and others. Like most faculty members of my generation, I was exposed to none of this in graduate school, nor was any of it an important part of the conversation among the faculty at IU in my early years here. What conversation we had about teaching focused largely on teaching tricks, when it was positive, and on students' failings when it was not. In the last several years there have been major improvements. IU's nationally recognized SOTL program has provided a forum where research on teaching is taken quite seriously. Participants have conversations about teaching that are heavily evidence-based and theory-framed, thus laying the base for possibly including SOTL as one of the areas of their research expertise.

More importantly, many departments here and elsewhere now offer SOTL-based courses to their Ph.D. students. Some departments at IU also have participated in the Preparing Future Faculty Program or are participating in the new Carnegie Initiative on the Doctorate. This may ultimately resolve an apparent paradox. Although I have read the literature on the scholarship of teaching broadly and with no attention to its origins, writing this chapter has led me to a new observation: A disproportionate number of the studies and examples that have had the most profound influence on me have been done at research universities. Key examples include Herron (1975) at Purdue, McKeachie (2002) at the University of Michigan, Perry (1970) at Harvard Univerisity, Rose (1989) at the University of California at Los Angeles, Steele (1997) at Stanford University, Svinicki and Dixon (1987) and Levinson (1985) at the University of Texas, and Treisman (1992) at the University of California at Berkeley.

The proliferation of graduate courses on pedagogy and other programs for better preparing faculty should lead to a gradual decrease in the extent to which scholars at research universities predominate in this area, as faculty members at institutions of diverse types become more scholarly in their approach to teaching and more inclined to treat their teaching as real experiments leading toward formal scholarship. If so, this will become the greatest of all contributions of research universities to the improvement of teaching.

References

Adams, M., ed. 1992. *Promoting diversity in college classrooms: Innovative responses for the curriculum, faculty and institutions.* San Francisco: Jossey-Bass.

Basseches, M. 1984. *Dialectical thinking and adult development.* Norwood, NJ: Ablex Publishing.

Baxter Magolda, M. B. 1992. *Knowing and reasoning in college: Gender-related patterns in students' intellectual development.* San Francisco: Jossey-Bass.

———. 1999. *Creating contexts for learning and self-authorship: Constructive-developmental pedagogy.* Nashville, TN: Vanderbilt University Press.

———. 2001. *Making their own way: Narratives for transforming higher education to promote self-development.* Sterling, VA: Stylus Publishing.

Belenky, M. F., B. M. Clinchy, N. R. Goldberger, and J. M. Tarule. 1986. *Women's ways of knowing: The development of self, voice and mind.* New York: Basic Books.

Feldman, K. A. 1987. Research productivity and scholarly accomplishment of college teachers as related to their instructional effectiveness: A review and exploration. *Research in Higher Education* 26 (3): 227–98.

Fullilove, R. E., and P. U. Treisman, 1990. Mathematics achievement among African American undergraduates at the University of California, Berkeley: An evaluation of the Mathematics Workshop Program. *Journal of Negro Education* 59 (3): 463–78.

Hattie, J., and H. W. Marsh. 1996. The relationship between teaching and research: A meta-analysis. *Review of Educational Research* 66 (4): 507–42.

Herron, J. D. 1975. Piaget for chemists: Explaining what "good" students cannot understand. *Journal of Chemical Education* 52 (2): 146–50.

Hofer, B. K., and P. R. Pintrich. 1997. The development of epistemological theories: Beliefs about knowledge and knowing and their relation to learning. *Review of Educational Research* 67 (1): 88–140.

King, P. M., and K. S. Kitchner. 1994. *Developing reflexive judgment: Understanding and promoting intellectual growth and critical thinking in adolescents and adults.* San Francisco: Jossey-Bass.

Kurfiss, J. G. 1989. *Critical thinking: Theory, research, practice, and possibilities.* College Station, TX: Association for the Study of Higher Education.

Levinson, S. 1985. On interpretation: The adultery clause of the Ten Commandments. *Southern California Law Review* 58:719–25.

McKeachie, W. J. 2002. *McKeachie's teaching tips: Strategy, research and theory for college and university teachers.* 11th ed. Boston: Houghton Mifflin.

Milton, O., H. R. Pollio, and J. A. Eison. 1986. *Making sense of college grades: Why the grading system does not work and what can be done about it.* San Francisco: Jossey-Bass.

Nelson, C. E. 1986. Creation, evolution, or both? A multiple model approach. In R. W. Hanson, ed., *Science and creation: Geological, theological, and educational perspectives.* New York: Macmillan.

———. 1989. Skewered on the unicorn's horn: The illusion of a tragic trade-off between content and critical thinking in the teaching of science. In L. Crowe, ed., *Enhancing critical thinking in the sciences.* Washington, DC: Society of College Science Teachers.

———. 1994. Critical thinking and collaborative learning. In K. Bosworth and S. Hamilton, eds., *Collaborative learning and college teaching.* San Francisco: Jossey-Bass.

———. 1996. Student diversity requires different approaches to college teaching, even in math and science. *American Behavioral Scientist* 40 (2): 165–75.

———. 1997. Tools for tampering with teaching's taboos. In W. E. Campbell and K. A. Smith, eds., *New paradigms for college teaching.* Edina, MN: Interaction Book Company.

———. 2000. Effective strategies for teaching evolution and other controversial subjects. In J. Skehan and C. E. Nelson, *The creation controversy and the science classroom.* Arlington, VA: NSTA Press.

Nelson, C. E., and M. K. Nickels. 2001. Using humans as a central example in teaching undergraduate biology labs. *Tested studies for laboratory teaching (Association for Biology Laboratory Education)* 22:332–65.

Nelson, C. E., M. K. Nickels, and J. Beard. 1998. The nature of science as a foundation for teaching science: Evolution as a case study. In W. F. McComas, ed., *The nature of science in science education: Rationales and strategies.* Boston, MA: Kluwer Academic Publishers.

Nickels, M. K., C. E. Nelson, and J. Beard. 1996. Better biology teaching by emphasizing evolution and the nature of science. *American Biology Teacher* 58 (6): 332–36.

Perry, W. G., Jr. 1970. *Forms of intellectual and ethical development in the college years: A scheme.* New York: Holt, Rinehart and Winston.

Rose, M. 1989. *Lives on the boundary: A moving account of the struggles and achievements of America's underclass.* New York: Penguin Books.

Rosser, S. V. 1986. *Teaching science and health from a feminist perspective: A practical guide.* New York: Pergamon Press.

Russell, I. J., W. D. Hendricson, and R. J. Herbert. 1984. Effects of lecture information density on medical student achievement. *Journal of Medical Education* 59 (11): 881–89.

Steele, C. M. 1997. A threat in the air: How stereotypes shape intellectual identity and performance. *American Psychologist* 52 (6): 613–29.

Sundberg, M. D., and M. L. Dini. 1993. Science majors vs nonmajors: Is there a difference? *Journal of College Science Teaching* 1993 (Mar/Apr): 299–304.

Svinicki, M. D., and N. M. Dixon. 1987. The Kolb model modified for classroom activities. *College Teaching* 35 (4): 141–46.

Tobias, S. 1990. *They're not dumb, they're different: Stalking the second tier.* Tucson, AZ: Research Corporation.

Treisman, U. 1992. Studying students studying calculus: A look at the lives of minority mathematics students in college. *College Mathematics Journal* 23 (5): 362–72.

Seven

The Three Faces of SOTL

The Contribution of the Summer Freshman Institute Project to Service, Teaching and Research

Bernice A. Pescosolido

Jeni Loftus

Stacy Scherr

Laura Fingerson

Kathryn Gold Hadley

Jenny Stuber

Paul Ruggerio Namaste

In the final decades of the 20th century, educators witnessed a fundamental reexamination of higher education in America (e.g., Levine 1997). Although Sullivan (1999, p. 32) notes U.S. colleges and universities are "generally recognized as one of the wonders of the modern world," they have been roundly criticized for "rising tuition, declining access, aloofness from the larger community, and mismanagement." Whatever the list of problems, Sullivan goes further to say that the heart of the critique centers on the "suspicion" that universities and their professors have turned too much of their attention away from the central mission of educating students. There has always been a lively exchange in sectors of the professoriate about the improvement of teaching, yet the recent range of discussion, debates, and suggestions is, perhaps, unprecedented. The shift in emphasis from faculty teaching to student learning; the accent on active learning and critical thinking; the concern with diversity; the focus on assessment (both formative and summative); and the widespread advent of pedagogical workshops and training programs at the graduate level all represent significant institutional social change (Adelman 1986; Cohen 1995; Gaff, Pruitt-Logan and Weibl 2000; Myers and Jones 1993; Paul 1990).

Perhaps no reconceptualization captures this flurry of activity and

alteration more than Boyer's (1990) *Scholarship Reconsidered*. Character-
izing the debate about the relative importance of teaching and research
as overdone and unproductive, he develops a four-celled typology of the
types of scholarship that better define and describe the work of faculty
in colleges and universities. The *scholarship of discovery* recasts basic research as the most essential form of scholarship. The *scholarship of application* brings that basic knowledge to real-world problems in the effort to improve the lives of individuals, organizations and societies. The
scholarship of integration places that knowledge in context, elaborating its
fit with other insights and sharing them with audiences outside the university. Finally, and most central to our concerns here, is the *scholarship of teaching*, which acknowledges the need to develop a base of research and creative activity about the effective transmission of that
knowledge. Perhaps the brilliance of Boyer's approach is its insistence
that these four forms of knowledge should not only co-exist, but mutually strengthen one another.

In this chapter, we focus on a collaborative project undertaken as the
scholarship of teaching, now most often referred to as the scholarship
of teaching and learning (SOTL). SOTL reflects the shift from a concern with what professors are teaching to what students are learning
(Barr and Tagg 1999). We first outline the basic contours of the Summer Freshman Institute (SFI) Project, and follow this description with
a discussion on how this effort of discovery articulated with the three
basic missions of the university—teaching, service and research. We
conclude with a discussion of the potential of SOTL to foster "stewards" of higher education and bodies of knowledge.

"Turning On the Light Bulb"

One source of criticism from inside and outside higher education has
been the attrition among students early in their college careers (Pascarella and Terenzini 1991). Recognizing the potential importance of
a good start to a successful college trajectory, the freshman-year experience became a topic of widespread, intense discussion as well as the
subject for development of theoretical perspectives, demographic pro-
filing, and institutional program efforts (see, e.g., Koch [2001] for an
annotated bibliography of the substantial body of work in this area).
Drawing together the expertise of nationally recognized leaders in higher
education such as John N. Gardner, Arthur Levine, Alexander Astin,
Stephen Brookfield and Sheila Tobias, the decade of the 1990s saw rapid
growth in a national conversation on the changing demographics of entering college students; the importance of campus climate; a reconsid-

eration of class sizes, approaches and topics; and an examination of the role of academic advising and faculty development on the retention of freshmen (e.g., Boyer et al. 1992; Cuseo 1991; Fidler 1991; Shanley and Hearns 1991; Smith 1993; Strommer 1993; Upcraft and Gardner 1989; Zeller 1991). Colleges and universities have reconfigured their orientation programs; introduced freshman seminars on special substantive topics, basic study skills, and career development; reexamined approaches in courses for high-risk students; and overhauled their advising programs (Barefoot and Fidler 1992; Martin and Arendale 1992; Upcraft and Kramer 1995).

In light of these national conversations and other local efforts, the College of Arts and Sciences, under the leadership of Associate Dean Lisa Pratt, embarked on an effort to improve the educational experience and success of freshmen at Indiana University's flagship campus in Bloomington. The major target of this effort was the concern that the freshman year was too often marked by the absence of a coherent and stimulating set of experiences that would draw students into the intellectual life of the university and compete more successfully with its nonacademic attractions.

Over the course of a number of months in the early part of the academic year 1999–2000, a series of decisions were made that shaped the nature of the SFI. With each decision, the circle of individuals involved grew. All were invited to subsequent meetings to take part in the participatory approach of program planning. First, the decision was made to pilot the project as a summer experience and, if successful, to implement it in the University as a freshman academic year experience. Second, the question of which students would be involved in the SFI shaped how the pilot would proceed. In the end, the decision was made to work with the Admissions Office to focus on a group of applicants who, by the end of December of the 1999–2000 year, had not been admitted through the regular process. These students, who numbered approximately 500, were held in a pool, with admissions decisions often awaiting their fall semester session grades. This pool was not a homogeneous group. Some lacked a required course; others had a pattern of improvement from a "bad start" in high school; and still others had some anomaly that put them in this gray area between accept and reject. After considering their records further, the admissions office admitted approximately one-third of these students. They became a natural control group for the SFI project. Others were offered the SFI program option, whereas others were ultimately rejected.

Third, once the decision was made to invite these students, the question of why they would agree to participate was answered by offering them an incentive: Students who successfully completed the SFI would be admitted to IUB in the Fall semester. Those who were not successful in the program would still qualify for admission in the fall at one of Indiana University's seven regional campuses. Fourth, the decision was made to focus on two basic courses and one other that would represent a new subject to many, if not most, freshmen. In the end, English composition, mathematics and psychology became the academic core of the SFI. The chairs of these departments were contacted. All agreed to participate and put their lead teachers of Writing, Finite Mathematics and Introductory Psychology in touch with the individuals developing the pilot program. Fifth, these instructors would serve as team leaders with a set of associate instructors (i.e., graduate student instructors) to keep the classes small. Sixth, the program would be a six-week residential program and include current IUB students as residence hall counselors. Finally, there would be an emphasis on advising (for the Fall semester) and study skills; some of the courses and activities also focused on time management and other more practical information for college life.

In the end, the SFI program was a joint effort of the College of Arts and Science, Summer Programs (which would run the SFI under its purview), and the Office of Admissions. Despite their diverse vantage points and interests in the outcomes, the major players in this effort were all committed to the essential goal of designing and piloting a new approach to improve learning outcomes and the intellectual development of freshmen in higher education, to "turn on the light bulb."

The Summer Freshman
Institute Project and SOTL

Very early in the process of developing this project, the leadership in the College of Arts and Sciences sought an evaluation of the SFI project. From the onset, the research connected with the SFI had two goals: 1) to provide an assessment of institutional efforts drawing theoretical insights and methodological rigor from disciplinary-based basic research (i.e., the scholarship of application), and 2) to advance the profession of teaching and improve learning outcomes for students (e.g., the scholarship of teaching, see Hutchings 2000). Some (e.g., Atkinson 2001) argue that pairing these dual goals is inevitable because SOTL lies at the juncture of teaching and other forms of scholarship but differs from good teaching, or even scholarly teaching (Hutchings and Shulman 1999; Smith 2001). Further, considered by the evaluation team as an opportunity to explore basic issues in organizational innovation, individual motivation, and the influence of social factors, the SFI project also offered a case study of basic social science processes.

Thus, in its development, execution and dissemination, the SFI project represented an effort to contribute to service, most explicitly; to teaching, both directly and indirectly; and to research that feeds back into basic social science research on education. We describe the contribution to each mission, in turn, in the sections that follow.

Assessing Institutional Social Change through Undergraduate Outcomes

The basic question regarding the institution and the academic and program units involved was straightforward: Did the SFI "work"? In other words, did students who attended and passed the experimental pilot program have better chances of success than regular college students? Whereas the question appeared to be simple, the answer was complex and we will provide only suggestive evidence here. As Figures 1 and 2 illustrate for the two cohorts of SFI students, there is a strong correlation between performance in the SFI program and overall grade point average (GPA) in the first year.[1] That is, students who did well in the SFI tended to do well in their first year at Indiana University. This finding held for both the students who went through the SFI in its first year (Summer 2000, Figure 7.1) and those who went through a slightly modified version in its second (Summer 2001, Figure 7.2).[2] Thus, if the question was whether SFI success was a good predictor of college success, the answer appeared to be yes. Whatever the SFI measured in terms of ability to do college work, it did so fairly well based on simple correlation analysis.[3]

However, the goal of the SFI was never intended to be a screener for those students who fell in the marginal admissions pool. It was designed to provide a model of intellectual engagement, giving those students involved an intellectual head start. To answer the question of efficacy, then, the retention and grades of students in the SFI were compared to the control group.[4]

Retention data for both cohorts of SFI students compared to the control group are presented in Table 7.1. The percentages of students in all three groups who completed the various semesters at Indiana University are virtually identical. Thus, the students in the SFI were retained at the same rate as students who were admitted to IUB through standard procedures. However, as indicated in Table 7.2, the performance of the first cohort of SFI students was significantly worse than the control

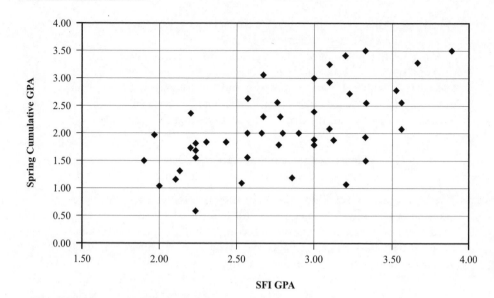

Figure 7.1 SFI grades by end of first year grades for cohort 1 ($r = .59$)

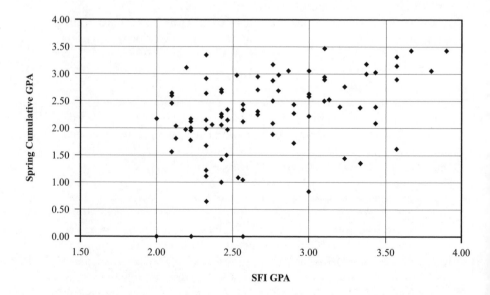

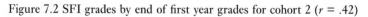

Figure 7.2 SFI grades by end of first year grades for cohort 2 ($r = .42$)

Table 7.1. Retention Data Comparing SFI 2000, SFI 2001 Students to Student Control Group

	Control Group		SFI 2000		SFI 2001	
	N	Percentage	N	Percentage	N	Percentage
Starting enrollment Fall 2000	162	100	54	100		—
Completed Fall 2000	159	98.1	53	98.1		—
Completed Spring 2001	148	91.4	49	90.7		—
Starting enrollment Fall 2001	137	84.6	45	83.3	102	100
Completed Fall 2001	Not available		41	75.9	101	99.0

Table 7.2. Comparison of Performance of SFI Students to Control Group

	GPA (Means)		
	Control Group	SFI 2000	SFI 2001
Cumulative GPA Year 1 without SFI GPA	2.66	2.14	2.24
with SFI GPA	—	2.26	2.37

group, and there was little difference between the SFI cohorts that experienced the original versus the modified, second summer version.

In sum, from a service perspective, the SFI project fulfilled its assessment goal, providing the institution with data that could be used to determine the effects of the program on traditional measures of student achievement. It documented that the SFI program was a good "litmus test" for marginal applicants because it provided a fairly good predictor of how undergraduates would fare in college courses. Further, both the anecdotal evidence from students, instructors and administrators as well as the student satisfaction data from a pencil-and-paper survey, which are the most typical forms of assessment in such programs, suggested that the program was a positive experience (details on request). However, those involved in the SFI from the Admissions Office were not interested in using this program to select applicants to admit to Indiana

University. The goal has been to find a way to intellectually engage students, to "turn on the light bulb." From that perspective, the SFI did not succeed. Students who participated were retained at the same rate as those most similar to them in terms of criteria for admissions, yet as a group their eventual grades were significantly poorer.

As a result of these analyses, all parties involved in the SFI agreed that it should not be continued and, as presently conceived and executed, could not serve as a model for the freshman-year experience. They decided to go back to the drawing board armed with these data and others (reported in later sections) to design another pilot project, benefiting from the lessons learned in this research (discussion follows).

Research Practicum:
Modeling Cutting-Edge, Multi-Method
Sociological Research

The basic question for research was "What can the scholarship of teaching and learning in the SFI project contribute to basic knowledge and to research training for Ph.D. students?" Although graduate students often work collaboratively on faculty projects, the primary mode of dissertation work among the graduate students in Indiana University's Department of Sociology is theory-driven, basic research, which addresses an important question in sociology. More often than not, it involves individual projects and uses a single method of inquiry. The SFI project offered research training and experience that was collaborative, applied and integrated methodologically.

Cast primarily as the scholarship of teaching, the SFI project's goal was to engage in research about the effective transmission of knowledge. However, to accomplish that single goal, those involved in the SFI project were required to acknowledge, appreciate, employ and contribute to each of the other forms of scholarship. From the beginning, the SFI project was an exercise in the scholarship of application. Reviewing both the basic research literature in sociology and past SOTL research on "bridging" programs, the Department of Sociology's SFI evaluation team's task was to bring basic knowledge to real-world problems to improve the educational experience and success of freshmen. These students considered past theoretical work in social psychology (e.g., on motivation), social networks (e.g., support influences in the family, the program), the sociology and social science of education (e.g., the predictive ability of SAT scores, classroom dynamics, the Tinto [1975] model of student achievement), and SOTL (e.g., learning styles). The students considered and brought a basic, multi-method approach to the SFI project. They determined what kind of institutional records or data would be needed; developed both a baseline and an exit survey instrument; interviewed the instructors; and adopted a rigorous sampling scheme to conduct an ethnography that observationally captured the SFI project meetings, the classroom experience, and some of the formal and informal meetings that the SFI students attended.

By doing so, the students on the SFI project gained training and insights in applied research, which are rarely part of the graduate experience in the top departments in Sociology. Further, they experienced, firsthand, the power of bringing together quantitative and qualitative approaches in sociology, a cutting-edge approach that is more often recommended than used. An analysis of data from institutional records and surveys allowed a quantitative evaluation of basic outcomes on the efficacy of the SFI ("what worked" and "what mattered"). But it was an analysis of data from ethnographic observations that allowed the formulation of the implicit hypotheses that the participants (both instructors and students) brought to the SFI program. This analysis also provided a textured understanding of "why" the SFI program outcomes were not as planned, and it offered direction on where its planning and execution needed to be rethought.

For example, observations of the planning meetings revealed that the lead instructors held ideas about what would matter. In particular, various instructors, during the planning phase, ventured claims that success in the SFI would reflect both SAT scores and psychological motivation. By listening to the working assumptions of the participants, the SFI project team was able to ensure that quantitative data were collected on these implicit hypotheses. In the end, both were refuted with quantitative data from student applications and the surveys. Further, both the planning meeting and classroom observations marked important discrepancies between the goals of the SFI and its execution. Whereas the SFI project was conceived as an intellectual experience that would turn students to scholarly pursuits, the instructors for the SFI program were drawn from those whose primary experience was in remedial programs. The flavor and tone of the classroom often reflected this influence. Also, although the SFI program's intent was intellectual excitement, the students' orientations were pragmatic. The qualitative analyses brought forward the importance of considering the concept of "resistance"— questioning and challenging the premise of the class and/or program (e.g., Higginbotham 1999).[5] SFI participants were resentful of their contingent status as Indiana University students, expressing comments about their need to "jump through hoops," and being considered "marginal" (see Hadley and Fingerson 2003).

Finally, the combination of multi-disciplinary and multi-method approaches offered insights to the SFI program team about how and where to go back to the drawing board. For example, research has suggested the importance of learning styles with studies documenting how a better fit between students' learning styles and teaching approaches would improve students' outcomes (e.g., see Powers [1999] for a review and successful application). This might have been an obvious explanation for the lack of the SFI's success and a direction for revision. However, taking the scholarship of application seriously, the SFI evaluation team borrowed these ideas from past SOTL theory and research, collected data and documented that there was no relationship between the fit of learning styles and student achievement. Neither would targeting their psychological motivations offer a fruitful future direction. Rather, both the qualitative and quantitative data suggested that the organizational constraints under which the SFI was required to operate (e.g., as a summer program for students who were not admitted through the regular process and drawing from instructors whose primary experience was in remedial courses) set a tone in the SFI that its benefits could not override (Pescosolido et al. 2003).

In particular, this latter point reflected one of the many potential contributions of the SFI project to the *scholarship of discovery*. Ignoring the program's applied intent and recasting research concerns in terms of organizational theory, the SFI project provided a window into organizational processes. As a case study, the SFI project demonstrated the role of organizational culture and climate on organizational outcomes. Further, data on the concept of resistance contributes to both the understanding of social psychological mechanisms and responses to dynamics of power.

Finally, and perhaps just as importantly, the SFI project experience allowed the graduate students to consider and gain experience in the *scholarship of integration*. They were required to take existing basic, applied and SOTL research and place that knowledge in context. They had to elaborate how these insights fit together in order to determine the nature and scope of the scholarship they would pursue. The SFI project pushed them to consider and develop an effective way to share their findings with audiences outside their usual realm of presentation (e.g., other sociologists in their disciplinary research and students in their teaching). With administrators, program participants and others in attendance, the SFI project evaluation group catalogued, summarized and presented the most central SFI project findings.[6]

In sum, while some of the critics of Preparing Future Faculty (PFF) programs in Research I universities cling to the notion that anything that takes graduate students' time and energy away from their dissertations or related basic research is problematic, the SFI project demonstrates the power of SOTL to create more sophisticated, better trained researchers and faculty. Unlike much of the work and training in the traditional graduate student program, participation in the SFI introduced sociology graduate students to the entire range of "scholarships" and exemplified their overlapping and mutually reinforcing nature. Such experiences may hold the potential to create a new generation of scholars, a goal of some of the leading innovators in higher education. We return to one of these views in the following section.

Service Learning: Teaching and Learning through Community Involvement

The basic question for teaching was "What learning goals were accomplished through the SFI project?" Here, the focus is not on the undergraduate students who enrolled in the SFI program but the graduate students who were members of the research team of the SFI project. In essence, this effort offered an opportunity for learning using the active strategy of service learning. Traditionally, service learning is conceived of as improving student learning by connecting the classroom in the academy to the community outside its walls. Not surprisingly, those in the academy are often better at conceiving of "community" in this way. Less often do they consider the possibility of using the university as a case of community, turning the analytic lens inward (Pescosolido 1991). Suggesting that graduate students can learn by becoming involved in the larger community of the university offers a unique but underused strategy for service learning. Thus the scholarship of teaching and learning marks a connection to service. By doing research that benefits the needs of the university, the SFI project was as able as other examples of service learning to provide graduate students with its documented benefits—personal and social development, improved achievement, a heightened sense of civic responsibility, and career awareness (Billig 2002; Boyer 1987; Hedin and Conrad 1987).

The SFI project was undertaken as part of the PFF program in the Department of Sociology. That program is composed of a sequence of three courses. The first course, S506, Teaching Undergraduate Sociology, accompanies graduate students' first experience in teaching their own courses and is preceded by workshops in the summer that assist them in the preparation and approval of classroom materials. Graduate student instructors, known as A.I.s, or Associate Instructors, master the "techniques of teaching" in S506 (Lowman 1995). It introduces students to basic issues in pedagogy (e.g., concepts of learning styles, the Perry scheme), and serves as a sounding board and support group during this first semester the Associate Instructors teach their own classes. It is required for all students who teach in the Sociology Department. The next two courses are optional but completion results in PFF certification. Sociological Issues in Higher Education, S606, places the teaching of sociology in context. It expands beyond the classroom to explore issues of the presentation of sociological material to a variety of audiences (e.g., students at different levels, other sociologists, those outside the academy); to ask students to connect their personal experiences and future plans to the larger landscape of higher education and society in general; to consider in greater depth issues in the ethics of sociological work, including but not limited to teaching; and to grapple with current debates in the discipline, the university and society. Research in Higher Education, S706, is most relevant to our discussion here. It requires students to engage in research and creative activity, broadly defined under the Boyer scheme. Students are allowed to work as individuals, in partnerships of varying size or as a cohort. In sum, S706 is a course in the scholarship of teaching and learning.

This third course offered one avenue to respond to the request of the College of Arts and Sciences to assist them in evaluating the SFI project. Further, given the limited resources typically available to pilot programs, it provided one of the few feasible ways to do such an assessment with any level of depth. The request was presented to the advanced graduate students enrolled in the Fall 1999 S606 course. The instructor, Pescosolido, made clear the nature of the SFI program and its early stage of development, the potential advantages and disadvantages of "adopting" this as a group project for S706, and the voluntary nature of participation in this project as their SOTL experience. The graduate students, in response, raised a number of issues—including summer funding (which was cobbled together from a variety of sources). Because the SFI program itself was in early stages of development and the instructor had agreed to provide some assistance as part of her service obligations whether or not the students participated, no immediate decision was required.[7]

Perhaps the single most unique aspect of learning for the graduate students involved a sense of empowerment and the potential of scholarship to result in institutional social change. The SFI project had an immediate and direct effect on University policy and direction. Rarely in the early careers of graduate students or junior faculty do they have the opportunity to see the connection between their research and the real world. This included an appreciation of the power of assessment in situations where the participants often have a limited, and usually positive, personal assessment of the efforts in which they have invested so much time and energy. In the course of preparing the protocol for the

SFI project, the students heard from other administrators and faculty at the University about the success of other programs, even though this depended solely on perceptions and did not include rigorous and independent assessment. Those with this positive view ultimately had to confront the discrepancies that became evident from including institutional, observational, interview and survey data.

Further, the SFI project offered a unique window into the operation of the University, its power structure and its decision-making processes. The students negotiated access to information, from both the University (e.g., Admissions and the Registrar) and the SFI participants (e.g., instructors as well as students).[8] For some students whose own dissertation research was in the planning stages or who had been involved with only secondary (i.e., already collected) data from large data sets or historical archives, this was the first serious discussion and application of issues of the protection of human subjects, confidentiality, and the operation of Indiana University's Institutional Review Board. The SFI project also offered a platform to discuss issues of service, higher education's internal version of civic responsibility, in a more active and concrete way. Finally, the SFI project allowed students to experience both the possibility of the integration of teaching, research and service, *and* to experience, firsthand, the pressures of trying to balance all three of these faculty roles.

In these ways, the scholarship of teaching and learning initiative enhanced these graduate students' awareness of the service aspect of their careers, whether they intended to become faculty or to go into more applied areas where they would have clients for whom they did research. The issue of service has traditionally been a topic raised by students in the PFF sequence. Graduate students read about issues in service; heard from the instructor in the S706 course and other faculty in the Teaching Brown Bag Series about their views, recollections and responses to service requests; and, perhaps, even had a passing experience with it (e.g., the Graduate Student Association in the Sociology Department elects students to almost all of its operating committees). However, the SFI project opened up the opportunity for active learning and reflective thinking in a way that brought the advantages and disadvantages of service into clearer perspective.

Conclusion

According to the Carnegie Foundation's new Initiative on the Doctorate, which is designed to reengineer the Ph.D. in American universities, the goal of doctoral training is not to simply produce professionals qualified to do various jobs in the labor force (http://www.

carnegiefoundation.org/CID). Rather, it aims to produce stewards who embrace four fundamental propositions about their responsibilities to their disciplines, to higher education, and to the society at large. First, stewards generate new knowledge. Research lies at the heart of training the next generation of scholars and those who receive graduate training for work outside the university. Second, stewards conserve the important ideas that are a legacy of the past. Understanding the fundamental contributions of past theory and research prevents wasted "rediscovery" and builds the store of intellectual contribution. Third, stewards are responsible for understanding how to transform that knowledge into explaining and connecting the field to others. This marks the importance of teaching, broadly conceived as passing on insights learned, not only to our undergraduate and graduate students, but to broader audiences, including the general public and those in a position to apply that knowledge to social problems. Fourth and finally, stewards are required to understand how disciplines fit together into the intellectual and social landscape. Most dilemmas that societies face do not fit neatly into the territorial divisions marked by disciplinary boundaries. Ideas and methods often liberally traverse these boundaries, marking the potential of internal, integrating conversations to more successfully address issues in their totality (Golde 2002).

Perhaps no better vehicle exists to fulfill these goals than the scholarship of teaching and learning (see Atkinson 2001). Although SOTL may be narrowly conceptualized as one form of scholarship, by its very nature, it requires thinking about discovery, application, integration and teaching as an interrelated set of activities. In that sense and in our experience of its practice, it holds the potential to create Eugene Rice's (1999) "complete scholars" who are encouraged and rewarded for teaching excellence, instructional scholarship and public service as well as research. In a fundamental way, SOTL connects Ph.D. students and faculties to the places where they labor, giving them a greater sense of ownership and community. This sense of engagement lies not only at the heart of student learning, but at the center of addressing the "disconnects" that capture much of the angst reflected in critiques, from inside and out, of higher education (e.g., see Baker 1999; Pescosolido and Aminzade 1999).

Acknowledgments

We acknowledge support from the Vice Chancellor's Office and the College of Arts and Sciences, Indiana University, as well as the American Sociological Association's Preparing Future Faculty Program Grant. We thank Lisa Pratt, Les Coyne, Travis Paulin, Sara Hinkle, Don Hossler, Terry Brown, and the instructors and students involved in the Summer Freshman Institute program for their time and co-operation.

Notes

1. This overall average did not include the SFI grade.
2. The psychology course, for example, went from small classes to a larger single lecture with discussion sections.
3. See Pescosolido et al. (2003) for more detail on the statistical analysis.
4. Recalling that the SFI students were drawn from those who fell, for some reason, *below* the admission bar, the control group was drawn from the same group of students but who were admitted, for a variety of reasons, under routine admissions procedures. We were able to compare some socio-demographic characteristics between the SFI participants and the cohort of entering freshman. We expected some differences from the start because SFI invitations were extended only to prospective students from Indiana. Overall, the SFI group included more members of under-represented minority groups than the freshman class. Further, 45 percent of SFI students' mothers and 41 percent of SFI students' fathers had college degrees, which is lower than the 58 percent and 64 percent respectively of IU freshmen students' parents. In subsequent multivariate analyses for SFI-I students, we included controls for race and gender, but they were not significant factors in predicting SFI participation on GPA for this small group.
5. Resistance may be vocal or expressed through nonparticipation (i.e., silence or absence). This is not to be confused, according to Higginbotham (1999, p. 475), with differences of opinion.
6. A chapter reviewer asked how the graduate student members of the SFI project team evaluated this experience. Although there was no formal summative assessment, the students gathered together (without the instructor, Pescosolido) to discuss our reactions.

   We believe that this experience has begun the development of our career path as stewards of the discipline. We have seen the positive and negative aspects of collaboration with each other, with University officials, with the instructors and students who were the subjects of the SFI, and with research strategies that go beyond the routine to creative integration. We learned a variety of lessons, including how to work on a research team, how to work with people who hold many different kinds of positions within a university, and how academics balance their research, teaching, and service obligations.

   Despite the many lessons learned, a number of important questions remain. We are still intrigued by the question of how pre-college summer programs can effectively "turn on the light bulb." Because of our exposure to this project, we better understand the role that SOTL may play throughout our academic lives. Most of all, however, we are interested in the question of how SOTL can be used to effect real change within educational institutions. After seeing our research findings play a part in the University's decision to discontinue the SFI program, we hope that the research that we and other scholars of teaching and learning produce will have a positive impact on educational institutions and the students who inhabit them.

7. Over the four cohorts that have completed the entire PFF sequence in the Department of Sociology, all have been offered the option of a collaborative experience as their SOTL project. Two cohorts have taken this option; one worked as individuals; and one opted for a mixture of individual and small group projects.

8. For example 5 out of 65 students and 1 out of 15 instructors did not consent to be included in the research study.

References

Adelman, C., ed. 1986. *Assessment in higher education: Issues and contexts.* Washington, DC: U.S. Department of Education, Office of Research and Improvement.

Atkinson, M. P. 2001. The scholarship of teaching and learning: Reconceptualizing scholarship and transforming the academy. *Social Forces* 79 (June): 1217–29.

Barefoot, B. O., and P. P. Fidler. 1992. *National survey of freshman seminar programming, 1991. Helping first year college students climb the academic ladder.* The Freshman Year Experience: Monograph Series No. 10. South Carolina University: Center for the Study of the Freshman Year Experience.

Baker, P. 1999. Creating learning communities: The unfinished agenda. In B. A. Pescosolido and R. Aminzade, eds., *The social worlds of higher education.* Thousand Oaks, CA: Pine Forge Press.

Barr, R. B., and J. Tagg. 1999. From teaching to learning: A new paradigm for undergraduate education. In B. A. Pescosolido and R. Aminzade, eds., *The social worlds of higher education.* Thousand Oaks, CA: Pine Forge Press.

Billig, S. H. 2002. Support for K–12 service-learning practice: A brief review of the research. *Educational Horizons* 80 (Summer): 184–89.

Boyer, E. 1987. Service: Linking school to life. *Community Education Journal* 1:7–9.

Boyer, E. 1990. *Scholarship reconsidered: Priorities of the professoriate.* Princeton: Carnegie Foundation for the Advancement of Teaching.

Boyer, E. et al. 1992. *Perspective on the freshman year: Volume II. Selected major addresses from freshman year experience conferences.* The Freshman Year Experience: Monograph Series No. 8. South Carolina University: Center for the Study of the Freshman Year Experience.

Cohen, L. 1995. Facilitating the critique of racism and classism: An experiential model for Euro-American middle-class students. *Teaching Sociology* 23:87–93.

Cuseo, J. 1991. *The freshman orientation seminar: A research-based rationale for its value, delivery, and content.* The Freshman Year Experience: Monograph Series No. 4. South Carolina University: Center for the Study of the Freshman Year Experience.

Fidler, D. S., ed. 1991. *Perspectives on the freshman year.* The Freshman Year Experience: Monograph Series No. 2. South Carolina University: Center for the Study of the Freshman Year Experience.

Gaff, J. G., A. S. Pruitt-Logan, and R. A. Weibl. 2000. *Building the faculty we need: Colleges and universities working together.* Washington, DC: Council of Graduate Schools and Association of American Colleges and Universities.

Golde, C. 2002. Looking beyond the finish line. Keynote Address at the Eighth Annual Preparing Future Faculty Campus-Wide Conference, Indiana University, February 28th.

Hadley, K., and L. Fingerson. 2003. Teachers train while students resist in the SFI classroom. Unpublished manuscript, Indiana University.

Hedin, D., and D. Conrad. 1987. Service: A pathway to knowledge. *Community Education Journal* 1:10–14.

Higginbotham, E. 1999. Getting all students to listen: Analyzing and coping with student resistance. In B. A. Pescosolido and R. Aminzade, eds., *The social worlds of higher education.* Thousand Oaks, CA: Pine Forge Press.

Hutchings, P., ed. 2000. *Opening lines: Approaches to the scholarship of teaching and learning.* Princeton, NJ: Carnegie Foundation for the Advancement of Teaching.

Hutchings, P., and L. S. Shulman. 1999. The scholarship of teaching: New elaborations, new developments. *Change* 31 (Sept-Oct): 10–15.

Koch, A. K. 2001. *The first-year experience in American higher education: An annotated bibliography.* 3rd ed. The First-Year Experience Monograph Series, No. 3. South Carolina University: Center for the Study of the Freshman Year Experience.

Levine, A. 1997. Point of view: Higher education's new status as a mature industry. *Chronicle of Higher Education,* January 31, p. A48.

Lowman, J. 1995. *Mastering the techniques of teaching,* 2nd ed. San Francisco: Jossey-Bass.

Martin, D. C., and D. R. Arendale. 1992. *Supplemental instruction: Improving first-year student success in high-risk courses.* The Freshman Year Experience: Monograph Series No. 7. South Carolina University: Center for the Study of the Freshman Year Experience.

Myers, C., and T. B. Jones. 1993. *Promoting active learning: Strategies for the classroom.* San Francisco: Jossey-Bass.

Pascarella, E. T., and P. T. Terenzini. 1991. *How college affects students: Findings and insights from twenty years of research.* San Francisco: Jossey-Bass.

Paul, R. 1990. *Critical thinking: What every person needs to survive in a rapidly changing world.* Rohnert Park, CA: Center for Critical Thinking and Moral Critique, Sonoma State University.

Pescosolido, B. A. 1991. The sociology of the professions and the profession of sociology: Professional responsibility, teaching, and graduate training. *Teaching Sociology* 19:351–61.

Pescosolido, B. A., and R. Aminzade. 1999. *The social worlds of higher education.* Thousand Oaks, CA: Pine Forge Press.

Pescosolido, B. A., J. Loftus, S. Scherr, P. R. Namaste, and J. M. Stuber. 2003. Why the "light bulb" didn't turn on: Stakeholder and institutional influences on a failed pilot program for the freshman year experience. Unpublished manuscript, Indiana University.

Powers, G. T. 1999. Teaching and learning: A matter of style? In B. A. Pescosolido and R. Aminzade, eds., *The social worlds of higher education.* Thousand Oaks, CA: Pine Forge Press.

Rice, R. E. 1999. Rethinking faculty careers. In B. A. Pescosolido and R. Aminzade, eds., *The social worlds of higher education.* Thousand Oaks, CA: Pine Forge Press.

Shanley, M., and R. Hearns, eds. 1991. *The freshman year experience in American higher education: An annotated bibliography. Suggested readings and resources for higher education faculty and administrators involved in promoting student success during the freshman year and beyond.* The Freshman Year Experience: Monograph Series No. 3. South Carolina University: Center for the Study of the Freshman Year Experience.

Smith, R. 2001. Formative evaluation and the scholarship of teaching and learning. *New Directions for Teaching and Learning* 88 (Winter): 51–62.

Smith, T. B. 1993. *Gateways: Residential colleges and the freshman year experience.* The Freshman Year Experience: Monograph Series No. 14. South Carolina University: Center for the Study of the Freshman Year Experience.

Strommer, D. W. 1993. *Portals of entry: University colleges and undergraduate divisions.* The Freshman Year Experience: Monograph Series No. 12. South Carolina University: Center for the Study of the Freshman Year Experience.

Sullivan, T. 1999. Higher education and its social contracts. In B. A. Pescosolido and R. Aminzade, eds., *The social worlds of higher education.* Thousand Oaks, CA: Pine Forge Press.

Tinto, V. 1975. Dropout from higher education: A theoretical synthesis of recent research. *Review of Educational Research* 45:89–125.

Upcraft, M. L., and J. N. Gardner. 1989. *The freshman year experience. Helping students survive and succeed in college.* San Francisco, CA: Jossey-Bass.

Upcraft, M. L., and G. L. Kramer, eds. 1995. *First-year academic advising: Patterns in the present, pathways to the future.* The Freshman Year Experience: Monograph Series No. 18. South Carolina University: Center for the Study of the Freshman Year Experience.

Zeller, W., ed. 1991. *Residence life programs and the first-year experience.* The Freshman Year Experience: Monograph Series No. 5. South Carolina University: Center for the Study of the Freshman Year Experience.

Eight

The Contributions of the Research University to Assessment and Innovation in Undergraduate Education

George D. Kuh

Shibboleths and contradictions abound in American higher education. The research university is the subject of its fair share. On the one hand, American research universities are the envy of the world in terms of important discoveries in virtually all fields of human endeavor and high-quality graduate programs (Geiger 1993; Graham and Diamond 1997; Noll 1998; Rosovsky 1990). On the other hand, research universities are presumed to be—at best—indifferent to undergraduates (Brooks 1994; Education Commission of the States 1995; Kellogg Commission 1997; Wingspread Group 1993). The Boyer Commission on Educating Undergraduates in the Research University (1998) gave credence to this latter view, concluding that baccalaureate education at research universities is sub-par. If this judgment is accurate, it points to a national problem, given that research universities award almost one-third of all baccalaureate degrees annually (even though they comprise only about 6 percent of baccalaureate degree-granting institutions).

But not everyone agrees with the Boyer Commission and other like-minded observers (Kuh 2001a). Some credible sources go so far as to assert that research universities also provide a superior undergraduate education, both in terms of educational and economic value (Noll 1998; Vincow 1997). In addition, there is evidence that research universities are leaders in efforts to improve the quality of the college experience as many innovations in undergraduate education, such as learning communities and first-year student seminars currently being used in all types of institutions, were developed by and first implemented at research universities.

The research university generates such bi-polar characterizations for two reasons. First, it is the standard to which most other colleges and universities aspire (Geiger 1986, 1993; Graham and Diamond 1997; Lipset 1994; Rosovsky 1990). For decades, all types of colleges and universities have been trying to emulate aspects of the research university because it epitomizes academic values, including a deep, abiding commitment to academic freedom and excellence in scholarship (Geiger 1986; Rosovsky 1990). Small teaching-oriented colleges as well as larger master's degree-granting state universities compete for faculty members who will publish and obtain external funds to support various activities including research.

The second reason the research university receives so much attention is because most of the scholars who systematically study and write about American higher education (including undergraduate education) work in such settings. In fact, despite the widespread belief that research universities tend to be indifferent to the quality of undergraduate education, scholars at these institutions have produced most of what is known about the undergraduate student experience including research on effective pedagogical practices. That many vibrant Carnegie Scholarship of Teaching and Learning chapters are found at research universities is another indication that these institutions take teaching and learning seriously.

In this chapter I review some of the more important contributions of the research university to improving student learning and institutional effectiveness through assessing dimensions of quality in undergraduate education. After setting the context for why assessment in higher education is important and defining key terms, I trace the intellectual roots of institutional assessment in American higher education with particular attention to the role of research universities in developing many of the most widely used assessment tools and approaches. I then discuss selected findings from national research and assessment programs that provide a balanced picture of the current performance of research universities in undergraduate education. I close with some implications for how assessment can support the scholarship of teaching and other institutional improvement efforts.

What's All the Fuss About?
The Assessment Mandate

In simple terms, assessment is collecting evidence of student and institutional performance (Banta 1988; Ewell 1988). Although many academics say they do this when grading student work, few outcome measures are available that allow meaningful comparisons of student learning within or between institutions. As a result, colleges and universities cannot make definitive statements about whether their students are learning what they need to know and what they will be able to do after college; there is no measure of learning that can be applied across institutions and states. The latter point was underscored by the National Center on Public Policy and Higher Education (2002), which again assigned an "incomplete" to the student learning category in its recent state-by-state report card, *Measuring Up*.

The demand for student and institutional performance measures has steadily increased since the mid-1980s when several influential reports appeared, beginning with *A Nation at Risk* (National Commission on Excellence in Education 1983) and its postsecondary counterpart, *Involvement in Learning* (Study Group on the Conditions of Excellence in American Higher Education 1984). One of the key themes in the latter report was that colleges and universities should systematically determine the degree to which students were learning what they needed to become economically self-sufficient and responsible citizens after college. Other national reports, such as *Integrity in the Curriculum* (Association of American Colleges 1985), *Time for Results* (National Governors' Association 1986), and *An American Imperative* (Wingspread Group 1993), subsequently echoed this theme.

Regional accreditation associations are other sources of external pressure for institutions of higher education to take responsibility for student learning. Unlike national reports, regional accreditation bodies cannot easily be ignored. Authorized by the federal government to assure quality in higher education, these agencies historically asked schools they were reviewing for information about almost everything *except* evidence of student learning. But by the late 1990s, all six of the regional accreditation associations finally were requiring that re-accreditation applications include institutional level information about the nature and quality of the student experience (Gray 2002). Accreditors' unified demands for assessment data have made assessment at institutions of higher education a priority. Discipline-based organizations in fields such as engineering, nursing, and teacher education also now expect to see evidence that students meet recommended standards (Palomba and Banta 2001).

Though perennially predicted to fade (Ewell 2002), assessment is now firmly established as a field of professional practice in postsecondary education. Annual assessment conferences, such as the one sponsored by the American Association for Higher Education, draw more than 1500 for a three-day meeting. *Change* magazine features assessment-related articles, and Jossey-Bass, a major publishing house specializing in higher education titles, circulates *Assessment Update,* a bimonthly newsletter containing short, practical essays on relevant topics. All of these examples are evidence that assessment has now become part of the landscape of American higher education.

Despite the substantial amount of activity around the country in virtually every type of institution, research university faculty members and—to a lesser extent—academic administrators have been slow to embrace assessment as a core responsibility (Ewell 2002). Classroom research met with a similar reception when it was introduced in the early 1990s (Angelo and Cross 1993). The subsequent designation of classroom research as an integral aspect of the scholarship of teaching helped to legitimize such activities (Angelo 2002). Banta and associates (2002) propose to redefine assessment as a form of scholarship with the goals of legitimizing assessment in the eyes of faculty members and increasing the value and utility of assessment results.

The scholarship of assessment is designed to deepen and extend the foundation of knowledge underlying assessment of student learning through systematic inquiry (Banta and associates 2002). It is based on the premise that faculty and student behaviors can be measured in ways that estimate what and how much students are learning—information that is necessary and relevant to improve the teaching and learning process (Ewell 2002). This definition also emphasizes that scholarly assessment is more than collecting information; such work must also contribute to the knowledge and best practices of the field, and assessment results are to be used to improve student learning and institutional effectiveness.

As Angelo (2002) observed, both the scholarship of teaching and a scholarly approach to assessment are broad-based reform movements fueled by the shift underway in the academy from emphasizing instruction to emphasizing learning (Barr and Tagg 1995; Tagg 2003). That is, in the learning paradigm, what matters is not what the teacher knows or can do, but what the student learns and can do after completing a program of study. And as with the scholarship of teaching (Boyer 1990; Glassick, Huber and Maeroff 1997), good assessment work is guided by relevant theory and reflective practice, is evidence based, and is vetted with colleagues who have similar interests and goals. In this sense, the scholarship of assessment is similar to conducting good discipline-based research. Both require good questions, appropriate investigative methods, representative data sources, good measures of quality, and effective communication of the findings (Pike 2002).

Intellectual Roots of the Scholarship of Assessment

Although the scholarship of assessment is a new concept, it draws on decades of scholarship in allied fields, one of which is student development during the college years (Kuh, Gonyea and Rodriguez 2002). "Student development" is a generic term that represents the host of desirable skills, knowledge, competencies, beliefs, and attitudes students are expected to acquire during college. These include: (a) complex cognitive skills such as reflection and critical thinking; (b) an ability to apply knowledge to practical problems encountered in one's vocation, family, or other areas of life; (c) an understanding and appreciation of human differences; (d) practical competencies such as decision-making, conflict resolution and teamwork, and (e) a coherent integrated sense of identity, self-esteem, confidence, integrity, aesthetic sensibilities, spirituality, and civic responsibility (American College Personnel Association 1994; Kuh and Stage 1992).

Efforts to measure student development first appeared in the literature in the 1930s with studies of both currently enrolled students (e.g., Jones 1938; McConnell 1934; Pressy 1946) and alumni (Havemann and West 1952; Newcomb 1943). Through most of the 1960s, the focus of this work was on measuring attitudes, interests, and other aspects of personality functioning of traditional-age college students, such as authoritarianism and motivation for learning. The two most frequently used instruments for these purposes during this formative period were the Omnibus Personality Inventory (OPI) and the Minnesota Multiphasic Personality Inventory (MMPI), developed respectively at the Center for the Study of Higher Education at the University of California, Berkeley and the University of Minnesota. The OPI became the instrument of choice for multi-institutional studies of student development (Clark, Heist, McConnell, Trow and Yonge 1972). Though many of the studies were intended to be used for improving the college experience, these early discipline-based efforts emphasized hypothesis testing and theory building much more than application.

A parallel line of inquiry emerged in the late 1950s and early 1960s to take into account student characteristics and behaviors as well as features of the college environment that were associated with adjustment to college, achievement, satisfaction, and persistence. The pioneering efforts in this area included the development of the College Characteristics Index (CCI) by Syracuse University's George Stern (with assistance from C. Robert Pace) and the College and University Environment Scales (CUES) by Pace who by this time had moved to UCLA. Both these tools were widely used (e.g., CUES was subsequently copyrighted by the Educational Testing Service) to measure "student-institution fit" which, it was later determined, directly and indirectly affected various aspects of student development (Pascarella and Terenzini 1991) as well as student satisfaction and retention (Astin 1977, 1993; Bean 1986; Pascarella and Terenzini 1991; Tinto 1993).

Interest in measuring the impact of college on students came of age in the 1960s, stimulated in large part by the publication of such classics as *Changing Values in College* (Jacob 1957), *The American College* (Sanford 1962), *The Impact of College on Students* (Feldman and Newcomb 1969), *Education and Identity* (Chickering 1969), *No Time For Youth* (Katz and Korn 1968), and *Growing Up in College* (Heath 1968). Student self-report questionnaires based on theory and research from educational and developmental psychology provided most of the data for these efforts, though some definitive studies by scholars such as Newcomb (1943) at the University of Michigan were done using qualitative methods (interviews). Some groundbreaking work was also produced by a handful of scholars working at selective liberal arts colleges, including Heath (1968) at Haverford College and Sanford (1962) at Vassar College.

Before the 1960s ended, Astin (1977, 1993) established the Cooperative Institutional Research Program (CIRP) with the support of the American Council on Education. Based at UCLA's Higher Education Research Institute, the CIRP study is the nation's longest-running student survey of college students. Annually administered to several hundred thousand first-year students, the project pairs the CIRP entering student survey with its follow-up survey of seniors allowing for longitudinal examinations of the impact of college.

By the late 1960s the student development research literature was robust enough to permit the much-needed formulation and testing of developmental theories that describe the complex, holistic processes by which students grow, change and develop during the college years. Scholars at research universities were also at the forefront in this line of research. To assess psychosocial development, or how individuals resolve challenges and personal growth issues at different stages or periods during the life cycle, Prince, Miller, and Winston (1974) at the University of Georgia developed the Student Developmental Task Inventory. Complementary work was done by Hood and several of his University of Iowa doctoral students who developed the Iowa Student Development Inventories. As the characteristics of students began to change, theories emerged to describe developmental issues common to diverse groups of students, such as adult learners (Gould 1978; Levinson 1978) and, more recently, students of color (Cross, Strauss and Fhagen-Smith 1999; Sue and Sue 1990).

Theories and instruments were also developed to measure cognitive development—the processes by which students move from fairly simplistic, dualistic ("right" or "wrong") judgments and reasoning abilities to more complicated, reflective understandings and constructions of reality. The most prominent work in this area was done by Gilligan (1982), Kohlberg (1981) and Perry (1970) from Harvard University, King and Kitchener (1994) who began their collaboration at the University of Minnesota in the 1970s, Baxter Magolda (1992) from Miami University, and Fowler (1981) from Emory University. Another example of this genre is from the University of Missouri–Columbia where Wood (1983) developed a pencil and paper instrument to measure higher order critical and reflective thinking in order to improve instruction in his psychology department. The results of his research exposed questionable assumptions about teaching, learning, and student behavior, such as the limited capacity of first-year students for reflective thinking, given their developmental level. This prompted discussions about whether traditional teaching approaches, such as emphasizing memorization in first-year survey courses, were having the desired effects, given student characteristics and developmental levels. Wood incorporated this information in his teaching practicum for psychology teaching assistants, a tactic that has since migrated to TA training in other departments (Kuh, Gonyea and Rodriguez 2002). Erwin and Wise (2002) among others are also testing instruments to measure critical thinking, problem-solving skills, and subject matter knowledge in different fields.

Student Engagement

At the intersection of student development research, assessment practice, and the scholarship of teaching is the concept of student engagement. Student engagement represents the combination of time and energy that students devote to educationally purposeful activities, and the policies and practices that institutions and faculty members use to induce students to take part in such activities. The student engagement premise is deceptively simple, even self-evident: the more students do something, the more proficient they become (Kuh 2003). That is, the more students study a particular subject, the more they learn about it, and the more students practice a particular skill such as reading, writing and problem-solving, the more adept they become at those activities. The empirical relationship between "time on task" and learning was originally established in the 1930s by the eminent educational psychologist Ralph Tyler (Merwin 1969) and made prominent as noted below by the work of Pace (1982) and Astin (1984).

This principle has since been corroborated countless times by research studies that show that educationally purposeful activities are precursors to student learning and personal development (Banta and associates 1993; Ewell and Jones 1996). Moreover, engaging in these effective educational practices seems to benefit all students to about the same degree (Kuh 2003; National Survey of Student Engagement 2002). Thus, in the absence of actual measures of student learning, student engagement data are "process indicators" that can be thought of as proxies for learning. Among the better known process indicators are the seven "good practices" in undergraduate educations, such as setting high expectations and providing prompt feedback (Chickering and Gamson 1987). The use of process indicators as part of an institutional assessment program is very appealing because it provides information that schools can use immediately to identify areas where student and institutional performance are falling short of desired levels (Kuh 2001b; National Survey of Student Engagement 2002).

The conceptual underpinning for student engagement is Pace's (1982) "quality of effort" concept, which is consistent with Astin's (1984) "theory of involvement," and the "involving colleges" framework described by Kuh, Schuh, Whitt and associates (1991). The use of student engagement to estimate institutional performance has been popularized by the widespread use of the National Survey of Student Engagement (Kuh 2001b, 2003), an assessment tool that is based in large part on the College Student Experiences Questionnaire (Pace and Kuh 1998).

In summary, scholars at research universities have produced the bulk of the student development theory and research (as well as psychometric analyses and construction of discipline-specific measures) that are the foundation for contemporary approaches to assessing student learning and institutional effectiveness. In the 1950s and 1960s the Center for the Study of Higher Education at UC Berkeley, Syracuse University, and the University of Minnesota were leaders in the field. Today, the major centers of student development research and assessment of student learning are the Indiana University Center for Postsecondary Research, Policy and Planning (spanning the Bloomington and Indianapolis campuses), UCLA's Higher Education Research Institute, the Penn State Center for the Study of Higher Education, and the University of Michigan Center for the Study of Higher and Postsecondary Education. Other noteworthy contributors to the field include Pascarella and Terenzini (1991), of the University of Iowa and Penn State University respectively, who authored the classic volume, *How College Affects Students*, the definitive work on the impact of college on students.

Scholars at research universities have not done all the pioneering work in assessment and institutional improvement, of course. Efforts have also been made at Alverno College, Empire State College, and Evergreen State College among others; for example, Dary Erwin at James Madison University founded the first Ph.D. program specifically focused on assessment (Ewell 2002).

Student Engagement at Research Universities

In this section I summarize selected findings from several recent studies of student engagement at research universities (Kuh 2001b, 2003; Kuh and Gonyea 2003; Kuh and Hu 2001; National Survey of Student Engagement 2000, 2001, 2002). This information comes from two national research programs based at the IU Center for Postsecondary Research, Policy and Planning mentioned earlier, the National Survey of Student Engagement and the College Student Experiences Questionnaire project. The NSSE data are from 265,000 randomly sampled first-year and senior students from about 620 four-year colleges and universities collected between 2000 and 2002. The CSEQ data represent two overlapping samples of undergraduates. The first CSEQ sample is made up of more than 300,000 students from about 300 different four-year colleges and universities who completed the second, third, and fourth editions of the CSEQ over a 19-year period (1984 through 2002). The second sample is composed of more than 80,000 full-time students from 131 baccalaureate degree-granting institutions who completed the fourth edition of the CSEQ between 1998 and 2002. Both NSSE and CSEQ measure the extent to which students participate in educationally purposeful activities. In addition, both surveys ask students to report the progress they've made during college in key areas. And both have undergone extensive psychometric testing and are considered to be valid and reliable measures (Ewell and Jones 1996; Kuh et al. 2001; Kuh, Gonyea and Rodriguez 2002).

To provide a lexicon for faculty members, administrators, parents, students, and external stakeholders to talk with one another about student engagement, we created five clusters of effective educational practices from selected NSSE items (Kuh 2001b) (Figure 8.1). The benchmarks are level of academic challenge, student interactions with faculty members, active and collaborative learning, enriching educational experiences and supportive campus environment.

The NSSE and CSEQ studies lead to four conclusions about student engagement in general and the quality of undergraduate education in research universities in particular. First, students at research universities are less engaged overall on the five NSSE benchmarks compared

Level of Academic Challenge

Challenging intellectual and creative work is central to student learning and collegiate quality. Colleges and universities promote high levels of student achievement by emphasizing the importance of academic effort and setting high expectations for student performance.

- Preparing for class (studying, reading, writing, rehearsing, and other activities related to your academic program)

- Number of assigned textbooks, books, or book-length packs of course readings

- Number of written papers or reports of 20 pages or more

- Number of written papers or reports between 5 and 19 pages

- Number of written papers or reports fewer than 5 pages

- Coursework emphasizes: Analyzing the basic elements of an idea, experience or theory

- Coursework emphasizes: Synthesizing and organizing ideas, information, or experiences

- Coursework emphasizes: Making judgments about the value of information, arguments, or methods

- Coursework emphasizes: Applying theories or concepts to practical problems or in new situations

- Worked harder than you thought you could to meet an instructor's standards or expectations

- Campus environment emphasizes spending significant amounts of time studying and on academic work

Continued on the next pages

Figure 8.1 Benchmarks of effective educational practice

Active and Collaborative Learning

Students learn more when they are intensely involved in their education and are asked to think about and apply what they are learning in different settings. Collaborating with others in solving problems or mastering difficult material prepares students to deal with the messy, unscripted problems they will encounter daily during and after college.

- Asked questions in class or contributed to class discussions

- Made a class presentation

- Worked with other students on projects during class

- Worked with classmates outside of class to prepare class assignments

- Tutored or taught other students

- Participated in a community-based project as part of a regular course

- Discussed ideas from your reading or classes with others outside of class (students, family members, co-workers, etc.)

Student Interactions with Faculty Members

Through interacting with faculty members inside and outside the classroom, students see firsthand how experts think about and solve practical problems. As a result their teachers become role models, mentors, and guides for continuous, life-long learning.

- Discussed grades or assignments with an instructor

- Talked about career plans with a faculty member or advisor

- Discussed ideas from your reading or classes with faculty members outside of class

- Worked with faculty members on activities other than coursework (committees, orientation, student-life activities, etc.)

- Received prompt feedback from faculty on your academic performance

- Worked with a faculty member on a research project

Figure 8.1 (continued on the next page)

Enriching Educational Experiences

Complementary learning opportunities inside and outside the classroom augment the academic program. Experiencing diversity teaches students valuable things about themselves and other cultures. Used appropriately, technology facilitates learning and promotes collaboration between peers and instructors. Internships, community service and senior capstone courses provide students with opportunities to synthesize, integrate, and apply their knowledge. Such experiences make learning more meaningful and, ultimately, more useful because what students know becomes a part of who they are.

- Talking with students with different religious beliefs, political opinions, or values

- Talking with students of a different race or ethnicity

- An institutional climate that encourages contact among students from different economic, social, and racial or ethnic backgrounds

- Using electronic technology to discuss or complete assignments

- Participating in: internships or field experiences
community service or volunteer work
foreign language course work
study abroad
independent study or self-designed major
culminating senior experience
co-curricular activities

Figure 8.1 (continued on the next page)

with their counterparts attending other types of institutions. This is evident from the NSSE data shown in the series of box and whisker charts in Figure 8.2 (National Survey of Student Engagement 2002) and is corroborated by the CSEQ data (Kuh and Gonyea 2003; Kuh and Hu 2001).

Second, although smaller is generally better in terms of student engagement, the highest-scoring research universities were as engaging as many small colleges. This, too, is evident from Figure 8.2 and from CSEQ-based studies (Kuh and Hu 2001). One of the most distinctive features of high performing research universities, after controlling for selectivity and other institutional and student characteristics, is that they are typically perceived by their students to place a strong emphasis

Supportive Campus Environment

Students perform better and are more satisfied at colleges that are committed to their success and cultivate positive working and social relations among different groups on campus.

- ▣ Campus environment provides support you need to help you succeed academically

- ▣ Campus environment helps you cope with your nonacademic responsibilities (work, family, etc.)

- ▣ Campus environment provides the support you need to thrive socially

- ▣ Quality of relationships with other students

- ▣ Quality of relationships with faculty members

- ▣ Quality of relationships with administrative personnel and offices

---

Figure 8.1 (continued). Benchmarks of effective educational practice

on developing intellectual and analytical qualities. Apparently, engaging research universities are marked by campus cultures that send strong, consistent messages about the importance of academic performance and scholarship.

Third, the quality of the student experience at research universities varies less than at other types of institutions. That is, the range of student engagement scores tends to be more compressed at research universities than at other types of institutions on four of the five benchmarks of effective educational practice (Figure 8.2). Only on the supportive campus environment measure do research university students show a greater range in scores compared with other types of institutions.

Finally, student engagement varies more within institutions than between institutions or even institutional types. At first blush this may appear counterintuitive, but it is consistent with other research (Pascarella and Terenzini 1991). To illustrate, the range of academic challenge benchmark scores of seniors at 15 different research universities, ranging from the lowest-scoring school on this benchmark to the highest-scoring, is shown in Figure 8.3. (Only the middle 80 percent of students at each institution is shown so that outliers do not skew the display.) The difference in mean scores between the lowest- and highest-

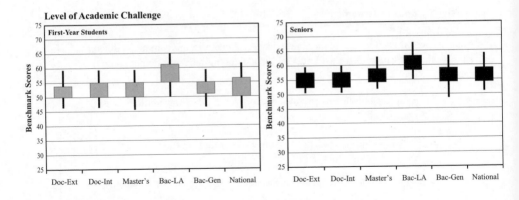

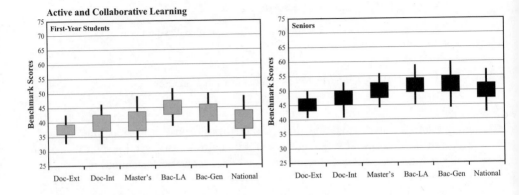

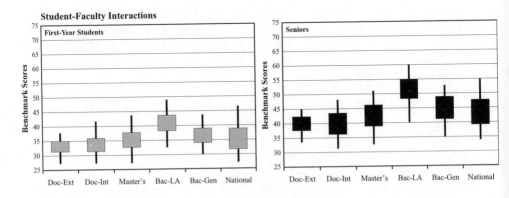

Figure 8.2 National benchmarks of effective educational practice

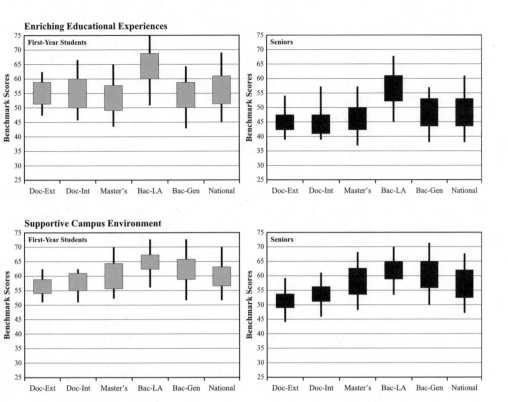

Enriching Educational Experiences

Supportive Campus Environment

Figure 8.2 (continued). National benchmarks of effective educational practice

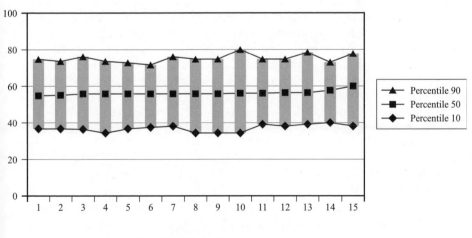

Doc-Extensive Institutions

Figure 8.3 Levels of academic challenge: Seniors at doctoral–extensive instutions

scoring schools is only about 10 points, or 10 percent of the 100 point scale. However, the engagement levels of students within each institution are much greater. The pattern represented here is similar for all five NSSE benchmarks and for all other institutional types.

These results suggest that one immediate step colleges and universities can take to improve undergraduate education is to identify students who score in the lowest deciles on engagement measures—those who are essentially disengaged—and develop strategies to involve them in educationally purposeful activities (Kuh, Hu and Vesper 2000). But this cannot simply be done by student category (younger and older, full-time and part-time), because this assumes that students in these groups are more alike than they actually are (Kuh 2003).

Information Literacy and Library Use

The shift from teaching to learning as the primary goal of undergraduate education (Barr and Tagg 1995; Tagg 2003) has implications for many aspects of the university including the library. CSEQ trend data show that student use of the library declined between 1984 and 2001, especially as a venue for reading and studying (Kuh and Gonyea 2003). This is due in large part to the explosion of the World Wide Web in the mid-1990s, allowing students to access information and library resources online from their dorm rooms, fraternity and sorority houses, other campus locations, and off-campus residences. Even so, students at research universities use the library less frequently compared with students attending other types of institutions, net of other factors such as institutional size and student characteristics. At the same time, though, students at research universities report the greatest gains in information literacy during college, perhaps because research universities typically are better wired for technology than other types of institutions, with broadband access to computer networks, excellent online library search engines, and network access from residence hall rooms, academic support centers, and study lounges in campus unions (Kuh and Gonyea 2003).

Diversity Experiences

Understanding the importance of and learning to work effectively with people from different backgrounds is an essential set of skills and competencies for college students. Along with their counterparts at baccalaureate liberal arts colleges, students at research universities more frequently engage in such diversity-related activities as having serious conversations with students from backgrounds different than their own, whereas students at master's-granting institutions are the least likely to engage in such activities. In part this is a function of "density" of racial and ethnic groups, as students are somewhat more likely to engage in diversity-related activities on campuses where there are larger proportions of students of color. Research universities tend to enroll relatively high numbers of students of color (Kuh 2003; National Survey of Student Engagement 2002).

The quality of undergraduate education at research universities is not as strong as some observers expect (Boyer Commission 1998), given their resources and enviable position in the institutional pecking order. They have improved their relative performance during the last decade by requiring students to do more reading and writing and making faculty members more accessible (Boyer Commission 2002), two effective educational practices that are positively associated with desired outcomes of college (Kuh and Hu 2001). For example, the frequency of student-faculty contact increased at research universities between the mid-1980s and the mid-1990s, perhaps in part because of changing reward systems that place a greater emphasis on instruction (Diamond and Adam 1997) and other efforts to improve the baccalaureate experience (Kuh 2001a). These include using more active and collaborative pedagogical approaches in large introductory classes (Boyer Commission 2002). In the next section I describe a few other promising practices at research universities that are being implemented at other types of institutions.

Efforts to Enhance Student Learning at Research Universities

As mentioned at the outset, many of the current initiatives to improve undergraduate education originated at research universities. I'll describe three that have been empirically linked with student success (Education Commission of the States 1995; Hossler, Kuh and Olsen 2001; Upcraft, Gardner and Barefoot in press). They include small seminars for first-year students taught by regular faculty members, learning communities such as Freshmen Interest Groups and linked course learning options, and student collaboration with faculty members on research.

First-Year Seminars

About 30 years ago, at the University of South Carolina, John Gardner introduced the forerunner to the now widely adopted University 101 course that is focused primarily on orienting new students to college life and teaching them survival and academic success skills (Upcraft, Gardner and Barefoot in press). Another form of the first-year seminar is a discipline-based course with 25 or fewer students taught by a faculty member. The basic model, in place at Harvard University since the 1950s, features senior faculty teaching in their specialty area to first-year students (Light 2001). The University of Michigan recently revitalized its version wherein senior faculty members teach discipline-based freshman seminars for students entering the College of Literature, Science and the Arts and introductory courses in the recently revised engineering curriculum.

Learning Communities

A shibboleth that haunts universities is that learning is fundamentally a solitary intellectual activity. Recent research demonstrates that this is not the case (Bransford, Brown and Cocking 2002). Rather, deep learning is a product of social interaction, and often most productively occurs when certain conditions are present—learners are known by name and respected as individuals, feel comfortable, interact with people from backgrounds different than their own, take intellectual risks, assume responsibility for their learning and social welfare, and participate in community affairs. To intentionally create these conditions, the University of Washington developed learning communities in the 1980s. Learning communities take different forms; some are exclusively classroom-based and others have a residential component where participants live in close proximity. But all are typically made up of small numbers of students who are co-enrolled in two or more courses. The organizing principle is to create "communities of learners" whereby the network of social relations connects students to one another and to the course content. An implicit goal of many forms of learning communities is to teach students the skills and understandings they need to succeed academically and to participate fully in institutional life (which we used to take for granted several decades ago when colleges were small and primarily residential).

Learning communities are positively related to all five benchmarks of effective educational practice as well as diversity experiences, gains in personal and social development, practical competence, and general education, and overall satisfaction with the undergraduate college experience (National Survey of Student Engagement 2002). Nationally, almost a third (31 percent) of first-year students at research universities report participating (or planning to participate) in some type of learning community. This is the highest rate of any type of four-year college or university, consistent with the Boyer Commission's (2002) observation that more research universities provide such opportunities. The University of Missouri–Columbia and Indiana University Bloomington are among the research universities offering residential freshman interest groups (FIGS), clusters of about 20 students co-enrolled in the same 2–3 courses who also live in close proximity in campus housing (Kuh 2001a).

Student-Faculty Collaboration on Research

Although research universities did not invent the concept, they have a competitive advantage in terms of the number of opportunities they afford undergraduates to conduct research with experts who are at the cutting edge of their fields. About 27 percent of seniors at research universities say they've worked on a research project with a faculty member, a somewhat smaller portion than the one-third of seniors at baccalaureate liberal arts colleges who do so (National Survey of Student Engagement 2002). But at about one-sixth of research universities, most (75 percent or more) undergraduates apparently have such an experience (Boyer Commission 2002). In some disciplines, such as science and engineering, substantial proportions of undergraduate majors engage in research, but for those in the social sciences and humanities the numbers are much lower.

In addition to the federally funded McNair Scholars program and institutionally sponsored Summer Research Opportunity Programs, universities have used seed money creatively to promote more student-faculty collaboration on research. For example, upon discovering that NSSE data showed that the frequency of student collaboration with faculty members on research was unacceptably low, given the institution's mission, the president of Georgia Tech University created a $250,000 grant fund as an incentive to stimulate more of this activity. The University of Montana–Missoula issues an annual request for proposals for "Engagement Awards." Academic departments apply for up to $3,000 for projects that promise to enhance students' academic experiences. The projects are also supposed to lead to permanent changes in faculty and student behavior in at least three of the five NSSE benchmarks of effective educational practice, one of which must be student-faculty interaction. Units get $2,000 up front with the remaining $1,000 coming after assessing the effect of the award. In 2001 and 2002, full awards were made to four departments and partial awards to two others, including the geology department, which created additional student-faculty research opportunities and hosted a conference for all undergraduates in the state to present their research. As a result 60 undergraduates are engaging in faculty-led research, and the Geology Club has been revitalized (www.cs.umt.edu/geology).

Examples of Other Effective Educational Practices at Research Universities

Getting students off to a good start at college is important to developing a foundation for success (Kuh 2001a). Texas A&M pulls many levers to welcome and introduce newcomers to its rich traditions, beginning with Fish Camp (a popular, highly engaging orientation program in which about 4700 students participate), an array of multicultural and mentoring services, and an intrusive, effective academic advising system that is reviewed periodically by the faculty senate.

The University of Kansas intentionally promotes student-faculty contact by mandating that students constitute 20 percent of the members of campus policy-making committees and sponsoring "Meet-a-Professor" nights in the residence halls. Most classes (79 percent) have fewer than 30 students.

At the University of Missouri–Columbia 89 percent of seniors have a capstone experience, required by its Hesburgh award-winning general education program. Also, almost two-thirds of all students frequently use electronic technology to discuss or complete assignments as more than 60 percent of all classes have a built-in Web component.

Georgia Tech's optional coop program involves more than 3,500 students and 600 employing organizations (including some international placements). Most engineering programs require a senior design project capstone experience that requires students to work in small teams and publicly present their work.

Institutional research at IU Bloomington showed that student use of an academic skills center increased when the center was moved closer to where students lived; also, students in high-risk courses were almost twice as likely to seek tutoring when it was available in their own residence hall as when the same service was provided in other campus locations. Now, three academic skills centers have been placed in residence halls in different parts of the campus. Students who use these skill centers for mathematics and writing skills improvement are much more likely to persist to the second year and get higher grades than peers who do not, even though they are similar in most background characteristics including academic ability (Hossler, Kuh and Olsen 2001; Smith 2003).

Adding Value to Assessment at Research Universities

The challenge of effectively integrating a scholarship of assessment with scholarship of teaching is not unique to research universities. In this section I offer seven principles to enhance the efficacy of assessment efforts and create a culture of evidence that is the cornerstone of institutional improvement (see also Angelo 2002).

Enlist Support

Enlist the support of influential stakeholders before, during, and after data collection. Faculty members, administrative leaders, and others who occupy gate-keeping roles need to be informed and involved for the assessment process to succeed and for results to be used productively. For those leading assessment projects, one promising start is to meet with deans and department chairs and to invite them to share their ideas and concerns about student engagement. What kind of information about student learning and institutional effectiveness do they find compelling and useful? What can be done individually, at the department level and at the institutional level, to take more responsibility for student learning? What tactics might be used to induce students to take greater advantage of institutional resources for learning?

Faculty members often suspect that the assessment results will be used primarily in their reviews as a measure of accountability, rather than to identify areas where institutional effort might be directed to improve student learning. In other instances, faculty members may be skeptical of the validity and utility of assessment tools. To allay these fears administrators should ensure that faculty members have an opportunity to influence the design of the assessment process; this will increase the probability that the results will be taken seriously.

Talking about student engagement promotes talking about teaching and learning. To assist in this effort, NSSE has developed a faculty version of the student engagement survey that can help stimulate and focus substantive conversations about student learning. Among its uses are to compare faculty responses to student responses, which may identify gaps between faculty expectations and student behaviors that can be addressed to improve student learning (http://www.collegereport.org/faculty/).

Faculty development is a key lever for advancing the value of assessment, one that the University of Missouri (UM) is using to realize its aspiration to become "nationally recognized as an eminent learner-centered research university" (*2001 University of Missouri Strategic Plan*, 1). Toward that end the UM system introduces the student engagement concept to new faculty members through the system's New Faculty Teaching Scholars program to help them better understand what it means to create a "learner-centered environment" and to identify practical ways that they can infuse effective educational practices in their work with students inside and outside the classroom. By comparing campus results with benchmark scores from similar institutions, the Teaching Scholars are able to determine what their campus was doing well and areas where improvement would be welcome.

The Dean of Faculties at Indiana University Bloomington, Moya Andrews, sponsors an annual Freshman Learning Project where 15 or so faculty members come together for a two-week intensive seminar to explore in depth their assumptions about teaching and learning and the changing characteristics of today's students. As a result, the structure and pedagogy used in large introductory courses is beginning to change, consistent with promising educational practice (Smith 2003).

Approach Assessment as a Scholarly Activity

Approach assessment as a scholarly activity and link it to the scholarships of teaching, application, and integration. One reason assessment falters is because few faculty members either are aware of, or care about, the results. Assessment can have the intended impact only if many faculty members view assessment as a productive activity, consistent with their scholarly interests, and apply assessment results to their teaching (Angelo 2002). For a scholarship of assessment to take root, a network of faculty members, instructional development specialists, and academic administrators must work together to point out explicitly the shared goals of the scholarships of assessment, teaching, discovery and application. Boyer (1990, p. 21) suggests some guiding questions to point the way: "How can knowledge responsibly be applied to consequential problems? How can it be helpful to individuals as well as institutions, and how can specific problems themselves define an agenda for scholarly investigation?"

Just as the scholarship of teaching "involves question asking, inquiry, and investigation" (Hutchings and Shulman 1999, p. 13), the scholarship of assessment focuses on whether: (1) the assessment measures address the key questions; (2) the data answer the questions being asked; and (3) the data are sensitive to students' educational experiences and the effects of teaching and learning (Pike 2002). For both the scholarship of teaching and the scholarship of assessment to flourish, a culture of evidence must be cultivated that will encourage and support the search for applications of answers to these kinds of questions.

Another key task is to create synergy between these two sets of activities that makes both the scholarship of teaching and assessment rewarding and productive. Palomba (2002) offers an array of suggestions toward this end, including performance measures for assessing general education and major field outcomes, capstone exercises whereby graduating students demonstrate proficiency and comprehensive learning, student portfolios that show evidence of learning, and individual course-imbedded assessments based on classroom assessment and classroom research.

Sample to Enable Disaggregation

Sample strategically to insure that enough data are available to disaggregate at the department or program level. Faculty enthusiasm for digging into assessment results is difficult to sustain if only a handful of students from their department are among the respondents. Institution-wide averages are typically meaningless to faculty and staff groups charged with improving some aspect of the undergraduate program. One of the keys to promoting use of assessment data is getting department-level buy-in so that the sample is representative and the numbers of students participating are large enough to enable dissagregation at the unit level where faculty members can examine performance results of their own students. This means that enough students in specific cohorts or major fields must be sampled. For this reason institutions such as Brigham Young University, Indiana University Bloomington, Indiana University Purdue University Indianapolis, North Dakota State University, South Dakota State University, University of Delaware, and the University of Missouri–Columbia are randomly selecting for the NSSE survey more students than called for by the project's standard random sampling strategy (which is adequate to produce acceptable point estimates at the institutional level). A large sample size reduces sampling error and is more likely to yield enough respondents to be able to "drill down" to the department or major field level. Another example is Southwest Texas State University where department chairs invite faculty to complete the faculty version of the NSSE mentioned earlier in order to estimate levels of student engagement and the relative value of certain student engagement activities. In 2002 about 300 tenure-track faculty members from 13 different departments participated.

Examine Results

Examine the results from multiple perspectives. The initial assessment results of student learning or other areas of institutional performance should be viewed as a baseline indication. One set of findings may be enough to mobilize action, especially when comparisons with other departments or peer institutions confirm or challenge prevailing views. But equally meaningful discussions result when colleagues take a criterion-referenced view of student engagement in the context of the school's mission and then determine reasonable expectations for student engagement in various educational practices.

Experience so far shows that, in general, faculty members and students tend to respond the same way to about half of the questions on the NSSE, and concordance is highest for the areas where student engagement is either quite high or fairly low. For about a quarter of the items, faculty members overestimate student engagement. Some of these differences are understandable, such as faculty reporting much more class discussion than students report. Faculty may devote a considerable amount of class time to discussion and answering questions, but in a class of 40 students, only about 10 students may dominate much of the discussion. Thus, 30 of 40 students responding could accurately report "never" or "occasionally" when asked about participating in class discussions. Similarly, faculty members say more students frequently come to class without completing readings or assignments than students report. This makes sense because what faculty members may consider being "prepared" is probably more rigorous than is students' understanding of adequate preparation.

By focusing on the gaps between student and faculty responses investigators can help establish and more clearly communicate appropriate expectations for student performance, especially the extent to which memorization is emphasized relative to higher-order mental activities of analysis and synthesis. In addition, certain engagement activities are more important in faculty members' eyes for first-year students (class discussion, prompt feedback) and others for seniors (class presentations, talking about career plans). This criterion-referenced approach to using assessment data can increase faculty ownership in the process of improvement and appreciation for the value of student engagement. Academic and student affairs deans and department chairs find it compelling to prioritize improvement initiatives based on what their colleagues agree is important and what their students say they are or are not doing very often. In addition, focus groups with students almost always yield pithy insights into what results mean and pertinent suggestions for increasing engagement in specific areas.

Link Different Sources of Relevant Data

Link results to other information about the student experience and complementary initiatives. Student learning is enhanced when students engage in a variety of complementary activities inside and outside the classroom (Pascarella and Terenzini 1991). In a similar vein, the positive impact of student engagement results will be multiplied if the data can be made relevant to groups of faculty and staff members spearheading different reform efforts around the campus. Targets of opportunity include colleagues working on general education and core curriculum issues as well as service learning opportunities; students, faculty, and staff who are responsible for diversity programming; and participants in Scholarship of Teaching and Learning activities. By finding a common interest, such as student engagement, individuals and groups can mutually support and learn from one another's work, which will increase the positive impact on teaching and learning that any single effort might produce on its own. In addition, with appropriate clearance from institutional review boards, assessment information can be linked with information from academic transcripts, retention studies, focus groups, and results from other surveys to develop a rich, comprehensive picture of the undergraduate experience.

Form Partnerships

Form partnerships with other universities and agencies to support improvement. Universities often get stymied in their efforts to improve because they encounter inevitable obstacles and drags on their will and resources. It is difficult to sustain energy and commitment in the face of daily distractions and multiple competing priorities inherent in contemporary academic life. The chances of successful innovation improve when campus teams are formed and institutions work together in consortial arrangements on topics of mutual interest (Ewell 1997). Institutional teams linked to partners at other schools insinuate a measure of peer accountability into the process and provide much-needed support and encouragement to persevere. In addition, participation in a consortium may increase the number of institutionally compatible, transportable exemplars that are uncovered, as more people are looking for them. Variants of this model are being used by such national associations as the American Association for Higher Education and the Association of American Colleges and Universities in their summer workshops and institutes.

Project BEAMS (Building Engagement and Attainment of Minority Students) has adopted a similar strategy. AAHE, NSSE, and the Alliance for Equity in Higher Education (Alliance), with support from Lumina Foundation for Education, have joined forces to help reduce the national gap in educational attainment for African Americans, Hispanics, and Native Americans by increasing the number of students from these groups who earn a bachelor's degree. BEAMS will enable up to 150 Alliance member institutions to focus on enhancing student engagement, learning and success. Participating schools will administer NSSE twice between 2003 and 2006, first to identify priorities for action and a second time to estimate progress. A key aspect of the strategy is for participating schools to assemble teams that will then participate in a variety of institutional improvement activities as a member of a 6–8 school consortium.

Among the two dozen institutional consortia that have used NSSE since 2000, two are composed of research universities that exchanged student-level records after removing individual student identification information. One group was made up of the four public universities in Ohio, the other of about 15 AAU institutions from around the country. These institutions agreed to share data with the understanding that the information would be used only for internal purposes, and not made public. This was a precedent-setting move for these schools, although private research universities in the Consortium on Financing Higher Education have shared information in the past.

Develop Feedback Loops

Concentrate on developing and sustaining productive feedback loops between assessment processes, results, and changes in policy and practice. As mentioned earlier, it is essential that the right people—faculty members and academic administrators especially—pay attention to and use assessment results. Here are several of the noteworthy efforts that are underway at research universities.

The University of Wisconsin system is using student engagement data to compare institutional values and priorities with actual practice. The results prompted considerable discussion and several campuses are administering the NSSE annually to learn more on an ongoing basis about how their students are experiencing their educational programs. The UW system also administered a subset of NSSE questions to the

2001–02 graduates from all campuses to learn if there is a difference in the responses between students who followed a traditional path to completing a degree and those who followed a nontraditional path.

Student engagement results at the University of Utah showed that student use of technology was not at a level that the institution considered acceptable. This prompted information technology staff to design additional staff training and planning efforts.

IUPUI (www.imir.iupui.edu/imir/) and the University of Colorado-Boulder (www.colorado.edu/pba/outcomes/) post assessment results on the Internet to make them more widely and immediately available. Appalachian State University is a pioneer in the use of database applications and the Internet to report assessment results and has developed an interactive site (www.appstate.edu/www_docs/depart/irp/irp.html) from which individuals obtain survey results by major field, year, or other cross sections. The annual reports of the National Survey of Student Engagement (2000, 2001, 2002) provide additional examples of how institutions are using assessment results to improve the quality of the undergraduate experience.

Conclusion

Although maligned for ignoring undergraduate education, research universities actually have been at the forefront of developing approaches for assessing student learning and institutional effectiveness, and in the formulation of theories that describe student development during the college years. In fact, it is hard to imagine what the state of assessment of student learning and institutional effectiveness would be today without the contributions of scholars from these institutions. Research universities also have introduced a number of practices to enhance the quality of the undergraduate experience.

However, despite many noteworthy contributions, research universities do not uniformly offer the highest-quality undergraduate experience for the typical student. Nevertheless, some institutions perform surprisingly well, given their size, organizational complexity, and multiple missions, in comparison to liberal arts colleges, which as a group have the highest scores on measures of student engagement. More importantly, scholars at research universities have been instrumental in raising issues and providing the vision for undergraduate reforms in all sectors of American higher education. For this alone, the research university deserves recognition for enhancing the quality of the undergraduate experience nationally.

References

American College Personnel Association. 1994. *The student learning imperative: Implications for student affairs.* Washington, DC: American College Personnel Association.

Angelo, T. A. 2002. Engaging and supporting faculty in the scholarship of assessment: Guidelines from research and best practice. In T. W. Banta, ed., *Building a scholarship of assessment.* San Francisco: Jossey-Bass.

Angelo, T. A., and K. P. Cross. 1993. *Classroom assessment techniques: A handbook for college teachers.* San Francisco: Jossey-Bass.

Association of American Colleges. 1985. *Integrity in the curriculum: A report to the academic community.* Washington, DC: Association of American Colleges.

Astin, A. W. 1977. *Four critical years.* San Francisco: Jossey-Bass.

———. 1984. Student involvement: A developmental theory for higher education. *Journal of College Student Development* 40 (5): 518–29.

———. 1993. *What matters in college: Four critical years revisited.* San Francisco: Jossey-Bass.

Banta, T. W., ed. 1988. *Implementing outcomes assessment: Promise and perils.* New Directions for Institutional Research, no. 59. San Francisco: Jossey-Bass.

Banta, T. W., and associates. 1993. *Making a difference: Outcomes of a decade of assessment in higher education.* San Francisco: Jossey-Bass.

———. 2002. *Building a scholarship of assessment.* San Francisco: Jossey-Bass.

Barr, R. B., and J. Tagg. 1995. From teaching to learning—A new paradigm for undergraduate education. *Change* 27 (6): 12–25.

Baxter Magolda, M. B. 1992. *Knowing and reasoning in college: Gender-related patterns in students' intellectual development,* 1st ed. San Francisco: Jossey-Bass.

Bean, J. P. 1986. Assessing and reducing attrition. In D. Hossler, ed., *Managing college enrollments.* New Directions for Higher Education, no. 53. San Francisco: Jossey-Bass.

Boyer Commission on Educating Undergraduates in the Research University. 1998. *Reinventing undergraduate education: A blueprint for America's research universities.* Stony Brook, NY: The Carnegie Foundation for the Advancement of Teaching.

———. 2002. *Reinventing undergraduate education: Three years after the Boyer report.* Stony Brook, NY: The Carnegie Foundation for the Advancement of Teaching.

Boyer, E. L. 1990. *Scholarship reconsidered: Priorities for the professorate.* Princeton, NJ: Carnegie Foundation for the Advancement of Teaching.

Bransford, J. D., A. L. Brown, and R. R. Cocking, eds. 2000. *How people learn: Brain, mind, experience, and school.* Washington, DC: National Research Council/National Academy Press.

Brooks, H. 1994. Current criticisms of research universities. In J. R. Cole,

E. G. Barber, and S. R. Graubard, eds., *The research university in a time of discontent,* pp. 231–254. Baltimore: The Johns Hopkins University Press.

Chickering, A. W. 1969. *Education and identity.* San Francisco: Jossey-Bass.

Chickering, A. W., and Z. F. Gamson. 1987. Seven principles for good practice in undergraduate education. *AAHE Bulletin* 39 (7): 3–7.

Clark, B., P. Heist, T. McConnell, M. Trow, and G. Yonge. 1972. *Students and colleges: Interaction and change.* Berkeley: University of California, Center for Research and Development in Higher Education.

Cross, W. E., L. Strauss, and P. Fhagen-Smith. 1999. African American identity development across the life span: Educational implications. In R. Sheets and E. Hollins, eds., *Racial and ethnic identity in school practices.* Mahwah, NJ: Erlbaum.

Diamond, R. M., and B. E. Adam. 1997. *Changing priorities at research universities: 1991–1996.* Syracuse, NY: Syracuse University Center for Instructional Development.

Education Commission of the States. 1995. *Making quality count in undergraduate education.* Denver, CO: Education Commission of the States.

Erwin, T. D., and U. Delworth. 1980. An instrument to measure Chickering's vectors of identity. *NASPA Journal* 17 (3): 19–24.

Erwin, T. D., and S. I. Wise. 2002. A scholar-practitioner model for assessment. In T. W. Banta and associates, *Building a scholarship of assessment,* pp. 67–81. San Francisco: Jossey-Bass.

Ewell, P. T. 1988. Implementing assessment: Some organizational issues. In T. W. Banta, ed., *Implementing outcomes assessment: Promise and perils.* New Directions for Institutional Research, no. 59. San Francisco: Jossey-Bass.

———. 1997. Organizing for learning: A new imperative. *AAHE Bulletin* 50 (4): 10–12.

———. 2002. An emerging scholarship: A brief history of assessment. In T. W. Banta, ed., *Building a scholarship of assessment.* San Francisco: Jossey-Bass.

Ewell, P. T., and D. P. Jones. 1996. *Indicators of "good practice" in undergraduate education: A handbook for development and implementation.* Boulder, CO: National Center for Higher Education Management Systems.

Feldman, K. A., and T. M. Newcomb. 1969. *The impact of college on students.* San Francisco: Jossey-Bass.

Fowler, J. W. 1981. *Stages of faith: The psychology of human development and the quest for meaning.* 1st ed. San Francisco: Harper and Row.

Geiger, R. L. 1986. *To advance knowledge: The growth of the American research universities.* Oxford: Oxford University Press.

———. 1993. *Research and relevant knowledge: American research universities since World War II.* Oxford: Oxford University Press.

Gilligan, C. 1982. *In a different voice: Psychological theory and women's development.* Cambridge: Harvard University Press.

Glassick, C. E., M. T. Huber, and G. I. Maeroff. 1997. *Scholarship assessed: Evaluation of the professoriate.* San Francisco: Jossey-Bass.

Gould, R. L. 1978. *Transformations: Growth and change in adult life.* New York: Simon & Schuster.

Graham, H. D., and N. Diamond. 1997. *The rise of American research universities: Elites and challengers in the postwar era.* Baltimore: The Johns Hopkins University Press.

Gray, P. J. 2002. The roots of assessment: Tensions, solutions, and research directions. In T. W. Banta, ed., *Building a scholarship of assessment.* San Francisco: Jossey-Bass.

Havemann, E., and P. West. 1952. *They went to college.* San Diego: Harcourt Brace Jovanovich.

Heath, D. H. 1968. *Growing up in college: Liberal education and maturity,* 1st ed. San Francisco: Jossey-Bass.

Hossler, D., G. D. Kuh, and D. Olsen. 2001. Finding fruit on the vines: Using higher education research and institutional research to guide institutional policies and strategies. (Part II) *Research in Higher Education* 42 (2): 223–35.

Hutchings, P., and L. S. Shulman. 1999. The scholarship of teaching: New elaborations, new developments. *Change* 30 (5): 11–15.

Jacob, P. 1957. *Changing values in college: An exploratory study of the impact of college teaching.* New York: Harper & Row.

Jones, V. A. 1938. Attitudes of college students and changes in such attitudes during four years in college. *Journal of Educational Psychology* 29:14–35.

Katz, J., and H. A. Korn. 1968. *No time for youth: Growth and constraint in college students.* 1st ed. San Francisco: Jossey-Bass.

Kellogg Commission on the Future of State and Land-Grant Universities. 1997. *Returning to our roots: The student experience.* Washington, DC: National Association of State Universities and Land-Grant Colleges.

King, P. M., and K. S. Kitchener. 1994. *Developing reflective judgment: Understanding and promoting intellectual growth and critical thinking in adolescents and adults.* San Francisco: Jossey-Bass.

Kohlberg, L. 1981. *The philosophy of moral development: Moral stages and the idea of justice.* 1st ed. San Francisco: Harper and Row.

Kuh, G. D. 2001a. College students today: Why we can't leave serendipity to chance. In P. Altbach, P. Gumport, and B. Johnstone, eds., *In defense of the American university.* Baltimore: The Johns Hopkins University Press.

———. 2001b. Assessing what really matters to student learning: Inside the National Survey of Student Engagement. *Change* 33 (3): 10–17, 66.

———. 2003. What we're learning about student engagement from NSSE. *Change* 35 (2): 24–32.

Kuh, G. D., and R. M. Gonyea. 2003. The role of the academic library in promoting student engagement in learning. *College and Research Libraries* 64 (4): 256–82.

Kuh, G. D., and S. Hu. 2001. Learning productivity at research universities. *Journal of Higher Education* 72 (1): 1–28.

Kuh, G. D., and F. K. Stage. 1992. Student development theory and research. In B. R. Clark and G. Neave, eds., *Encyclopedia of higher education.* Oxford and New York: Pergamon. [updated 1996 for CD-ROM]

Kuh, G. D., R. M. Gonyea, and D. P. Rodriguez. 2002. The scholarly assessment of student development. In T. W. Banta, ed., *Building a scholarship of assessment*. San Francisco: Jossey-Bass.

Kuh, G. D., S. Hu, and N. Vesper. 2000. "They shall be known by what they do": An activities-based typology of college students. *Journal of College Student Development* 41 (2): 228–244.

Kuh, G. D., J. H. Schuh, E. J. Whitt, and associates. 1991. *Involving colleges: Encouraging student learning and personal development through out-of-class experiences*. San Francisco: Jossey-Bass.

Kuh, G. D., J. C. Hayek, R. M. Carini, J. A. Ouimet, R. M. Gonyea, and J. Kennedy. 2001. *NSSE technical and norms report*. Bloomington, IN: Indiana University Center for Postsecondary Research and Planning.

Levinson, D. J. 1978. *The seasons of a man's life*. New York: Knopf.

Light, R. J. 2001. *Making the most of college: Students speak their minds*. Cambridge, MA: Harvard University Press.

Lipset, S. M. 1994. In defense of the research university. In J. R. Cole, E. G. Barber, and S. R. Graubard, eds., *The research university in a time of discontent*. Baltimore: The Johns Hopkins University Press.

McConnell, T. 1934. Changes in scores on the psychological examination of the American Council on Education from freshman to senior year. *Journal of Educational Psychology* 25:66–69.

Merwin, J. C. 1969. Historical review of changing concepts of evaluation. In R. L. Tyler, ed., *Educational evaluation: New roles, new methods*. The 68th Yearbook of the National Society for the Study of Education, Part II. Chicago: University of Chicago Press.

National Center on Public Policy and Higher Education. 2002. *Measuring up 2002: The state-by-state report card for higher education*. San Jose, CA: The National Center on Public Policy and Higher Education. [www.highereducation.org]

National Commission on Excellence in Education. 1983. *A nation at risk*. Washington, DC: U.S. Department of Education.

National Governors' Association. 1986. *Time for results: The governors' report on education*. Washington, DC: National Governors' Association.

National Survey of Student Engagement. 2000. *The NSSE 2000 Report: National benchmarks of effective educational practice*. Bloomington, IN: Indiana University Center for Postsecondary Research and Planning.

———. 2001. *Improving the college experience: National benchmarks for effective educational practice*. Bloomington, IN: Indiana University Center for Postsecondary Research and Planning.

———. 2002. *From promise to progress: How colleges and universities are using student engagement results to improve collegiate quality*. Bloomington, IN: Indiana University Center for Postsecondary Research and Planning.

Newcomb, T. M. 1943. *Personality and social change*. New York: Dryden.

Noll, R. G. 1998. *Challenges to research universities*. Washington, DC: Brookings Institution Press.

Pace, C. R. 1982. *Achievement and the quality of student effort*. Washington, DC: National Commission on Excellence in Education.

Pace, C. R., and Kuh, G. D. 1998. *College student experiences questionnaire*, 4th ed. Bloomington, IN: Indiana University Center for Postsecondary Research and Planning.

Palomba, C. A. 2002. Scholarly assessment of student learning in the major and general education. In T. W. Banta, ed., *Building a scholarship of assessment*. San Francisco: Jossey-Bass.

Palomba, C. A., and T. W. Banta. 2001. *Assessing student competence in accredited disciplines: Pioneering approaches to assessment in higher education*. Sterling, VA: Stylus.

Pascarella, E. T., and P. T. Terenzini. 1991. *How college affects students*. San Francisco: Jossey-Bass.

Perry, W. G. 1970. *Forms of intellectual and ethical development in the college years: A scheme*. New York: Holt, Rinehart and Winston.

Pike, G. R. 2002. Measurement issues in outcomes assessment. In T. W. Banta, ed., *Building a scholarship of assessment*. San Francisco: Jossey-Bass.

Pressy, S. L. 1946. Changes from 1923 to 1943 in the attitudes of public school and university students. *Journal of Psychology* 21:173–88.

Prince, J. S., T. K. Miller, and R. B. Winston, Jr. 1974. *Student developmental task and lifestyle inventory*. Athens, GA: Student Development Associates.

Rosovsky, H. 1990. *The university: An owner's manual*. New York: Norton.

Sanford, N. 1962. The developmental status of the freshman. In N. Sanford, ed., *The American College: A psychological and social interpretation of the higher learning*. New York: Wiley.

Smith, W. R. 2003. Changing institutional culture for first-year students and those who teach them. *About Campus* 8 (1): 3–8.

Study Group on the Conditions of Excellence in American Higher Education. 1984. *Involvement in learning*. Washington, DC: U.S. Department of Education.

Sue, D. W., and D. Sue. 1990. *Counseling the culturally different: Theory and practice*. 2nd ed. New York: John Wiley & Sons.

Tagg, J. 2003. *The learning paradigm college*. Williston, VT: Anker.

Tinto, V. 1993. *Leaving college: Rethinking the causes and cures of student attrition*. 2nd ed. Chicago: University of Chicago Press.

University of Missouri. 2001. *2001 University of Missouri Strategic Plan*. Columbia: University of Missouri.

Upcraft, L., J. N. Gardner, and B. O. Barefoot, eds. In press. *Meeting challenges and building support: Creating a climate for first-year student success*. San Francisco: Jossey-Bass.

Vincow, G. 1997. The student-centered research university. *Innovative Higher Education* 21 (3): 165–78.

Wingspread Group on Higher Education. 1993. *An American imperative: Higher expectations for higher education*. Racine, WI: Johnson Foundation.

Wood, P. 1983. Inquiring systems and problem structure: Implications for cognitive development. *Human Development* 26 (5): 249–65.

Nine

"In My Class? No."

Professors' Accounts of Grade Inflation

Janice McCabe

Brian Powell

One need only mention the phrase "grade inflation," also referred to as "grade compression," to a group of professors to elicit an unusually strong reaction. Grade inflation—often defined as grades being unjustifiably higher than they were in the past—continues to occupy the attention of the academy, the media, and the public at large (Adelman 1995; Anglin and Meng 2000; Kuh and Hu 1999; Rosovsky and Hartley 2002). Media accounts in as diverse an array of outlets as the *New York Times*, the *Chronicle of Higher Education*, the *National Review*, and *USA Today* suggest that rampant grade inflation is an increasing problem for colleges and universities. Often these reports highlight grade inflation in elite schools, as evidenced by the recent media flurry surrounding the number of "Honors" distinctions and A's given at Harvard, Princeton, and Stanford (Archibald 1998; Franks 2002; Mansfield 2001; Matthews 2002; Newcomb 2002; Rutenberg 2002), but others contend that this problem is prevalent in all types of postsecondary institutions (Kuh and Hu 1999).

Concerns, of course, about grade inflation are not new. Similar criticisms have been expressed for more than a century: at Harvard University in 1894, for example, some professors bemoaned the ease by which students could earn an A or B (Report of the Committee on Raising the Standards, Harvard University 1894, cited in Kohn 2002). In fact, our ongoing analysis of media accounts of grade inflation over the last few decades shows dips and rises in the frequency of articles on grade inflation. One peak in media coverage occurred in the mid-1990s, and an examination of the frequency of articles from the past two years shows another rise in the early 2000s.

Much of this recent discussion asserts that grade inflation is the inevitable result of increasing leniency by professors, which in turn is a function of the increasingly prominent role that student evaluations play in faculty reviews and hiring (and retention). Other factors also have been implicated, for example, the transformation of higher education into a "business" and, in turn, students from learners to "consumers" of education and the increasing diversity of college students (Leik 1998; Staples 1998). One of the primary themes suggested in the literature is that professors purposefully or unknowingly are "buying" higher student evaluations with easier grading (Goldman 1985; Greenwald and Gillmore 1997; Wilson 1998; Wilson 1999).

Others, however, disagree. Some, pointing to analyses of data collected by the U.S. Department of Education (1999, 2002), argue that reports of grade inflation, rather than grade inflation itself, are inflated (Kohn 2002; Shoichet 2002). We also have been involved in this debate and, in a previous examination of grades at Indiana University, have contended that most claims of grade inflation, at least at our institution, are overstated: little grade inflation has occurred in the twenty-plus years studied (1973–1997), and what has occurred can be mostly accounted for by demographic and institutional changes in higher education (e.g., changes in the gender, racial and age composition of students and instructors; changing student credentials; the shift in the type of courses students take; the rise in professional schools; and "withdrawal inflation") (Freese, Artis and Powell 1999; Powell and McCabe 2003).

Despite the recent heated rhetoric about grade inflation and grading practices in postsecondary education, we find it perplexing that the voices of professors have been mostly absent from this discussion. To be sure, many of the self-appointed "experts" on this topic are from colleges and universities (ourselves included), but it is unclear whether their views represent those of faculty members who do not participate in the public debate. Instead, the opinions of this latter group, at least regarding their perceptions of and experiences with grades and grade inflation, have been virtually unexplored. We believe that one of the most fundamental lessons to be learned from the Scholarship of Teaching and Learning is the importance of exploring professors' accounts of their day-to-day experiences in the classroom. To that end, in this chapter, we report on the first wave of a series of in-depth interviews with professors at Indiana University and the insights that these interviews offer for our understanding of grading and grade inflation.

Research Design

The first author conducted 25 in-depth interviews with faculty members at Indiana University, a public flagship research university in which concerns over grade inflation have been part of the public discourse (e.g., Jaqua 2002; Powell 1999; Silas 2001). A Carnegie Foundation Research I institution with many graduate and professional programs ranked in the top tier, Indiana University also has been a leader in the promotion of the Scholarship of Teaching and Learning. We recognize that no one setting can represent the views of professors at the diverse range of postsecondary institutions in the U.S., a point we return to later. Our choice of Indiana University as the first institution to include in our ongoing project was based in part on convenience (our home institution), but also to counterbalance what we believe has been an overemphasis on the experiences in Ivy League and other elite private schools.[1]

The sample included faculty members from six units[2] within the university: three departments from the College of Arts and Sciences (one in the natural sciences, one in the social sciences, and one in the humanities),[3] as well as three professional schools on campus (the Business School, the School of Health, Physical Education and Recreation, and the School of Education). We also restricted our sample to full-time, tenure-track faculty members who taught at least one undergraduate class in the last three years.[4] With stratified random sampling, we tried to maximize the diversity of our sample (by gender, rank, substantive interests within units, administrative experiences, and course sizes taught). This sampling strategy allowed us to check for commonalities (and heterogeneities) both within and between these diverse units and groups. Forty-two professors were contacted by e-mail and invited to participate in the interview.[5] The tape-recorded and transcribed interviews[6] with the 25 faculty ranged from 45 minutes to 3½ hours in length. Most interviews were 60 to 90 minutes in length. Interviews were conducted in settings chosen by the respondents; all but one interview were conducted in the professors' offices. At least four faculty members were interviewed in each of the six academic units. Fifteen respondents were male and ten were female.[7] There were five assistant professors, 13 associate professors and seven full professors, ranging in age from 34 to 69 with a mean age of 48.[8]

In reaching our decision to use a qualitative research design incorporating in-depth interviews, we recognized the utility of other approaches, such as standardized questionnaires administered to a larger group of professors.[9] Although these approaches may provide valuable insight into professors' views regarding grade inflation (and we certainly encourage other scholars to capitalize on such approaches), we were convinced (and became even more so during the interviews) that the approach we selected would enable us to go beyond professors' automatic responses to questions and instead to explore their more reflective accounts and, indeed, the meanings underlying professors' beliefs about grading and grade inflation. The tradeoff with choosing interviews over questionnaires was a smaller sample, but much richer and more in-depth data. By uncovering the complexities and contradictions inherent in professors' accounts of grading and grade inflation, we hope to add to our understanding of the discourse surrounding grading inflation and more broadly of the Scholarship of Teaching and Learning.

The interview instrument included a series of questions focusing on teaching, grading, and grade inflation at the undergraduate level.[10] The interview began with a general discussion of the respondent's experiences with and general satisfaction with teaching, and more specifically with grading, and proceeded to include questions about, among others, professors' perceptions of and explanations for grade inflation, views regarding actual and ideal grade distributions, opinions regarding the implications of faculty gender, race, and rank for teaching and grading practices, beliefs regarding the teaching, research, and service expectations in their department or school, and recommendations regarding grading policies. Our analysis was supplemented by an examination of grade distributions for Indiana University and the respondents' grade distributions, which are publicly available.

From these interviews several themes emerged. In this chapter, we highlight the five most salient themes regarding faculty members' (1) perceptions of grade inflation at their university, school and department as well as in their own classes; (2) explanations for the existence of, or perception of, grade inflation; (3) accounts of the relationship between grades and student evaluations; (4) perceptions of ideal grade distributions for themselves and for others (other professors, departments, schools, and/or universities); and (5) views regarding the role of university and departmental policies to address the "problem" of grade inflation.

Perceptions of Grade Inflation

Of the 25 interviewees, six (24 percent) responded that they did not believe that grade inflation was occurring at their home institution, whereas five (20 percent) were equivocal (e.g., "Possibly, but I really don't tune into it a lot so I don't really know." "Don't know, wouldn't be surprised if it is."). The remaining 14—that is, over half (56 percent) of the respondents—were convinced that grade inflation existed at their university. Not only did the majority of respondents perceive grade inflation at their university, they also were more animated and emphatic in their responses (e.g., "No Doubt." and "Absolutely!") than were those who believed that accounts of grade inflation were overstated (e.g., "No, I don't think so." and "No, not really."). As one professor observed:

> I know that it [grade inflation] goes on. I think there is a greater and greater willingness to—and I'm going to come off here like a stodgy old . . . —but I think there is a greater willingness to accept mediocrity. (assistant professor, female, humanities)

We suspect that the 56 percent figure may underestimate faculty perceptions of grade inflation because of a unique situation regarding one of the focal departments (in the social sciences): one professor in that department has written and spoken publicly against the existence of grade inflation at the university and, perhaps as a result of his work, none of the five professors from that department claimed that grade inflation was prevalent at the university. Although this situation speaks to interdepartmental variation in perceptions of grade inflation, it is instructive that if we excluded this department from our analysis, the percentage of interviewees who believed grade inflation occurred at the university would surge to 70 percent.

Although the above discussion suggests that a majority of faculty members believed or at least did not categorically dispute that grade inflation was widespread, there was less consensus whether grade inflation actually occurred in their own schools or departments. Many reacted strongly to these questions as they came closer to home, as in the case of a professor who responded "hell no!" to the question whether grade inflation was occurring in his department. Apparently, the faculty members make a clear distinction between the university as a whole and their school/department per se: that is, in the eyes of several of the interviewees, grade inflation is a problem that occurs at other units/schools in their institution instead of their own.

At least some professors do not make the aforementioned distinction, yet nearly all professors differentiate their own grading practices from those in their department, school, and/or university. Only two respondents admitted that grade inflation occurred in their classes, but even these two thought their grades had changed only marginally and only among the more marginal students. One indicated that over his 30 years of teaching in the humanities, his grades had increased just slightly and that he remained consistent in his allocation of A's, whereas the other professor observed:

> I think there probably is a small degree of grade inflation, so, an example might be the writing assignment we had this semester that I was prepared to give several D's on and my associate instructors [teaching assistants] talked me out of some D's to C–'s, so not big, but I think that, in particular I think there is an unwillingness to fail people and that brings the average up, so there may not be a great difference in what earns an A, but I think that the lower end up to C has been compressed. (associate professor, male, sciences)

More typical, however, were responses such as:

> I can assure you . . . that the average grades in my classes tend to be lower than those of a significant number of my colleagues. (assistant professor, female, humanities)

> I have a tendency to be critical. So, in my classes grade inflation can never be an issue. (associate professor, male, health/physical education/recreation)

> My class? No, because I control it. And I make sure that I keep a challenge to the students. And I will not, really, even though I adjust the grading by adjusting the intensity of the exam to sort of try to come to some happy medium. I don't make anything really easy because I don't want to deal with this. I don't want to, I mean, I have students that I know are getting through without challenge, without learning and it's, at this point, when I get them, I don't want to let that happen again. (associate professor, male, sciences)

In other words, our interviewees saw grade inflation as a problem that did not occur in their neighborhood, and especially not in their own household.

Although most respondents denied the existence of grade inflation in their own classes, they apparently disagreed about what constituted grade inflation. For some, it was equivalent to high grades, whereas for others it was defined as an increase in grades over time. Still, another group contended that high grades or even an increase in grades over time did not represent grade inflation by itself. Rather, the high grades or increase in grades had to be, as in the words of one professor, "unjustifiable." For example, in the following quote, a professor explained a seeming discrepancy: that grade inflation occurred at the university level, that his grades were higher than those typically given at the university, and yet he still believed that his grades were not indicative of grade inflation:

> Not at all. . . . No. If there is anything, my students are motivated to work hard. Because, you know, I work hard for them. (associate professor, male, health/physical education/recreation)

Another professor expressed similar sentiments:

> I require more work and give more A's, but require harder thinking. (professor, male, sciences)

Consistent with their beliefs that they played little role in grade inflation, approximately half of our respondents, when asked to identify their grading as "easy," "moderate" or "tough," chose "tough" or a combination of tough with some modification (e.g., "tough with heart"). In contrast, none chose "easy" by itself, although three respondents, perhaps recognizing the complexity of grading, indicated that they were both "easy" and "tough" in their grading, depending upon which component of grading was being assessed: one professor saw himself as an admixture of tough, moderate, and easy:

> I'm just comparing myself to my own inner standard of knowing how tough I could be versus how tough I am, so somewhere between Santa Claus and the Grinch, I guess. (assistant professor, male, business)

Although the terms "tough," "moderate," and "easy" might be seen as absolute or relative standards, over three-fourths of the interviewed professors claimed that their self-assessment was based on a comparison to their department and/or university, as illustrated by the following assessment:

> Yes, I would probably say I'm moderately tough compared to [department] and probably sciences in general and closer to tough on a broader scale. So I think that sciences tend to be a little harder in their grading than some disciplines. (associate professor, male, sciences)

When they were asked how their grades fared compared to others in their department, three respondents said that they did not know.[11] Of the remaining 22, only three volunteered that they believed their grades were higher than the departmental average, and 11 (i.e., 50 percent) reported that their grades were lower (and in some unsolicited responses "much lower"). Commenting about her grades compared to others in her department, one instructor claimed:

Well, they are tougher. Getting an A in my class is extremely difficult. I would say, on average, my mean grade is lower . . . and I tell
my students, "A C is good. A C is average. You're doing what
you're supposed to be doing. A B is going to be exceptionally well
done. And an A, it's out of this world." And so, very few people are
going to put in the work that it requires to do out-of-this-world
work. And, so I talk with them about it and they understand that
a C, a C+ is probably going to be the modal grade in my class.
(assistant professor, female, education)

Certainly a few of our interviewees may have given lower grades than
have their peers, yet there is no reason to believe that the interviewees as
a group actually were "tougher" than others in their own department—
indeed, our examination of the grade distributions for their undergraduate courses confirms that the average grades from this sample are on par
with those in their department. This, along with the aforementioned
tendency among our interviewees to see grade inflation at the university
level but not in their class, corresponds with what some social psychologists refer to as a self-enhancing tendency (Hedley 1986; Taylor and
Brown 1988). This is the social psychological equivalent of the Lake
Wobegon Effect, "where all the children are above average" (interestingly, the invocation of the Lake Wobegon Effect is ubiquitous in the
public discourse on grade inflation; however, in those discussions, the
students, but not the professors, are the ones who are above average).
Social psychological scholarship is replete with examples of individuals
differentiating their behavior, attitudes, and other personal attributes
from those of others. Individuals see themselves as "better than average" with respect to, among others, academic ability, general happiness,
marital happiness, job performance, earnings potential, compassion,
and even driving ability (Hedley 1986; Smith and Powell 1990; Taylor
and Brown 1988; Westie 1973). Although one might dismiss these tendencies as delusional, scholars have argued that such tendencies are so
prevalent because they promote our mental health and well-being, as
well as our productivity (Taylor and Brown 1988).

Still, this self-enhancing tendency among professors might occur in
part because most professors do not have or do not choose to have complete information regarding the grading practices of other professors in
their department, yet alone on the campus as a whole. But, do professors
engage in the same self-enhancing tendencies under conditions in which
they do have full information?

The interviewees were asked to estimate their average course grades
for a "typical" undergraduate course. They were given a sheet of a paper
with letter grades and asked to "indicate on this sheet what a typical

grade distribution would look like." They could specify course level (e.g., introductory, upper-level) and could choose to use only whole letter grades (A, B, C, D, and F) or the full range of grades (i.e., including pluses and minuses).[12] They appeared to take this task quite seriously, although one declined to provide grade information regarding her undergraduate classes because she believed that she had not taught undergraduate courses often enough in recent years to be able to accurately recall her average grades.[13] Several attempted to look up their grades, but we reassured them that because the university already made grades publicly available, we were more interested in their best recollection of the grades they assign. In many cases, this question was the most time-consuming and, in the view of several of the interviewees, among the most difficult to answer. One respondent (in health/physical education/recreation), for example, initially thought the task at hand was easy: "This won't be that hard. In fact, I developed my grade scale with this somewhat in mind." After several minutes of revising her scale, she responded, "You're right. It *is* hard." This pattern was quite common: many worked and reworked their distribution until it looked "about right."

In contrast to some schools, information on course grade distributions is made publicly available at Indiana University. Consequently, we were able to compare our interviewees' self-reports of grade distributions with their actual distributions. For each respondent (except for the professor who did not feel comfortable estimating her grades in her undergraduate classes), we computed the actual average of his/her undergraduate courses during the past three years (1999 to 2002).[14]

Nearly all of the interviewed professors believed their grades were lower than they actually were: they underestimated the number of A's and overestimated the number of lower grades in their classes. The most extreme example was a professor who estimated her grades for her undergraduate courses as follows:

11 percent A, 24 percent B, 53 percent C, 7 percent D, and 4 percent F[15]

These grades translate into a 2.31 average, or approximately a C+. An inspection of the grades she actually assigned, however, reveals a markedly different pattern:

62 percent A, 33 percent B, 3 percent C, 1 percent D, 1 percent F

These grades convert into a 3.53 average (between a B+ and an A−). That is, the professor underestimated the average by 1.22 points, more than a full letter grade.

The degree to which this respondent miscalculated her grades was greater than that done by the others, but the direction of this miscalculation was mirrored among nearly every respondent (22 out of the 24 professors, or 92 percent). This pattern occurred regardless of whether the instructor believed grade inflation was occurring and regardless of whether the grade point average in their class was comparatively high or low (the grade point averages from our sample ranged from 2.4 to 3.5).

A typical response, in fact, one that almost perfectly fits the average pattern of the interviewed professors, was by a social science professor who estimated his grade distribution as:

13 percent A (3 percent A and 10 percent A−)
60 percent B (20 percent B+, 20 percent B, and 20 percent B−)
25 percent C (10 percent C+, 10 percent C, and 5 percent C−)
3 percent D (2 percent D+ and 1 percent D)
0 percent F[16]

His actual grades[17] were:

34 percent A (1 percent A+, 11 percent A, and 22 percent A−)
50 percent B (17 percent B+, 23 percent B, and 10 percent B−)
14 percent C (6 percent C+, 5 percent C, and 3 percent C−)
1 percent D
1 percent F

As demonstrated by these figures, the professor underestimated the percentage of A's he assigned (13 percent vs. 34 percent) and overestimated the percentage of C's and below (28 percent vs. 16 percent). His estimated distribution translates into a 2.76 grade point average, in contrast to his actual 3.11 grade point average. The difference between these two averages (.35) is extremely close to the average difference (.37) we found among our respondents. To put this figure in perspective, this figure far outdistances the reported rise in grade point average that has occurred at Indiana University during the past 30 years (i.e., what some people have referred to as rampant grade inflation)![18]

We might be tempted to dismiss these differences by arguing that respondents were disingenuous in their interviews, but we do not believe this to be the case. To the contrary, as indicated above, the respondents seemed to take this task especially seriously and spent a great deal of time working and revising their estimates. That several wanted to look at their records to be more accurate, and that they were informed that we could already access their grades, discounts the possibility that they were attempting to deceive the interviewer. Instead, we believe that, echoing the self-enhancing tendencies we discussed earlier, the professors genuinely believed they were giving lower grades than they actually did.

Explanations for Grade Inflation

There seemed to be a general consensus among the interviewees that grade inflation exists (albeit not in their classroom). There was at the same time considerably greater heterogeneity in their specific explanations for its presence. Many of the interviewees initially raised the notion of declining standards as a critical factor.

> There's a . . . kind of grade inflation that's due to people just giving grades away, lowering standards. (professor, male, sciences)

> If there is grade inflation it means that the faculty don't care as much about student learning. . . . So, giving grades based on showing up . . . I would say grades are not party favors. I don't give them out as party favors (*laughs*). (associate professor, female, sciences)

As seen in these quotes, and in virtually every interview in which lowering standards was mentioned, instructors attributed responsibility for the declining standards to others, a pattern that is consistent with the self-enhancing distinctions that we discussed earlier. When contrasting others with themselves, respondents often underscored their reliance on higher standards:

> I've always believed in holding students, I guess, to high standards. I always felt that if you expect ultimately more than perhaps students are capable of, that's finally kind of a compliment to them. To expect anything less, I think, is always insulting. So, I expect a great deal out of my students and I want, I especially want, those high grades, I want an A, to mean something. (assistant professor, female, humanities)

Still, the respondents' use of the "declining standards" explanation to some degree begs the question, as it is unclear whether declining standards are a cause, a covariate, or merely an indicator of grade inflation. When the interviewer probed further, however, respondents identified a wide range of factors that paralleled those identified in scholarly writing and media accounts elsewhere: for example, the lingering effects of the Vietnam War and the student movement, the elimination of certain curricular requirements, the changing student clientele, and the demands of the economy and job market. Despite the range in explanations provided, the most common broad explanation falls under the rubric of increasing student pressure, as described by the following quotes:

. . . And pressure from students too. Because they are much more grade conscious, it seems to me, than they used to be, [and] much more likely to come in and challenge, it's a lot more like they think there's a "Let's Make a Deal" sort of atmosphere. I run into that all the time. Particularly in a large class. (professor, male, social sciences)

One of the things that is different from 20 years ago is that I have more students—a higher proportion of students and more students —complaining about their grades, come to me with what are not bad grades and asking—and in some cases demanding—that their grades be changed . . . And it's not the D's and the F's that are busy with this activity. It is the B's . . . I feel there is more begging and a more confrontive environment. . . . I think that more students are coming to college with higher visions . . . more students who see themselves as A students . . . who expect A's, for whom a B is a bad grade, because of their, perhaps their histories in high school, junior high and so forth. Perhaps because of the good job we, as parents, have done to raise self-assured children and confident children. I don't know. Of course, I don't know why, but it seems that the pressure for higher grades is greater. . . . I think that enters your psyche and you know that the tougher grades that you give, the more you're going to have to face the onslaught of complaints. And maybe it works kind of insidiously and subconsciously. (professor, female, health/physical education/recreation)

Some instructors ascribed student pressure to external, societal factors:

I think there are a lot of pressures in society, which are passed on to students, to achieve high grades. There is just an expectation that it's your right to get a good grade if you work hard. Seems to me to be more of an entitlement mentality, related to effort. So, the argument that I hear from students frequently is "I spent time on this . . . [and] tried very hard therefore I deserve a good grade." (associate professor, female, education)

This description of "generic" student pressure is much more complex than it appears at first glance. Every respondent frequently made comments reflecting their awareness of student pressure, for example, "it's a hell of a lot easier just to give them a B and let them go" (professor, male, humanities). Yet, paradoxically, when we asked them directly whether they felt "implicit or explicit pressure, demands, or expectations regarding grades," approximately half of the interviewees responded no. It is possible that they believed that an affirmative response to this question implied that student pressure played a role in their grading practices, when it was apparent that most felt that they, unlike their peers, were not swayed by student pressure. This issue appears as follows, in the words of one professor:

> So I think that there are people who succumb to that. They don't want to get into battles with students. They don't want to be perceived as the one who ruined their potential shot to get into medical school or something like that. (associate professor, male, sciences)

However, when asked if he personally felt such pressure, he replied:

> No, and I make it very clear to the students that I don't take the grades as that important. I think their learning is more important than how they perform on exams. And that comes across in many ways, in class like when an exam is coming, they all want to know what's on it and I tell them, "everything that we've been talking about in class," I will not tell them specifics . . . the whole point is to learn the material and don't worry about the grade. If you learn the material, it's not an issue. (associate professor, male, sciences)

This professor's position was that to the extent that student pressure occurred, he, unlike other professors, was immune to it. This response, however, is not idiosyncratic, but rather is similar to that expressed in most faculty interviews. Admittedly, a few (very few) respondents at least acknowledged some level of student pressure influencing them, but in a more subtle way.

One, for example, described the demands he experienced:

> I would say it's closer to implicit and it's probably internal and it mostly stems from the emotional effect of delivering a particular grade. For example, if you give somebody a D on a paper, you know it's going to ruin that person's day, maybe their week, and that's a hard thing. We're not here 'cause we don't like students. 'Cause we *like* students. And we *like* to do this. And I'm conscious of what grades I give because if you give a bunch of people a really low grade, you can really lose their attention for the rest of the course . . . so in that sense, it's internal and implicit. I don't think there's any explicit [pressure] other than the occasional student who says, "I didn't deserve this." And that's just, that's a fight that you can't really wage. (associate professor, male, sciences)

To summarize, then, interviewees collectively viewed student pressure as a powerful—if not the key—factor fueling grade inflation, but many still denied that they experienced this pressure themselves. Of those who admitted this experience, even fewer acknowledged that they were influenced by it, although they were convinced that others were. And of those who indicated such influence, most stated that student pressure operated in a more indirect way than what they believed occurred with other professors. These discussions of student pressures seem contradictory, yet are consistent with the aforementioned self-enhancing tendency, which allows them to acknowledge the powerful effect of student pressure without admitting (or feeling) that they themselves are contributing to the "problem."

Grades and Student Evaluations

Inextricably linked to the topic of student pressure is that of end-of-the-semester student evaluations. In the public discourse over grade inflation, many have contended that grade inflation is the inevitable result of an increasingly student-based or client-based postsecondary system in which student evaluations play an ever more prominent role in faculty hiring (and firing) and rewards. Although this contention has been viewed with skepticism by some (one of the co-authors included),[19] we were interested in the extent to which interviewees agreed with the purported link between grades and student evaluations.

The majority of respondents were convinced or found it plausible that grades are strongly correlated with student evaluations. For example, in her discussion of grade inflation and student evaluations, one professor of education commented, "those two come hand in hand." Another female associate professor (humanities) maintained that grade inflation occurs because professors "unjustifiably give high grades to students because they want higher evaluations." Another professor agreed:

> There's certainly that part where, you know, a lot of good grades results in great teaching evaluations, which drives some people to grade inflation, without consciously doing it. I think that they are. And many times, I think they delude themselves into thinking that they're great teachers because the students write good evaluations. But, I mean, there's no question that the quality of your evaluations follows the grades. (associate professor, male, sciences)

Not only did instructors assert that this link between grades and student evaluations exists, many also believed that others exploited it. In relating his experiences at his previous university, one respondent offered the example of a former colleague who ostensibly raised his grades and then saw his evaluations increase:

It occurred to me that, you know, he started talking about how his evaluations were getting a lot better and it's right along with him raising his grades. . . . So we learn, hey, there are certain ways to raise those evaluations. And I don't think, probably, anyone would admit to it, but you see everyone around you doing certain things. You see the average grade going up from semester to semester. It's hard to be the guy that's way lower, because then students will hate you. And it impacts evaluations. (associate professor, male, business)

But while interviewees believed that others might be inflating their grades in order to improve their teaching evaluations, they did not implicate themselves in this. Rather, they claimed that their teaching evaluations, although very good—indeed "better than average,"[20] would be even more positive if they gave higher grades:

I think if my grade point averages were higher, as strong as my course evaluations are, I think they would be even higher. (assistant professor, female, humanities)

In my evaluations I tend to get really positive comments evaluating the teaching style and the content and basically everything except tests and grading and those comments bring the average down. . . . People have suggested that if I just lighten up on students then my evaluations would be a little higher. (associate professor, male, sciences)

At the same time, however, interviewees believed that others, and perhaps themselves as well, were suspicious of high evaluations:

If you go too high and you do well with the teaching ratings, people will *immediately* assume it's the grades you're giving. Now, that may or may not be the case. There is the social pressure—people will view you as being soft and buying the students. (assistant professor, male, business)

Building on this idea, another instructor contended:

It might . . . but I don't think that faculty here, including myself, would want to get their evaluations higher through that means [i.e., higher grades]. 'Cause it would be pretty obvious (*laughs*) for one thing, I mean, people could check that out . . . there are a few checks and balances out there. People could look at the quality of your course and what you require. (professor, female, social sciences)

So, most respondents appeared to believe that there is a link between grades and evaluations, but that their good evaluations were not a function of these grades and, in fact, would be higher if they were more lenient (although we noted earlier their grades actually are not lower than average). They also thought that others tried to improve their evaluations through more generous grading practices, but, at the same time, believed that such efforts resulted in high evaluations being discredited.

Further inspection, however, suggests that respondents were even more equivocal about the alleged link between teaching evaluations and grades. When asked specifically whether the professors in their department who earned the highest evaluations were the ones who also gave the highest grades in their courses, only two responded affirmatively. Instead, they discussed other factors that were much more pivotal in yielding positive student feedback. For example, one, who earlier in the interview agreed that evaluations were affected by grades, commented, "The ones I have reviewed in all the times [I have been] reviewing teaching . . . are excited about learning and that's the biggest reason they get better evaluations. The subject content, far more than the grades they get . . . " influence students' evaluations (professor, female, social sciences).

By the same token, when asked whether instructors in their department who earned the worst evaluations were the ones who assigned the lowest grades, only one respondent pointedly agreed. One respondent, acknowledging the contradictory nature of her responses to the questions regarding the link between grades and evaluations, noted:

> This may sound like a contradiction, but I think students can tell when their instructor doesn't know what they're doing, doesn't know the subject matter, doesn't have the command of the subject matter, and they pick on them for that in the evaluations, even if they got A's. (professor, female, health/physical education/recreation)

This quote also speaks to a recurrent theme expressed by many respondents: that despite their negative portrayal of students and student pressures (as discussed earlier), instructors recognized that:

> Students are more savvy than you think. . . . They don't like someone who will give them a high grade, but they don't learn anything. (professor, male, education)

Thus, despite initially asserting a straightforward link between grades and evaluations, upon further probing by the interviewer, most respondents revealed a good deal of faith in their students and their evaluations' ability to distinguish the best and worst teachers.

Ideal Grade Distributions

Public discussions of grade inflation suggest that to the extent that grade inflation has occurred and is a significant problem, then any solution would result in a lowering of grades on campuses. Correspondingly, we asked interviewees what they believed a grade distribution for their classes *should* look like, regardless of their actual distribution. Of the 24 interviewees who offered a distribution, only two thought their grades should be lower (the other responded, "I don't know what ideal is. I promise you, I don't grade with the idea of producing a particular distribution" [assistant professor, female, humanities]). Surprisingly, almost two-thirds would like to see a *higher* grade distribution.

Yet, when asked to describe the grade distribution that should be given at the university, almost two-thirds of the respondents proposed *lower* grades.[21] For example, one responded that the distribution of grades in his class should be 50 percent A's, 25 percent B's, and 25 percent C's (a grade point average of 3.25) but that the grades at the university level should be 15 percent A's, 15 percent B's, 40 percent C's, 15 percent D's, and 15 percent F's (a grade point average of 2.00). Another thought the ideal distribution for her class should be 100 percent A's (a grade point average of 4.00), but for the university should be 30 percent A's, 20 percent B's, and 50 percent C's (a grade point average of 2.80). Another professor thought that the grades in her class should average in the B range, but at the university level, students were a "C-minus bunch" overall. Ironically, only two professors even acknowledged the seeming discrepancy in these two distributions. These overall responses, though, suggest once again that instructors did not see their courses as contributing to grade inflation (and, if anything, they would like to see higher grades) and that they viewed their own classes as qualitatively different, so different that they warranted a higher grade distribution.

Policies to Address the "Problem" of Grade Inflation

From our interviews, it was apparent that faculty members believed that grade inflation existed, although not in their classrooms, and that something should be done to address the problem. That said, respondents were unclear what constituted something. Nevertheless, nearly all noted a conspicuous silence on this topic that has promoted a culture in which grade inflation, or a perception of grade inflation, could flourish:

> I don't really know that much about how other people do their grading within the school. It's not something that I talk with people about too much. (assistant professor, male, business)

> Nobody—faculty usually don't talk about how they grade at all even in the department, never mind cross-department. (professor, male, social sciences)

Among the few respondents who commented that they had any conversations about grading with others, these discussions were with individual faculty members who were friends or shared common interests. In other words, discussions of grades were not part of any common culture:[22]

> I don't sit and talk about it with other tenure-track people or others . . . so I don't think we've developed a kind of culture. Not that I know of. (professor, female, social sciences)

More broadly, however, respondents volunteered that little discussion on pedagogy actually occurred, even at a university that is increasingly recognized for its emphasis on teaching. The absence of discussion did not appear to be a function of the faculty's (or the university administration's) disinterest in teaching. To the contrary, throughout the interviews, the respondents expressed a great deal of enthusiasm about and satisfaction from teaching.[23] They instead located the problem in the individualistic nature of teaching. That is, despite the frequent portrayal of research as solitary and private, the ostensibly more social component of teaching seems equally if not more individualistic, as indicated by the following responses:

> The problem with teaching at the university . . . teaching becomes a very private enterprise. You rule the roost in your class, very few people know what you actually do. Nobody looks over your shoulder when you're grading. Nobody says "Can I see a stack of your papers . . . " That just never happens. It's a very private thing. And I think there are some real disadvantages of that. (assistant professor, female, humanities)

> For better or worse, teaching at the faculty level is an individualistic thing. (professor, female, social sciences)

Given how little dialogue on grading—and teaching—reportedly occurred, it is not surprising that respondents also felt that more conversations on this topic and more information regarding grading and grade distributions would be useful. With one exception, respondents revealed that they had received either no information or very limited information about grading and grade inflation at their university.[24] Consequently, several emphasized the need for basic information about teaching, grading, and assessment:

There is a bunch of basic information on grading that could save people a lot of pain and effort. (professor, male, sciences)

Data about how grades actually are assigned, and then advice about ways to assess students might be useful. Sometimes people simply are replicating the grading schemes that they knew when they were students. If they had more information . . . (associate professor, female, education)

According to these interviewees, the collection and dissemination of information on how their grades compare to others (for the same course, department, school, and/or university, as well as other universities) would be an important step in helping instructors assess the possibility of grade inflation:[25]

I think some department statistics of grade distributions would be neat to see. Then professors could say, "Where do I stand?" (assistant professor, male, social sciences)

I think it would be nice to know what other colleges, what other universities give [and] what we have historically given, just to provide some data on whether grade inflation is an issue. (assistant professor, male, business)

Ironically, much of the information that professors said that they desired was available already at the university. A few recognized this fact:

I think this is one of the friendliest new faculty places with lots of support. . . . You have to ask for the help, I mean, it's not forced on you—rightfully so. (professor, female, health/physical education/recreation)

In addition, information about grade distributions for each professor, each course, each department, and each college were readily available, as discussed earlier in this chapter. So, it seemed that the problem was not the unavailability of such material, but the perception of unavailability. Regardless of the cause, however, professors' lack of knowledge about grades raises an interesting puzzle: To the extent they claimed that they knew little about the grading distributions at the university, why did so many of these interviewees believe that grade inflation was so rampant at the university?

Professors were not shy in articulating grade inflation as a serious concern, yet they were hesitant in endorsing specific policies for staving off grade inflation. Most did not advocate much beyond conversations. In the words of one, "I think talking about it is all they should do" (associate professor, male, sciences). We specifically asked for reactions to proposals to limit the number of particular grades (e.g., 20 percent A's), to provide enforced rules for grading, and to establish formal recommendations regarding grades. Only one respondent supported any plan to set limits on specific grades.[26] All others opposed such a plan, some vehemently so (e.g., "Absolutely, not!" and "No, that's terrible!"). Respondents repeatedly stressed the primacy of academic freedom ("No, I think it's an academic freedom issue" [professor, female, health/physical education/recreation]), a principle so fundamental that it trumped any concern about grades, "no matter how much I squawk about the high grades here" (professor, male, education).

Approximately two-thirds of the respondents did not even support the establishment of recommendations regarding grading practices, once again citing the importance of maintaining academic freedom. Others questioned whether any set of agreed-upon guidelines could be established given the substantial variations in classroom structure, course content, and pedagogical styles, among other factors, at the university:

> No . . . I don't think there's a common enough experience teaching to do that sort of thing. (associate professor, male, sciences)

Even among the respondents who supported some type of guidelines, there were reservations over how overarching these guidelines should be:

> If there were anything like that it would have to be level specific. I wouldn't support any kind of guidelines that were university wide and across departments because, for example, in my class, if I was told if I had 10 students I could only have 1 A, and it's an elective, that's totally wrong. If it's a group of incoming freshmen who represent the average population of the state, I could see how you would say, you really have to have your average a C and a normal distribution . . . Maybe I'd be really reluctant to do even that though. I think faculty just need to be educated about the danger of grade inflation and what's their purpose here. (associate professor, male, sciences)

It appeared that despite concerns over grades and grade inflation, most respondents felt that any systematic and formal check on grades was either unfeasible or indefensible. Rather, it appeared that the interview-ees preferred a less formal, and, in turn less consequential, approach:

> No, not really, I think there should be informal pressure brought to bear on people who are way out of line. (professor, male, social sciences)

Despite the instructors' reluctance to support any formal mechanism to check for abuses or inconsistencies in grading, some recognized their own complicity in what they perceived to be a serious problem:

> I think grade inflation is sort of like discrimination. You know it exists, but you can't really point your finger at it. It's partly be-cause we're cowards, and I know I'm included in it. I won't go to my colleagues and say, "Hey, I noticed that you gave a student an A and I don't think it's an A," because of that trust and that, I guess, freedom that we give each other that we're not going to in-terfere with their assessment of performance. (assistant professor, female, education)

Conclusion

The broad themes presented in this chapter suggest that many if not most of the interviewed faculty members believe that grade inflation is prevalent at the university level, but believe that it is less of a problem in their department than elsewhere and even less so for themselves. In fact, respondents' reports of their own grades are considerably lower than their actual grades, a discrepancy that is larger than the docu-mented rise in grade point average (referred to by some as rampant grade inflation) at this institution over the last 30 years. Respondents typically believe that student pressure occurs and contributes to grade inflation, but do not believe they are personally influenced by it. They believe that there is a link between grades and student evaluations, but do not believe that their evaluations are higher than they should be, and do not believe that those with the best evaluations give the highest grades or that those with the worst evaluations give the lowest. Instruc-tors believe grade inflation should be curtailed and there should be a lower grade distribution at the university as whole, but prefer a higher grade distribution for their classes. Finally, they believe that something should be done to address the "problem" of grade inflation, but do not believe that policies to control grades are the answer.

These seeming contradictions demonstrate perhaps the application of the self-enhancing tendencies noted by social psychologists and discussed earlier in this chapter. It is important to recognize that these patterns are not apparently related to self-delusion or lack of self-reflection on the part of our sample of professors. To the contrary, we were impressed by our interviewees' thoughtful, detailed, and complex responses. The seeming contradictions we noted may illustrate a general tendency identified in the social psychological literature: the idea that individuals believe they are better than average and that their situation is distinct from others. The self-enhancing tendency helps explain why professors in a research university would believe grade inflation exists, but that their grades do not contribute to it and why perhaps people overestimate the degree to which low grades were typical in universities several decades ago.

The results of our interviews are instructive regardless of whether one views grade inflation as a "scandal" (Mansfield 2001) or a "dangerous myth" (Kohn 2002). These interviews may offer insight into why faculty members and institutions may be resistant to proposals to control grade inflation. Indeed, the interviews suggest that because instructors see grade inflation as "someone else's fault," few are willing to take responsibility for the alleged problem (of course, this is true even among those who in their written work have decried grade inflation, as these critics, just like our interviewees, routinely identify themselves as "tough" graders). In addition, these interviews show how professors can readily believe that grade inflation is a problem despite their admission that they have limited, if any, information on grade distributions of their peers, their firm belief that they are not inflating grades in their own classes, and the reality that their grades do not deviate considerably from others in the university. We attribute professors' receptiveness to claims of grade inflation to two factors: the recurrent discussions of the grade inflation "crisis" in the media and professors' imperfect knowledge, for example, reliance on student accounts of other professors' grades. As one noted:

> The only lens I have to see this is through the students. (assistant professor, male, social sciences)

These factors speak to a climate in which teaching is viewed as solitary and individualistic. They also suggest that departmental and university-wide conversations about grades and grade inflation, as well as improved dissemination of information on this topic and greater attention to these issues in the training of graduate students, may cultivate a culture that not only helps us more informatively and reflectively assess whether grade inflation is real or artificially constructed but also makes teaching less isolating.

Because our interviewees were professors at a research university, it is possible that their peers from other academic settings (e.g., liberal arts colleges) may not share the views presented in this chapter. To the extent that the research community does not reward teaching, faculty members at more teaching-oriented schools may view assessment as a more critical component of their job and, in turn, may more frequently and comprehensively communicate with each other regarding grading practices and philosophies. Of course, because professors at most postsecondary institutions were trained at research universities, their views may have been shaped to a large degree by their experiences as graduate students. Our ongoing project is in its early stages and we look forward to interviewing a broader range of instructors on these topics to assess whether the patterns identified here can be generalized to other educational institutions.

The themes emerging from the interviews attest to the dangers of relying on media accounts or "spokespeople" for the academy to represent faculty opinions about topics such as grade inflation. Equally important, these results underscore the need for academicians to more fully engage in the Scholarship of Teaching and Learning. Although we believe that the complex patterns revealed here would have been difficult to capture without the use of in-depth interviewing, we believe that a wide range of data collection efforts as part of initiatives in the Scholarship of Teaching and Learning will lead us to improved understanding about assessment in general, and, more specifically, about grade inflation, as well as other issues that affect the professional lives of faculty and students.

Notes

This research was supported in part by a Scholarship of Teaching and Learning Grant from the Office of the Vice Chancellor for Academic Affairs and Dean of the Faculties. We thank Jo Dixon, R. D. Fulk, Bernice Pescosolido, David Dean Seckman and Alicia Suarez for their helpful comments, and the professors we interviewed for their willingness to share their thoughtful views regarding grade inflation.

1. Indeed, Ivy League schools have been the epicenter for most media accounts of grade inflation (e.g., Hartocollis 2002; Healy 2001, 2002; "Ivy League Grade Inflation" 2002; Margolick 1994; Toby 1994). Accordingly, we also have conducted several informal interviews with professors from two Ivy League schools and another elite private institution. Although professors from those schools were even more adamant about the existence of

grade inflation than were professors from Indiana University (as one professor indicated, "you have a better chance of winning the lottery than getting a C"), the themes we discuss in this chapter also emerged in those discussions.

2. These units were chosen in part to reflect that variation in grading at the institution, with the professional schools having a slightly or considerably higher grade distribution than the College of Arts and Sciences (Indiana University Office of the Registrar 2002). To account for variation within the College of Arts and Sciences (in which the grades in the humanities tended to be higher than those in the social sciences that in turn generally were higher than those in the sciences), we chose departments with grade distributions in line with their general area (i.e., humanities, social sciences, or sciences).

3. Given the relatively small size of some of the departments in the College of Arts and Sciences and our desire to protect the confidentiality of our interviewees, we do not identify the departments in the College of Arts and Sciences. This is less of a concern with the three professional schools, which are larger.

4. Not interviewed in this study were clinical, adjunct, and graduate student instructors. Recognizing their growing presence and the posited relationship between faculty status and grading practices (e.g., Fedler, Counts and Stoner 1989; Moore and Trahan 1998; Sonner 2000; Wendell 2001), we intend to interview members of these groups in the future. In our interviews, we also asked professors their opinions about the implications of the increase in clinical, adjunct, and graduate student instructors on university grades; results will be discussed in subsequent work.

5. Ten professors declined to be interviewed, four agreed to be interviewed at a later date (either because they were on sabbatical or had a heavy teaching load), and three did not respond to our e-mail request. This response rate is in line with other studies of professionals. We also found no evidence that the nonrespondents differed from our respondents in gender, rank, or grade point average.

6. Quotations presented here exclude identifying information (such as specific faculty, department, and course names), and verbal utterances, such as "uh-huh," "you know," and "um," typically are omitted for clarity.

7. At Indiana University Bloomington, 27.9 percent of tenured and tenure-track faculty were women (Bloomington Office for Women's Affairs 2002). We purposely oversampled women, who constituted 40 percent of our sample.

8. Twenty of the 25 professors self-identified as white or Caucasian. Of the remaining five professors, three were African American, one was Hispanic and one was Asian American. Given the fairly small number of professors of color at Indiana University and our commitment to ensuring confidentiality, professors are not identified by race in this chapter.

9. As part of our ongoing project, we also have conducted archival analysis and analyzed grades and grade trends from Indiana University.

10. The interview also included a more limited set of questions regarding the grades and grade inflation at the graduate student level.

11. Ironically, of these three, two earlier had responded that they compared themselves to other professors in their department when assessing whether they were "tough," "moderate," or "easy."

12. In some cases, respondents chose to estimate grades for more than one level of classes they taught. In this case, all levels they estimated were compared to their actual grades. Regardless of level of the course (e.g., introductory or upper-level undergraduate courses), the same general pattern emerged (discussion follows).

13. She, however, wrote her average grades for a graduate-level course instead.

14. Excluded from these analyses were labs, internships, and individual study, as well as courses with fewer than five students enrolled, as the grades distribution reports are not made available for classes of this size.

15. She chose not to differentiate within a letter grade (e.g., B+).

16. When estimating these figures, the professor realized and even wrote that they added to 101.

17. Like most professors at this university, he taught a mix of introductory and upper-level undergraduate courses. The average grades differed very little between the introductory and upper-level courses; figures presented here are for all sections combined.

18. From the *2002–2003 Fall Enrollment Report* from the Indiana University Office of the Registrar, the average undergraduate grades in 2001–2002 was 3.01, .16 points higher than the comparable grades in 1973–74 (2.86). The lowest reported grades occurred in 1983–84 (2.72), .29 lower than in 2001–2002.

19. In an analysis of the authors' department of sociology, Freese, Artis and Powell (1999) found that instructors who won departmental, college, or university awards assigned slightly *lower* grades than did their peers who had not won such awards, that the correlation between average grades and student evaluations for graduate student instructors was slightly *negative*, and that student-predicted course grades were less strongly linked to their overall evaluation of their instructor than were students' assessment of instructors' clarity, enthusiasm, fairness, and impartiality.

20. Consistent with the self-enhancing tendencies identified earlier, approximately three-fourths of the interviewed professors reported that their teaching evaluations were higher than average, or as one professor described himself, "I'm the man." With the exceptions of a professor who admitted that his evaluations were lower than others in his department and another who described her evaluations as "just average," the others indicated that although they were average compared to one group (e.g., their department), they were above average compared to another (e.g., their school).

21. Three professors did not believe that there was an ideal distribution at the university level.

22. In the one exception, a professor indicated that she had frequent formal and informal conversations about grading and assessment, although she too believed that even more discussion was necessary.

23. When asked to rate their teaching experiences on a scale from 1 (extremely unhappy or dissatisfied) to 5 (extremely happy or satisfied), nearly all (22 out of 25) responded with ratings of 4 or 5. Moreover, every interviewee indicated that s/he thought teaching was important or very important in his/her life.

24. Of those who indicated that they received any information, two were from departments in which target grade ranges for specific courses or sets of courses were provided, one professor mentioned advice regarding grades that he received from a colleague, one referred to a handbook provided by her school, and two professors mentioned basic information on assessment issues that they had received either in graduate school or at the university.

25. In one exception, however, a professor commented that because grading strategies are so heterogeneous, he believed providing information on other professors' grading would not be helpful and, in fact, would be "confusing" to new professors.

26. In this one case, he endorsed the establishment and enforcement of grade ranges, similar to those strongly recommended in his department, within which professors' course grades should fall (e.g., having a class average between 2.7 and 3.0).

References

Adelman, C. 1995. A's aren't that easy. *New York Times*, May 17: A19.

Anglin, P. M., and R. Meng. 2000. Evidence on grades and grade inflation at Ontario's universities. *Canadian Public Policy* 26 (3): 361–68.

Archibald, R. C. 1998. Just because the grades are up, are Princeton students smarter? *New York Times*, Feb. 18: A1.

Bloomington Office for Women's Affairs. 2002. *Report on the status of women.* September 2002.
(http://www.indiana.edu/~owa/Status %20 Report %20on%20Women.pdf).

Edwards, C. H. 2000. Grade inflation: The effects on educational quality and personal well being. *Education* 120 (3): 538–46.

Fedler, F., T. Counts, and K. R. Stoner. 1989. Adjunct profs grade higher than faculty at three schools. *Journalism Educator* 44 (2): 32–37.

Franks, T. 2002. Grades row at Harvard. *BBC News*, Jan. 14. (http://news.bbc. co.uk/1/hi/world/americas/1760531.stm).

Freese, J., J. E. Artis, and B. Powell. 1999. Now I know my ABC's: Demythologizing grade inflation. In B. A. Pescosolido and R. Aminzade, eds., *The social worlds of higher education: Handbook for teaching in a new century*, pp. 185–94. Thousand Oaks, CA: Pine Forge Press.

Goldman, L. 1985. The betrayal of the gatekeepers: Grade inflation. *Journal of General Education* 37 (2): 97–121.

Greenwald, A. G., and G. M. Gillmore. 1997. Grading leniency is a removable contaminant of student ratings. *American Psychologist* 52 (11): 1209–17.

Hartocollis, A. 2002. Harvard faculty votes to put the excellence back in A. *New York Times,* May 22. (http://www.nytimes.com/2002/05/22/education/ 22HARV.html).

Healy, P. 2001. Harvard's quiet secret: Rampant grade inflation. *The Boston Globe,* Oct. 7. (http://www.boston.com/globe/metro/packages/harvard_honors).

———. 2002. Harvard looks to raise bar for graduating with honors. *The Boston Globe,* Jan. 31. (http://www.boston.com/globe/metro/packages/harvard_ honors/follow_up_3.htm).

Hedley, R. A. 1986. Everybody but me: Self-other referents in social research. *Sociological Quarterly* 56 (2): 245–58.

Indiana University Office of the Registrar. 2002. *2002–03 fall enrollment report: A summary of first semester with a historical overview.* Bloomington, IN: Indiana University.

Ivy League Grade Inflation. 2002. *USA Today,* Feb. 7. (http://www.usatoday. com/news/comment/2002/02/08/edtwof2.htm).

Jaqua, N. 2002. 'Making' the grade. *Indiana Daily Student,* May 20: 1. (http:// www.idsnews.com/story.php?id=10217).

Kohn, A. 2002. The dangerous myth of grade inflation. *The Chronicle Review,* Nov. 8: B7–B9.

Kuh, G. D., and S. Hu. 1999. Unraveling the complexity of the increase in college grades from the mid-1980s to the mid-1990s. *Educational Evaluation and Policy Analysis* 21 (3): 297–320.

Leik, R. K. 1998. There's far more than tenure on the butcher block: A larger context for the recent crisis at the University of Minnesota. *Sociological Perspectives* 41 (4): 747–55.

Mansfield, H. C. 2001. Grade inflation: It's time to face the facts. *The Chronicle of Higher Education,* April 6: B24.

Margolick, D. 1994. Stanford U. decides to make courses harder to drop but easier to fail. *The New York Times,* June 4: 7.

Matthews, S. 2002. Leave no child unsuccessful? *Education Week,* Jan. 9. (http:// www.edweek.org/ew/newstory.cfm?slug=16matthews.h21&keywords= grade%20inflation).

Moore, M., and R. Trahan. 1998. Tenure status and grading practices. *Sociological Perspectives* 41 (4): 775–81.

Newcomb, A. 2002. Everyone's a star. *The Christian Science Monitor,* Feb. 5. (http://www.csmonitor.com/2002/0205/p11s01-legn.html).

Powell, B. 1999. Now we know our ABC's: Demythologizing grade inflation. Presented at *Indiana University Scholarship of Teaching and Learning Lecture Series,* November 19.

Powell, B., and J. McCabe. 2003. Grade inflation revisited. Presented at *Indiana University Scholarship of Teaching and Learning Lecture Series,* March 7.

Rosovsky, H., and M. Hartley. 2002. *Evaluation and the academy: Are we doing the right thing? Grade inflation and letters of recommendation.* Cambridge, MA: American Academy of Arts & Sciences.

Rutenberg, D. 2002. Grade inflation at Ivies has shown upward trend. *The Daily Pennsylvanian,* Feb. 8. (http://www.dailypennsylvanian.com/vnews/display.v/ART/2002/02/08/3c63878a32533).

Shoichet, C. E. 2002. Reports of grade inflation may be inflated, study finds. *Chronicle of Higher Education,* July 12: A37.

Silas, A. 2001. Grade inflation on the rise: Increasing GPAs may point to lowered expectations. Indiana Daily Student, May 10. (http://www.idsnews.com/story.php?id=4768).

Smith, H. L., and B. Powell. 1990. Great expectations: Variations in income expectations among college seniors. *Sociology of Education* 63 (3): 194–207.

Sonner, B. S. 2000. A is for 'adjunct': Examining grade inflation in higher education. *Journal of Education for Business* 76 (1): 5–9.

Staples, B. 1998. Why colleges shower their students with A's. *New York Times,* March 8: 4, 16.

Taylor, S. E., and J. D. Brown. 1988. Illusion and well-being: A social psychological perspective on mental health. *Psychological Bulletin* 103 (2): 193–210.

Toby, J. 1994. In war against grade inflation, Dartmouth scores a hit. *The Wall Street Journal,* Sept. 8: A18.

U.S. Department of Education. 1999. *The new college course map and transcript files: Changes in course-taking and achievement, 1972–1993,* 2nd ed. Washington, DC: U.S. Department of Education.

U.S. Department of Education, National Center for Education Statistics. 2002. *Profile of undergraduates in U.S. postsecondary education institutions: 1999–2000.* (http://nces.ed.gov/pubsearch/pubsinfo.asp?pubid=2002168).

Wendell, B. 2001. Can untenured faculty members stop grade inflation? *The Chronicle of Higher Education: Daily News,* Dec. 13. (http://www.chronicle.com/jobs/2001/12/2001121301c.htm).

Westie, F. R. 1973. Academic expectations for professional immortality: A study of legitimation. *American Sociologist* 8 (1): 19–32.

Wilson, B. 1999. The phenomenon of grade inflation in higher education. *National Forum* 79 (4): 38–41.

Wilson, R. 1998. New research casts doubt on value of student evaluations of professors. *The Chronicle of Higher Education,* Jan. 16: 12–14.

Ten

Educational Assessment and Underlying Models of Cognition

Lei Bao

Edward F. Redish

Many existing quantitative assessment tools focus on a binary question: Have the students applied the knowledge correctly or have they not? The results of such a measurement are the percentage of students who get the correct answer. The fact that each student may simultaneously possess alternate frameworks or misconceptions is not reflected in the measurement. In addition, assessment tools seldom address the context issue or whether students may apply the correct knowledge in some situations and alternative types of knowledge in others.

Many assessment tools assume that students possess internal models or have general ability levels. Under this assumption, those doing assessment look for consistency between student responses on correlated items in a test in order to infer the existence and quality of those internal models or abilities. Inconsistent data may be rejected as noise. However, research in education, cognitive science, and neuroscience shows that the cognitive response is a dynamic context-dependent process. Results from a measurement instrument depend on the interactions between students' internal characteristics and the specific settings of the instrument. Inconsistent student behavior on correlated items not only represents a common phenomenon but provides important information about the state of the student's thinking. From this perspective, the inconsistency of student behavior becomes part of the signal rather than noise.

In this chapter, we introduce a new quantitative method based on analogies with methods of quantum physics that works with research-based multiple-choice questions to give insight into students' conceptual states. Both the consistent and inconsistent features of student behaviors are interactively represented under a coherent theoretical basis, which can be used directly to provide direction for instructional interventions.

Student Behavior in Learning (Physics)
and the Goals for Assessment

The recent decades of education research have illuminated a rich collection of student difficulties in learning science and mathematics and many cognitive theories have been developed to interpret them. These yield implications for assessment in four general areas:

- Learning is affected by students' previous knowledge.
- Students can create new alternative ideas which can be different from both their previous knowledge and the community-accepted scientific ones.
- Students' knowledge structures can be different from that of experts in many ways.
- There are commonly observed inconsistencies in students' use of their knowledge in equivalent contexts.

Effects on Learning from Students' Previous Knowledge

It is well established that students come to new learning experiences in possession of a system of knowledge developed from personal experience and previous learning. Such knowledge, often referred to as preconceptions, misconceptions, or alternative conceptions by physics educators, can have significant effects on students' learning. Many studies in physics education have shown that certain preconceptions can pose strong barriers to understanding physics knowledge correctly (Viennot 1979; Clement 1982; McDermott 1984; Halloun and Hestenes 1985). Researchers in other areas of science education have also found similar results where students' misconceptions were found to be "entrenched" and difficult to change by conventional instruction (Posner et al. 1982; Scott, Asoko and Driver 1991; Bransford, Brown, and Cocking 1999). There is a large body of literature in physics education research documenting common types of students' prior knowledge and ways to develop instructional strategies to deal with them (McDermott and Redish 1999).

Students' Creation of Alternative Ideas

During instruction, it is widely observed that students can create new alternative conceptual understandings that are different from both their previous knowledge and the scientific knowledge introduced in the instruction. One form of such creation is the development of synthesized (or hybrid) models of a concept during learning. For example, Vosniadou (1994) investigated children's development of the concept of earth and identified a unique situation: during learning children can develop synthesized mental models to reconcile the conflicts between their initial naive models and the evidences that support the scientific model. Students' hybrid mental models incorporate some pieces of the correct understandings but keep large parts of their existing knowledge systems unchanged. Because it has some part of the correct understandings, a hybrid model can provide explanations consistent with some parts of correct knowledge. This creates a temporary solution for solving the conflicts created by using one's prior knowledge and thus can be used as a quick (and easy) fix when cognitive conflicts are encountered in learning.

Vosniadou and Brewer (1992) reported that children often have an initial model of a "rectangular earth" which reflects the common sense of land being flat. Through learning, a child started to recognize that the earth has to be a sphere. To reconcile the conflict between a spherical earth and the experience of land being flat, children can develop a hybrid model of a "hollow sphere" where people can stand inside the sphere on a flat plane.[1]

The creation of knowledge can also take place at an implicit and abstract level where the prior knowledge involved is not school based but comes directly from implicit interpretations of experience. DiSessa, investigating people's sense of physical mechanism, that is, their understanding of why things work the way they do, found that many students, even after instruction in physics, often come up with simple statements that describe the way they think things function in the real world. They often consider these statements to be "irreducible"—as the obvious or ultimate answer; that is, they can't give a "why" beyond it. "That's just the way things work," is a typical response. DiSessa refers to such statements as *phenomenological primitives* or *p-prims* (diSessa 1993). Minstrell observed that students' responses to questions about physical situations can frequently be classified in terms of reasonably simple and explicit statements about the physical world or the combination of such statements. Minstrell refers to such statements as *facets* (Minstrell 1991).

Sometimes diSessa's p-prims are general in character and sometimes they refer to specific physical situations and are similar to Minstrell's facets. We restrict the term "primitive" to describe the abstract reasoning primitive behind diSessa's p-prims. We use the term "facet" to refer to the mapping of a reasoning primitive into a physical situation. An example of where we would separate differently from diSessa is in the p-prim "continuous push"—a constant effort is needed to maintain motion. We would refer to this as a facet, which is a mapping of the reasoning primitive: a continued cause is needed to maintain a continued effect.

During instruction, the mapping of a reasoning primitive from students' prior knowledge system with newly encountered contexts can create new types of facet-like knowledge. Students are typically explicit about the facet they use but are much less, if at all, aware of the primitive they are using to create the new facet. A primitive such as "more cause leads to more effect" represents a general reasoning pattern of proportionality. A facet based on this primitive in the context of mechanics would be "more mass produces more force." (This is often considered as one of the more entrenched naive preconceptions in mechanics.) Later, when students start to learn electricity, the same p-prim can be mapped to create new knowledge such as "more resistance indicates more difficulty to conduct the current and thus causes less current," which is correct in many situations.

The creation of hybrid models is an explicit creation process in which students are explicitly aware of reassembling pieces of prior and new knowledge. A second type of creation is more implicit. Abstract reasoning primitives are remapped to new contexts to form new facets. In such cases, students may be able to identify the particular abstract reasoning pattern they have used—rather than, "it's just the way it works."

Students' Knowledge Structures

In studies of students' approaches to solving problems, differences were found between experts and novices that provide useful information about how knowledge may be structured by the two populations. Experts not only have more physics knowledge than novices, but also their knowledge is better organized. Experts categorize problems based on the principles used in their solutions whereas novices tend to categorize problems using surface features of the problem situations (Chi, Feltovich and Glaser 1981). Experts store information in chunks whereas novices have the information stored individually (Larkin 1979). Experts solve problems first by determining the underlying principles useful to a solution whereas novices jump directly to trying to relate the unknowns to memorized mathematical equations (Chi, Feltovich and Glaser 1981; Larkin 1979, 1983).

It is also observed that novice students' knowledge tends to be linked to a particular context. For example, mathematics students who have been trained in traditional instruction do very poorly on nonroutine problems (Eisenberg and Dreyfus 1985). A large part of the difficulties for students facing nonroutine problems in mathematics is their inability to recognize the deep-level mathematical structure of the problems, confusing contextual information with superficial features (Gliner 1989, 1991). This same confusion of mathematical and surface structure was found to have a large effect on attempts to transfer problem-solving procedures between different disciplines (Bassok 1990; Bassok and Holyoak 1989): When problems were given in similar contexts, students were able to transfer their knowledge between different disciplines. On the other hand, when the surface details were different, students were unable to recognize that the new problems were similar to ones they had seen before. Clearly a deeper conceptual understanding is necessary for students to go beyond the surface details to succeed in transferring knowledge.

Inconsistency of Students Using Their Knowledge in Equivalent Contexts

In research on student learning of science and mathematics, it is well documented that students can use inconsistent reasoning (Clough and Driver 1986; Palmer 1997; Bao and Redish 2001). When measuring students' knowledge, we often give several questions that are related to a single concept topic that an expert would solve using a single model. We call a set of such questions *expert-equivalent*. However, when presented with such a set of questions, a student who does not see the coherent deep structure may call on different (and often contradictory) types of understandings.

Many studies have been conducted to model this situation. Maloney and Siegler (1993) proposed a framework of *conceptual competition*. They suggested that a student might maintain several different understandings of a concept that would coexist and compete with, rather than replace, the student's previous understandings. The understanding that wins the competition on a given problem will depend on an interaction between the understandings and the features of the problem.

In a similar study, Thornton (1994) used the term *student views* to represent the different understandings of a physics concept. He developed a phenomenological framework to explore the dynamic process by which these views are transformed in learning. He found students to have different views coexisting at the same time during instruction and referred to such mixing as a *transitional state*. His research suggests that in the learning process many students move from a consistent but incorrect view, through a transitional state, towards a consistent and correct view.

These results imply that students may simultaneously hold more than one type of understanding in their minds. Which type they choose to apply is likely to depend on the presented context and their experiences with similar contexts. At the time of instruction, we cannot expect students to change suddenly to a new, more generalized model. Students will apply the newly learned model to some situations while retaining their previous model for others. Because the mixed learning state will occur as the students make the transition, detecting it can be an important indicator for students' progress.

Expectations on Assessment

To help students learn more effectively, we need not only to understand the learning process but to equip the instructors with effective assessment instruments so that they can obtain timely feedback during the course of instruction. Because of the complexity of possible student behaviors during learning, assessment instruments need to:

- measure the existence and prevalence of students' prior and newly created knowledge,
- measure and distinguish structural information about students' knowledge such as deep-level understanding vs. superficial understanding, and
- properly respond to the "inconsistency" of students using their knowledge in equivalent contexts.

To do this, we need a model of the cognitive process so that we can identify the needed information and understand how to extract it. Based on this model we then identify what variables we can control and how to obtain robust measurement results.

Understanding Student Behaviors in Terms of Context Dependence

To achieve the goals we set for assessment, we have to understand the effects of contexts in learning and in measurement. In the literature, there are multiple perspectives of what can be defined (or included) as a context. Contexts include the specific properties and content of the material presented to the student, the elements of the physical learning environment, and the cognitive states of both student and teacher when the material is presented.

Students' and instructors' internal mental states may be activated or formed as a result of interactions with the content and learning environment contexts. These internal states may not be easily changed over a short period of time (e.g., in a class session period). Students will often maintain, either explicitly or implicitly, their views and attitudes throughout a class session unless they are significantly manipulated (e.g., the class explicitly emphasizes a particular view or attitude that is not normally activated by the students). Either way, the time required for general views to change are often longer than that for students to change understandings of one piece of content knowledge. Therefore, during the learning of a particular piece of content knowledge, one can consider the general views and attitudes as a slow-changing background of the learning process, which can also have significant effect on the learning.

On the other hand, when students have mixed, possibly contradictory elements of knowledge that may arise from partial or incomplete learning, local cues can strongly affect which elements are activated. This adds a short-term, rapidly changing fluctuation of the student response.

The Effects of Contexts on Learning

In this section, we consider the role of context dependence on four categories of student behaviors.

Inconsistency of student behaviors. The contextual features of physics scenarios presented in class can cause students to activate different types of knowledge. For example, in our study on Newton's Third Law, after instruction we provide students a set of expert-equivalent questions in which the objects, the mass, and the velocity of the objects would vary. Both the choice of object (e.g., a football or a cart) and the features of the object (e.g., mass and/or velocity) were able to evoke different types of knowledge in a single student (Bao, Hogg and Zollman 2002). Other research also suggested similar results (Palmer 1997; Schecker and Gerdes 1999).

When presented with a physics scenario, students who have not yet developed a principle-level understanding of the concept often make associations to their prior knowledge developed from real-world experience based on the surface features of the contexts. We observed in our interviews that when students were presented with a scenario of a collision between two carts similar to the demonstration shown in class, most were able to invoke correct expert knowledge (Bao 2002b). In the same interview with the same student, when presented with scenarios of collisions between common objects such as footballs, cars, etc., the student would often use commonsense (non-Newtonian) knowledge. Contexts similar to everyday situations seen outside of class tend to activate students to use everyday knowledge; whereas contexts similar to the ones used in class often activate the knowledge discussed in class. We also found that the students did not actively seek consistency among the set of scenarios given; however, when requested, some of them were able to note the similarity and develop a more generalized understanding that was consistent to all scenarios. In such cases, students usually started to realize that their prior knowledge was inappropriate.

These studies suggest that the features of the context scenarios related to the teaching and learning of a concept are an important factor causing the inconsistency in students' uses of their knowledge. Based on the same idea, we can interpret the phenomenon of entrenched misconceptions and the fragmentations (and transfer) of knowledge in terms of context dependence. Before we do so, it is useful to further inspect the deeper-level causes of the context dependence.

The underlying mechanisms of context dependence. The origin of context dependence may be traced directly to the brain's ability to develop associations between sensory input and stored information. In neural science, the learning process and knowledge are usually modeled with forms of associational networks such as pattern association networks (Rolls and Treves 1998). One way to model learning at the cognitive level is to use the constructive process of knowledge development in terms of associative networks (Rumelhart, Hinton and McClelland 1986). Extending this idea to the macroscopic cognitive level, we can then consider mental associations between hypothetical cognitive constructs such as episodic memories (images) of context scenarios, mental models, facets and p-prims. Then a particular type of student understanding of a concept can be represented in terms of networks of associations connecting the different elements (Bao 2002a,b). The phenomenon of context dependence can then be interpreted as the results of patterns of association connecting episodic images of context scenarios and more abstract level constructs such as mental models.

In Figure 10.1, we illustrate how we can use association patterns to represent features of context dependence. In this example, C_i, $i = 1 \ldots$ 4, represent four expert-equivalent context scenarios related to a single

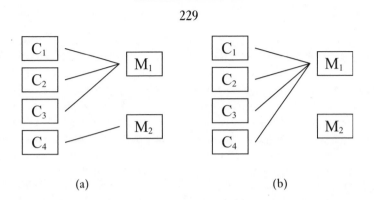

(a)   (b)

Figure 10.1 Patterns of associations between contexts and student models

concept. M_j, j = 1, 2 are two dominant types of understandings of the concept: here we may refer to M_1 as the correct expert mental model and M_2 as the naive model. The lines connecting C_i and M_j represent the associations a single student or a population may develop between context scenarios and conceptual understandings. In practice, such an association represents a probability that a context scenario would activate a student or a population to use a specific type of knowledge, which can be measured using conceptual surveys and interviews (Bao 2002b). Part (a) of the diagram shows an association pattern reflecting inconsistent use of different types of knowledge; that is, some of the scenarios activate the correct model in a student and others activate the naive model. On the other hand, part (b) of the diagram shows a consistent use of the correct knowledge in all given contexts.

During learning, the brain receives inputs from virtually all association areas in the neocortex (Van Hoesen 1982; Squire, Shimamura and Amaral 1989), and has available highly elaborated multimodal information from different sensory pathways. The brain integrates these inputs to form multimodal representations, which are further processed to create episodic memories. Therefore, all the physical features of the context scenarios can be part of the cues that are integrated in the formation of the conceptual knowledge and that can later cause the activation of the previously formed knowledge.

Interpreting preconceptions, fragmentation, and transfer. Students' preconceptions are formed through everyday experiences both inside and outside the formal school environment, which establish extensive association networks based on a wide variety of real-life scenarios. These scenarios and their features can then act as cueing agents to activate a student's knowledge to deal with given situations. When students are presented with scenarios similar to those from previous experience, they can be expected to activate their preconceptions with high probability. Because the students' preconceptions can provide practical explanations that are validated through large amounts of experience, the association networks developed with the preconceptions can be very difficult to modify. (A conceptual-level modification might require restructuring the network that connects many different pieces of the knowledge system developed based on considerable personal experience.)

During instruction, physics knowledge is often introduced with abstract scientific representations and unrealistic, overly simplified examples. It is then likely for students to develop an association network that only connects the correct physics knowledge with the in–class–context scenarios. As a result, students can develop a fragmented view treating physics as unrealistic and only applicable to the situations presented in class.

Because learning is a gradual constructive process, students may first develop somewhat incomplete association networks, which can function successfully within small localized domains of contexts. When the context domains are crossed, problems can happen in the form of failure to activate the related knowledge or the activation of inappropriate knowledge. This may explain the phenomenon of students developing fragmented conceptual knowledge and the difficulties in transfer of knowledge.

To create or to activate. The phenomenon of students creating knowledge is also dependent on the context. Here we distinguish two mental processes: activation and creation. Suppose a student is given a context scenario. If the setting of a new context is similar to the ones in the student's experience, this context can activate existing knowledge that is then applied to create a response. If the new context has no good matches from the ones in the student's experience, it is then more likely for the student to create on the spot a new type of understanding based on certain features of the new context. Depending on the familiarity of the content knowledge to the student, one process can dominate the other. For example, in learning many topics in classical mechanics, the dominant process is the activation of previously developed knowledge. On the other hand, in learning quantum mechanics, students often create new types of interpretations of the physical settings on the spot using both classical ideas and quantum mechanical ones (Bao 1999, 2002c).

The arguments of this section lead to two major conclusions: (1) the creation process and the activation process are both important in learning; and (2) context dependence is a significant part of the mechanism underlying the activation and the creation processes. Using the context dependence framework, both the activation and the creation processes can be interpreted coherently as indispensable parts of a complete learning process.

Developing a Measurement Variable and a Measurement Representation

Our goal is to develop assessment methods and instruments that provide information about student learning that can be interpreted within our cognitive model. We started by looking at the inconsistency issue, which led us to investigate the effects of context in learning. Our second look at the inconsistency issue revealed ways to explain the inconsistency as the results of the learning being context dependent. Now we take a third look at the inconsistency issue to treat inconsistency as "signals" that contain important information about the status of students' knowledge and the learning process, and we will develop assessment methods that measure and utilize such information.

Developing a Measurement Variable

We begin by making a list of requirements on a measurement variable. First, it should contain quantitative information on specific types of knowledge that are possible for a student to activate or to create during learning. These often include various types of preconceptions, the correct expert knowledge and possible forms of students' creations. Second, the measurement variable should contain quantitative information on the ways that students use their knowledge—that is, the information about the consistency of student behaviors. Finally the contextual information of the measurement instruments needs to be integrated in the analysis as an important part of the signal.

We can code richer information about student knowledge in our model by taking our measurement variable beyond the one-dimensional type (a score) to a multi-dimensional form (a vector). To construct such a vector, we need first to identify the types of knowledge that are to be represented. This requires a detailed cognitive representation for the relevant knowledge.

A Cognitive Representation and the Inferential Measurement

In previous research, we developed a cognitive representation in the form of associative networks (Bao 1999; Bao and Redish 2001; Bao

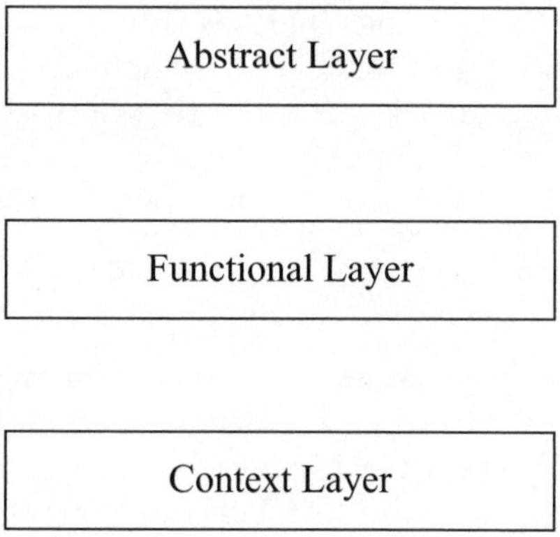

```
┌─────────────────────────────────┐
│          Abstract Layer          │
└─────────────────────────────────┘


┌─────────────────────────────────┐
│          Functional Layer        │
└─────────────────────────────────┘


┌─────────────────────────────────┐
│          Context Layer           │
└─────────────────────────────────┘
```

Figure 10.2 Layers of mental constructs in the order of context dependence and measurement

2002a) that infers cognition from observations of student behaviors. The representation framework we use has three general layers of elements based on their relations with the contexts (see Figure 10.2).

The *context layer* consists of the actual physically determinable (controllable) entities such as a student's raw responses to given tasks and concrete features of the contexts, which may include the specific scenarios, tasks, settings of a scenario and settings of the learning environment.

The *functional layer* contains a category of functional mental constructs that can be activated by the contexts or created for the contexts. The applications of these functional constructs in the related contexts are directly responsible for the specific responses students create in responding to the given tasks. Students are explicitly aware of their use of such mental constructs. Examples of these elements include mental models, facets (Minstrell 1991), or simply propositional or statement-like ideas that can be directly applied in the context. The feature of direct application is crucial, because it establishes the causal relation between such a mental construct and the student's responses. Notice that a functional construct is not just a recalled fact. It has certain generality over a domain of contexts (it can often be applied to more than one context setting).

Finally, we have an *abstract layer*—mental constructs that are general over a large domain of contexts, for example, ontology, general beliefs, and reasoning primitives such as mathematical and logical reasoning patterns. These elements may not be directly applicable to particular contexts, but contribute to the formation of constructs in the functional layer. For instance, in the example discussed earlier, a reasoning primitive such as "more cause indicates more effect" is simply a general reasoning pattern of proportionality, which can be related to virtually all situations, but is not directly applicable in any contexts before the actual objects or entities to be associated with the "more" is determined. A facet based on this primitive in the context of mechanics would be "more mass indicates more force," which is directly applicable in many contexts of mechanics to produce responses. The use of a functional construct such as this facet is explicit to the student. On the other hand, the involvement of the general elements such as a reasoning primitive can be implicit to the student. Therefore, the existence and characteristics of a general element cannot be obtained directly from analyzing the student responses. Such an inference must be based on the analysis of a range of functional constructs that involve the same general element.

We can now begin to identify variables from the three layers and to develop a cognitive representation for assessment. The process starts with systematic qualitative research studies emphasizing the context issues. From the results of these qualitative studies, we identify a set of context variables. We can then change the context variables to form measurement settings and use them to observe student behaviors in different settings. These results are analyzed to infer possible functional constructs and the probabilities for the different functional constructs to be used by the students in those contexts. We can infer the possible higher-order abstract constructs and their relations with the lower-order variables. A flow chart of the general process of inferential measurement for the different layers of cognitive constructs is shown in Figure 10.3.

Developing a Measurement Representation:
The Basic Ideas of Model Analysis

For a particular physics concept, questions designed with different context settings can cause a student to use different types of knowledge. In our research, we are particularly interested in the functional layer of cognitive constructs. This layer forms functional packages of knowledge interpolating between the abstract and the particular. Elements of this layer can be created, stored and retrieved, and once activated they can be applied by students to create explanatory understandings of the contexts. For simplicity, we call such a package of knowledge a *model*.

Common models. Our measurement variable needs to represent informa-

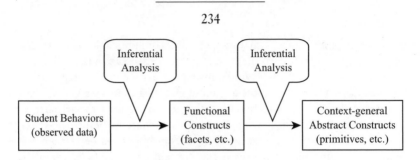

Figure 10.3 Inferential measurement of mental constructs

tion about the existence and use of specific models in contexts. We combine qualitative and quantitative methods to develop our approach to measurement: we use qualitative instruments such as interviews and open-ended surveys to identify the possible types of models that are typically activated or created by students in our particular population. We then develop quantitative instruments to probe how individual students or a population may use these different models in changing contexts.

For example, for a particular concept topic we prepare a sequence of expert-equivalent questions or scenarios in which an expert would use a single, coherent model. During learning, the particular pieces of knowledge or models that are activated by one of these expert-equivalent questions can be highly dependent on the settings of the specific question. Research also suggests that when studying a particular student population, a small number of different models often accounts for the behavior of most students in most common contexts (Halloun and Hestenes 1985; Marton 1986). Then, based on systematic qualitative studies we can often identify a small set of models that have nontrivial probabilities to be activated or created by our population. As a practical matter, we often lump all low probability models or models that are yet to be identified and that have a total probability smaller than 5 percent into a single *null model*. With the null model included, the set of models becomes complete; that is, any student response can be categorized.[2] We use the term *common models* to represent this set of models related to a single concept topic. These models include the null model, the models held by the students with nontrivial probabilities and an expert model (if not already included in the models held by the students).

Model space and student model state. We have observed two ways in which a single student may use his/her models when presented with a set of expert equivalent questions (Bao 1999; Bao and Redish 2001; Bao, Hogg and Zollman 2002). Each of the situations is defined as a *model state:*

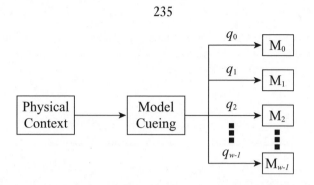

Figure 10.4 Different student model states, $M_0 \ldots M_{w-1}$ may be cued with probabilities $q_0 \ldots q_{w-1}$ depending on cues in the context and how the student interacts with them

1. The student consistently uses one of the common models in answering all questions. When this is measured, we call it a *pure model state* (or a consistent state).
2. A set of expert-equivalent questions may activate different models. We call this a *mixed model state* representing inconsistent use of models.

If a set of questions has been carefully designed to probe a particular concept, we can estimate the probabilities for a single student to activate the different common models in response to these questions and we can use these probabilities to represent the student's model state. Thus, a student's model state can be represented by a specific configuration of the probabilities for the student to use different common models in a given set of situations related to a particular concept.

We show in Figure 10.4 a schematic of the process of cueing and activating a student's model, where $M_0 \ldots M_{w-1}$ represent the different common models (assuming a total of w common models including the null model), and $q_0 \ldots q_{w-1}$ represent the probabilities that a particular situation will result in a student activating the corresponding model. Note that given different sets of questions, the measured probabilities can be different. The measured student model state is a result of the interaction between the individual student and the instrument used in the measurement, and should not be taken as a property of the student alone. For convenience, we consistently define M_0 to be the null model and M_1 to be the expert model.

By putting this set of probabilities in a w-dimension vector, we can develop a mathematical representation for the model state (Strang 1988).

This vector is in a linear space spanned by a set of basis vectors that each represents a unique common model. We call such a space the *model space* (Bao 1999; Bao and Redish 2001).

Model Analysis: Mathematical Representations and Analysis Methods

The vector representing a single student's model state can be expressed as a linear combination of the basis vectors of the model space. For example, suppose we give a student m multiple-choice (single-response) questions on a single concept for which there exist w common models. First, let us consider the *probability vector*. Define $\vec{Q}_k$ as the kth student's probability distribution vector measured with m questions, where q_η^k represents the probability for the kth student to use the ηth model in solving these questions and n_η^k represents the number of questions in which the kth student applied the ηth common model. We write (using the "arrow" notation commonly used in physics to indicate a quantity with direction as well as magnitude),

$$\vec{Q}_k = \begin{pmatrix} q_0^k \\ q_1^k \\ \vdots \\ q_{w-1}^k \end{pmatrix} = \frac{1}{m} \begin{pmatrix} n_0^k \\ n_1^k \\ \vdots \\ n_{w-1}^k \end{pmatrix}. \tag{1}$$

We also have

$$\sum_{\eta=0}^{w-1} n_\eta^k = m. \tag{2}$$

In equation (1) we have taken the probability that the kth student is in the ηth model state to be $q_\eta^k = n_\eta^k / m$. Note that q_η^k is affected by the specific question set chosen.

We do not choose to use $\vec{Q}_k$ to represent the model state of the kth student. Instead, we choose to associate the student state with a vector consisting of the *square root* of the probabilities, which has unit length in the model space, u_k. We choose this by analogy with quantum physics, where probabilities are commonly described in terms of the squares of state vectors. This has a number of advantages over using probabilities directly.[3]

$$|\mathbf{u}_k\rangle = \begin{pmatrix} \sqrt{q_0^k} \\ \sqrt{q_1^k} \\ \vdots \\ \sqrt{q_{w-1}^k} \end{pmatrix} = \frac{1}{\sqrt{m}} \begin{pmatrix} \sqrt{n_0^k} \\ \sqrt{n_1^k} \\ \vdots \\ \sqrt{n_{w-1}^k} \end{pmatrix} \tag{3}$$

where

$$\langle \mathbf{u}_k | \mathbf{u}_k \rangle = \sum_{\eta=0}^{w-1} q_\eta^k = 1 \tag{4}$$

We choose to represent the vector using the "bra-ket" notation where the ket state $|\mathbf{u}_k\rangle$ represents the column vector defined as the model state vector of the kth student. The bra state $\langle \mathbf{u}_k |$ is a row vector which is the transpose of the ket state. By the standard rules of matrix multiplication, the two put together in "bra-ket" form give the dot product of the two vectors, which is 1 in this case; that is, the model state vector is unitary.

The student model state represents an interaction between the student and the particular instrument chosen. Because we are concerned with evaluating normative instruction, in which the student is being taught a particular model or set of models, the choice of the proportion of questions depends on normative goals—what the instrument (test) designer considers important for the student to know. *The student state should therefore be thought of as a projection of student knowledge against a set of normative instructional goals, not as an abstract property belonging to the student alone.* For the purpose of assessment, researchers can develop a standardized set of questions based on the normative goals. These questions can then be used to provide comparative evaluation on situations of student models for different populations.

When using models and model states, it is important to distinguish the difference between a hybrid model and a mixed model state (Bao 2002b): a hybrid model is an attempt by the student to make coherent a number of distinct models. We treat is as we do any other type of model and give it a unique dimension in the model space. The mixed (and inconsistent) use of different models is a distinct type of student behavior.

Measuring Students' Model States with Multiple-Choice Instruments

We use multiple-choice instruments as an example to show how to apply our mathematical representation to measure and analyze learning. The development of an effective instrument should always begin with systematic qualitative investigations (interviews) on student difficulties in understanding a particular concept to identify common models that students may form before, during and after instruction. Using the results from this research, multiple-choice questions can be developed where the choices are designed to activate the different common models. Then interviews are again used to confirm the validity of the instrument and elaborate what can be learned from the data. This process can then be cycled repeatedly until it converges.

In physics education, widely accepted research-based multiple-choice instruments exist on a variety of topics. The two most popular instruments on concepts in Newtonian mechanics are the force concept inventory (FCI) (Hestenes, Wells and Swackhamer 1992) and the force-motion concept evaluation (FMCE) (Thornton 1994). The questions are designed to probe critical conceptual knowledge and their distracters are chosen to activate common naive conceptions. As a result, many of the questions on these tests are suitable for use with the model analysis method. In this chapter, we use data from the FCI test taken by engineering students in the calculus-based physics class at the University of Maryland. Results of the FMCE test with students from other schools are discussed in Bao (1999).

The force-motion concept: Student understanding of the concept of force-motion connection has been thoroughly studied for the past two decades and researchers have been able to develop a good understanding of the most common student models (Viennot 1979; Champagne, Klopfer and Anderson 1980; Clement 1982; Galili and Bar 1992; Halloun and Hestenes 1985). A commonly observed student naive model is "motion indicates force"—that is, there is always a force in the direction of motion. For the population in our introductory physics class, this is the most common incorrect student model related to the force-motion concept. The correct expert model would state that an unbalanced force is associated with a change in the velocity—an acceleration. Therefore, for this concept, we can define three common models: Model 0: the null model; Model 1: the expert model (an object can move with or without a net force in the direction of motion); Model 2: the common naive model (there is always a force in the direction of motion).

In the FCI, five questions activate models associated with the force-motion concept (questions 5, 9, 18, 22, 28). As an example, consider question 5 (see Figure 10.5). The distracters "a," "b," and "c" represent three different responses associated with the same incorrect student model (Model 2). All of the three choices involve a force in the direction

A boy throws a steel ball straight up. Consider the motion of the ball only after it has left the boy's hand but before it touches the ground, and assume that forces exerted by the air are negligible. For these conditions, the forces(s) acting on the ball is (are):

a. a downward force of gravity along with a steadily decreasing upward force.

b. a steadily decreasing upward force from the moment it leaves the boy's hand until it reaches its highest point; on the way down there is a steadily increasing downward force of gravity as the object gets closer to the Earth.

c. an almost constant downward force of gravity along with an upward force that steadily decreases until the ball reaches its highest point; on the way there is only a constant downward force of gravity.

d. an almost constant downward force of gravity only.

e. none of the above. The ball falls back to ground because of its natural tendency to rest on the surface of the Earth.

Figure 10.5 Question 5 of the FCI (Hestenes, Wells and Swackhamer 1992)

of motion. If a student selects one of these three choices, we consider that the student is using Model 2. To use this method, we have to assume that if a student is cued into using a particular model, the probability for the student to apply the model inappropriately is small (less than 10 percent). Such probabilities can often be evaluated with interviews. With this method, if a student answers "d" on this question, we assume that it is very likely that the student has a correct model. A method to estimate the probability for such inference can be found in Bao (1999). Choice "e" is rarely held by students in our introductory physics class and thus categorized as reflecting a null model.

The associations between the three models and the responses corresponding to the five FCI questions are listed in Table 10.1. Notice that the mappings between model and item do not have to be one-to-one. However, to ensure that meaningful inference can be made, it is appropriate to map several choices to one model but not one choice to multiple models. Using Table 10.1, we can obtain a quantitative estimation of individual students' model states from the students' responses. For example, if a student answers the five questions with "d," "a," "b," "d" and "c,"

**Table 10.1. Associations between the Physical Models
and the Choices of the Five FCI Questions on the
Force-Motion Concept**

Questions	Model 0	Model 1	Model 2
5	e	d	a, b, c
9	e	a, d	b, c
18	c, d	b	a, e
22		a, d	b, c, e
28	b	c	a, d, e

we may infer (from Table 10.1) that the student has used the expert model (Model 1) on all five questions. Thus, the student probability vector is

$$\vec{Q}_k = \frac{1}{5}\begin{pmatrix} 0 \\ 5 \\ 0 \end{pmatrix} = \begin{pmatrix} 0 \\ 1 \\ 0 \end{pmatrix}, \tag{5}$$

which shows that the student has the probability of 100 percent to use the expert model and the probability of zero to use either the null model (Model 0) or the naive model (Model 2). The corresponding model state vector is

$$|\mathbf{u}_k\rangle = \begin{pmatrix} 0 \\ 1 \\ 0 \end{pmatrix}. \tag{6}$$

This state can be described as a pure expert state—the student consistently applies the expert model on all five questions related to the concept being probed.

Similarly, if the student answers the questions with "b," "b," "a," "c" and "d," we may infer that the student has used the naive model (Model 2) on all five questions, which will produce a pure naive state

$$|\mathbf{u}_k\rangle = \begin{pmatrix} 0 \\ 0 \\ 1 \end{pmatrix}. \tag{7}$$

The student consistently applies the naive model on all five questions.

More interestingly, if the student answers the five questions with "a," "d," "a," "d" and "b," we will obtain a probability vector consisting of the relative frequencies of model use (interpreted as likelihoods)

$$\vec{Q}_k = \frac{1}{5}\begin{pmatrix} 1 \\ 2 \\ 2 \end{pmatrix}, \tag{8}$$

which gives a model state vector

$$|\mathbf{u}_k\rangle = \frac{1}{\sqrt{5}}\begin{pmatrix} 1 \\ \sqrt{2} \\ \sqrt{2} \end{pmatrix}. \tag{9}$$

Compared to the two model states discussed above, this state vector has multiple nonzero components, which reflects that the student is using multiple models on this set of expert-equivalent questions. This is what we call a mixed model state.

As we can see, using the model state vector, we can represent quantitatively two types of information: (1) which models (and their probabilities) the student is using in responding to a set of questions; (2) whether the student uses the models consistently or inconsistently (and how inconsistently in terms of probabilities).

Notice again that the state is measured using a finite number of questions. Therefore, it is the outcome of the student interacting with the given questions. If a different set of questions were used with the same student, we expect the result to yield a different model state. However, through multiple measurements with diverse contexts, we expect to approach a stable value of the model state for a student or a population.[4]

Analyzing a Population with the Model Density Matrix

As discussed above, we can use model state vectors to represent how a single student is responding to a set of questions. Now we want to analyze the same types of information for a population. We could simply add all the individuals' state vectors together and obtain an average vector for the class. However, this would "erase" the information on the consistency of individual students' uses of models. For example, suppose a class has two groups of students of the same size. Students in one group all have a pure expert model state (equation 6) and the students in the other group all have a pure naive state (equation 7). Then the average state for the class obtained by summation of all the individuals' states is

$$\left|\mathbf{u}_{avg}\right\rangle = \frac{1}{\sqrt{2}}\begin{pmatrix}0\\1\\1\end{pmatrix}. \tag{10}$$

Now consider another situation in which all the students in the class have the identical mixed state

$$\left|\mathbf{u}_k\right\rangle = \frac{1}{\sqrt{2}}\begin{pmatrix}0\\1\\1\end{pmatrix}. \tag{11}$$

The above two situations will produce the same average state for the class. Therefore, the summation of the individuals' states will eliminate the information about the mixing carried by the individuals' states.

One can also perform statistical analysis or cluster analysis of the individuals' states (Bao 2002b). These analyses can provide detailed information about the class and the individual students. However, as the dimension of the model space increases, the orders of the calculation and the total number of possible combinations of states will increase exponentially (in the form of $2^w Nm$ where w is the dimension of the model space, N is the number of students, and m is the number of questions used). Here we describe a method, the model density matrix, which can retain information on the individuals' states without much increase of the complexity in calculation. (The increase of calculation is in the order of $w^2 Nm/2$.)

With the individual students' model states measured, we can calculate a matrix for the class denoted $\mathbf{D}$ (equation 12 is based on the same example discussed above and N is the total number of the students in a class):

$$\mathbf{D} = \frac{1}{N}\sum_{k=1}^{N}\left|\mathbf{u}_k\right\rangle\left\langle\mathbf{u}_k\right| = \frac{1}{N}\sum_{k=1}^{N}\frac{1}{m}\begin{bmatrix} n_0^k & \sqrt{n_0^k n_1^k} & \sqrt{n_0^k n_2^k} \\ \sqrt{n_1^k n_0^k} & n_1^k & \sqrt{n_1^k n_2^k} \\ \sqrt{n_2^k n_0^k} & \sqrt{n_2^k n_1^k} & n_2^k \end{bmatrix}. \tag{12}$$

We refer to this matrix as a *model density matrix* (by analogy with the terminology for a similarly structured object in quantum physics). The class model density matrix is a symmetric matrix. The diagonal elements of the matrix add to 1 and give the probabilities of how the class of students altogether uses the different models, which is equivalent to the summation of the model probability vectors. The off-diagonal ele-

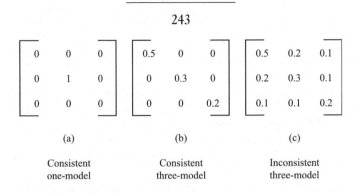

$$\begin{bmatrix} 0 & 0 & 0 \\ 0 & 1 & 0 \\ 0 & 0 & 0 \end{bmatrix} \quad \begin{bmatrix} 0.5 & 0 & 0 \\ 0 & 0.3 & 0 \\ 0 & 0 & 0.2 \end{bmatrix} \quad \begin{bmatrix} 0.5 & 0.2 & 0.1 \\ 0.2 & 0.3 & 0.1 \\ 0.1 & 0.1 & 0.2 \end{bmatrix}$$

(a)   (b)   (c)

Consistent   Consistent   Inconsistent
one-model   three-model   three-model

Figure 10.6 Examples of student class model density matrices

ments are not probabilities but represent one way of expressing correlations between probabilities. They retain the information about whether the individual students use their models consistently. For example, consider a class of students with diverse backgrounds. In responding to the set of questions, the class behavior can be interpreted as a combination of three types of situations (see Figure 10.6):

1. All students in a class use the same model (not necessarily a correct one) and are individually consistent in using it. The students all have the same pure model state. (Figure 10.6, case a.)
2. The class population holds three different models but each student only uses a single model consistently. Each student has a pure model state, but the class does not have a single state. (Figure 10.6, case b.)
3. Many individual students have several models and use them inconsistently. Many individual students have mixed model states. (Figure 10.6, case c.)

As shown in this example, the diagonal elements of the **D** give the inferred probabilities for the class of students to use the different models and the off-diagonal elements reflect the consistency of the individual students' uses of their models. Notice that in the latter two of the three situations shown in Figure 10.6 the diagonal elements are the same but the off-diagonal elements are different. Large off-diagonal elements indicate that low consistency (more mixing) for individual students in their model uses is common in the class. Because the matrix is symmetric, the effective number of elements that need to be calculated is $w(w+1)/2$. This is larger than what is needed for the model state vector, but much less than the total possible combinations of the model states needed in performing cluster analysis.

Extracting Information from the Model Density Matrix

There are multiple ways to extract information from the model density matrix (Bao 1999, 2002b). Here, we will show examples using the method of eigenvector analysis.[5]

Because a class model density matrix is symmetric, we can obtain a complete set of eigenvalues and eigenvectors (Bao and Redish 2001). The magnitude of an eigenvalue is affected by the similarity between the individual student's model vectors and the number of students that have similar model state vectors. Thus if we obtain a large eigenvalue (>0.8) from a class model density matrix, it implies that many students in the class have similar individual model state vectors. On the other hand, if we obtain several small eigenvalues, it indicates that students in the class behave differently from one another. Therefore, we can use the magnitudes of the eigenvalues to evaluate the diversity of a class.

The information contained in the eigenvectors reflects a set of features of the individual model states that need to be interpreted in combination with the eigenvalues.[6] For example, if there is an eigenvector with a large eigenvalue (>0.8), it represents a dominant state vector that is similar to most individual states. In this case, we refer to this as a *primary* eigenvector. The additional eigenvectors act as corrections to the primary state reflecting less common features.

When considering the class as a single unit, a primary eigenvector gives a good evaluation of the overall structure of the class. However, if we regard the class as a composition of individual students, there can be interesting details that cannot be extracted with a simple eigenvalue decomposition. For instance, suppose we have a class that can be divided into several groups of students, where students in each group all have similar model states and students from different groups have significantly different model states. In this situation an eigenvalue decomposition can provide good results for two cases:

1. When the model states from different groups are nearly orthogonal, the eigenvalue decomposition will produce eigenvectors that are similar to these model states. In this case, the eigenvalues reflect the sizes of the different groups.
2. When one of these student groups has a dominant population, the eigenvalue decomposition will produce a primary vector with a large eigenvalue, very close to the model state held by this dominant group.

In the case where students are different but not so different (for example, they have a range of different but non-orthogonal model states), an eigenvector analysis will not yield appropriate model states. If the eigenvalues are small, we can do a scatter plot of the individual students' model state vectors, which can further suggest whether it might be useful to perform a cluster analysis, separating the class into distinct subgroups. In general, when the eigenvalue of a primary eigenvector is less than 0.65 and the student model states are mixed, it indicates that the students in the class have a less concentrated distribution of non-orthogonal model states.

Representing the Class Model State—The Model Plot

In many situations we have encountered, students often have two dominant models: a correct expert model and a common misconception. To conveniently represent and study the student model states and the changes of the states in this situation, we construct a two-dimensional graph called a *model plot* to represent the student usage of the two models (Bao 1999; Bao and Redish 2001). For example, suppose we study model 1 and model 2 in a three-model situation (model 0 is a null model). A class model state, $v_\mu = (v_{0\mu}, v_{1\mu}, v_{2\mu})^T$ with an eigenvalue λ_μ, can be represented as a point in a two-dimensional space in which the two axes represent the probabilities[7] that a student in the class will use the corresponding models on one of the items of the probe instrument. The state is represented by a point (point B in Figure 10.7) on a plot with $P_1 = \lambda_\mu v_{1\mu}^2$ as the vertical component and $P_2 = \lambda_\mu v_{2\mu}^2$ as the horizontal component.

When the eigenvalue of a class model state is small (the class has no dominant mode), the class model point will be close to the origin. On the other hand, a state with a large eigenvalue will be close to the line going through (0, 1) and (1, 0), which is the upper boundary of the allowed region of the model plot. In the case when a class model state vector has small elements on model dimensions that are not considered ($v_{0\mu}$ in this case), we can make an approximation letting $\lambda_\mu(1 - v_{0\mu}^2) \cong \lambda_\mu$. Then the distance between a model point and the upper boundary can be used to estimate the eigenvalue of the corresponding model state.

We divide the model plot into four regions: the consistent model 1 region, the consistent model 2 region, the mixed region, and the small eigenvalue region. When a class has a primary model state plotted in the model 1 region (or model 2 region), it indicates that most students have comparatively consistent model states with a dominant probability on model 1 (or model 2). When a class has a primary model state plotted in the mixed region, most of the individual students have mixed model states, that is, most of the individual students are inconsistent in using

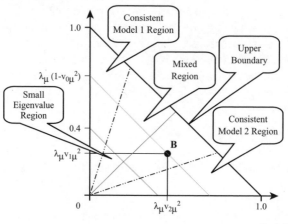

Figure 10.7 Model regions on model plot

their models. The small eigenvalue region represents model states with small eigenvalues (<0.4), which reflect less popular features of the class behavior. In the example reported in the next section, the primary eigenvalue is close to 0.8, which indicates that most students have similar model states and the primary eigenvector can represent most of the information of the class.

The model plot is a useful tool that can visually present a variety of information which includes the diversity (or similarity) of the population, the consistency of individual students in using their models, the types of models used by individual students, and the probabilities for individual students and the class population to use the different models. We can also put the pre and post model states from different classes together on the same plot to study the patterns and shifts of the different classes' model states.

Examples Using Model Analysis Methods

Model Analysis of FCI Data

The results shown below are based on FCI data from the pre- and post-testing of 14 introductory mechanics classes at the University of Maryland. The students are mostly engineering majors. All of the classes had

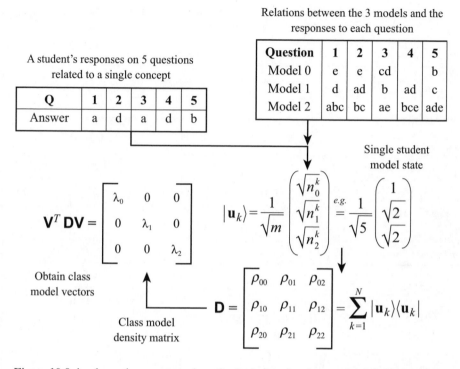

Figure 10.8 A schematic representation of calculating the class model density matrix and extracting the class's model states

traditional lectures three hours per week and were assigned weekly readings and homework consisting of traditional textbook problems. All of the students also had one hour per week of small group ($N\sim30$) recitation led by teaching assistants (TAs). For half of the classes, recitations were traditional TA-led problem-solving sessions (students asking questions and the TA modeling solutions on the board). The other half received recitations taught with *Tutorials in Introductory Physics* (McDermott and Shaffer 1998). These sessions consisted of students working together in groups of three to five on research-based guided-discovery worksheets. The worksheets often used a cognitive conflict model and helped students develop qualitative reasoning about fundamental physics concepts. In the following analysis, we use the five FCI questions on the force-motion concept as an example to demonstrate methods of class model density matrix and eigenvector analysis, which are summarized in Figure 10.8.

Table 10.2. Class Model Density Matrices and Model States on Force-Motion Concept (N~800)

Force-Motion	Tutorial					
	Pre			Post		
Density Matrix	$\begin{bmatrix} 0.04 & 0.02 & 0.07 \\ 0.02 & 0.27 & 0.23 \\ 0.07 & 0.23 & 0.69 \end{bmatrix}$			$\begin{bmatrix} 0.03 & 0.03 & 0.02 \\ 0.03 & 0.66 & 0.28 \\ 0.02 & 0.28 & 0.31 \end{bmatrix}$		
Eigenvalues	0.03	0.80	0.17	0.03	0.82	0.15
Eigenvectors	$\begin{pmatrix} 0.03 \\ -0.12 \\ 0.99 \end{pmatrix}$	$\begin{pmatrix} 0.40 \\ 0.91 \\ 0.09 \end{pmatrix}$	$\begin{pmatrix} -0.92 \\ 0.39 \\ 0.07 \end{pmatrix}$	$\begin{pmatrix} 0.03 \\ 0.04 \\ -0.99 \end{pmatrix}$	$\begin{pmatrix} 0.87 \\ 0.48 \\ 0.05 \end{pmatrix}$	$\begin{pmatrix} -0.49 \\ 0.87 \\ 0.02 \end{pmatrix}$
Force-Motion	Traditional					
	Pre			Post		
Density Matrix	$\begin{bmatrix} 0.05 & 0.03 & 0.08 \\ 0.03 & 0.27 & 0.22 \\ 0.08 & 0.22 & 0.68 \end{bmatrix}$			$\begin{bmatrix} 0.04 & 0.03 & 0.05 \\ 0.03 & 0.46 & 0.25 \\ 0.05 & 0.25 & 0.50 \end{bmatrix}$		
Eigenvalues	0.04	0.79	0.17	0.03	0.74	0.23
Eigenvectors	$\begin{pmatrix} 0.02 \\ 0.12 \\ -0.99 \end{pmatrix}$	$\begin{pmatrix} 0.40 \\ 0.91 \\ 0.12 \end{pmatrix}$	$\begin{pmatrix} -0.92 \\ 0.39 \\ 0.03 \end{pmatrix}$	$\begin{pmatrix} 0.01 \\ 0.10 \\ -0.99 \end{pmatrix}$	$\begin{pmatrix} 0.67 \\ 0.73 \\ 0.08 \end{pmatrix}$	$\begin{pmatrix} -0.74 \\ 0.67 \\ 0.06 \end{pmatrix}$

Details of the calculations are discussed in the references (Bao 1999; Bao and Redish 2001). We show in Table 10.2 the eigenvectors of the pre and post student model density matrices obtained by combining all classes together ($N \sim 800$).

From Table 10.2, we can see that the eigenvalues for the eigenvectors corresponding to the null models are small. This indicates that most students use either the correct expert model or the incorrect naive model (or both), and the model space defined from the qualitative research matches well with this population. In addition, the primary class model states (state with the largest eigenvalue) of all classes have eigenvalues around 0.8. Therefore, the primary state alone gives a fairly good description of the class. The student class model states on the force-

Model 1 (Correct)

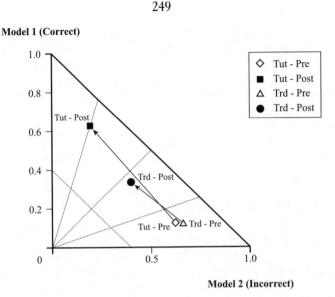

Model 2 (Incorrect)

Figure 10.9 Model plot of class model states on force-motion with FCI data

motion concept are displayed on a model plot in Figure 10.9. For each type of class (traditional or tutorial), we plot the class's primary model states for both pre- and posttests. The initial states of both types of classes are nearly the same and in the consistent model 2 region indicating that before instruction most students in the two classes consistently use the incorrect model on all the questions related to force-motion.

After instruction, the model state of the tutorial class moves to the consistent model 1 region indicating that most students use the correct model rather consistently. On the other hand, the primary model state of the traditional class is mixed, which suggests that most students in the class are inconsistent in using their models. Because the model state is nearly a perfect mix, a student randomly selected from the class would have equal probability to use either the expert model or the naive model on a question arbitrarily selected from this set of five questions on force-motion.

Assessing the Fine Details of Context Dependence:
Effects of Specific Context Features

To investigate the finer details of context dependence, we conducted an experiment at Kansas State University in which we implemented a new measurement instrument designed to isolate the effects of different contextual features of expert-equivalent scenarios (Bao, Hogg and Zollman 2002). This research demonstrates that context scenarios can involve multiple contextual aspects, which we refer to as *physical features*. These features of the contexts can be integrated in students' reasoning as part of the knowledge or as cues to activate their knowledge. For example, in learning Newton's Third Law, for a given context scenario, students usually attend to four physical features including the mass, the velocity, the object that is actively pushing, and the acceleration. Students can activate a naive model when cued with one physical feature and an expert model when cued with another physical feature as if the physical features are independent variables.

To probe this phenomenon, we developed a multiple-choice instrument that isolates the different physical features in measuring the student model states. Existing instruments such as FCI often mix several physical features in a single question. For example, the two situations shown in Figure 10.10 can be used to design questions to measure students' understandings of Newton's Third Law. Students are often asked to compare the forces exerted by the two persons on each other. There are usually two naive models involved: (1) the person who pushes exerts a larger force; (2) the person with larger mass exerts a larger force. It mixes the two physical features, mass and pushing, together. If a student answers item a) saying that Bob exerts a larger force, no further evidence can be obtained to infer if the incorrect response is generated based on consideration of mass, of pushing or of both.

In our new multiple-choice instrument, each question only measures students' reasoning related to a single physical feature of Newton's Third Law. Figure 10.10 (b) is a modified version of the two persons pushing each other, in which both now push at the same time. If a student responds that Bob exerts a larger force, we then have evidence to infer that this student is using an incorrect model based on the physical feature of mass. The question can now isolate the physical feature of mass and allow the probing of the students' models involving only mass. In order to measure the possible mixing of students' use of their models, we designed three questions using different context settings for each of the four physical features (Bao, Hogg and Zollman 2002).

With our new instrument, we studied five introductory physics courses at Kansas State University, all taught with traditional lecture-recitation type instruction. These courses are:

• Physical World (PW), a conceptual physics course for nonscience majors with no math prerequisites;

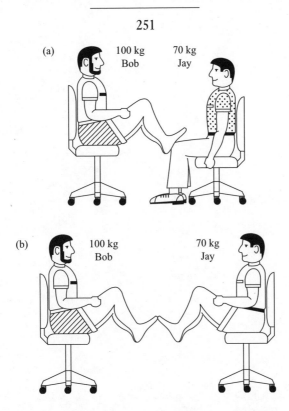

Figure 10.10 Question design isolating context features in Newton's Third Law, (a) from the FCI, (b) modified to isolate a single physical feature

- General Physics 1/2 (GP1/2), the first/second semester of a two-semester, algebra-based physics course;
- Engineering Physics 1/2 (EP1/2), the first/second semester of a two-semester, calculus-based course for physics and engineering majors.

Among these classes, only GP2 and EP2 had previously received instruction on mechanics; therefore, we treat the results of GP2 and EP2 as post-instructional data and the results from PW, GP1 and EP1 as pre-instructional data. In addition, the level of students' preparation/background on physics knowledge can be described in an increasing order from PW → GP1 → EP1 for pre-instruction classes and from GP2 → EP2 for post-instruction classes.

The results are shown in four model plots each representing the classes' primary model states for one physical feature (see Figure 10.11).

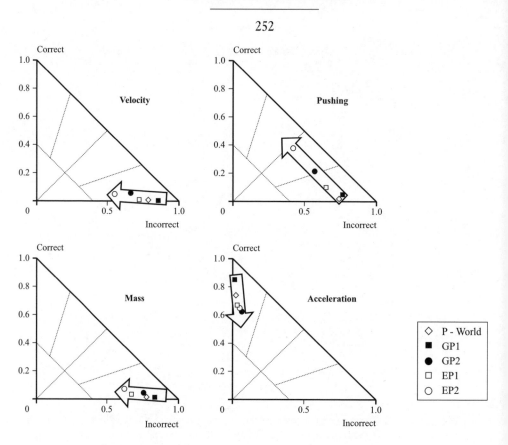

Figure 10.11 Student class model states on Newton's Third Law with the four physical features

Each point on one model plot represents a class's primary state (there are five points in each plot representing five classes). The arrow in the diagram shows how the model states of different classes change as the level of the class increases.

From Figure 10.11, we can see that for the physical features of mass and velocity, the model states of all the classes stay in the consistent model 2 region. This indicates that most students have a consistently dominant incorrect model—*the object with the larger mass or velocity exerts a larger force during an interaction.* The general direction of the changes of the model states is horizontal and towards 0. This suggests that the popularity of the incorrect model decreases with higher-level courses—from 90 percent (GP1) to 70 percent (EP2), but the model states stay in the model 2 region showing that most students in these five classes apply their models consistently; that is, there is little mixed use of different models. The process can be interpreted that a small fraction of students totally understand the concept and became very consistent in using an expert model. The remaining students, whose fraction of the population decreases as the level of the class increases, didn't get it at all and were very consistent in using the naive model.

Student model states with the physical feature of acceleration appear to be in the opposite situation where most students hold a consistent "correct" model considering acceleration irrelevant. In this case, the pattern of the changes in model states suggests that higher-level students started to have less confidence on this model. The cause of this phenomenon is still being studied. Our current results suggest that the lower-level students (who often have difficulty with the concept of acceleration) respond to the questions with their dominant attentions on mass and velocity, and ignore acceleration. As students gain more knowledge from instruction on mechanics, they can get confused on the correct relations among acceleration, force, and velocity and thus develop an incorrect model that treats acceleration as a factor that affects the forces during the interaction.

With the physical feature of pushing, student model states show a different structure. The low-level classes still consistently have a dominant incorrect model. As the level of class becomes more advanced, student model states become more mixed. The most advanced class (EP2) has nearly a perfectly mixed model state. This is very different from the situations with the other physical features and implies a different process in conceptual development. As clearly shown in the model plot, the three classes without instruction all stay in the region representing a consistent incorrect model. The two classes with instruction are in the mixed region. The shifts of the class model states suggest the process in which students start with a consistent incorrect model and go through stages of mixed model states towards building a consistent correct model (e.g., see the previous example with tutorial instruction shown in Figure 10.9). This is a different process of conceptual development compared to the students' models on the other three physical features.

From the research results using both qualitative and quantitative methods, we can infer a possible explanation. It appears that "pushing" is often the first and the most common issue in examples used to introduce Newton's Third Law. More importantly, most students have the experience of being pushed back when they are pushing an object. Most students remembered the sentence "when you push something, you get pushed back" introduced by the instructors, and believed it because they can easily relate this to their personal experience. Integrating this as an example in instruction can link the concept directly to a student's life experience and presumably help them make sense of it. Therefore, students show significant changes of their models on this physical feature even with traditional instruction. On the other hand, students' strong naive models associated with mass and velocity often receive inadequate (or ineffective) treatment through traditional instruction and students' changes on their models with these physical features are small.

This example shows clearly the context dependence of learning with respect to the formation and activation of students' prior knowledge and the formation of conceptual knowledge during the instruction. It is particularly interesting that for the same concept students can develop very different models for subsets of the context features and can also go through a completely different conceptual change process on different contextual features. This is strong evidence suggesting that we have to address the context issues in assessment and in instruction with care and completeness.

Cognitive Models and Treatments
on Information from Measurement

The results we obtained using model analysis methods are often difficult to get from any one-dimensional measurement variables such as a score. The mixed state of students' use of their knowledge is fundamental to the learning process and is part of the information that needs to be assessed. Such information cannot be obtained through analysis that assumes consistency of student behaviors. Therefore, we provide an example that compares model analysis with factor analysis.

Factor analysis uses a correlation matrix to analyze the consistency of student behaviors in terms of covariance and correlations of student responses on different test items. Usually, the measurement variable is the score on an item. By analyzing the covariance or correlation matrix of students' responses on test items, a set of "factors" can be obtained, which are often interpreted as representing certain latent abilities or conceptual constructs possessed by the students. There are many concerns about this method. For example, the factors are nonunique and can be rotated, which can cause arguments on what the factors actually represent. Here we emphasize the connection to the underlying cognitive model. If one uses factor analysis or similar methods that attempt to extract hidden variables from analyzing correlations of student behaviors, it is implicitly assumed that hidden variables should lead to a consistency in student behaviors in given contexts, which produces the correlation.

To show how factor analysis may fail to produce meaningful results, we reference a study conducted by Huffman and Heller (1995) who used factor analysis to explore whether the results of the FCI can reveal any factors and patterns along the six conceptual dimensions based on which the FCI was designed (Hestenes, Wells and Swackhamer 1992). After performing a factor analysis on a data set from nearly 1000 students, no factors could be extracted to match the specific conceptual dimensions. They concluded that "the questions on the FCI are only loosely related to each other" (p. 140) and that the FCI "actually measures bits and pieces of students' knowledge that do not necessarily form a coherent force concept." (p. 141) In our view, this research result is strong evidence showing that the activation of conceptual knowledge is context dependent and thus causing inconsistency of students' responses on expert-equivalent items. Therefore, the correlations between students' responses on a cluster of questions designed to measure a single concept dimension can be insignificant unless the students are all in pure model states.

With the same data used in the above examples, we calculated the correlation matrices for getting the correct answer on four questions on the force-motion concept (see Table 10.3). We used only the data from the classes under traditional instruction. The correlations on the pretest are somewhat higher than on the posttest. This makes sense since model analysis shows (see Figure 10.9) that most students appear to have a pure naive model state on pretest and mixed states on the posttest. With such correlations, it is very hard to extract any meaningful factors.

We carried out the analog of a model analysis: we wanted to study how students use both the expert model and the naive model, because the two models both describe rational and stable reasoning patterns. Here the null model is treated as pieces and bits of rather random ideas that are less rational and less stable. In the calculation, if we find a student giving a response that reflects *either* the naive model or the expert model, we assign a model score of 1 to the student. Similarly, if a student uses the null model, we assign 0 to the student. Then we calculate the correlations between students' model scores on the four questions. The correlation matrices are shown in Table 10.4.

These data show much stronger correlations between the model scores on the four questions, which indicates that most students used either the naive model or the expert model on the set of questions. Based on such correlations, we would find one strong factor showing commonalities between the four questions (see Table 10.5).

From many examples we have studied, we find that the use of null models on the FCI questions is less than 5 percent. Therefore, we can conclude that the majority of students we studied would use either the

Table 10.3. Correlation Matrix of Correct Answers on Four Questions on the Force-Motion Concept (traditional instruction only)

Pre-instruction					Post-instruction				
R	Q5	Q9	Q18	Q28	R	Q5	Q9	Q18	Q28
Q5	1	0.64	0.47	0.42	Q5	1	0.51	0.31	0.33
Q9	0.64	1	0.54	0.55	Q9	0.51	1	0.38	0.34
Q18	0.47	0.54	1	0.51	Q18	0.31	0.38	1	0.44
Q28	0.42	0.55	0.51	1	Q28	0.33	0.34	0.44	1

Table 10.4. Correlation Matrix of Model Choice (correct or naive) on Four Questions on the Force-Motion Concept (traditional instruction only)

Pre-instruction					Post-instruction				
R	Q5	Q9	Q18	Q28	R	Q5	Q9	Q18	Q28
Q5	1	0.97	0.86	0.74	Q5	1	0.96	0.86	0.90
Q9	0.97	1	0.82	0.70	Q9	0.96	1	0.83	0.89
Q18	0.86	0.82	1	0.67	Q18	0.86	0.83	1	0.78
Q28	0.74	0.70	0.67	1	Q28	0.90	0.89	0.78	1

expert model or the naive model on the two clusters of FCI questions we studied. When many individual students are inconsistent in using the different models on the set of questions related to a single concept as a result of context dependence, low correlations between student scores on the questions will result. In this case, factor analysis will not produce meaningful results.

Values of Measuring Mixed Model States

Empirical Observations of Students' Conceptual Development Process

Based on the literature and our own investigations on student models of physics (Thornton 1994; Maloney and Siegler 1993; Bao and Redish 2001; Bao, Hogg and Zollman 2002), we can put together a picture to

Table 10.5. Factor Loading Obtained from Model Choice on Four Questions on the Force-Motion Concept (traditional instruction only)

Pre-instruction					Post-instruction				
Loading	F1	F2	F3	F4	Loading	F1	F2	F3	F4
Q5	0.97	−0.14	0.15	−0.10	Q5	0.98	−0.06	0.14	−0.15
Q9	0.95	−0.17	0.22	0.11	Q9	0.97	−0.10	0.18	0.13
Q18	0.91	−0.18	−0.37	0.01	Q18	0.91	0.40	−0.08	0.02
Q28	0.84	0.55	−0.02	0.01	Q28	0.94	−0.23	−0.25	0.01

characterize the different stages of conceptual development in terms of the situations of students' use of models. For a particular concept topic, a student's learning can be described with five typical stages shown in Figure 10.12 (Bao 2002b). The process represents a general progressive learning path and a student can begin and end with any one of the stages.

The first is the pre-naive stage, which represents the situation where students by themselves won't be able to develop/possess a logically consistent model of the concept topic. Many examples of this situation have been observed in our interviews, where students fail to provide any logically sound reasoning for a physical phenomenon. Many students just can't provide reasoning of any kind. Some students attempt to put together reasoning but they usually fail to recognize the relevant variables from the context and do not have appropriate causal relations in their reasoning—for example, a result can also be the cause of itself. Basically, these students have limited logical manipulation ability. Students in this stage can also be measured with a model-based, multiple-choice instrument, which will show a high probability on the null model dimension (an example of this is shown in Bao, Hogg and Zollman 2002).

The second is the naive model stage. In this case students consistently hold one or several models of the concept topic. These models are often developed by students based on their real-life experience and previous school learning. Although these models may have a similar level of coherence and robustness as an expert's model, they can produce correct results in a limited set of cases and may not interface well with scientific models.

The third stage corresponds to mixed model states. The last stage is the expert model state in which the students are able to apply the expert

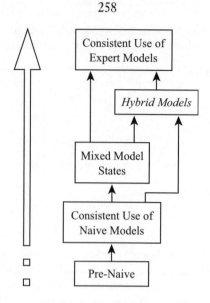

Figure 10.12 Stages of conceptual development

models of the concept topic consistently in a wide variety of appropriate context settings. Starting from the third stage, it is possible to bring students into explicit awareness of conflicts of the different models with carefully prepared context settings. Also starting from the third stage, students may develop hybrid models as a result of instruction.

From many examples in the literature (McDermott and Redish 1999), it appears that an average undergraduate population in an introductory physics course often starts with the naive model state and ends up somewhere in the mixed stages. Our previous research indicates that with traditional instruction, students often move to the middle of the mixed stages, and with research-based instructions (e.g., tutorials), students can move very close to the expert state.

Possible Applications in Instruction

As indicated by many studies on students' conceptual change process, when students hold naive models, effective teaching strategies often require bringing students into explicit awareness of the conflicts of their existing naive models (Posner, Strike, Hewson and Gertzog 1982; McDermott and Shaffer 1998). Therefore, the measurement of what

types of context settings can cue multiple models and the explicit awareness of conflicts can play a valuable role in instruction. It provides useful information on both the students' states of understanding and on
whether (or which ones of) the context scenarios of the questions are
appropriate to be incorporated in teaching to help students. The possible
instructional applications of the results of such measurements are summarized below (Bao 2002b)

(1) When students are measured as in the pre-naive stage, the first task
of the instruction is often to help students recognize the relevant
variables of the contexts and understand the basic causal relations
that the students will need to manipulate the variables and to put
together some reasoning, that is, to help them make observations of
the basic characteristics of the physical phenomenon. At this stage,
because many students' reasoning capabilities are quite "fragile,"
encouragement and facilitation of students' development of the
ability to do logical reasoning (not necessarily the correct types) is
often the major theme of the instruction. Activities to confront students' incorrect ideas should be carefully controlled to avoid causing frustrations among students.

(2) If a pure naive model is detected, the instructor can begin with
helping students develop some basic understanding of the expert
model and/or confronting students' naive models. In this stage,
strong confrontation of students' existing models can cue students'
desire to change their current understandings; however, because the
students don't have much of the correct model yet, it is often difficult for them to quickly change in the correct direction and they
may become frustrated. Therefore, it may work better if the instruction first helps students learn some new ideas in reasoning
without being troubled by any contradiction. Later, the instruction
can guide the students to re-interpret their existing examples (including the ones used in the questions) and see the conflicts of using their old models.

(3) If a mixed model state is detected, it shows that the students have
started to understand the expert model but such understandings
are often strongly tied to limited contexts and students may treat
different expert-equivalent contexts as unrelated situations (context-
dependent fragmentation of knowledge). It also implies that the
context scenarios of the questions won't spontaneously activate explicit awareness of multiple models and the conflicts between these
models. To use these context scenarios in instruction, it is often

necessary to use several questions that each may cue a different model and guide the students to realize the conflicts by comparing their reasoning on the different questions.

(4) As a related issue, we may find students developing hybrid models during instruction. In this situation, it is important to identify the specific contexts in which the hybrid models are developed. Because a hybrid model is often locally consistent within the contexts in which it is developed, to create cognitive conflicts it is necessary to prepare different context settings that the students can recognize as equivalent and that the application of the hybrid model will produce contradictory results.

In the third and fourth cases, since the students already know the correct model (or parts of the correct model), the instructor can more directly confront the students' naive models and guide them to apply the correct model under different contexts. Regardless of the states the students are in, the instruction should always involve as many real-life examples as possible (because most of the students have rich experience and also incorrect interpretations with such examples), and guide the students to re-interpret these examples using the correct models developed in learning. Without a rigorous re-interpretation process, it is often difficult for students to develop a robust understanding of the concept (rather students can develop fragmented knowledge strongly tied to specific contexts). That is, the features of the contexts that may cue a student into using naive models need to be systematically addressed so that they would consistently cue a student into using the correct model. Similarly, the instruments used in the measurement should also involve diverse context settings to ensure a more complete evaluation of students' understanding.

Summary

In this chapter, we take a theoretical perspective built on the context dependence of learning to interpret the student learning behaviors. Based on this framework, we find explanations for a range of phenomena observed in research, which include students' misconceptions and pre-conceptions, students' creations of alternative conceptions, fragmentation of students' knowledge, difficulties in transfer of students' knowledge, and inconsistency in students' use of their knowledge in equivalent contexts. These are important issues that need to be explicitly addressed in assessment and instruction. Building on the theoretical understanding of the context dependence issue, we developed model analysis, which combines both qualitative and quantitative methods to form a measurement representation and numerical methods for conducting quantitative assessment on the probabilities for students to apply specific pieces of knowledge and the ways that students use the knowledge. In particular, we are now able to quantitatively measure and evaluate the inconsistency of student behaviors in terms of mixed model states. Such inconsistency often causes difficulties for methods such as factor analysis that rely on the existence of correlations in student behaviors. As shown by research, the mixed states represent crucial information about the conceptual development process, which needs to be included in the assessment as part of the signal rather than random errors. The assessment of the mixed states can also provide direct guidance for instruction.

Acknowledgment

The authors thank the members of the research groups at The Ohio State University and at the University of Maryland. The related research is supported in part by the NSF grants REC-0087788, REC-0126070, and REC-0087519.

Notes

1. It is not only children who develop such hybrid models. In a study of student understanding of quantum mechanics, we observed senior-level undergraduate students also developing hybrid models to reconcile quantum phenomena with their classical intuitive beliefs (Bao 1999).

2. Of course, in addition to collecting random and incoherent student responses, models that have not yet been understood as a stable construct by researchers may well be classified initially as null. When a significant fraction of student responses on a particular question winds up being classified as null, it becomes an indicator suggesting that a better understanding of the range of student responses needs to be developed through qualitative research.

3. We choose to define the square root vector so that when the inner and outer product of this vector is taken with itself it yields useful and straightforward relationships. The inner product, equation (4), leads to the sum of probabilities constraint and the outer product produces the density matrix defined in equation (12). Although there could be many ways of constructing a density matrix from probabilities and their joint products, we choose to build with the square root vector. This construction respects the symmetry of the space with respect to the exchange of the models, and the use of a matrix built by outer products permits useful manipulative techniques.

4. The measurement of the state also has uncertainties resulting from a variety of additional factors, some of which are discussed by Bao (1999).

5. An eigenvector of a matrix is a vector which, when acted upon by the matrix, yields a vector of the same direction but of (possibly) different length. The change in scale is referred to as the eigenvalue belonging to the eigenvector. A symmetric matrix has a basis of orthogonal eigenvectors (Strang 1988).

6. Because the total number of eigenvectors equals the number of dimensions of the model space, they cannot retain all the detailed information about the individual model states. Such information can be extracted through statistical methods or through cluster analysis methods that allow the clusters to be non-orthogonal and unlimited in number—the only constraint is the measurement precision that determines the resolution of a measured model state, which further determines the number of total distinguishable state vectors. In general, this resolution is inversely proportional to the number of questions used in a measurement. (See Bao 1999 for details on the measurement resolution.)

7. In a basis where the density matrix is diagonal, the diagonal elements are the eigenvalues of the matrix. It is this feature that allows us to identify the eigenvalues as probabilities.

References

Bao, L. 1999. Dynamics of student modeling: A theory, algorithms, and application to quantum mechanics. Ph.D. dissertation, University of Maryland.

———. 2002a. Quantum cognition: Are we ready? AAPT National Conference, *Announcer* 31 (4): 67.

———. 2002b. Explicit and implicit states of model mixing in conceptual development. *American Journal of Physics, Physics Education Research Supplement*, submitted.

———. 2002c. States and perturbations of cognitive processes in learning quantum mechanics. Physics Research and Education: Quantum Mechanics. Gordon Research Conferences.

Bao, L., and E. F. Redish. 2001. Concentration analysis: A quantitative assessment of student states. *American Journal of Physics, Physics Education Research Supplement* 69 (7): S45–53.

Bao, L., K. Hogg, and D. Zollman. 2002. Model analysis of fine structures of student models: An example with Newton's Third Law. *American Journal of Physics, Physics Education Research Supplement* 70 (7): 766–78.

Bassok, M. 1990. Transfer of domain-specific problem-solving procedures. *Journal of Experimental Psychology: Learning, Memory, and Cognition* 16: 522–33.

Bassok, M., and K. Holyoak. 1989. Interdomain transfer between isomorphic topics in algebra and physics. *Journal of Experimental Psychology: Learning, Memory, and Cognition* 15:153–66.

Bransford, J., A. L. Brown, and R. Cocking, eds. 1999. *How people learn: Brain, mind, experience, and school.* Washington DC: National Academy Press.

Champagne, A., L. Klopfer, and J. Anderson. 1980. Factors influencing the learning of classical mechanics. *American Journal of Physics* 48 (11): 1074–79.

Chi, M. T. H., P. J. Feltovich, and R. Glaser. 1981. Categorization and representation of physics problems by experts and novices. *Cognitive Science* 5:121–52.

Clement, J. 1982. Students' preconceptions in introductory mechanics. *American Journal of Physics* 50 (1): 66–71.

Clough, E., and R. Driver. 1986. A study of consistency in the use of students' conceptual frameworks across different task contexts. *Science Education* 70 (4): 473–96.

diSessa, A. 1993. Towards an epistemology of physics. *Cognition and Instruction* 10:105–225.

Eisenberg, T., and T. Dreyfus. 1985. Toward understanding mathematical thinking. In L. Streefland, ed., *Proceedings of the Ninth International Conference for the Psychology of Mathematics Education*, pp. 241–46.

Galili, I., and V. Bar. 1992. Motion implies force: Where to expect vestiges of the misconception? *International Journal of Science Education* 14 (1): 63–81.

Gliner, G. 1989. College students' organization of math word problems in relation to success in problem solving. *School Science and Mathematics* 89 (4): 392–404.

———. 1991. College students' organization of math word problem solving in terms of mathematical structure versus surface structure. *School Science and Mathematics* 91 (2): 105–110.

Halloun, I. A., and D. Hestenes. 1985. Common sense concepts about motion. *American Journal of Physics* 53 (11): 1043–55.

Hestenes, D., M. Wells, and G. Swackhamer. 1992. Force concept inventory. *The Physics Teacher* 30:141–58.

Huffman, D., and P. Heller. 1995. What does the force concept inventory actually measure? *The Physics Teacher* 33:138–43.

Larkin, J. H. 1979. Processing information for effective problem solving. *Engineering Education* 79:285–88.

———. 1983. The role of problem representation in physics. In D. Gentner and A. L. Stevens, eds., *Mental models*, pp. 75–99. Hillsdale, NJ: Lawrence Erlbaum Associates.

Maloney, D. P., and R. S. Siegler. 1993. Conceptual competition in physics learning. *International Journal of Science Education* 15 (3): 283–95.

Marton, F. 1986. Phenomenography—A research approach to investigating different understandings of reality. *Journal of Thought* 21 (3): 28–49.

McDermott, L. C. 1984. Research on conceptual understanding in mechanics. *Physics Today* 27:24–32.

McDermott, L. C., and E. F. Redish. 1999. Resource Letter PER-01: Physics Education Research. *American Journal of Physics* 67 (8): 755–67.

McDermott, L. C., and P. S. Shaffer. 1998. *Tutorials in introductory physics*. New York: Prentice Hall.

Minstrell, J. 1991. Facets of students' knowledge and relevant instruction. In R. Duit, F. Goldberg, and H. Niedderer, eds., *Research in physics learning: Theoretical issues and empirical studies*. Proceedings of an International Workshop, Bremen, Germany, March 4–8, pp. 110–28. University of Kiel, Germany: IPN.

Palmer, D. 1997. The effect of context on students' reasoning about forces. *International Journal of Science Education* 19 (6): 681–96.

Posner, G. J., K. A. Strike, P. W. Hewson, and W. A. Gertzog. 1982. Accommodation of a scientific conception: Toward a theory of conceptual change. *Science Education* 66 (2): 211–27.

Rolls, E. T., and A. Treves. 1998. *Neural networks and brain function*. Oxford: Oxford University Press.

Rumelhart, D. E., G. E. Hinton, and J. L. McClelland. 1986. A general framework for parallel distributed processing. In D. E. Rumelhart, J. L. McClelland, and The PDP Research Group, *Parallel distributed processing: Explorations in the microstructure of cognition*, Vol. 1, *Foundations*. Cambridge: MIT Press.

Schecker, H., and J. Gerdes. 1999. Messung von konzeptualisierungsfähigkeit in der mechanik. Zur aussagekraft des Force Concept Inventory. *Zeitschrift für Didaktik der Naturwissenschaften* 5 (1): 75–89.

Scott, P., H. Asoko, and R. Driver. 1991. Teaching for conceptual change: A review of strategies. In R. Duit, F. Goldberg, and H. Niedderer, eds., *Research in physics learning: Theoretical issues and empirical studies*. University of Kiel, Germany: IPN.

Squire, L. R., A. P. Shimamura, and D. G. Amaral. 1989. Memory and the hippocampus. In J. Byrne and W. O. Berry, eds., *Neural models of plasticity: Theoretical and empirical approaches*, pp. 208–239. New York: Academic Press.

Strang, G. 1988. *Linear algebra and its applications*, 3rd ed. San Diego: Harcourt Brace Jovanovich.

Thornton, R. K. 1994. Conceptual dynamics: Changing student views of force and motion. *Proceedings of the International Conference on Thinking Science for Teaching: The Case of Physics*. Rome, Sept.

Van Hoesen, G. W. 1982. The parahippocampal gyrus: New observations regarding its cortical connections in the monkey. *Trends in Neurosciences* 5 (4): 345–50.

Viennot, L. 1979. Spontaneous reasoning in elementary dynamics. *European Journal of Science Education* 1 (2): 205–21.

Vosniadou, S. 1994. Capturing and modeling the process of conceptual change. *Learning and Instruction* 4 (1): 45–69.

Vosniadou, S., and W. F. Brewer. 1992. Mental models of the earth: A study of conceptual change in childhood. *Cognitive Psychology* 24 (4): 535–85.

Eleven

Quantitative Research on Teaching Methods in Tertiary Education

William E. Becker

Advocates and promoters of specific education methods are heard to say "the research shows that different teaching pedagogy really matters." Education specialist Ramsden (1998, p. 355) asserts: "The picture of what encourages students to learn effectively at university is now almost complete." Anecdotal evidence and arguments based on theory are often provided to support such claims, but quantitative studies of the effects of one teaching method versus another are either not cited or are few in number. DeNeve and Heppner (1997), for example, found that only 12 of the 175 studies identified in a 1992 through 1995 search for "active learning" in the Educational Resources Information Center (ERIC) database made comparisons of active learning techniques with another teaching method. An ERIC search for "Classroom Assessment Techniques" (CATs) undertaken for me by Jillian Kinzicat in 2000 yielded a similar outcome. My own (March 2000) request to CATs specialist Tom Angelo for direction to quantitative studies supporting the effectiveness of CATs yielded some good leads, but in the end there were few quantitative studies employing inferential statistics.

Even when references to quantitative studies are provided, they typically appear with no critique. When advocates point to individual studies or to meta-analyses summarizing quantitative studies, they give little or no attention to the quality or comparability of studies encompassed. When critics, on the other hand, point to a block of literature showing "no significant difference," the meaning of statistical significance is overlooked.[1]

In this study I address the quality of research aimed at assessing alternative teaching methods. I advance the scholarship of teaching and learning by separating empirical results with statistical inference from conjecture about the student outcomes associated with CATs and other teaching strategies aimed at actively engaging students in the learning process. I provide specific criteria for both conducting and exploring the strength of discipline-specific quantitative research into the teaching and learning process. Examples employing statistical inference in the teaching and learning process are used to identify teaching strategies that appear to increase student learning. I focus only on those studies that were identified in the literature searches mentioned above or were called to my attention by education researchers as noteworthy.

Although my review of the education assessment literature is not comprehensive and none of the studies I reviewed were perfect when viewed through the lens of theoretical statistics, there is inferential evidence supporting the hypothesis that periodic use of things like the one-minute paper (wherein an instructor stops class and asks each student to write down what he or she thought was the key point and what still needed clarification at the end of a class period) increases student learning. Similar support could not be found for claims that group activities increase learning or that other time-intensive methods are effective or efficient. This does not say, however, that these alternative teaching techniques do not matter. It simply says that there is not yet compelling statistical evidence saying that they do.

Criteria

A casual review of discipline-specific journals as well as general higher education journals is sufficient for a reader to appreciate the magnitude of literature that provides prescriptions for engaging students in the educational process. Classroom assessment techniques, as popularized by Angelo and Cross (1993), as well as active learning strategies that build on the seven principles of Chickering and Gamson (1987) are advanced as worthwhile alternatives to chalk and talk. The relative dearth of quantitative work aimed at measuring changes in student outcomes associated with one teaching method versus another is surprising given the rhetoric surrounding CATs and the numerous methods that fit under the banner of active and group learning.

A review of the readily available published studies involving statistical inference shows that the intent and methods of inquiry, analysis, and evaluation vary greatly from discipline to discipline. Thus, any attempt to impose a fixed and unique paradigm for aggregating the empirical work on education practices across disciplines is destined to fail.[2] Use of flexible criteria holds some promise for critiquing empirical work involving statistical inferences across diverse studies. For my work here, I employ an 11-point set of criteria that all inferential studies can be expected to address in varying degrees of detail:

1) Statement of topic, with clear hypotheses;
2) Literature review, which establishes the need for and context of the study;
3) Attention to unit of analysis (e.g., individual student versus classroom versus department, etc.), with clear definition of variables and valid measurement;
4) Third-party supplied versus self-reported data;
5) Outcomes and behavioral change measures;
6) Multivariate analyses, which include diverse controls for things other than exposure to the treatment that may influence outcomes (e.g., instructor differences, student aptitude), but that cannot be dismissed by randomization (which typically is not possible in education settings);
7) Truly independent explanatory variables (i.e, recognition of endogeneity problems including simultaneous determination of variables within a system, errors in measuring explanatory variables, etc.);
8) Attention to nonrandomness, including sample selection issues and missing data problems;
9) Appropriate statistical methods of estimation, testing, and interpretation;
10) Robustness of results—check on the sensitivity of results to alternative data sets (replication), alternative model specifications, and different methods of estimation and testing; and
11) Nature and strength of claims and conclusions.

These criteria will be discussed in the context of selected studies from the education assessment literature.

Topics and Hypotheses

The topic of inquiry and associated hypotheses typically are well specified. For example, Hake (1998) in a large-scale study involving data from some 62 different physics courses seeks an answer to the single question: "Can the classroom use of IE (interactive engagement of students in activities that yield immediate feedback) methods increase the effectiveness of introductory mechanics courses well beyond that attained by traditional methods?" (p. 65) The Hake study is somewhat unique in its attempt to measure the learning effect of one set of teaching strategies versus another across a broad set of institutions.[3]

In contrast to Hake's multi-institution study are the typical single-institution and single-course studies as found, for example, in Harwood (1999). Harwood is interested in assessing student response to the introduction of a new feedback form in an accounting course at one institution. Her new feedback form is a variation on the widely used one-minute paper (a CAT) in which an instructor stops class and asks each student to write down what he or she thought was the key point and what still needed clarification at the end of a class period. The instructor collects the students' papers, tabulates the responses (without grading), and discusses the results in the next class meeting (Wilson 1986, p. 199). Harwood (1999) puts forward two explicit hypotheses related to student classroom participation and use of her feedback form:

> H_1: Feedback forms have no effect on student participation in class.
> H_2: Feedback forms and oral in-class participation are equally effective means of eliciting student questions. (p. 57)

Unfortunately, Harwood's final hypothesis involves a compound event (effective and important), which is difficult to interpretation:

> H_3: The effect of feedback forms on student participation and the relative importance of feedback forms as compared to oral in-class participation decline when feedback forms are used all of the time. (p. 58)

Harwood does not address the relationship between class participation and learning in accounting, but Almer, Jones, and Moeckel (1998) do. They provide five hypotheses related to student exam performance and use of the one-minute paper:

> H_1: Students who write one-minute papers will perform better on a subsequent quiz than students who do not write one-minute papers.
> H_1a: Students who write one-minute papers will perform better on a subsequent essay quiz than students who do not write one-minute papers.
> H_1b: Students who write one-minute papers will perform better on a subsequent multiple-choice quiz than students who do not write one-minute papers.
> H_2: Students who address their one-minute papers to a novice audience will perform better on a subsequent quiz than students

who address their papers to the instructor.

H₃: Students whose one-minute papers are graded will perform better on a subsequent quiz than students whose one-minute papers are not graded. (p. 493)

Rather than student performance on tests, course grades are often used as an outcome measure and explicitly identified in the hypothesis to be tested. For example, Trautwein, Racke, and Hillman (1996/1997, p. 186) ask: "Is there a significant difference in lab grades of students in cooperative learning settings versus the traditional, individual approach?" The null hypothesis and alternative hypotheses here are "no difference in grades" versus "a difference in grades." There is no direction in the alternative hypothesis so, at least conceptually, student learning could be negative and still be consistent with the alternative hypothesis. That is, this two-tail test is not as powerful as a one-tail test in which the alternative is "cooperative learning led to higher grades," which is what Trautwein, Racke, and Hillman actually conclude. (More will be said about the use of grades as an outcome measure later.)

Not all empirical work involves clear questions and unique hypotheses for testing. For example, Fabry et al. (1997, p. 9) state "The main purpose of this study was to determine whether our students thought CATs contributed to their level of learning and involvement in the course." Learning and involvement are not two distinct items of analysis in this statement of purpose. One can surely be involved and not learn. Furthermore, what does the "level of learning" mean? If knowledge (or a set of skills, or other attributes of interest) is what one possesses at a point in time (as in a snapshot, single-frame picture), then learning is the change in knowledge from one time period to another (as in moving from one frame to another in a motion picture). The language employed by authors is not always clear on the distinction between knowledge (which is a stock) and learning (which is a flow) as the foregoing examples illustrate.

Literature Review

By and large, authors of empirical studies do a good job summarizing the literature and establishing the need for their work. In some cases, much of an article is devoted to reviewing and extending the theoretical work of the education specialists. For instance, Chen and Hoshower (1998) devoted approximately one-third of their 13 pages of text to discussing the work of educationalists. Harwood (1999), before or in conjunction with the publication of her empirical work, co-authored descriptive pieces with Cottel (1998) and Cohen (1999) that shared their views and the theories of others about the merits of CAT. In stark contrast, Chizmar and Ostrosky (1999) wasted no words in stating that as of the time of their study no prior empirical studies addressed the learning effectiveness (as measured by test scores) of the one-minute paper (see their endnote 3); thus, they established the need for their study.[4]

Valid and Reliable Units of Analysis

The 1960s and 1970s saw debate over the appropriate unit of measurement for assessing the validity of student evaluations of teaching (as reflected, for example, in the relationship between student evaluations of teaching and student outcomes). In the case of end-of-term student evaluations of instructors, an administrator's interest may not be how students as individuals rate the instructor but how the class as a whole rates the instructor. Thus, the unit of measure is an aggregate for the class. There is no unique aggregate, although the class mean or median response is typically used.[5]

For the assessment of CATs and other instructional methods, however, the unit of measurement may arguably be the individual student in a class and not the class as a unit. Is the question: how is the ith student's learning affected by being in a classroom where one versus another teaching method is employed? Or is the question: how is the class's learning affected by one method versus another? The question (and answer) has implications for the statistics employed.

Hake (1998) reports that he has test scores for 6,542 individual students in 62 introductory physics courses. He works only with mean scores for the classes; thus, his effective sample size is 62, and not 6,542. The 6,542 students are not irrelevant, but they enter in a way that I did not find mentioned by Hake. The amount of variability around a mean test score for a class of 20 students versus a mean for 200 students cannot be expected to be the same. Estimation of a standard error for a sample of 62, where each of the 62 means receives an equal weight, ignores this heterogeneity.[6] Francisco, Trautman, and Nicoll (1998) recognize that the number of subjects in each group implies heterogeneity in their analysis of average gain scores in an introductory chemistry course. Similarly, Kennedy and Siegfried (1997) make an adjustment for heterogeneity in their study of class size on student learning in economics.

Fleisher, Hashimoto, and Weinberg (2002) consider the effectiveness (in terms of course grade and persistence) of 47 foreign graduate student instructors versus 21 native English-speaking graduate student instructors in an environment in which English is the language of the majority of their undergraduate students. Fleisher, Hashimoto, and Weinberg recognize the loss of information in using the 92 mean class grades for these 68 graduate student instructors, although they do report aggregate mean class grade effects with the corrected heterogeneity adjustment for standard errors based on class size. They prefer to look at 2,680 individual undergraduate results conditional on which one of the 68 graduate student instructors each of the undergraduates had in any one of 92 sections of the course. To ensure that their standard errors did not overstate the precision of their estimates when using the individual student data, Fleisher, Hashimoto, and Weinberg explicitly adjusted their standard errors for the clustering of the individual student observations into classes using a procedure developed by Moulton (1986).[7]

Whatever the unit of measure for the dependent variable (aggregate or individual) the important point here is recognition of the need for one of two adjustments that must be made to get the correct standard errors. If an aggregate unit is employed (e.g., class means) then an adjustment for the number of observations making up the aggregate is required. If individual observations share a common component (e.g., students grouped into classes) then the standard errors reflect this clustering. Computer programs like STATA and LIMDEP can automatically perform both of these adjustments.

No matter how appealing the questions posed by the study are, answering the questions depends on the researcher's ability to articulate the dependent and independent variables involved and to define them in a measurable way. The care with which researchers introduce their variables is mixed, but in one way or another they must address the measurement issue: What is the stochastic event that gives rise to the numerical values of interest (the random process)? Does the instrument measure what it reports to measure (validity)? Are the responses consistent within the instrument, across examinees, and/or over time (reliability)?[8]

Standardized aptitude or achievement test scores may be the most studied measure of academic performance. I suspect that there are nationally normed testing instruments at the introductory college levels in every major discipline—at a minimum, the Advanced Placement exams of ETS. There are volumes written on the validity and reliability of the SAT, ACT, GRE, and the like. Later in this chapter I comment on the appropriate use of standardized test scores, assuming that those who construct a discipline-specific, nationally normed exam at least strive for face validity (a group of experts say the exam questions and answers are correct) and internal reliability (each question tends to rank students as does the overall test).

Historically, standardized tests tend to be multiple-choice, although national tests like the advanced placement (AP) exams now also have essay components. Wright et al. (1997) report the use of a unique test score measure: 25 volunteer faculty members from external departments conducted independent oral examinations of students. As with the grading of written essay-exam answers, maintaining reliability across examiners is a problem that requires elaborate protocols for scoring. Wright et al. (1997) employed adequate controls for reliability but because the exams were oral, and the difference between the student skills emphasized in the lecture approach and in the cooperative learning approach was so severe, it is difficult to imagine that the faculty member examiners could not tell whether each student being examined was from the control or experimental group; thus, the possibility of contamination cannot be dismissed.

Whether multiple-choice (fixed response) questions, essay (constructed response) questions or oral exams measure different dimensions of knowledge is a topic that is and will continue to be hotly debated. Becker and Johnston (1999) address the simultaneity between alternative forms of testing and the lack of information that can be derived from the simple observation that essay and multiple-choice test scores are correlated. As this debate continues researchers have no choice but to use the available content tests or consider alternatives of yet more subjective forms. Self-created instruments must be treated as suspect. Fabry et al. (1997), for example, focus their analysis on student answers to the question: "Do you think CATs enhanced your learning/participation in the course?" (p. 9). Written responses were converted to a three-point scale (yes, maybe/somewhat, no). Although Fabry et al. report only the number of yes responses, converting these responses to a numerical value on a number line is meaningless. Any three ordered values could be used, but the distance between them on the number line is irrelevant. To explain unordered and discrete responses, researchers should consider the estimation of multinomial logit or probit models discussed in Greene (2003).

More troubling with respect to the study by Fabry et al. are the facts that they never define the word "enhance," and they do not specify whether learning and participation are to be treated as synonyms, substitutes, or as an and/or statement. In addition, there is a framing problem. The scale is loaded away from the negative side. By random draw there is only a one-third chance of getting a response of "no enhanced learning/participation." These are classic problems found in invalid instruments; that is, a one-to-one mapping does not exist between the survey question and the responses.

Fabry et al. (1997) also aggregated student responses over four instructors who each used a different combination of CATs in the four different courses each taught. How can we distinguish if it is the effect of the instructors or the set of techniques that is being captured? This is a clear problem of aggregation that cannot be disentangled to get a valid answer about what is being measured.

Student evaluations of teaching are often used to answer questions of effectiveness, which raises another issue of validity: Do student evaluations measure teaching effectiveness? Becker (2000) argues that there is little reason to believe that student evaluations of teaching capture all the elements or the most important elements of good teaching. As measured by correlation coefficients in the neighborhood of 0.7, and often less, end-of-term student evaluation scores explain less than 50 percent of the variability in other teaching outcomes, such as test scores, scores from trained classroom observers, post-course alumni surveys, and so on.[9]

Other questions of validity arise when course grades are used as the measure of knowledge. Are individual exam grades just a measure of student knowledge at the time of the assessment? Do course grades reflect student end-of-term knowledge, learning (from the beginning to the end of the term), rate of improvement, or something even more subjective? Finally, grades may not be reliably assigned across instructors or over time. To establish validity of grades among a group of instructors elaborate protocols would have to be in place. Each student would have to be graded by more than one evaluator with the resulting distribution of students and their grades being roughly the same across evaluators.

Indices of performance are sometimes created to serve as explanatory variables as well as the outcome measure to be explained. Indices used to represent an aggregate can be difficult if not impossible to interpret. Kuh, Pace, and Vesper (1997), for example, create a single index they call "active learning," from 25 items related to student work and student personal development interests. They then use this active learning index score as one of several indices included as independent variables in a least-squares regression aimed at explaining an index of what students perceive they gained from attending college. Their estimated slope coefficient for females tells us that a one unit increase in the active learning index increases the predicted student's gain index by 0.30, holding all else fixed.[10] But what exactly does this tell us?

Kuh, Pace, and Vesper (1997) provide multivariate analysis of students' perceived gains, including covariate indices for student back-ground variables, and institutional variables as well as the measures for good educational practices such as active learning. Their study is in the tradition of input-output or production function analysis advanced by economists in the 1960s. Ramsden (1998, pp. 352–354), on the other hand, relies on bivariate comparisons to paint his picture of what en-courages university students to learn effectively. He provides a scatter plot showing a positive relationship between a y-axis index for his "deep approach" (aimed at student understanding versus "surface learning") and an x-axis index of "good teaching" (including feedback of assessed work, clear goals, etc.), Figure 11.1.

Ramsden's regression ($y = 18.960 + 0.35307x$) implies that a zero on the good teaching index predicts 18.960 index units of the deep ap-proach. A decrease (increase) in the good teaching index by one unit leads to a 0.35307 decrease (increase) in the predicted deep approach index. The predicted deep approach index does not become negative (surface approach?) until the good teaching index is well into the nega-tive numbers (bad teaching?) at a value of -53.605.[11] What is the pos-sible relevance of these numbers for the instructor? What specific infor-mation does this yield that could guide institutional policy?

Self-Reported Data

Frequently in classroom assessment work, data on students are obtained from the students themselves even though students err greatly in the data they self-report (Maxwell and Lopus 1994) or fail to report infor-mation as requested (Becker and Powers 2001).

Kuh, Pace, and Vesper (1997) recognize the controversial nature of using self-reported data but in essence argue that it is not unusual and that in the absence of other options it has become accepted prac-tice. When the problems of self-reported data are considered, it is the validity and reliability of the dependent variable (self-reported achieve-ment, gain, satisfaction, etc.) that is typically addressed. Overlooked is the bias in coefficient estimators caused by measurement errors in the explanatory variables. An ordinary least-squares estimator of a slope co-efficient in a regression of y on x is unbiased if the x is truly indepen-dent (which requires that causality runs from x to y, and not simultane-ously from y to x, and/or that x is measured with no error). As long as the expected value of y at each value of x is equal to the true mean of y conditioned on x, measurement error in y is not a problem in regression analysis. It is the measurement error in x that leads to the classic regres-sion to the mean phenomenon that plagues education-achievement-

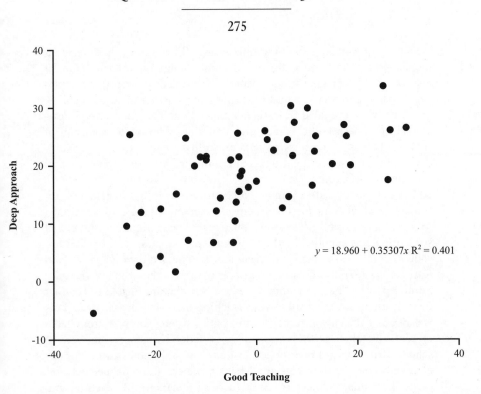

Figure 11.1 Deep approach and good teaching

equation estimates (as demonstrated mathematically in several endnotes to this chapter).

Institutional procedures regarding human subject research and registrars' misconceived policies blocking access to student data in the name of the Buckley Amendment may be the biggest obstacles to quality evaluation of CATs and other active learning methods. (The Family Educational Rights and Privacy Act explicitly enables teachers to have access to student information for the purpose of improving instruction, http://www.ed.gov/offices/OM/fpco/ferpa/ferparegs.html#9931.) Many authors report that they were prevented from getting actual individual student data from university records but were free to seek self-reported data from students. For example, Almer, Jones and Moeckel (1998) report that institutional policy precluded them from directly obtaining SAT and GPA information from student records (p. 491). They obtained 539 self-reported GPAs and 295 SAT scores from the 867 students in their final sample. Both measures of ability were found to be highly significant in explaining quiz scores. They report, however, that inclusion of either ability measure did not change the interpretation of results: the use of one-minute papers raises student performance. Because of the potential for bias resulting from missing data, both ability measures were excluded from their reported analyses. Becker and Powers (2001), on the other hand, find that the inclusion or exclusion of potentially biased and missing data on ability measures and other standard covariates was critical to accuracy in assessing the importance of class size in learning.

There is no consistency among institutions regarding instructors' access to student data for classroom assessment studies. For example, Maxwell and Lopus (1994) were able to get access to actual individual student data as supplied by their institution's registrar in their study to show the misleading nature of student self-reported data. Chizmar and Ostrosky (1999) also obtained registrar data for their study of the one-minute paper. The complaints of educators who are unable to conduct investigations aimed at improving teaching are well documented. This is especially the case at research universities where administrators' fears of reprisals (such as the withholding of federal funds to the medical school) drive institutional policies in any and all studies involving human subjects. Legal experts are debating the extension of medical protocols in human subject research to the scholarship of teaching and learning (Gunsalus 2002). The expansion and rigid application by institutional review boards of policies intended for medical clinical trials involving human subjects to studies aimed at teaching and learning, and the erroneous application of the Family Educational Rights and Privacy Act (Buckley Amendment) barring the release of student information for studies that are explicitly aimed at improving instruction are two hurdles that are causing some scholars to abandon efforts to undertake empirical study of the educational process.

Outcomes and Study Design

As already discussed, numerous measures have been proposed and used to assess knowledge (cognitive domain) and attitudes (affective domain) relevant to student development. If truly randomized experiments could be designed and conducted in education, as advanced by Campbell, Stanley, and Gage (1963) for example, then a researcher interested in assessing cognitive-domain or affective-domain outcomes of a given classroom treatment need only administer an achievement test or attitude survey at the end of the program to those randomly assigned to the treatment and control groups. There would be no need for pre-treatment measures. Consequences other than the treatment effect could be dismissed with reference to the law of large numbers (i.e., the distribution of a statistic to be calculated from a random sample degenerates or collapses on its expected value as the sample size increases).

Unfortunately, no one has ever designed an absolutely perfect experiment—randomization is not an absolute; it is achieved in degrees. The best we can do in social science research is to select the treatment and control groups so that they are sharply distinct and yet represent events that could happen to anyone (Rosenbaum 1999). The difficulty is finding a believable counterfactual: If the ith person is in the control (experimental) group, what would have happened if someone like this person had been in the experimental (control) group?[12]

Instead of talking about final achievement, researchers attempt to adjust for lack of randomness in starting positions by addressing the learning effect of one treatment versus another. The most obvious measure of the learning outcome is the difference between a pretest (test given to students at the start of a program or course of study—i.e., pretreatment) and posttest (test given at the end—i.e., post-treatment). Similarly, for changes in attitudes an instrument to assess the difference between a "presurvey" and "postsurvey" can be constructed. The study design for assessing the treatment effect is then called "a difference in differences design" in which the difference between the pretest and posttest differences for the treatment and control groups is compared. Unfortunately, calculation and comparison of these "change scores" or "value-added measures" are fraught with problems that go beyond the psychometric issues of the validity and reliability of the instruments (as already discussed).

Researchers interested in examining the effect of a treatment occasionally use the final grade in a course. As already stated, it is never clear whether the course grade is intended to measure the student's final position (post-knowledge) or improvement (post-knowledge minus pre-knowledge). Whether it is assigned on a relative basis (one student's performance versus another's) or absolute scale has implications as to what can be assessed by a comparison of grades. For many statistical procedures, a normal distribution is assumed to be generating the outcome measures. When grades are used as the outcome measure, the researcher must be concerned about the ceiling (typically 4.00) and the discrete nature of grades (as in A, B, C). The normal distribution is continuous with an infinite number of values and thus it is not appropriate when letter grades are the outcome measure.

Anaya (1999, p. 505) proposes the use of a "residual gain score" for assessing the entire undergraduate experience. She regresses end-of-undergraduate experience GRE scores on pre–undergraduate SAT scores, obtains residuals from this regression, which she calls the "residual gain score," and then regresses these residuals on explanatory variables of interest. Conceptually, one can easily adopt this process to individual courses using GPA or other aggregates. For example, in stage one, end-of-term numerical course grades can be regressed as a postscore on matched students' GPAs at the start of the course as a prescore. In stage two, the residuals from this regression are regressed on a zero- or one-valued covariate (for control or experimental identification) and other explanatory variables. Unfortunately, this "residual gain score" model is inconsistent. If the residual gain score is a function of known explanatory variables, why isn't the posttest a function of these same variables?[13]

Numerous transformations of test scores have been proposed as the student outcome of the teaching process. Becker (1982), for example, put forward a theoretical model of student achievement associated with the optimum allocation of time in which the appropriate outcome is a logarithmic transformation of student achievement. This model was estimated by Gleason and Walstad (1988). A log transformation has the greatest effect on extreme high values. Often, when the posttest or the posttest-minus-pretest change score is used as the dependent variable, extreme high values are not a problem because the maximum score on a test is achieved (the ceiling effect). This truncation causes a special problem in modeling achievement and learning because an achievable ceiling implies that those with high pretest scores cannot become measurably better. It also implies that test scores cannot be assumed to be normally distributed as required for most testing situations.

One modern way to handle ceiling effects is to estimate a Tobit model (named after Nobel Laureate in economics James Tobin), which involves an estimate of each student achieving the ceiling and then simultaneously adjusting the regression in accordance. Before maximum likelihood computer programs were readily available to estimate Tobit models, a few psychologists and economists advanced a gap-closing measure as the dependent variable for studies of educational methods where ceiling effects +might be present:

$$g = gap\ closing = \frac{posttest\ score - pretest\ score}{maximum\ score - pretest\ score}$$

The three test scores (*maximum score, posttest score,* and *pretest score*) could be defined for the individual student or as average measures for a group of students. The "average *g*" assigned to a group could be obtained from averaging the g calculated for each student in the group or it could be obtained from the test score averages for the group. The resulting average g from these two methods need not be the same; that is, results may be sensitive to the average method employed.

Hake (1998) measured the pretest and posttest scores by the respective classroom averages on a standardized physics test. Unfortunately, in 1998 Hake was unaware of the literature on the gap-closing model. The outcome measure g is algebraically related to the starting position of the student as reflected in the pretest: g falls as the *pretest score* rises, for *maximum score* > *posttest score* > *pretest score*.[14] Any attempt to regress a posttest-minus-pretest change score, or its standardized gap-closing measure g on a pretest score yields a biased estimate of the pretest effect.[15]

Almost universally now researchers in education attempt to measure a treatment effect by some variant of student behavioral change over the life of the treatment. They seldom address what the value of that change score is to the student and society. Students may place little value on performing well on an exam that does not count. The market for undergraduates does not place a value on change; it values the final level of accomplishment. Employers buy graduates' contemporaneous aptitudes and skills, not the change in test scores or change in opinions. What the student knew four years ago in the first semester of the freshman year or what he or she may have learned in any given course is irrelevant to the employer, except insofar as it affects the rate of learning. Knowing the level of a test score or the difference between test scores is of little career help to a student or society without knowing the value the market places on these measures.

Knowledge of test scores may have administrative value to the classroom teacher, but that may have little relationship to the economic concept of value. Just as water has a high "value in use" but a low "value in exchange," some basic skills, such as an ability to reconcile a checkbook, may have high value in use but low value in exchange. Other skills may have a high value at one point in time and little value at another; for example, the ability to manipulate a slide rule fell in value with the availability of the inexpensive hand calculator; the ability to manipulate the handheld calculator fell in value with the advance of spreadsheets, MathCAD, and statistical computer packages. Although some skills may be viewed as essential for education, their market value is determined by demand and supply. The normative beliefs of a faculty member, department chair, curriculum committee, central administrator or university board of governance member about the importance of intellectual skills are elusive without reference to what employers are paying for the bundle of skills embodied in graduates, and what skills they desire from the graduates. (The satisfaction derived from learning and its change score measurement modeled in Becker [1982] is ignored here in the interest of brevity.)

Hansen, Kelley, and Weisbrod (1970) called attention to the problem of valuing multi-dimensional student learning and its implications for curriculum reform but few have followed their lead. As they state, who receives the benefits of instruction and how they weight those benefits will affect the valuation. In assessing benefits, researchers can explore the effect of instruction in a specific subject on the decisions of unequally endowed students to go to university and to major in that subject. The study by Beron (1990) on student knowledge and the desire to take additional courses is a good beginning in seeking answers to questions about the alternative ways in which students and teachers value discipline-specific knowledge. Fournier and Sass (2000) provide a good example of modeling student choice in course selection and persistence.

Once we move beyond looking at a single teaching outcome, the question is: using multiple outcomes and multiple inputs, are the teachers and/or students technically efficient in combining the inputs and the outcomes? A teacher and/or student is technically inefficient if, when compared to other teachers and/or students with similar levels of inputs, greater student outcomes could be achieved without increasing input use, or equivalently the same level of student outcomes could be achieved with fewer inputs. Conceptually, although this is difficult in practice as seen in the production function estimates of Anaya (1999), Kuh, Pace, and Vesper (1997), and others, regression residuals could be used to suggest inefficiencies. DEA (data envelope analysis) is a linear programming technique for evaluating the efficiency of decision-makers when there are multiple outcomes. DEA could be used to determine whether the teacher and/or student exhibits best practices or, if not, how far from the frontier of best practices the teacher and/or student lies.

Unfortunately, no one engaged in education research on teaching and learning has yet used DEA in a meaningful way for classroom teaching practices. Lehmann and Warning (2003) attempt to assess efficiency of United Kingdom universities in producing research and teaching but their teaching input measures (e.g., number of teachers and expenditures on libraries) and the teaching outputs measures (e.g., drop-out rate, employment of grads) are too broad to extract recommendations about teaching practices. Johnes and Johnes (1995) and Thursby (2000) provide applications to research outputs and inputs of economics departments in the United Kingdom and the United States, respectively, where the research outputs are counts on department publications, citations, and numbers of Ph.D.s awarded in a fixed time period, but again no implications for teaching can be extracted. Surveys of the DEA method are provided by Lovell (1993) and Ali and Seiford (1993).

Input Covariates in Multivariate Analyses

If truly random experiments could be designed and conducted in education, then a multivariate analysis with covariates to control for consequences other than the treatment effects would not be needed. But, as already stated, no one has ever designed and no one likely ever will design a perfect experiment in education: recall that randomization should be thought of in degrees rather than as an absolute.

Almer, Jones, and Moeckel (1998) provide a good example of a study in accounting classes that attempts to randomize applications of multilevel treatments (different combinations of types of one-minute paper and quiz types) across classrooms. But even following the random assignment of treatments, Almer, Jones, and Moeckel recognize the need to control for differences in student ability, as well as other covariates believed to influence student performance. They use analysis of variance (ANOVA) to determine the effect of different types of one-minute papers on multiple-choice and essay response quiz scores. This type of study design and method of analysis is in keeping with the laboratory science view advanced by Campbell, Stanley, and Gage (1963).

As noted early, educationalists have adopted the economist's view that learning involves a production function in which student and teacher inputs give rise to outputs. A regression function is specified for this input-output analysis. For example, Kuh, Pace, and Vesper (1997) estimate a regression in which students' perceived gains (the outputs) are produced by input indices for student background variables, institutional variables and measures for good educational practices (active learning). A traditional ANOVA table, like that found in Almer, Jones, and Moeckel (1998), can be produced as a part of any regression analysis. Unlike the traditional ANOVA analyses, however, regression modeling makes assumptions explicit, provides estimates of effect sizes directly, and extends to more complex analyses necessitated by data limitations and violations of assumptions that are algebraically tractable. Traditional ANOVA is driven by the design of the experiment whereas production function and regression equation specifications are driven by theory.

In a typical production function (or input-output) study, a standardized multiple-choice test is used to measure each student's knowledge of the subject at the beginning (pretest) and end of a program (post-test). A change score for each student is calculated as the difference between his or her post-program score and pre-program score. The post-program scores, the change scores, or any one of several transformations of post and pre-program scores are assumed to be produced by human-specific attributes of the students (called human capital: e.g., SAT or ACT scores, initial subject knowledge, grade points, previous courses of study), utilization measures (e.g., time spent by student or teacher in given activities), and technology, environment or mode of delivery (e.g., lectures, group work, computer use). Of all the variations considered by researchers, the only consistently significant and meaningful explanatory variables of student final achievement are pre-aptitude/achievement measures such as SAT/ACT scores, GPA, class rank, etc. (As discussed in the next section, even the importance of and the manner in which time enters the learning equation is debated.) The policy implications could not be more clear: in order to produce students who are highly knowledgeable in a subject, start with those who already have a high ability.[16] The implications for educational research are likewise clear: unless covariates for students' aptitudes and/or prior skill levels are included in the explanation of learning, the results are suspect.[17]

The input-output approach (as well as traditional ANOVA) has five problems. First, production functions are only one part of a student's decision-making system. Observed inputs (covariates) are not exogenous but are determined within this system. Second, data loss and the resulting prospect for sample-selection bias in the standard pretest and posttest design are substantial, with 20 to 40 percent of those enrolled in large classes who take a pretest no longer enrolled at the time of the posttest. Third, from probability and statistical theory, we know that failure to reject the null hypothesis does not imply its acceptance. Because an experimental teaching method shows no statistically significant improvement over the lecture does not imply that it is not better. Fourth, although an aptitude/ability measure is essential in the explanation of final student achievement, how this covariate enters the system is not trivial because measurement error in explanatory variables implies bias in the coefficient estimators. Fifth, as already discussed, education is a multi-product output that cannot be reflected in a single multiple-choice test score. These problems with the application of the production function mind-set are being addressed by econometricians and psychometricians, as seen for example in the new RAND corporation study of class size in California and the exchange between Rosenbaum (1999) and four commenters in *Statistical Science* (August 1999) on design rules and methods of estimation for quasi-experiments.

Endogeneity in a Student Decision-Making Framework

There are theoretical models of student behavior that provide a rationale for why researchers fail to find consistent evidence of the superiority of one teaching technique over another in the production of learning. For example, Becker (1982) constructed a model in which a student maximizes the utility (or satisfaction) of different forms of knowledge, current consumption, and expected future income.[18] This utility maximization is subject to a time constraint, to the production relationships that enable the student to acquire knowledge and to consume out of income, and to the manner in which the different forms of knowledge are measured and enter into future income. The "prices" of different forms of knowledge reflect opportunity costs generated by the time constraint, production functions, and uncertain future income. The desired student outcomes and time allocation decisions are endogenous or determined simultaneously within the system.

Becker's (1982) model shows that improved teaching technology that enables students to more efficiently convert study time into knowledge in one subject need not result in any change in student desire for more of that knowledge. The time savings that result from the more efficient pedagogy in one course of study may be invested by the student in the acquisition of knowledge in other subjects or may be used for market work or leisure. The "prices" of the different forms of knowledge and the marginal utility of each form of knowledge, leisure, and future income in equilibrium determine student choices. It is not only the production function relationship that gives rise to a certain mix of inputs being combined to produce a given output. The levels of the outputs and inputs are simultaneously determined; the inputs do not cause the outputs in the unidirectional sense that independent variables determine the dependent variable.

Allgood (2001) modifies Becker's (1982) model to show the lack of student effort when students are targeting grade levels in a given subject for which a new teaching or learning technology has been introduced. These models make explicit how rewards for academic achievement in one subject affect achievement in that subject as well as other subjects that jointly enter a student's decision-making framework as endogenous inputs that are simultaneously determined in the student's choices. Researchers working with the test-score data are thus wise to check if students take the tests seriously. Unfortunately, many educators continue to overlook the effect of incentives on measured student performance.

In their study of time on task, Admiraal, Wubbels, and Pilot (1999) do not recognize that observed student allocation of time and output produced are endogenous. An observation of a reduction in time students devote to a subject (following the introduction of an alternative teaching technique in the subject) without a decrease in achievement can result from the introduction of an efficient teaching/learning technique. On the other hand, observing no difference in achievement but an increase in time students devote to the subject suggests the introduction of an inefficient method. Such may be the case for the cooperative learning, group-oriented, and open-ended question approach (structured active learning sections, SAL) versus the lecture style, and challenging quantitative, individualized homework and test questions (response learning, RL) in the work of Wright et al. (1997). They report that after an experiment at the University of Wisconsin-Madison in which SAL and RL sections in chemistry were taught at the "high end of the performance scale . . . students in both sections had performed equivalently" (p. 4), but SAL students spent 15 percent more time in out-of-class work than RL students.[19] Although Wright et al. report other worthwhile affective domain differences, on the basis of the oral examination results, the cooperative learning, group-oriented, and open-ended question approach of the structured active learning approach was inefficient. Proponents of cooperative learning such as Klionsky (1998, p. 336), when confronted with their own students' negative reaction regarding time usage, quip: "they have a hard time objectively judging its advantages or disadvantages."

Data Loss and Sample Selection

Becker and Powers (2001) show how studies including only those students who provide data on themselves and persist to the end of the semester are suspect in assessing the contribution of class size in student learning.[20] Missing data points could be caused by students failing to report, data collectors failing to transmit the information, the researcher "cleaning the data" to remove unwanted items, or students simply not providing the data. Unlike inanimate objects or animals in a laboratory study, students as well as their instructors can self-select into and out of studies.

Well-designed studies such as that of Wright et al. (1997) address issues of self-selection into treatment groups. But few studies outside of economics consider the fact that a sizeable proportion of students who enroll in introductory courses subsequently withdraw, never completing the end-of-course evaluation or final exam. A typical study of the gain or change scores from the beginning to the end of the course excludes all who do not complete a posttest. The process that determines which students quit between the pretest and the posttest is likely related to the process that determines test scores. That is, both persistence and final exam score are related in the student decision-making process (they are endogenous). Becker and Powers provide probit model estimates (which are simultaneously done with the estimation of the achievement equation via maximum likelihood routines) showing, all else equal, that individual students with higher pre-course knowledge of economics are more prone to persist with the course than those with lower pre-course knowledge; and those in smaller classes are likewise more likely to persist to the final exam.[21] Controlling for persistence, class size does affect student learning.

When studies ignore the class size and sample selection issues, readers should question the study's findings regardless of the sample size or diversity in explanatory variables.[22] Hake (1998), for example, does not call attention to the fact that his control group, which made little or no use of interactive-engaging teaching methods, had a mean class size of 148.9 students (14 classes and 2,084 students), but his experimental class size average was only 92.9 students (48 classes and 4,458 students). Hake gives us no indication of beginning versus ending enrollments, which is critical information if one wants to address the consequence of attrition. Admiraal, Wubbels, and Pilot (1999) acknowledge that missing data could be a problem but have no idea of how to deal with the fact that in their two courses only 44.2 percent (349 of 790 students) and 36.6 percent (133 of 363 students) of enrolled students attended the exam and the seminar where questionnaires were administered. This is particularly troubling because one of the objectives of their study is to see how time on task, as reported on the questionnaires, affects exam performance.

The timing of withdrawal from a course is related to many of the same variables that determine test scores (Anderson, Benjamin and Fuss 1994). For example, taking high school calculus and economics contributed greatly to a student's desire to complete the entire two-semester college economics course. However, more experienced students were more likely to drop sooner; they did not stick around if they saw "the handwriting on the wall." Consistent with these results, Douglas and Sulock (1995) conclude that prior experience with economics, accounting, and mathematics, as well as class attendance, all increase the probability of a student completing an economics course. They also show how correction for self-selection out of the course influenced the production function relationship between the standard input measures and the course grades of those who stayed, even though the course drop rate was only 12 percent. Becker and Walstad (1990) reveal yet another source of selection bias when test scores are to be explained; if test administration is voluntary, teachers who observe that their average class score is low on the pretest may not administer the posttest. This is a problem for multi-institution studies, such as that described in Hake (1998) where instructors elected to participate, administer tests and transmit data.

As already stated, missing observations on key explanatory variables can also devastate a large data set. Students and their instructors are selective in what data they provide, and those collecting and processing the data may be selective in what they report. Because there is no unique way to undo the censoring that is associated with missing data, any conclusion drawn only from students and their instructors who provide data must be viewed with skepticism regardless of the sample size. This point was lost on Piccinin (1999) in his study of how advocates of alternative teaching methods affect teaching and learning. His outcome measure was a classroom mean score from a multi–item student evaluation form. Of interest was whether any of three different levels of consultation by teaching resource center staff members with instructors had an effect on student evaluations of the instructors. (Levels of consultation: FC = interview/discussion between instructor and consultant; FCO = FC plus observation of classroom by consultant; and FCOS = FCO plus meeting between consultant and instructor's students.)

Of the 165 instructors who consulted the teaching center during a seven-year period, 91 had data at the time of consulting (Pre 2) and at the end of the semester or year after consulting (Post 1), and only 80 had data three years after consultation (Post 2). Although we do not have the individual instructor data (which is needed for an analysis of selection), the discussion provided by Piccinin gives some idea of the potential selection problems. Piccinin reports that assistant professors are overrepresented in FC group. That the t statistic (based on an assumption of identical population variances) rises from -0.3378 (for Post 1 minus Pre 2 mean changes) to a significant 2.2307 (for Post 2 minus Pre 2 mean changes) may be the result of three low-ranking faculty members being terminated. At the other extreme, the relatively low-scoring senior faculty member in the time-intensive FCOS group could be demonstrating nothing more than regression or self-selection into this group.

In the absence of perfect randomized experiments, with no entry or exit, selection problems at some point in the sampling process can always be identified. But should we care if we cannot teach a subject to the uninterested and unwilling? We are always going to be teaching to self-selected individuals, so why should our experiments not reflect the actual conditions under which we work? Why worry about what does not apply?[23] On the other hand, if building enrollment in our programs and departments is important, then the previously uninterested students are the ones that must be attracted. We need to understand the selection process in students choosing and persisting in courses, as well as in measuring their learning.

Tests for the Effects of Instructional Variables

Hanushek (1991, 1994) and others writing in the economics of education literature in the 1980s and early 1990s advanced the notion that instructional variables (class size, teacher qualifications, and expenditures on the like) are unimportant in explaining student learning.[24] More recently the vote-counting meta-analysis employed by Hanushek has come under attack by educationalists, Hedges, Lane, and Greeenwald (1994a,b), and economist Krueger (2000).[25] Regardless of the merits of the Hedges et al. and Krueger challenges, Hanushek's or any other researcher's conclusion that certain instructional variables are insignificant in explaining student test scores (and thus acceptance of the null hypothesis of no average effect in the populations is confirmed) is wrong.

Statisticians cringe at the idea of "accepting the null hypothesis." The null hypothesis of no learning effect can never be accepted for there is always another hypothesized value, in the direction of the alternative hypothesis, that cannot be rejected with the same sample data and level of significance. The Type II error inherent in accepting the null hypothesis is well known but largely ignored by researchers.

The power of the test (one minus the probability of not rejecting the null hypothesis when the null is false) can always be raised by increasing the sample size. Thus, if statistical significance is the criterion for a successful instructional method, then ever-larger sample sizes will "deliver the goods." Statistical significance of an instructional method might be demonstrated with a sufficiently large sample, but the difference in change scores will likely be trivial on multiple-choice tests with 25 to 40 items (the number of questions typically required to demonstrate an internally reliable test that able students can complete in a 50- to 75-

minute period). Differences of only a few correct answers in pretest and posttest comparisons of control and experimental group results are the rule, not the exception, even after adjusting for sample selection.

Similar to small changes in test scores producing statistically significant difference of no practical importance, student evaluations of instructors can produce statistically significant differences with no real difference in teacher performance. For instance, Piccinin (1999, pp. 77–78) reports that the 0.28 point increase in mean aggregated student evaluation scores from 3.77 to 4.05, for those consulting with a teaching specialist, is statistically significant, but the 0.16 point decrease from 4.01 to 3.85, for those also observed in the classroom, is not. What is the practical meaning of the 0.16 difference? As psychologist McKeachie (1997, p. 1223), a longtime provider of college teaching tips, puts it: "Presentation of numerical means or medians (often to two decimal places) leads to making decisions based on small numerical differences—differences that are unlikely to distinguish between competent and incompetent teachers."

That "practical importance" is more relevant than "statistical significance" does not tell us to ignore p-values, the standard errors on which they are based, or other measures of dispersion. Klionsky's (1998) failure to report standard errors or any other descriptive statistics related to variability makes it impossible to assess the sensitivity of the estimate to random sampling error. Recent emphasis on reporting "effect sizes" without reference to standard errors, statistical significance and the interpretation of unstandardized magnitudes, as seen for example in Admiraal, Wubbels, and Pilot (1999), ignores the insights that can be gained from this information. The point is not whether descriptive statistics (means, standard errors, etc.) of actual magnitudes should be reported—they should. The point is that researchers cannot blindly use the sharp edge of critical values in hypotheses testing.

As already suggested, one of the myths of educational research is that students in a classroom can be treated as if they were randomly assigned rats in a laboratory experiment where descriptive statistics are sufficient for analysis. This is seen in much of the discussions involving the reporting of "effect size" (e.g., a confidence interval: estimator + margin of error). These discussions typically focus on which one of the dozens of measures of effect size is best for meta-analysis (Elmore and Rotou 2001; Thompson 2002) with only passing reference to estimator bias resulting from sampling problems and model misspecifications.

Conceptually, results from multiple studies employing the same outcomes and descriptive statistics could be aggregated to form a meta-analysis; however, any statistician who has attempted to conduct a meaningful meta-analysis must be bothered by the fact that there is no unique way to perform the aggregation. The fact that there are numerous articles advocating one or another method of aggregation should lead even the naive researcher to be suspicious. When considering doing meta-analysis or relying on the results of a meta-analysis there are at least five issues to consider.

First, there may be no way to interpret combined results from studies employing diverse models and estimation methods. For example, what is the meaning of two apples plus three oranges equaling five fruit?

Second, the order in which comparisons are made may affect the results. For example, assume one researcher says teaching/learning method A is preferred to B, which is preferred to C. A second researcher says method B is preferred to C, which is preferred to A; and a third researcher says method C is preferred to A, which is preferred to B. What is the preferred teaching/learning method across these three researchers if we first assess whether A is preferred to B, with the winning A or B method then compared to C? Instead, what is the preferred teaching/learning method across these three researchers if we first ask if B is preferred to C, with the winning B or C method then compared with A? Nobel Laureate in economics Kenneth Arrow (1951) recognized this and related paradoxes of voting behavior and aggregation schema with his "Impossibility Theorem."

A third example of an aggregation problem in sampling was provided by Jessica Utts (1991) at a History of Philosophy of Science seminar at the University of California at Davis:

Professors A and B each plans to run a fixed number of Bernoulli trials to test

$$H_0: p = 0.25 \text{ versus } H_A: p > 0.25$$

Professor A has access to large numbers of students each semester to use as subjects. In his first experiment, he runs 100 subjects, and there are 33 successes (p-value = 0.04, one-tailed). Knowing the importance of replication, Professor A runs an additional 100 subjects as a second experiment. He finds 36 successes (p-value = 0.009, one-tailed).

Professor B teaches only small classes. Each quarter, she runs an experiment on her students to test her theory. She carries out ten studies this way, with the following results.

Attempted Replications by Professor B

n	Number of successes	One-tailed p-value
10	4	0.22
15	6	0.15
17	6	0.23
25	8	0.17
30	10	0.20
40	13	0.18
18	7	0.14
10	5	0.08
15	5	0.31
20	7	0.21

Which professor's results are "most impressive"?

(In addition to looking at the p-values, count up the relative number of successes of each professor.)

Nobel Laureate in economics Daniel Kahneman and longtime collaborator Amos Tversky provided a fourth problem involving aggregation when they demonstrated the importance of power and sample size in defining successful replications. Tversky and Kahneman (1982) distributed a questionnaire at a meeting of psychologists, with the following inquiry:

An investigator has reported a result that you consider implausible. He ran 15 subjects, and reported a significant value, $t = 2.46$ (one-tail p-value $= 0.0275$). Another investigator has attempted to duplicate his procedure, and he obtained a nonsignificant value of t with the same number of subjects. The direction was the same in both sets of data. You are reviewing the literature. What is the highest value of t in the second set of data that you would describe as a failure to replicate? (p. 28)

They reported the following results:

The majority of our respondents regarded $t = 1.7$ as a failure to replicate. If the data of two such studies ($t = 2.46$ and $t = 1.7$) are pooled, the value of t for the combined data is about 3.00 (assuming equal variances).[26] Thus, we are faced with a paradoxical state of affairs, in which the same data that would increase our confidence in the finding when viewed as part of the original study, shake our confidence when viewed as an independent study. (p. 28)

Fifth, a meta-analysis requires that the studies underlying the results do not have material faults; yet, those doing meta-analysis, like that of Springer, Stanne, and Donovan (1997) on the effect of learning in small groups, make no attempt to impose a quality criterion on the studies they consider. The quality of educational research is the focus of this chapter and its importance cannot be overestimated.

In closing this discussion of statistical tests, it is worth remembering that the use of the Z, T, χ^2, F or any other probability distribution requires that the sampling situation fits the underlying model assumed to be generating the data when critical values are determined or p-values are calculated. Every estimator has a distribution but it may not be the one assumed in testing. For example, the standardized sample mean, $Z = (\overline{X} - \mu)/(\sigma_X/\sqrt{n})$, is normally distributed if X is normally distributed or if the sample size n is large. The asymptotic theory underpinning the Central Limit Theorem also shows that for a sufficiently large sample size, Z is normal even if the population standard deviation σ_X is unknown. If the sample size is small and σ_X is unknown, then Z is not normal, but it may be distributed as Gosset's T if X is itself normally distributed. (Similar conditions hold for the other common distributions used in parametric hypotheses testing.) When mean sample scores are 4.01 and 4.05, on a 5-point scale, with sample standard deviations in the 0.37 and 0.38 range for the small sample shown in Piccinin's (1999) Table 3, the normality assumption is untenable. The ceiling of 5 must be treated as a readily reachable truncation point in the population distribution; thus, the population cannot be assumed to be normal.

Violations of distribution assumptions require more complex modeling or a move to nonparametric statistics, as demonstrated by Becker and Greene in this volume for estimating the likelihood that a student will increase his/her grade in a second course where course grades are discrete (A, B, C, D, or F) and bounded (A is an achievable maximum and F is an achievable minimum). Biometricians, psychometricians, econometricians, and like specialists in other disciplines are doing this in noneducation-based research. Outside economics, there is little indication that such is being done in the scholarship of teaching and learning research.

Robustness of Results

In the move to more complex modeling, it is always possible that the modeling and method of estimation, and not the data, are producing the results. For instance, labor economists are well aware that parametric sample-selection adjustment procedures (described in endnote 22) can produce spurious results. An option is to report results under alternative sets of assumptions or with different (parametric or nonparametric) estimators.

There are several examples of researchers reporting the consequence of alternative measures of the outcome measures. There are also a few examples of authors reporting results with and without key explanatory variables that are measured with error. As mentioned earlier, Almer, Jones, and Moeckel (1998) discuss the effect of the one-minute paper on student learning, with and without the use of student-reported GPA as a covariate.

Outside of economic education I could find no examples of education researchers checking alternative regression model specifications. Examples of such checking within economics can be seen in Chizmar and Ostrosky (1999) in their analysis of the one-minute paper reporting regression results for the posttest on the pretest, and other explanatory variables, and the change score on the other explanatory variables. Becker and Powers (2001) consider regressions of posttest on the pretest, and other explanatory variables, and the change score on the other explanatory variables, with and without the use of self-reported GPA, and with and without adjustment for sample selection.

Conclusion

In drawing conclusions from their empirical work, few authors are as blatant as Ramsden (1998, p. 355): "The picture of what encourages students to learn effectively at university is now almost complete." Yet, few either recognize or acknowledge the typical fallacies that result from using pre- and posttest, mean-different t tests to assess learning differences between a control and treatment group. Fewer still appreciate the complexity of specifying and estimating an appropriate population model that is believed to be generating the data; they neither address nor attempt to adjust for the many sample-selection problems associated with the testing of students in real educational settings.

Education is a multi-outcome endeavor. Researchers attempting to capture these varied outcomes with a single index will always be subject to aggregation problems. The untried DEA approach to multi-outcome production may be an alternative that does not require aggregation of outcomes and may provide easily interpretable measures of technical efficiency in teaching and learning. As authors acknowledge (but then proceed regardless), the use of the educational production functions with test scores as the only output measure is too narrow. Pretest and posttest, single-equation specifications, with potentially endogenous regressors, simply may not be able to capture the differences that we are trying to produce with diverse teaching methods. Adjustments for sample-selection problems are needed but even after these adjustments with large samples, failure to reject the null hypothesis of no instructional effect may point more to deficiencies in the multiple-choice test outcome measure or application of the classical experimental design than to the failure of the alternative instructional method under scrutiny.

The state of quantitative research has changed greatly in the past 30 years primarily through discipline-based scholarship in the social sciences at the major research universities. The movement primarily at lower tier universities to assess teaching and learning has ignored these developments in quantitative methods. Here I have provided only some of the mathematical and statistical shortcomings that education researchers are overlooking by not working from alternative and explicitly specified population models that may be generating the sample data on individuals and classes of those individuals. The next step for readers who want to learn more of the current state of the science for model specification, estimation and testing of education treatment effect might be to read a series of short articles on evaluating treatment effects by Manski (2001), Heckman and Vytlacil (2001), Smith and Todd (2001) and Ichimura and Taber (2001). We will not learn much, however, from continuing to apply a research paradigm intended for randomized laboratory experiments when our study designs are far from random.

Acknowledgment

Financial support was provided by an Indiana University Bloomington, Scholarship of Teaching and Learning Research Grant, and by the University of South Australia, School of International Business, Faculty of Business and Management. An earlier draft of this study was presented at the Scholarship of Teaching and Learning Colloquium, Indiana University Bloomington, March 2, 2001. Constructive criticism was provided by Suzanne Becker, George Kuh, and Samuel Thompson.

Notes

1. For example, before he closed his websites, Thomas Russell's "The No Significant Difference Phenomenon," http://cuda.teleeducation.nb.ca/nosignificantdifference/, had brief quotes from over 355 research reports, summaries and papers on the use of technology for distance education. His site at "Significant Difference" (http://cuda.teleeducation.nb.ca/

significantdifference/) had few. My review will not include studies of computer technology or distance learning. DeNeve and Heppner (1997, p. 232) report that in seven of the 12 studies they identified in their ERIC search "active learning techniques appear to have some benefits." Although they do not calculate it, there is a 0.387 probability of getting at least 7 successes in 12 trials in random draws, with a 0.5 probability of success on each independent and identical trial. A p-value of 0.387 is hardly sufficient to reject the chance hypothesis. My review is restricted to selections from the traditionally published studies.

2. There have been numerous attempts to force standards on journal editors in education and psychology in regard to what is and is not acceptable use of statistics. For example, although there was and continues to be a push to abandon statistical significance testing among educational researchers in psychology (Thompson 2002), the American Psychological Association Task Force on Statistical Inference did not endorse the banning or strict requirement for the use of any statistics: "Always provide some effect-size estimate when reporting a p value." (Wilkinson 1999, p. 599)

3. Other discipline-based studies employ nationally normed tests to explore various aspects of the teaching-learning environment. For example, in economics the three editions of the Test of Understanding of College Economics have been used to assess the learning effect of class size on student learning, native language of the teacher, student and instructor gender, and the lasting effect of a course in economics. Typically, these studies are institution specific.

4. Chizmar and Ostrosky (1999) was submitted to the *Journal of Economic Education* in 1997 before the publication of Almer, Jones, and Moeckel (1998), which also addresses the effectiveness of the one-minute paper.

5. Unlike the mean, the median reflects relative but not absolute magnitude; thus, the median may be a poor measure of change. For example, the series 1, 2, 3 and the series 1, 2, 300 have the same median (2) but different means (2 versus 101).

6. Let y_{it} be the observed test score index of the ith student in the tth class, who has an expected test score index value of μ_{it} That is, $y_{it} = \mu_{it} + \varepsilon_{it}$, where ε_{it} is the random error in testing such that its expected value is zero, $E(\varepsilon_{it}) = 0$, and variance is σ^2, $E(\varepsilon_{it}^2) = \sigma^2$, for all i and t. Let $\bar{y}_t$ be the sample mean of a test score index for the tth class of n_t students. That is, $\bar{y}_t = \bar{\mu}_t = \bar{\varepsilon}_t$ and $E(\bar{\varepsilon}_t^2) = \sigma^2/n_t$. Thus, the variance of the class mean test score index is inversely related to class size.

7. As in Fleisher, Hashimoto, and Weinberg (2002), let y_{gi} be the performance measure of the ith student in a class taught by instructor g, let F_g be a dummy variable reflecting a characteristics of the instructor (e.g., nonnative English speaker), let x_{gi} be a $(1 \times n)$ vector of the student's observable attributes, and let the random error associated with the ith student taught by the gth instructor be ε_{gi}. The performance of the ith student is then generated by

$$y_{gi} = F_g\, \gamma + x_{gi}\, \beta + \varepsilon_{gi}$$

where γ and β are parameters to be estimated. The error term, however, has two components: one unique to the ith student in the gth instructor's class (u_{gi}) and one that is shared by all students in this class (ξ_g): $\varepsilon_{gi} = \xi_g + u_{gi}$. It is the presence of the shared error ξ_g for which an adjustment in standard errors is required. The ordinary least squares routines employed by the standard computer programs are based on a model in which the variance-covariance matrix of error terms is diagonal, with element σ_u^2. The presence of the ξ_g terms makes this matrix block diagonal, where each student in the gth instructor's class has an off-diagonal element σ_ξ^2.

8. Discussions of the reliability of an exam are traced to Kelley (1927). Kelley proposed a way to visualize a test taker's "true score" as a function of his or her observed score in a single equation that relates the estimated true score ($\hat{y}_{true}$) to the observed score ($y_{observed}$). The best estimate comes from regressing the observed score in the direction of the mean score (μ) of the group from which the test taker comes. The amount of regression to the mean is determined by the reliability (α) of the test. Kelley's equation is

$$\hat{y}_{true} = \alpha y_{observed} = + (1-\alpha)\mu$$

If a test is completely unreliable (alpha is zero) the best predictor of a test taker's true score is the group mean. That is, the observed score is a random outcome that only deviated from the group mean by chance. If alpha is one (the test is perfectly reliable) then there is no regression effect and the true score is the same as the observed. Alpha between zero and one gives rise to the "errors in variables" problem discussed in later endnotes. Unfortunately, alpha is unknown and, as discussed in later endnotes, attempts to estimate it from observed test scores is tricky to say the least.

Reliability is often built into a test by placing questions on it that those scoring high on the test tend to get correct and those scoring low tend to get wrong. Through repetitive trial testing (called "test norming"), questions that contribute to differentiating students are sought in the construction of highly reliable tests. In the extreme case, this type of test construction can be expected to yield test scores that are close to 50 percent correct regardless of the number of alternatives provided on each of many multiple-choice questions.

For instance, if each question on an N question multiple-choice test has four alternatives, then the expected chance score is $0.25N$ items correct. But if some test takers are better guessers than others, or know more about the subject, then the test developer may experiment with repeated testing and place questions on the sequential exams that the q percent with the highest overall test score tend to get correct, and that the bottom q percent get wrong. As the identification of differentiating questions approaches perfection and as q approaches 0.5, the expected number of correct answers approaches $0.5N$. That is,

$$\lim_{\substack{l\to 0 \\ h\to 1 \\ q\to .5}}[qlN + 0.25(1-2q)N + qhN)] = 0.5N$$

where N is the number of multiple-choice questions, each with 4 alternative answers,

> q is the proportion of top and bottom scored exams used for question selection,
> h is the proportion of correctly answered questions by the top scorers, and
> l is the proportion of correctly answered questions by the bottom scorers.

9. A reviewer of this chapter argued, "an R-square of 0.5 is pretty good for social science work." But this statement does not recognize the distinction between the use of R^2 as a descriptive measure of a sample relationship (as it is used to describe the association between end-of-semester student evaluations and other outcomes) and a measure of goodness-of-fit in regression model building (where $R^2 \leq 0.5$ in cross-section studies is not unusual). R-square is relatively irrelevant in the latter context, as Goldberger (1991, p. 177) makes clear:

> From our perspective, R^2 has a very modest role in regression analysis. . . . Nothing in the CR (classical regression) model requires that R^2 be high . . . the most important thing about R^2 is that it is not important in the CR model. The CR model is concerned with parameters in the population, not with goodness of fit in the sample.

10. Kuh, Pace, and Vesper (1997) tell us that the probability of getting this coefficient estimate is significantly different from zero at the 0.0005 Type I error level (in a one- or two-tail test is not clear). They do not tell us how the standard errors were calculated to reflect the fact that their explanatory variables indices are themselves estimates. It appears, however, that they are treating the active learning index (as well as the other regressor indices) as if it represents only one thing whereas in fact it represents an estimate from 25 things. That is, when an estimated summary measure for many variables is used as a covariate in another regression, which is estimated with the same data set, more than one degree of freedom is lost in that regression. If the summary measure is obtained from outside the data set for which the regression of interest is estimated, then the weights used to form the summary measure must be treated as constraints to be tested.

11. Ramsden (1998) ignores the fact that each of his 50 data points represents a type of institutional average that is based on multiple inputs; thus, questions of heteroscedasticity and the calculation of appropriate standard errors for test statistical inference are relevant. In addition, because Ramsden reports working only with the aggregate data from each university, it is possible that within each university the relationship between good teaching (x) and the deep approach (y) could be negative but yet appear positive in the aggregate.

When I contacted Ramsden to get a copy of his data and his coauthored

"Paper presented at the Annual Conference of the Australian Association for Research in Education, Brisbane (December 1997)," which was listed as the source for his regression of the deep approach index on the good teaching index in his 1998 published article, he replied:

> It could take a little time to get the information to you since I no longer have any access to research assistance and I will have to spend some time unearthing the data. The conference paper mentioned did not get written; another instance of the triumph of hope over experience. Mike Prosser may be able to provide a quick route to the raw data and definitions. (e-mail correspondence 9/22/00)

Aside from the murky issue of Ramsden citing his 1997 paper, which he subsequently admitted does not exist, and his not providing the data on which the published 1998 paper is allegedly based, a potential problem of working with data aggregated at the university level can be seen with three hypothetical data sets. The three regressions for each of the following hypothetical universities show a negative relationship for y (deep approach) and x (good teaching), with slope coefficients of -0.4516, -0.0297, and -0.4664, but a regression on the university means shows a positive relationship, with slope coefficient of $+0.1848$. This is a demonstration of "Simpson's paradox," where aggregate results are different from dissaggregated results.

University One

$$\hat{y}(1) = 21.3881 - 0.4516x(1) \quad \text{Std. Error} = 2.8622 \quad R^2 = 0.81 \quad n = 4$$

$y(1)$: 21.8 15.86 26.25 14.72

$x(1)$: -4.11 6.82 -5.12 17.74

University Two

$$\hat{y}(2) = 17.4847 - 0.0297x(2) \quad \text{Std. Error} = 2.8341 \quad R^2 = 0.01 \quad n = 8$$

$y(2)$: 12.60 17.90 19.00 16.45 21.96 17.1 18.61 17.85

$x(2)$: -10.54 -10.53 -5.57 -11.54 -15.96 -2.1 -9.64 12.25

University Three

$$\hat{y}(3) = 17.1663 - 0.4664x(3) \quad \text{Std. Error} = 2.4286 \quad R^2 = 0.91 \quad n = 12$$

$y(3)$: 27.10 2.02 16.81 15.42 8.84 22.90 12.77 17.52 23.20 22.60

$x(3)$: -23.16 26.63 5.86 9.75 11.19 -14.29 11.51 -0.63 -19.21 -4.89

$y(3)$: 25.90

$x(3)$: -16.16

University Means

$$\hat{y}(means) = 18.6105 + 0.1848x(means) \quad \text{Std. Error} = 0.7973 \quad R^2 = 0.75 \quad n = 3$$

$y(means)$: 19.658 17.684 17.735

$x(means)$: 3.833 -6.704 -1.218

12. Although attempts at truly random selection are rare in educational research, an exception can be seen in the student/teacher achievement ratio (STAR), which was a four-year longitudinal class-size study funded by the Tennessee General Assembly and conducted by the State Department of Education. Over 7,000 students in 79 schools were randomly assigned into one of three interventions: small class (13 to 17 students per teacher), regular class (22 to 25 students per teacher), and regular-with-aide class (22 to 25 students with a full-time teacher's aide). Classroom teachers were also randomly assigned to classes. Although Finn and Achilles (1990), Krueger and Whitmore (2001), and others use these data to demonstrate the advantages of smaller classes, these researchers ignore the effects of nonrandom attrition and reassignment in later grades following the initial kindergarten random assignments. I know of no like attempts at tertiary level randomization.

13. According to Anaya (1999, p. 505), the first stage in assessing the contribution of teaching to learning, when the same instrument is not available as a pre- and posttest, is the calculation of a "residual gain score." This only requires the ability to regress some posttest score (y_1) on some pretest score (z_0) to obtain residuals. Implicit in this regression is a model that says both test scores are each driven by the same unobserved ability, although to differing degrees depending on the treatment experienced between the pretest and posttest, and other things that are ignored for the moment. The model of the ith student's pretest is

$$z_{0i} = \alpha(ability)_i + u_{0i},$$

where α is the slope coefficient to be estimated, u_{0i} is the population error in predicting the ith student's pretest score with ability, and all variables are measured as deviations from their means. The ith student's posttest is similarly defined by

$$y_{1i} = \beta(ability)_i + v_{1i}$$

Because *ability* is not observable, but appears in both equations, it can be removed from the system by substitution. Anaya's regression is estimating the reduced form:

$$y_{1i} = \beta_\alpha z_{0i} + v_{\alpha 1i}, \text{ for } \beta_\alpha = \beta/\alpha \text{ and } v_{\alpha 1i} = v_{1i} - (u_{0i}/\alpha).$$

Her least-squares slope estimator and predicted posttest score for the ith student is

$$b_\alpha = \sum_i y_{1i} z_{0i} / \sum_i z_{0i}^2 \text{ and } \hat{y}_{1i} = b_\alpha z_{0i} = \left[\sum_i y_{1i} z_{0i} / \sum_i z_{0i}^2 \right] z_{0i}$$

The ith student's "residual gain score" is $(y_{1i} - \hat{y}_{1i})$. In Anaya's second stage, this residual gain score is regressed on explanatory variables of interest:

$$(y_{1i} - \hat{y}_{0i}) = X_i \rho + w_{1i}$$

where X is the matrix of explanatory variables and here the subscript i indicates the ith student's record in the ith row. The ρ vector contains the population slope coefficients corresponding to the variables in X and w_{1i} is the error term. Unfortunately, the problems with this two-stage procedure start with the first stage: b_α is a biased estimator of β_α.

$$E(b_\alpha) = E\left(\sum_i y_{1i}\, z_{0i} \,/\, \sum_i z_{0i}^2 \right)$$

$$= \beta_\alpha + E\left\{ \sum_i [v_{1i} - (u_{0i}/\alpha)]_{1i}\, z_{0i} \,/\, \sum_i z_{0i}^2 \right\}$$

Although v_{1i} and z_{0i} are unrelated, $E(v_{1i}\, z_{0i}) = 0$, u_{0i} and z_{0i} are positively related, $E(u_{0i}\, z_{0i}) > 0$; thus, $E(b_\alpha) < \beta_\alpha$. As in the discussion of reliability in other endnotes, this is yet another example of the classic regression to the mean outcome caused by measurement error in the regressor. Notice also that the standard errors of the ordinary least-squares ρ vector estimator do not take account of the variability and degrees of freedom lost in the estimation of the residual gain score.

14. Let the change or gain score be, $\Delta y = [y_1 - y_0]$, which is the posttest score minus the pretest score, and let the maximum change score be $\Delta y_{max} = [y_{max} - y_0]$, then

$$\frac{\partial (\Delta y / \Delta y_{max})}{\partial y_0} = \frac{-(y_{max} - y_1)}{(y_{max} - y_0)^2} \leq 0, \text{ for } y_{max} \geq y_1 \geq y_0$$

15. Let the posttest score (y_1) and pretest score (y_0) be defined on the same scale, then the model of the ith student's pretest is

$$y_{0i} = \beta_0 (ability)_i + v_{0i},$$

where β_0 is the slope coefficient to be estimated, v_{0i} is the population error in predicting the ith student's pretest score with ability, and all variables are measured as deviations from their means. The ith student's posttest is similarly defined by

$$y_{1i} = \beta_1 (ability)_i + v_{1i}$$

The change or gain score model is then

$$y_{1i} - y_{0i} = (\beta_1 - \beta_0)ability + v_{1i} - v_{0i}$$

And after substituting the pretest for unobserved true ability we have

$$\Delta y_i = (\Delta\beta / \beta_0)y_{0i} + v_{1i} - v_{0i}[1 + (\Delta\beta / \beta)]$$

The least-squares slope estimator ($\Delta b / b_0$) has an expected value of

$$E(\Delta b / b_0) = E\left(\sum_i \Delta y_1 \, y_{0i} \,/ \sum_i y_{0i}^2 \right)$$

$$E(\Delta b / b_0) = (\Delta \beta / \beta_0) + E\left\{ \sum_i [v_{1i} - v_{0i} - v_{01}(\Delta \beta / \beta_0)]_{1i} \, y_{0i} \,/ \sum_i y_{0i}^2 \right\}$$

$$E(\Delta b / b_0) \le (\Delta \beta / \beta_0)$$

Although v_{1i} and y_{0i} are unrelated, $E(v_{1i} y_{0i}) = 0$, v_{0i} and y_{0i} are positively related, $E(v_{0i} y_{0i}) > 0$; thus, $E(\Delta b / b_0) \le \Delta \beta / \beta_0$. Becker and Salemi (1979) suggest an instrumental variable technique to address this source of bias and Salemi and Tauchen (1987) suggest a modeling of the error term structure.

Hake (1998) makes no reference to this bias when he discusses his regressions and correlation of average normalized gain, average gain score and posttest score on the average pretest score. In http://www.consecol.org/vol5/iss2/art28/, he continued to be unaware of, unable or unwilling to specify the mathematics of the population model from which student data are believed to be generated and the method of parameter estimation employed. As the algebra of this endnote suggests, if a negative relationship is expected between the gap closing measure

$$g = (\text{posttest} - \text{pretest})/(\text{maxscore} - \text{pretest})$$

and the pretest, but a least-squares estimator does not yield a significant negative relationship for sample data, then there is evidence that something is peculiar. It is the lack of independence between the pretest and the population error term (caused, for example, by measurement error in the pretest, simultaneity between g and the pretest, or possibly missing but relevant variables) that is the problem. Hotelling receives credit for recognizing this endogenous regressor problem (in the 1930s) and the resulting regression to the mean phenomenon. Milton Friedman received a Nobel Prize in economics for coming up with an instrumental variable technique (for estimation of consumption functions in the 1950s) to remove the resulting bias inherent in least-squares estimators when measurement error in a regressor is suspected. Later Friedman (1992, p. 2131) concluded: "I suspect that the regression fallacy is the most common fallacy in the statistical analysis of economic data . . ." Similarly, psychologists Campbell and Kenny (1999, p. xiii) state: "Regression toward the mean is an artifact that as easily fools statistical experts as lay people." But unlike Friedman, Campbell and Kenny do not recognize the instrumental variable method for addressing the problem.

In an otherwise innovative study, Paul Kvam (2000) correctly concluded that there was insufficient statistical evidence to conclude that active learning methods (primarily through integrating students' projects into lectures) resulted in better retention of quantitative skills than traditional methods, but then went out on a limb by concluding from a scatter plot of individual student pretest and posttest scores that students who fared worse on the first exam retain concepts better if they were taught using active learning methods. Kvan never addressed the measurement error problem inherent in using the pretest as an explanatory variable. Wainer (2000) calls attention to others who fail to take measurement error into account in labeling students as "strivers" because their observed test scores exceed values predicted by a regression equation.

16. Given the importance of pre-course aptitude measures, and the need to tailor instruction to the individual student, it is curious that faculty members at many colleges and universities have allowed registrars to block their access to student records for instructional purposes. As Maxwell and Lopus (1994) report, students are less than accurate in providing information about their backgrounds. Thus, as discussed in this chapter, using student self-reported data in regressions will always involve problems of errors in variables. Salemi and Tauchen (1987) discuss other forms of errors in variables problems encountered in the estimation of standard single-equation learning models.

17. The effect of omitting a relevant explanatory variable, such as aptitude, from a model of learning, as measured by the difference between the posttest score (y_1) and pretest score (y_0), depends on the relationship between the included and excluded variables. To see this assume the true linear model of the ith student's learning, $\Delta y_i = (y_{1i} - y_{0i})$, is a function of only two explanatory variables (x_{1i} and x_{2i}):

$$\Delta y_i = \beta_0 + \beta_1 x_{1i} + \beta_2 x_{2i} + \varepsilon_i$$

where the critical error term assumptions are $E(\varepsilon_i | x_{1i}, x_{2i}) = 0$ and $E(\varepsilon_i x_{ji}) = 0$. But if there is a suspected linear relationship between x_{1i} and x_{2i}, and if x_{2i} is omitted from the learning equation ($\Delta y_i = \beta_0 + \beta_1 x_{1i} + \varepsilon_i^r$), then the expected value of the x_{1i} coefficient estimator b_1^r is

$$E(b_1^r) = \beta_1 + \delta_1 \beta_2$$

where $x_{2i} = \delta_0 + \delta_1 x_{1i} + \eta_i$, the δ's are parameters, and η_i is the well-behaved error term for which $E(\eta_i | x_{1i}) = 0$, $E(\eta_i^2 | x_{1i}) = \sigma_\eta^2$, and $E(x_{1i} \eta_i) = 0$. Only if the x_{1i} and x_{2i} are not related ($\delta_1 = 0$), will b_1^r be an unbiased estimator of the x_{1i} coefficient when x_{2i} is omitted. The building of models based on data-mining routines such as stepwise regression are doomed by the omitted variable problem. If a relevant variable is omitted from a regression in an early step, and if it is related to the included variables, then the contribution of the included variables is estimated with bias. It does not matter with which of the related explanatory variables the model builder starts; the contribution of the included variables will always be biased by the excluded.

18. The word "knowledge" is used here to represent a stock measure of student achievement; it can be replaced with any educational outcome produced by the student with various forms of study time and technology, as measured at a single point in time.

19. Wright et al. (1997) report that 20 percent of the students in the SAL section continued to work independently (p. 4). Assuming that these students invested the same average time in out-of-class work as the RL students implies that those who truly worked together in the SAL section spent 18.75 percent more time on course work than those who worked independently.

20. To assess the consequence of the missing student data on estimators in the matched pre- and posttest learning models, for example, consider the expected value of the change score, as calculated from a regression of the difference in posttest score (y_1) and pretest score (y_0) on the set of full information for each student. Let Ω_i be the full information set that should be used to predict the ith student's change score $\Delta y_i = (y_{1i} - y_{0i})$. Let $P(m_i = 1)$ be the probability that some of this explanatory information is missing. The desired expected value for the ith student's learning is then

$$E(\Delta y_i | \Omega_i) = E(\Delta y_i | \Omega_{ci}) + P(m_i = 1)[E(\Delta y_i | \Omega_{mi}) - E(\Delta y_i | \Omega_{ci})]$$

where Ω_{ci} is the subset of information available from complete records and Ω_{mi} is the subset of incomplete records. The expected value of the change score on the lefthand side of this equation is desired but only the first major term on the righthand side can be estimated. They are equal only if $P(m_i = 1)$ is zero or its multiplicative factor within the brackets is zero. Because willingness to complete a survey is likely not a purely random event, $E(\Delta y_i | \Omega_{mi}) \neq E(\Delta y_i | \Omega_{ci})$.

21. Lazear (1999) argues that optimal class size varies directly with the quality of students. Because the negative congestion effect of disruptive students is lower for better students, the better the students, the bigger the optimal class size and the less that class size appears to matter: ". . . in equilibrium, class size matters very little. To the extent that class size matters, it is more likely to matter at lower grade levels than upper grade levels where class size is smaller." (p. 40) However, Lazear does not address how class size is to be measured or the influence of class size on attrition. Nor does his analysis address the dynamics of class size varying over the term of a course.

22. Why the ith student does ($T_i = 1$) or does not ($T_i = 0$) take the posttest is unknown, but assume there is an unobservable continuous dependent variable T_i^* driving the student's decision; that is, T_i^* is an unobservable measure of the student's propensity to take the posttest. As in Becker and Powers (2001), if T_i^* is positive, the student feels good about taking the posttest and takes it; if T_i^* is negative, the student is apprehensive and does not take it. More formally, if T^* is the vector of students' propensities to take the posttest, H is the matrix of observed explanatory variables including the pretest, α is the vector of corresponding slope coefficients, and ω is the vector of error terms, then the ith student's propensity of taking the posttest is given by

$$T_i^* = H_i \alpha + \omega_i$$

Taking of the posttest is determined by this selection equation with the decision rule

$$T_i = 1, \text{ if } T_i^* > 0, \text{ and student } i \text{ takes the posttest, and}$$

$$T_i = 0, \text{ if } T_i^* < 0, \text{ and student } i \text{ does not take the posttest.}$$

For estimation purposes, the error term ω_i is assumed to be a standard normal random variable that is independently and identically distributed with the other error terms in the ω vector.

The effect of student attrition on measured student learning from pretest to posttest and an adjustment for the resulting bias caused by ignoring students who do not complete the course can be summarized with a two-equation model formed by the above selection equation and the ith student's learning:

$$\Delta y_i = X_i \beta + \varepsilon_i$$

where $\Delta y = (y_1 - y_0)$ is a vector of change scores, X is the matrix of explanatory variables, and again the subscript i indicates the ith student's record in the ith row. β is a vector of coefficients corresponding to X. Each of the disturbances in vector ε are assumed to be distributed bivariate normal with the corresponding disturbance term in the ω vector of the selection equation. Thus, for the ith student we have

$$(\varepsilon_i, \omega_i) \sim \text{bivariate normal}(0, 0, \sigma_\varepsilon, 1, \rho)$$

and for all perturbations in the two-equation system we have

$$E(\varepsilon) = E(\omega) = 0, E(\varepsilon\varepsilon') = \sigma_\varepsilon^2 I, E(\omega\omega') = I, \text{ and } E(\varepsilon\omega') = \rho\sigma_\varepsilon I.$$

That is, the disturbances have zero means, unit variance, and no covariance among students, but there is covariance between selection and the posttest score for a student.

The linear specification of the learning equation specification and nonlinear specification of the selection equation ensure the identification of each equation. Estimates of the parameters in the learning equation are desired, but the ith change score (Δy_i) is observed for only the subset of n of N students for whom $T_i = 1$. The regression for this censored sample of n students is

$$E(\Delta y_i \mid X_i, \ T_i = 1) = X_i \beta + E(\varepsilon_1 \mid T_i^* > 0); i = 1, 2, \ldots, n < N.$$

Similar to omitting a relevant variable from a regression, selection bias is a problem because the magnitude of $E(\varepsilon_i \mid T_i^* > 0)$ varies across individuals and yet is not included in the estimation of the learning equation for the n students. To the extent that ε_i and ω_i (and thus T_i^*) are related, estimators are biased, and this bias is present regardless of the sample size.

The learning equation regression involving matched pretest and posttest scores can be adjusted for student attrition during the course in several ways. An early Heckman-type solution to the sample selection problem is to re-write the omitted variable component of the regression so that the equation to be estimated is

$$E(\Delta y_i \mid X_i, \ T_i = 1) = X_i \beta + (\rho \sigma_\varepsilon) \lambda_i; i = 1, 2, \dots, n$$

where $\lambda_i = f(-T_i^*)/[1 - F(-T_i^*)]$, and f(.) and F(.) are the normal density and distribution functions. The inverse Mill's ratio (or hazard) λ_i is the standardized mean of the disturbance term ω_i, for the ith student who took the posttest; it is close to zero only for those well above the $T = 1$ threshold. The values of λ are generated from the estimated probit selection equation. Each student in the learning regression gets a calculated value λ_i, with the vector of these values serving as a shift variable in the learning regression. The estimates of both ρ and σ_ε and all the other coefficients in selection and learning equations can be obtained simultaneously using the maximum likelihood routines in statistical programs such as LIMDEP or STATA.

23. Heckman and Smith (1995) show the difficulty in constructing a counter-factual situation for alternative instructional methods when participation is voluntary or random. Without a counterfactual situation (i.e., what would have happened if these same people were in the control group), it is impossible to do assessment.

24. Card and Krueger (1996) report a consistency across studies showing the importance of school quality on a student's subsequent earnings. They recognize that tests can be administered easily at any time in the education process and thus provide a cheap tool for monitoring programs. In recognition of the time lag for measuring earnings effects, they recommend the use of drop-out rates as an alternative to test scores for immediate and ongoing program assessment. After all, unless students finish their programs, they cannot enjoy the potential economic benefits.

25. Hedges, Lane, and Greenwald (1994a,b) use a meta-analysis involving an aggregation of p-values to cast doubt on Hanushek's assertion about the relevance of expenditures on instructional methods in generating test scores. Krueger (2000) reviews the Hanushek and Hedges et al. debate and contributes the observation that it is the peculiar weighting employed by Hanushek that is producing his vote-counting results. As demonstrated in this chapter, there is no unique way to do a meta-analysis.

26. The first t, $t_1 = 2.46$, and second, $t_2 = 1.7$, can be solved for $\bar{x}_1$ and $\bar{x}_2$ and then $\bar{x}_3$ can be created as $\bar{x}_3 = 0.5(\bar{x}_1 + \bar{x}_2)$ and t_3 can be determined as, where the population mean is set equal to zero under the null hypothesis:

$$t_3 = \frac{(0.5)\left[2.46\left(\frac{s}{\sqrt{15}} \right) + \mu + 1.7\left(\frac{s}{\sqrt{15}} \right) + \mu \right] - \mu}{\frac{s}{\sqrt{15}}} = 2.94 \cong 3$$

References

Admiraal, W., T. Wubbels, and A. Pilot. 1999. College teaching in legal education: Teaching method, students' time-on-task, and achievement. *Research in Higher Education* 40 (6): 687–704.

Ali, A. I., and L. Seiford. 1993. The mathematical programming approach to efficiency analysis. In H. Fried, C. A. K. Lovell, and S. Schmidt, eds., *Measurement of production efficiency*. New York: Oxford University Press.

Allgood, S. 2001. Grade targets and teaching innovations. *Economics of Education Review* 20 (October): 485–94.

Almer, E. D., K. Jones, and C. Moeckel. 1998. The impact of one-minute papers on learning in an introductory accounting course. *Issues in Accounting Education* 13 (3): 485–97.

Anaya, G. 1999. College impact on student learning: Comparing the use of self-reported gains, standardized test scores, and college grades. *Research in Higher Education* 40 (5): 499–526.

Anderson, G., D. Benjamin, and M. Fuss. 1994. The determinants of success in university introductory economics courses. *Journal of Economic Education* 25 (Spring): 99–121.

Angelo, T. A., and P. K. Cross. 1993. *Classroom assessment techniques: A handbook for college teachers*. San Francisco: Jossey-Bass.

Arrow, K. 1951. *Social choice and individual values*. Monograph No. 12. Cowles Commission for Research in Economics. New York: John Wiley and Sons.

Becker, W. E. 1982. The educational process and student achievement given uncertainty in measurement. *American Economic Review* 72 (March): 229–36.

———. 2000. Teaching economics in the 21st century. *Journal of Economic Perspectives* 14 (Winter): 109–19.

Becker, W. E., and W. H. Greene. 2001. Teaching statistics and econometrics to undergraduates. *Journal of Economic Perspectives* 15 (Fall): 169–82.

Becker, W. E., and C. Johnston. 1999. The relationship between multiple choice and essay response questions in assessing economics understanding. *Economic Record* 75 (December): 348–57.

Becker, W. E., and J. Powers. 2001. Student performance, attrition, and class size given missing student data. *Economics of Education Review* 20 (August): 377–88.

Becker, W. E., and M. Salemi. 1979. The learning and cost effectiveness of AVT supplemented instruction: Specification of learning models. *Journal of Economic Education* 8 (Spring): 77–92.

Becker, W. E., and W. Walstad. 1990. Data loss from pretest to posttest as a sample selection problem. *Review of Economics and Statistics* 72 (February): 184–88.

Beron, K. J. 1990. Joint determinants of current classroom performance and additional economics classes: A binary/continuous model. *Journal of Economic Education* 21 (Summer): 255–64.

Campbell, D., and D. Kenny. 1999. *A primer on regression artifacts*. New York: The Guilford Press.

Campbell, D., J. Stanley, and N. Gage. 1963. *Experimental and quasi-experimental design for research*. Boston: Houghton Mifflin.

Card, D., and A. Krueger. 1996. The economic return to school quality. In W. Becker and W. Baumol, eds., *Assessing educational practices: The contribution of economics*, pp. 161–82. Cambridge, MA: MIT Press.

Chen, Y., and L. B. Hoshower. 1998. Assessing student motivation to participate in teaching evaluations: An application of expectancy theory. *Issues in Accounting Education* 13 (August): 531–49.

Chickering, A. W., and Z. Gamson. 1987. Seven principles for good practice in undergraduate education. *AAHE Bulletin* 39 (7): 3–7.

Chizmar, J., and A. Ostrosky. 1999. The one-minute paper: Some empirical findings. *Journal of Economic Education* 29 (Winter): 3–10.

Cottel, P. G., and E. M. Harwood. 1998. Using classroom assessment techniques to improve student learning in accounting classes. *Issues in Accounting Education* 13 (August): 551–64.

DeNeve, K. M., and M. J. Heppner. 1997. Role play simulations: The assessment of an active learning technique and comparisons with traditional lectures. *Innovative Higher Education* 21 (Spring): 231–46.

Douglas, S., and J. Sulock. 1995. Estimating educational production functions with corrections for drops. *Journal of Economic Education* 26 (Spring): 101–13.

Elmore, P., and O. Rotou. 2001. A primer on basic effect size concepts. Paper presented at the April Annual Meeting of the American Educational Research Association, Seattle, WA.

Fabry, V. J., R. Eisenbach, R. R. Curry, and V. L. Golich. 1997. Thank you for asking: Classroom assessment techniques and students' perceptions of learning. *Journal of Excellence in College Teaching* 8 (1): 3–21.

Fleisher, B., M. Hashimoto, and B. Weinberg. 2002. Foreign GTAs can be effective teachers of economics. *Journal of Economic Education* 33 (Fall): 299–326.

Finn, J., and C. M. Achilles. 1990. Answers and questions about class size: A statewide experiment. *American Educational Research Journal* 27 (Fall): 557–77.

Fournier, G., and T. Sass. 2000. Take my course, please: The effect of the principles experience on student curriculum choice. *Journal of Economic Education* 31 (Fall): 323–39.

Francisco, J. S., M. Trautmann, and G. Nicoll. 1998. Integrating a study skills workshop and pre-examination to improve students' chemistry performance. *Journal of College Science Teaching* 28 (February): 273–78.

Friedman, M. 1992. Communication: Do old fallacies ever die? *Journal of Economic Literature* 30 (December): 2129–32.

Gleason, J., and W. Walstad. 1988. An empirical test of an inventory model of student study time. *Journal of Economic Education* 19 (Fall): 315–21.

Goldberger, A. S. 1991. *A course in econometrics*. Cambridge: Harvard University Press.

Greene, W. H. 2003. *Econometric analysis*. 5th ed. New Jersey: Prentice Hall.

Gunsalus, C. K. 2002. Rethinking protections for human subjects. *Chronicle of Higher Education* 49 (November 15): B24.

Hake, R. R. 1998. Interactive-engagement versus traditional methods: A six-thousand-student survey of mechanics test data for introductory physics courses. *American Journal of Physics* 66 (January): 64–74.

Hansen, W. L., A. Kelley, and B. Weisbrod. 1970. Economic efficiency and the distribution of benefits from college instruction. *American Economic Review Proceedings* 60 (May): 364–69.

Hanushek, E. 1991. When school finance 'reform' may not be a good policy. *Harvard Journal of Legislation* 28: 423–56.

———. 1994. Money might matter somewhat: A response to Hedges, Lane, and Greenwald. *Educational Researcher* 23 (May): 5–8.

Harwood, E. M. 1999. Student perceptions of the effects of classroom assessment techniques (CATs). *Journal of Accounting Education* 17 (4): 51–70.

Harwood, E. M., and J. R. Cohen. 1999. Classroom assessment: Educational and research opportunities. *Issues in Accounting Education* 14 (November): 691–724.

Heckman, J. 1979. Sample selection bias as a specification error. *Econometrica* 47: 153–62.

Heckman, J., and J. Smith. 1995. Assessing the case for social experiments. *Journal of Economic Perspectives* 9 (Spring): 85–110.

Heckman, J., and E. Vytlacil. 2001. Policy-relevant treatment effects. *American Economic Review Proceedings* 91 (May): 108–11.

Hedges, L., R. Lane, and R. Greenwald. 1994a. Does money matter? A meta-analysis of studies of the effects of differential school inputs on student outcomes. *Educational Researcher* 23 (April): 5–14.

———. 1994b. Money does matter somewhat: A reply to Hanushek. *Educational Researcher* 23 (May): 9–10.

Ichimura, H., and C. Taber. 2001. Propensity-score matching with instrumental variables. *American Economic Review Proceedings* 91 (May): 119–24.

Johnes, J., and G. Johnes. 1995. Research funding and performance in UK university departments of economics: A frontier analysis. *Economics of Education Review* 14 (3): 301–14.

Kennedy, P., and J. Siegfried. 1997. Class size and achievement in introductory economics: Evidence from the TUCE III data. *Economics of Education Review* 16 (August): 385–94.

Kelley, T. 1927. *The interpretation of educational measurement.* New York: World Book.

Klionsky, D. J. 1998. A cooperative learning approach to teaching introductory biology. *Journal of College Science Teaching* 28 (March/April): 334–38.

Krueger, A. B. 2000. Economic considerations and class size. Princeton University Industrial Relations Section Working Paper No. 477, www.irs.princeton.edu, September.

Krueger, A. B., and D. M. Whitmore. 2001. The effect of attending a small class in the early grades on college-test taking and middle school test results: Evidence from project STAR. *Economic Journal* 111 (January): 1–28.

Kuh, G. D., C. R. Pace, and N. Vesper. 1997. The development of process indicators to estimate student gains associated with good practices in undergraduate education. *Research in Higher Education* 38 (4): 435–54.

Kvam, P. 2000. The effect of active learning methods on student retention in
engineering statistics. *American Statistician* 54 (2): 136–40.

Lazear, E. 1999. Educational production. NBER Working Paper Series, National Bureau of Economic Research, No. 7349.

Lehmann, E., and S. Warning. 2003. Teaching or research? What affects the
efficiency of universities. Working Paper, Department of Economics, University of Konstanz, Germany.

Lovell, C. A. K. 1993. Production frontiers and productive efficiency. In
H. Fried, C. A. K. Lovell, and S. Schmidt, eds., *Measurement of production
efficiency*. New York: Oxford University Press.

Manski, C. 2001. Designing programs for heterogeneous populations: The
value of covariate information. *American Economic Review Proceedings* 91
(May): 103–106.

Maxwell, N., and J. Lopus. 1994. The Lake Wobegon effect in student self-
reported data. *American Economic Review Proceedings* 84 (May): 201–205.

McKeachie, W. 1997. Student ratings: The validity of use. *American Psychologist* 52 (November): 1218–25.

Moulton, B. R. 1986. Random group effects and the precision of regression
estimators. *Journal of Econometrics* 32 (August): 385–97.

Piccinin, S. 1999. How individual consultation affects teaching. In C. Knapper,
ed., *Using consultants to improve teaching. New Directions for Teaching and
Learning* 29 (Fall): 71–83.

Ramsden, P. 1998. Managing the effective university. *Higher Education Research
& Development* 17 (3): 347–70.

Rosenbaum, P. 1999. Choice as an alternative to control in observational studies. *Statistical Science* 14 (August): 259–78.

Salemi, M., and G. Tauchen. 1987. Simultaneous nonlinear learning models. In
W. E. Becker and W. Walstad, eds., *Econometric modeling in economic education research*, pp. 207–23. Boston: Kluwer-Nijhoff.

Smith, J., and P. Todd. 2001. Reconciling conflicting evidence on the performance of propensity-score matching methods. *American Economic Review
Proceedings* 91 (May): 112–18.

Springer, L., M. E. Stanne, and S. Donovan. 1997. Effects of small-group
learning on undergraduates in science, mathematics, engineering, and technology: A meta-analysis. ASHE Annual Meeting Paper. November 11.

Thompson, B. 2002. What future quantitative social science research could
look like: Confidence intervals for effect sizes. *Educational Researcher* 31
(April): 25–32.

Thursby, J. G. 2000. What do we say about ourselves and what does it mean?
Yet another look at economics department research. *Journal of Economic Literature* 38 (June): 383–404.

Trautwein, S. N., A. Racke, and B. Hillman. 1996/1997. Cooperative learning in the anatomy laboratory. *Journal of College Science Teaching* 26 (December/January): 183–89.

Tversky, A., and D. Kahneman. 1982. Belief in the law of small numbers. In D. Kahneman, P. Slovic, and A. Tversky, eds., *Judgment under uncertainty: Heuristics and biases*, pp. 23–31. Cambridge and New York: Cambridge University Press.

Utts, J. 1991. Replication and meta-analysis in parapsychology. *Statistical Science* 6 (4): 363–403.

Wilkinson, L. 1999. Statistical methods in psychology journals: Guideline and explanations. *American Psychologist* 54 (August): 594–604.

Wainer, H. 2000. Kelley's paradox. *Chance* 13 (1) Winter: 47–48.

Wilson, R. 1986. Improving faculty teaching effectiveness: Use of student evaluations and consultants. *Journal of Higher Education* 57 (March/April): 196–211.

Wright, J. C., R. C. Woods, S. B. Miller, S. A. Koscuik, D. L. Penberthy, P. H. Williams, and B. E. Wampold. 1997. A novel comparative assessment of two learning strategies in a freshman chemistry course for science and engineering majors. University of Wisconsin, Madison: LEAD Center.

Twelve

The Mathematics Throughout the Curriculum Project

Daniel P. Maki

Marc Frantz

Bart S. Ng

The importance of quantitative reasoning skills continues to grow with the complexity of our modern world. Increasing the effectiveness of undergraduate mathematics education is therefore an ongoing effort at virtually every college and university in America. In this chapter we show how aspects of research suggest ways to improve the mathematics curriculum for both majors and nonmajors.

Mathematics courses can imitate positive aspects of research by: (1) helping students discover worthwhile problems that are of interest to them; (2) motivating the learning of mathematics by linking it to the goals of the students; (3) requiring interdisciplinary work by groups of students with diverse skills; (4) requiring students to learn presentation skills for current and future use, and for the sense of satisfaction and closure known well to the researcher, but not found in traditional courses.

In this chapter we describe how faculty members at a research university enhanced undergraduate education through an interdisciplinary program aimed at advancing the teaching of mathematics. We also present some results from our evaluation team, and describe some of the faculty members' dissemination efforts.

The Origin of MTC

Participants and Support

The Indiana University Mathematics Throughout the Curriculum project (MTC) was initiated and sustained by a major grant from the Na-

311

tional Science Foundation's Division of Undergraduate Education (NSF-DUE), through an NSF-DUE initiative called Mathematical Sciences and Their Applications Throughout the Curriculum (MATC). The MATC initiative began in 1994. Its stated purpose was to promote systemic improvements in undergraduate education by increasing student understanding of, and ability to use, the mathematical sciences. The funded projects were to require collaboration of faculty in the mathematical sciences with faculty in other disciplines, and full support of the participating academic units. The projects were expected to result in national models of undergraduate curricula and instructional approaches that would have a profound impact on the participating and adopting institutions.

In response to the MATC initiative, more than 70 faculty members from the eight-campus Indiana University system met in November of 1994 and formed MTC. The group decided on its goals and chose a grant proposal-writing team. In 1996 NSF accepted the MTC proposal, and awarded Indiana University $2.8 million (NSF-DUE #455508) to support the project for five years, which officially began on September 1, 1996. Fellow MATC awardees included the University of Pennsylvania, Rensselaer Polytechnic Institute, Dartmouth College, a joint University of Nebraska/Oklahoma consortium, the State University of New York, and the United States Military Academy.

In addition to the grant from NSF, the principal investigators for MTC successfully applied for, and obtained in May of 1996, a grant of $300,000 from Indiana University's Strategic Directions Initiative, whose goal was to "Place student learning, intellectual exploration, persistence, and attainment at the center of the university's missions." Although the original time period for the NSF grant has expired, MTC is still operating under a three-year, no-cost extension granted by NSF until October 1, 2004. Moreover, MTC has continued to obtain additional outside support for its projects (see, for instance, the section "Mathematics and Art").

Besides the eight campuses of the Indiana University system, MTC participants include faculty from Franklin & Marshall College in Lancaster, Pennsylvania, and the University at Buffalo. Several other institutions have now adopted MTC courses or derivatives of them; we will discuss a few of these also.

The Goals of MTC

Traditional mathematics courses, designed and taught by mathematics faculty, are seldom perceived by students to be an integral part of an education that will prepare them for the challenge of an increasingly technological society. Often students view these classes as a set of hurdles to jump over prior to graduation—particularly those students not majoring in mathematics or in the physical sciences. Moreover, the lack of interaction between mathematics faculty and faculty from other disciplines results in a loss of opportunity for faculty members to convey the importance of mathematics in those disciplines, including the humanities and social sciences, the biological and health sciences, business and finance, and the physical and engineering sciences. Expertise in these disciplines can be exploited by faculty members teaching mathematics courses with exciting pedagogical results.

The primary aim of MTC is truly interdisciplinary course development to correct the students' perception that mathematics is something isolated from, if not irrelevant to, other disciplines, the real world, and their own ambitions and goals. To this end, MTC required its course developers to:

1. help students discover worthwhile problems that are of genuine interest to them;
2. motivate the learning of mathematics by linking it to goals of interest to the students;
3. require interdisciplinary work by groups of students with diverse skills;
4. require students to learn presentation skills for future use, and for the sense of satisfaction and closure known well to the researcher, but often lost in traditional courses;
5. disseminate these approaches nationwide through workshops, presentations at national meetings, scholarly publications, and the development of course materials.

Methods and Activities

We illustrate the methods of MTC by describing selected courses and the activities of their course developers, including classroom methods, materials development, and dissemination efforts. The project has fostered the development of two dozen interdisciplinary courses spanning disciplines as diverse as art, business, biology, journalism, history, politics, speech and hearing, criminal justice, and finance (a complete list of courses and instructors appears in the appendix). From these we have made a selection intended to suggest the range of instructional approaches, the diversity of targeted student audiences, and the challenges involved in truly interdisciplinary education. We also discuss some of the activities of the project's evaluation team, and the scholarly work that has resulted from their efforts.

314

The Prototype Course: Analytical Problem Solving

The prototype course for the MTC project was a course called Analytical Problem Solving (APS), developed and taught by mathematician Daniel Maki and business professor Wayne Winston at Indiana University's Bloomington campus (IUB). APS had already become a success at IUB by the time of the grant proposal, and was seen as a proof-of-concept course by NSF. The course has continued to flourish since its inception, and has continued to play a role as a model for course development.

The majority of the students who take APS are liberal arts majors (English, foreign languages, history, social sciences, etc.) in the Liberal Arts in Management Program who wish to learn how mathematics is used in business. The course was based on the idea that most students will appreciate mathematics more if they see an immediate use for it. With this in mind, the entire course was built around group projects. In addition, it had the following distinctive features which students have found especially appealing.

- Real problems, obtained from businesses and governmental units, were used to illustrate the relevance of the mathematical topics covered. The course was project-driven with topics matching the knowledge needed to complete the projects.
- All mathematical topics taught in the course were then used immediately in the projects; thus the students saw the usefulness of mathematics in solving a diverse set of real-life problems.
- Students worked in teams using computer software, primarily Microsoft Excel, to apply the mathematical tools developed in the class for the projects.
- Students were required to document, explain, and defend their mathematical work, thereby honing their communications skills and gaining a sense of closure and accomplishment.

An example of one project was the scheduling of tellers at a local credit union. Students began by collecting data on service times. Then they used hourly and daily customer data to develop a model that could be used to forecast the teller workload at the credit union at any time. Next, queuing theory was used to determine, as a function of the forecasted workload and service rate, the number of tellers needed at any given time. A user-friendly spreadsheet was developed that could be used by the credit union personnel manager to determine the manpower needs at any time. Finally, the students developed a linear programming model to determine the minimum cost of scheduling tellers to meet forecasted manpower needs. This single project required students to utilize basic statistics, regression analysis, queuing theory, advanced spreadsheet techniques, and linear programming.

Thus, from the students' point of view, the main goal of the project was not to pass an exam, but to produce a spreadsheet that could be (and actually has been) used by the credit union to minimize its costs and better serve its customers. In other words, students acted as real consultants conducting original research. Similar APS consulting projects have been done for the Indiana State Department of Health, K and W Corporation, A. C. Nielson, Otis Elevator, Summit Health Care, Cummins Engine, Steak N Shake, Applied Composites Engineering, Bedford Machine & Tool, and Applied Laboratories (pharmaceutical and health care products).

From the instructors' point of view, the projects must be carefully chosen so as to be manageable by the students, but challenging enough to require them to learn a significant amount of new mathematics. The work begins long before the start of the semester, with instructors meeting potential clients to discuss possible projects and other issues such as confidentiality requirements. The semester ends with student teams giving presentations to their clients, but the impact on the students extends well beyond that. Many students have gained the confidence to take further quantitative courses they had not originally planned on, and more than one graduate has returned to report that the deciding factor in a successful job interview was their report of the consulting project they did as a student.

Thus, despite the labor-intensive nature of APS, instructors at other campuses have enthusiastically adopted and adapted versions of the course. A version of the course has been adopted at Clarion University in Pennsylvania. At Indiana University Southeast, Kathryn Ernstberger (business) and Christopher Lang (mathematics) adapted the course as Applied Mathematics in Business. At Indiana University South Bend, Paul Kochanowski (economics) and Morteza Shafii-Mousavi (mathematics) have used the same class format with Mathematics in Action: Social and Industrial Problems. Although APS is aimed at upper-level undergraduate honors students, the latter course is a finite mathematics course for a broader base of students, and serves as our next example.

Course Adaptations

Mathematics in Action: Social and Industrial Problems. The audience for *Mathematics in Action* consisted of Indiana University South Bend (IUSB) students who normally took the IUSB courses Finite Mathematics (business and economics majors), Excursions in Mathematics (a course satisfying Liberal Arts and Sciences, along with other divisions' requirements), or Mathematics for Elementary Teachers (required for pre-service K–8 teachers). Mathematics in Action has attracted a diverse group of students from business, economics, liberal arts and sciences, nursing, and education. Student counselors advise students to enroll in Mathematics in Action, as an alternative to the above courses, because of its innovative nature and the success of former students. Former students advertised the course by writing articles in the student newspaper and by word of mouth. In addition, the instructors advertised the course as an innovative, exciting, real-world approach to learning mathematical tools; they posted course flyers around the campus and distributed the flyer in several classes.

Although the student audience was more broad-based than that of Analytical Problem Solving, the instructors were still able to teach a substantial amount of mathematics by linking it to real-world problems. Mathematical topics typically included data description, combinatorics, probability, conditional probability and Bayesian methods, network analysis, linear systems and matrices, optimization, project planning and control, inventory models, and queuing theory.

Like Analytical Problem Solving, Mathematics in Action was project-driven, with the students ultimately working on original problems. In the first semester of the course (spring 1997), the instructors recruited projects from seven local businesses and organizations, and each student worked on a team assigned to one of these projects. Given a particular project, student teams started by formulating research issues, problems, and questions. They then focused on data needs and on acquiring the mathematical, statistical, and computer skills necessary to solve these problems. For example, one team analyzed advertisements for the *South Bend Times*, a small publisher of weekly papers. The students conducted surveys to determine and compare readership and perceptions of the *Times–Penny Saver* publication with those of *the South Bend Tribune*, the major newspaper in the area, to evaluate the cost-effectiveness of advertising in the two publications. They showed that it was cheaper to advertise in the smaller newspaper; companies that did so reached more people who bought their specific products. The team documented its findings in a 47-page report and presented it to *Penny Saver.*

"We actually got to use things like probability and frequency tables and see that it worked," said one team member. "We were not just taking a test." This kind of practical experience is just what Shafii-Mousavi and Kochanowski had in mind when they developed the course. "These industry projects are so comprehensive," said Shafii-Mousavi. "The students learn how to deal with clients, with computers, with group projects, how to present the project, etc."

Mathematics in Action has been taught every spring since 1997. Recent projects included an indirect loan risk analysis for Teachers Credit Union, a copying cost analysis for Penn Harris Madison School Corporation, a mail delivery routing study for IUSB Special Services, a student retention analysis for IUSB, and a study for IUSB Security.

Kochanowski, Shafii-Mousavi, and Maki engaged in an extensive amount of dissemination of Mathematics in Action as well as Analytical Problem Solving, in the form of published and presented papers, workshops, and talks at national meetings. For a selection of published works, see Maki (2002) and Kochanowski and Shafii-Mousavi (1999a,b, 2000a,b).

Introduction to History. An example of an MTC course aimed at students with basic mathematics skills is Introduction to History, developed and taught at Indiana University Purdue University Indianapolis (IUPUI) by historian Monroe Little and statistician Jyotirmoy Sarkar of the IUPUI Department of Mathematical Sciences. This first-year course, offered for both history and mathematics credit, was composed primarily of high-risk freshmen—students who had little background in mathematics and whose motivational deficits added an extra challenge for the instructors. Again, the primary motivator was a focus on real-world applications.

The introductory assignment was drawn from an event garnering nationwide attention at that moment: the filmed story of the sinking of the Titanic. For their first assignment, students in the class analyzed passenger and crew records form the ill-fated ship, specifically focusing on the 15 members of the ship's band.

Although the class kept its focus narrow, the Titanic exercise helped the instructors to introduce students to the notion of historical debate. Debate about the Titanic, according to Little, has tended to fall into two camps. Although some historians believe survival of the shipwreck depended on chance, others believe survival reflected a social hierarchy among the first-, second-, and third-class passengers that reflected Victorian society. Rather than have students read one historian's interpretation of the event, however, Little and Sarkar equipped students with the data and basic statistical skills that allowed them to draw conclusions for themselves.

After completing this first assignment, the class moved on to more in-depth statistical studies of the 1860 census, provided by the IU Historical Society. These data, available to students through the course web site, provided unusually detailed information about individuals included in the census—information on a range of characteristics, from name, race, sex and marital status to the amount of real and personal property a person owned.

Students, who were then required to develop research proposals for themselves, delved into the census data to find areas of personal interest. The assignment also offered students the opportunity to explore more specialized paths of research, such as African-American history and women's history.

Catch the Waves to Calculus. In contrast to Introduction to History, the MTC course Catch the Waves to Calculus targeted freshmen who were exceptionally well prepared. This honors calculus course, developed by mathematician Peter Hamburger of Indiana University–Purdue University Fort Wayne (IPFW), gets its name from its central topic, Fourier analysis—the analysis of wave phenomena.

Hamburger got the idea for the course when his daughter, a Ph.D. student at Caltech, asked him for a crash course in Fourier analysis to help her in her biochemistry research. Although the "course" took only two weeks, Hamburger's lengthy preparation resulted in extensive lecture notes, which he realized could form the core of an exciting introduction to calculus for honor students. The catch to this "catching the waves" approach is that Fourier analysis, when presented rigorously, is as challenging as it is powerful. In fact, many mathematics majors do not encounter it until their junior or senior year. Add to that the fact that Hamburger's classes have been mainly composed of freshmen, high school students, and even a junior high school student, and the challenge becomes a formidable one.

Moreover, for Hamburger it was not enough for his honors calculus students to "turn the crank" of Fourier analysis, by merely applying the major results. He wanted them to be able to derive those results if asked. To meet this challenge, he presented the mathematics in two forms. First, he used a highly innovative textbook called *Who is Fourier? A Mathematical Adventure* (Gleason translation 1995). The authors of the textbook are not professors, but students of the Transnational College of LEX, a Japanese school where students as young as middle-school age study eleven foreign languages at once. In order to better understand the sounds of speech, the students learned Fourier analysis, treating mathematics as just another language to assimilate. *Who is Fourier?*, the result of their efforts, is likely the most intuitive text ever written on the subject.

In addition to formulas, the book contains countless illustrations, cartoon characters (children who teach the reader), and scissors-and-paper exercises. The text is not only inspiring, it's also humbling to anyone accustomed to the state of secondary mathematics education in America. On the same page where Euler's formula is derived using Maclaurin series, a little girl in a baseball cap enthusiastically quotes physicist Richard Feynman: "It's the most remarkable formula in mathematics. This is our jewel."

The text could not accomplish everything, however. To supplement the intuitive approach of the book, Hamburger supplied written lecture notes that add detail and rigor to the presentation.

There is yet a third dimension to the course, an interdisciplinary component that makes it a true MTC course. The students apply the mathematics they learn to undergraduate research projects that are supervised by faculty from other disciplines. Projects have resulted in publications and even a patent.

Can it all really work? To anyone who has seen presentations by Hamburger's students, the answer is self-evident. For example, on April 20, 2000, parents, students, and faculty from IPFW and IU Bloomington assembled at the IPFW campus to hear research presentations from the spring semester class. To give an idea of the results Hamburger has obtained, several of the talks are listed below. The reader should also take note of the ages of these honors students, as indicated by their class rank.

- Gregory Rohling (high school student), *Determination of Fracture Velocity along a Fault.* Project Supervisor: Dipak Chowdhury, Geology, IPFW.
- Stacy McVay (freshman mathematics/chemistry student), *Fourier Transform in NMR Measurements of Spin-Lattice Relaxation in Complex Hydrides.* Project Supervisor: Donald D. Linn, Chemistry, IPFW. McVay's work with Linn demonstrated the existence of a new type of chemical bond, and resulted in a joint paper with former Hamburger student Gabriel Skidd (Linn, Skidd, and McVay 2000).
- Richard Wartell (junior high school student), *Transforming Fourier Series.* Project Supervisor: Peter Hamburger, Mathematics, IPFW.
- Colin Heinmann (freshman engineering student), *Reconstructing Synthetic Radio Telescope Images.* Project Supervisor: Naresh Mathur, Electrical Engineering, IPFW.

The above results are typical of the success of Catch the Waves, which has been taught each semester since the fall of 1997. In recognition of the success of the course, the IPFW School of Arts and Sciences honored Hamburger with its 2001 Award for the Enhancement of

Learning. In November 2001, Hamburger and students Alex James and Richard Wartell (mentioned above) gave presentations of their work to the National Collegiate Honors Council Convention (Hamburger 2001; James 2001; Wartell 2001). James and fellow student Gabriel Skidd also gave a poster presentation of their research (in geology and chemistry, respectively) to a national meeting of all seven MATC consortia at IUB in 1999.

Each year, Hamburger offers, along with colleagues from IPFW, a workshop called "Physics-Based Calculus" (www.ipfw.edu/math/Workshop/PBC.html), designed to train high school and college instructors to implement the approach of Catch the Waves. The course home page is located at www.ipfw.edu/math/h-calculus/.

Speech and Hearing Sciences. Another MTC course with an emphasis on Fourier analysis and waves is the IUB course Mathematical Foundations for Speech and Hearing Sciences. This course, developed by speech and hearing sciences (SPHS) professors Diane Kewley-Port and David Eddins, and then mathematics education doctoral student Paul Kehle, debuted in the fall of 1997. It has become a required undergraduate SPHS course at IUB and also at the University at Buffalo where Eddins now teaches. SPHS spans two professions: speech and language pathology, and audiology. Entry-level career positions for each area require a master's degree. Foundations was designed to better prepare undergraduates to enter graduate school, and hence be competitive in these fields.

Analyzing sound waves from human speech in Microsoft Excel, the instructors have been able to present the difficult concept of Fourier analysis to the introductory-level class. To Eddins, the course could not have been as successful without the interdisciplinary collaboration. He and Kewley-Port had never taught mathematics as a primary topic before, and without the MTC project would not have been able to collaborate with Kehle. Eddins says this "one-of-a-kind" course that presents mathematics within the SPHS context was designed to make undergraduates more competitive as prospective graduate students in three ways: to better prepare students for the mathematics component of the GRE, to improve problem-solving skills needed for graduate courses, and to document strong mathematics skills on students' undergraduate transcripts.

Foundations is taught with interactive courseware that has been developed and published, with MTC support, as a compact disk (Eddins, Kewley-Port, and Kehle 2002). The course primarily consists of five projects on the topics of sound generation, vowel synthesis, hearing aids, clinical decision-making and voice disorders. Each student has a project, frequently done with the aid of advanced work with Excel. Problem sets to review and develop mathematics concepts accompany each project. Projects can be taught as stand-alone modules within other courses. The course home page is at www.indiana.edu/~acoustic/s319/s319home.html.

Kewley-Port, Kehle, and Eddins disseminate their techniques through residential workshops, for example, one held at IUB on May 24–25, 2003. They have also published expository articles about their course (Eddins, Kewley-Port, and Kehle 2000; Kehle, Kewley-Port, and Eddins 2001; Kehle, Eddins, and Kewley-Port in press).

Concepts of Biology. As with the SPHS course above, the content of the MTC course Concepts of Biology I: Plants was motivated by the perception that majors in this particular science needed better skills and greater confidence in their application of mathematics. In this case the audience was freshmen biology majors at IUPUI. Biologist Robert Keck had taught a more traditional version of this required course for many years, and had come to realize that students' lack of skill and confidence in approaching even basic quantitative problems in biology indicated that mathematics should be given more emphasis in the course. Thus in 1996 Keck teamed up with mathematician Richard Patterson, and with the support of MTC they wrote the textbook *Biomath: Problem Solving for Biology Students* (Keck and Patterson 2000), and built the course around the textbook.

The book and the course put a strong emphasis on quantitative problems for four reasons: to give students a deeper understanding of the biological concepts; to give them an appreciation for what biologists need to know about mathematics; to develop their critical thinking in questioning, analyzing data and evaluating assumptions; and to develop written presentation skills and the ability to work with others. The course has a 50-minute recitation section each week. A different problem was given to each group of four or five students. After grading, the solutions were posted on a bulletin board. The students could read the other problems and solutions, as well as see how their own problem was approached by groups from different sections of the course.

The book features self-contained problems such as the analysis of the enzymatic action of catalase, the pH of the stomach, and microtubules in mitosis. The basic mathematical topics include unit conversion and arithmetic, elementary algebra, geometry formulas, graphing and graph interpretation, logarithms, doubling time and half-life, and regression line analysis. The last part of every question asks what assumptions were made. Thus, students learn that problems can be solved in more than one way depending on the assumptions.

Biomath has been well received by other instructors who perceive the same need for quantitative skills on the part of their students. In the summer of 2000, more than 30 faculty from 13 schools attended an NSF-sponsored workshop titled "Partnerships: An Interdisciplinary Workshop for Faculty in Life Sciences and Mathematics" at Carroll College in Montana. At the end of the workshop, 13 faculty teams presented their plans for curricula development, and 12 of the plans incorporated *Biomath* as a textbook.

Mathematics and Statistics for Journalism. When Paul Voakes was an editorial writer for the *San Jose Mercury News,* and well into his 15-year journalism career, he began moonlighting as an adjunct professor at Stanford University. Having "caught the teaching bug," he eventually came to the Department of Journalism at IUB. His background had given him a broad view of things, including a conviction of the importance of writing clearly and accurately about quantitative issues. This made him an ideal partner for mathematics professor Chuck Livingston in the development of the MTC course Mathematics and Statistics for Journalism.

The course syllabus expresses the instructors' goals in a warning to the students:

> A large part of your professional responsibility will be to gather information independently and to present it accurately in a meaningful context. Without skills in mathematics or stats, journalists constantly have to rely on the calculations and interpretations of their sources, and they constantly hope and pray that the numbers they use in their writing are appropriate and correct. . . . However, journalists armed with some logic, some technique and some interpretive skills can analyze research, ask appropriate questions and understand the data well enough to tell readers and viewers clearly what the numbers mean.

When asked to name the single most important thing he would like to get across to his students, Voakes said it was the idea that "You can tell stories with numbers and do it with confidence." Confidence, of course, must come from skills. In that regard, Livingston acted as the "pioneer," teaching the course in its first semester in the fall of 1999. Voakes attended every class, and together the two instructors assessed the students' weaknesses and strengths. In the process, Voakes learned mathematics pedagogy from Livingston, which he says has made him a better teacher. The spring 2000 semester of the course was taught by Voakes, with Livingston observing on a regular basis. Mathematics topics in the course included probability and inferential statistics.

The course, which has now become a requirement for journalism majors, also covers descriptive statistics, with an emphasis on the graphical representation of data. Students polish their skills in weekly computer labs, using Microsoft Excel. According to Voakes, it is increasingly common for reporters to create the initial mathematical graphs and charts they need, before turning them over to an artist for embellishment and final polishing. Not surprisingly, writing is also a part of the course. Test, quiz and homework problems frequently end with the assignment of writing a short news story, or part of an imagined story, that explains the meaning of a numerical result.

Voakes has presented the results of the course at the National Journalism Educators Meeting (Voakes 1999).

The Mathematics of Finance. The level of undergraduate mathematics presented in MTC courses ranges from basic to advanced. An example of the latter is the course Introduction to the Mathematics of Finance, developed by IUB mathematics professors Victor Goodman and Joseph Stampfli. The prerequisites of this senior-level course include calculus, linear algebra, and probability and statistics, with ordinary differential equations considered helpful. Mathematics techniques introduced in the course include stochastic partial differential equations and Black-Scholes analysis, a key tool in modern finance. (In 1973, Fischer Black and Myron Scholes showed how a partial differential equation, surprisingly like a heat equation from physics, could be used to determine the fair market value for certain stock options. The method is widely used today.)

The financial topics covered include modeling, hedging, stochastic processes, arbitrage, Brownian-motion risk management, asset allocation, term structure of interest rates, option pricing, and market volatility. The focus is on real-world examples and applications, using basic stock, currency, and interest rate models. The course's Excel worksheets, for example, include actual data from the *Wall Street Journal.*

A substantial number of mathematics majors take the course, and for them the mathematics goes fairly smoothly. However, they face a barrage of new and unfamiliar financial terminology. Their fellow students from finance and economics are familiar with the terminology, but for them the mathematics tends to be more of a challenge. That's where the structure of the course helps out. Course grades are based on homework and group projects, so there is ample opportunity for students to collaborate and learn from each other. Final projects can be chosen from a list, but Stampfli says the students often come up with better ideas themselves. One group used time series methods to show a link between the stock prices of Compaq, Dell, and Gateway computer companies: it was possible to use the stock prices of one company to predict the change in those of another.

According to Goodman, the interdisciplinary atmosphere has affected students' decisions after taking the course. A graduate mathematics student, for instance, changed her career to finance and now works for a financial firm in Chicago. On the other hand, some finance students have decided to take more mathematics afterwards, for example, a student who subsequently enrolled in one of Goodman's probability courses. In fact, the course's success has spawned a new IUB graduate mathematics program in finance.

Goodman and Stampfli have written their own textbook for the course, as well as a detailed instructor's manual (Goodman and Stampfli 2001a,b). To insure that the approach of the textbook was both timely and realistic, Stampfli visited two leading financial institutions, Salomon Smith Barney and Goldman Sachs, to get advice from experts on the content.

On June 9–10, 2000, Goodman and Stampfli hosted the *Workshop in the Teaching of Financial Mathematics* at IUB. More than 25 faculty from various institutions around the country attended the workshop. Each workshop participant received a pre-publication copy of Goodman and Stampfli's textbook.

Mathematics and Art. The MTC course Mathematics and Art was designed to connect with a nontraditional audience including art majors. The course developers are both from mathematics departments: Marc Frantz, originally at IUPUI and now at IUB, and Annalisa Crannell of Franklin & Marshall College. Frantz's undergraduate degree is in fine arts, and he had a previous career in the arts before changing to mathematics.

There is a burgeoning interest in combining the two subjects, but few standard courses in the area. There is also considerable interest at many schools in promoting mathematics for liberal arts students, particularly in the form of freshman seminar courses. Thus, Frantz and Crannell saw an opportunity for a well-designed course, accompanied by appropriate materials, to proliferate beyond their own institutions; this has in fact been the case.

Although Frantz and Crannell teach the course somewhat differently at their respective schools, the two versions have much in common. For example, a major emphasis is placed on a true understanding of perspective that goes beyond memorizing the standard tricks taught to art students. Not only does this enable students to solve drawing problems that would stump most art majors, it also adds greatly to their appreciation of existing art.

For instance, one property of any perspective drawing or painting is that there is a unique point from which it should be viewed (with one eye closed) for the optimum experience of depth and realism. Although a few people are aware of this, practically no one knows how to find this special viewpoint. Nevertheless, anyone who understands the principles behind perspective can find the viewpoint with only a pair of shish kebab skewers (or pencils, etc.) and a little mathematical reasoning. An important highlight of the course is a field trip to a gallery or museum for perspective viewing. Frantz uses the Indianapolis Museum of Art and Crannell uses the Phillips Museum at Franklin & Marshall. This field experience invariably makes a lasting impression on students, for when a well-done perspective painting is viewed from the most appropriate viewpoint, the sense of depth is astonishingly greater than from anywhere else in the room.

This example highlights another similarity between the two versions of the course: they are both strongly activity-based. Both have a studio component, a computer lab component, a visit with a professional artist, and group and individual projects. Other topics include tilings, symmetry, coordinate and synthetic geometry, basic fractal geometry, affine transformations, limits, sequences, and series.

As an example of a student project, one of Frantz's students, a ceramics major, wanted to study the texture patterns on his own pottery. He designed a final project in which he digitally photographed three of his ceramic pieces and analyzed the texture patterns using a measurement called the box counting dimension. This empirical measurement gives an estimate of the fractal dimension, or space-filling tendency, of a pattern. He then used a software package called FractaSketch to create fractal patterns with the same dimensions, and embossed and colorized the fractal textures with Adobe Photoshop. The result was a trio of near-photographic images that so strongly resembled the original pieces that the student called them "virtual pottery."

Crannell's students have gone on to continue their explorations of the links between mathematics and art. In the fall of 1996, students Hayley Rintel and Melissa Shearer took Crannell's course in mathematics and art. In their sophomore year, they enrolled in Crannell's abstract algebra class, where they revisited tilings by looking at the algebraic structure of symmetry groups. A year later, the students obtained funding from their school to visit Spain and Italy during the summer of 1999. The goal of that trip was to document and compare the similarities and differences between Spanish and Italian architecture, using geometry and abstract algebra as tools for pattern analysis.

Their research resulted in an extensive collection of photographs, tutorials, and analyses that they presented as a series of web pages, and which formed the first part of a senior project that earned them honors in mathematics. Moreover, their web pages were subsequently accepted and published in the Mathematical Association of America's peer-reviewed *Journal of Online Mathematics* (Rintel and Shearer 2001).

In the summer of 2000, Frantz and Crannell began a series of residential mathematics and art workshops for teachers called VIEWPOINTS (php.indiana.edu/~mathart/viewpoints). The workshops have two components. The summer version consists of five days of intense activity-based training on the campus of Franklin & Marshall College. Each participant is provided with art supplies, course handouts, and a copy of the textbook *Lessons in Mathematics and Art* (Frantz 2001), written with MTC support. In the fall, participants reunite for a one-day follow-up workshop at IUB, where they give presentations on their use of VIEWPOINTS ideas and materials in their classes.

The follow-up workshop has helped motivate participants to implement mathematics and art projects in their classrooms. At Clarion University, mathematician Steve Gendler and artist Jim Rose have developed an intensive mathematics course for art majors that meets twice a week for mathematics classes run by Gendler, followed by studio sessions supervised by Rose. The class uses Frantz's *Lessons in Mathematics and Art*. Julie Labbiento, another VIEWPOINTS graduate at Clarion, developed VIEWPOINTS ideas and techniques into two sections of a mathematics course for liberal arts majors. Labbiento's students study symmetry, surrealism, optical art, tessellations, fractals, and perspective, as examples of mathematics in the arts. At Cardinal Stritch University in Milwaukee, mathematician Barbara Reynolds and artist Peter Galante are also developing a required mathematics course for art majors. Reynolds has already used VIEWPOINTS techniques in some of her other classes.

Other graduates who have employed VIEWPOINTS ideas and techniques in their classes include Michelle Penner (DePauw University), Ann Hanson (Columbia College), David Hartz (College of St. Benedict, Saint John's University), Patricia Hauss (Arapahoe Community College), Patricia Oakley (Goshen College), Jenni Rodin (Chadron State College), Robert Wolfe and Mary Jane Wolfe (University of Rio Grande), Ray Beaulieu (Sul Ross State University), Judy Meckley (Joliet Junior College), Dinesh Sarvate and Barbara Duval (College of Charleston), and Judy Silver (Marshall University).

The success of VIEWPOINTS, and the success of MTC in general have enabled Frantz and Crannell to obtain additional support. During 2001, the VIEWPOINTS workshops were supported by the Mathematical Association of America's Professional Enhancement Program. In the summer of 2002, Frantz and Maki successfully applied to NSF for supplemental funding to support VIEWPOINTS participants. Participants in VIEWPOINTS 2003 (June 8–13) received free tuition, lodging, meals, and art supplies.

In spring 2003, Frantz taught a new version of Mathematics and Art at IUB with Ayelet Lindenstrauss of the IUB mathematics department. For further information on the course, see Frantz (1998) and Crannell and Frantz (2000).

Evaluation

A key component of MTC is the project's evaluation team. Lead Evaluator Diana Lambdin, Associate Professor of Mathematics Education at IUB, and Ph.D. students Dasha Kinelovsky and Rajee Amarasinghe (now an Assistant Professor of Mathematics Education at California State University, Fresno) comprised the evaluation team. During each year of the original term of the grant, the evaluators prepared a detailed evaluation report for the National Science Foundation. The report is based on classroom observations, examination of course materials and student work, administration of questionnaires to students, and interviews of instructors and students.

In addition to this work, the evaluators brought the MTC project to the attention of educators nationwide through talks, presentations, and papers (Amarasinghe and Lambdin 2000; Kinelovsky, Amarasinghe, and Lambdin 2000). Amarasinghe, Kinelovsky, and Lambdin (2000) addressed what may be the most difficult part of the evaluators' job—assessing whether MTC courses make positive changes in students' attitudes toward mathematics. The authors ". . . documented [positive] changes in student attitudes about mathematics and mathematics learning in four key areas: connections, confidence, technology, and usefulness."

Amarasinghe in his Ph.D. thesis (Amarasinghe 2000) also examined the impact of MTC courses on student attitudes. Amarasinghe studied eight introductory-level MTC courses, including five of the courses described above (Applied Mathematics in Business, Mathematics in Action, Introduction to History, Mathematical Foundations for Speech and Hearing Sciences, and Mathematics and Art). The study, which recently won the Outstanding Dissertation Award from the IUB Department of Curriculum and Instruction, was in agreement with the conclusions of the American Educational Research Association paper: "Data indicated that students who completed [MTC] classes significantly changed their attitudes and beliefs positively while students in traditional classes did not" (Amarasinghe 2000, p. vi).

Amarasinghe concluded, "These results confirmed some of the results obtained in recent studies. For example, Blumenfeld et al. (1991) suggested that project based learning increases students' interest, Pea (1988) suggested that technology enhances students' interest, and Ames (1994) suggested that learning in group dimensions enhances mathematics learning. These results were supported in the data gathered" (Amarasinghe 2000, p. 155).

Conclusion

The idea of using projects and research to motivate students is not a new one. Faculty at research universities are potentially the most convincing proponents of the value of their subjects, having freely chosen to spend their professional lives immersed in them. However, there are two obstacles to this approach that are particularly formidable in mathematics. The first, which we have mentioned, is the traditional perception among students that mathematics is dry and remote from their own interests and the real world. The second obstacle stems from the maturity and success of the subject itself. With regard to pure mathematics, virtually all of the significant problems accessible to undergraduates have been posed and solved long ago. In fact, modern research in pure mathematics is generally not even readable by students with less than a first-year graduate education, let alone doable by undergraduate non-majors.

The interdisciplinary approach described in this chapter provided a way around both of these obstacles. As we have seen, it allowed instructors to connect mathematics in an authentic way with topics of interest to their students, with some freedom on the part of the students to choose the topics, just as a researcher does. Moreover, by connecting mathematics with other disciplines, the supply of accessible and genuinely interesting problems was greatly increased. Consequently, even introductory-level students could experience the excitement of tackling an original problem, and the satisfaction of bringing it to a well-written and/or well-presented conclusion. As the dissemination work of MTC continues during the grant extension, we hope and expect that other institutions will continue to adopt and adapt our courses, and share the benefits of this approach to mathematics education.

References

Amarasinghe, Rajee. 2000. A study of student attitudes and beliefs when learning introductory college mathematics in context. Ph.D. dissertation, Indiana University.

Amarasinghe, R., D. Kinelovsky, and D. Lambdin. 2000. Student motivation and attitudes in learning college mathematics through interdisciplinary courses. Paper presented at the annual conference of the American Educational Research Association (AERA), 25 April, New Orleans, Louisiana.

Amarasinghe, R., and D. Lambdin. 2000. Uses of computer technology in interdisciplinary mathematics learning. Paper presented at the annual International Conference on Learning with Technology, 8–10 March, at Temple University.

Ames, C. 1984. Achievement attributions and self-instructions under competitive and individualistic goal structures. *Journal of Educational Psychology* 76 (3): 478–87.

Blumenfeld, P. C., E. Soloway, R. W. Marx, J. S. Krajcik, M. Guzdial, and A. Palincsar. 1991. Motivating project-based learning: Sustaining the doing, supporting the learning. *Educational Psychologist* 26 (3&4): 369–98.

Crannell, A., and M. Frantz. 2000. A course in mathematics and art. *Journal of Geoscience Education* 48 (3): 313–16.

Eddins, D., D. Kewley-Port, and P. Kehle. 2000. Integrating math, physics, speech, hearing, computers and fun: Multimedia courseware. *ASHA Leader* 5 (16): 113.

———. 2002. Mathematics and physics for speech and hearing: A problem-based approach (CD-ROM). San Diego: Singular Publishing.

Frantz, M. 1998. How to look at art. *SIAM News* 31: 1–2. See also www.siam.org/siamnews/05-98/art.htm.

———. 2001. *Lessons in mathematics and art.* Online text at php.indiana.edu/~mathart/viewpoints/lessons/.

Gleason, A., trans. 1995. *Who is Fourier? A mathematical adventure.* Boston: Language Research Foundation.

Goodman, V., and J. Stampfli. 2001a. *The mathematics of finance: Modeling and hedging.* Pacific Grove, CA: Brooks/Cole.

———. 2001b. *Instructor's guide for Stampfli and Goodman's The Mathematics of Finance.* Pacific Grove, CA: Brooks/Cole.

Hamburger, P. 2001. Developing an honors calculus course. Paper presented at the National Collegiate Honors Council Convention, Chicago, Illinois.

James, A. 2001. Fractal power spectra and noise analysis. Paper presented at the National Collegiate Honors Council Convention, Chicago, Illinois.

Keck, R. W., and R. R. Patterson. 2000. *Biomath: Problem solving for biology students.* San Francisco: Benjamin/Cummings.

Kehle, P., D. Eddins, and D. Kewley-Port. In press. An interdisciplinary project-based approach to teaching the mathematical foundations of speech and hearing sciences. *Journal of the American Academy of Audiology.*

Kehle, P., D. Kewley-Port, and D. Eddins. 2001. Say ah: Identifying voice pathologies by studying harmonic-to-noise ratios. *Consortium* (Fall): 13–15.

Kinelovsky, D., R. Amarasinghe, and D. Lambdin. 2000. Multiple approaches to teaching interdisciplinary mathematics courses. Paper presented at Fifth Annual Conference and Meeting for the Southeastern Association of Educational Studies, 26–27 February, at the University of North Carolina, Chapel Hill.

Kochanowski, P., and M. Shafii-Mousavi. 1999a. Lessons learned from teaching an interdisciplinary course in economics and mathematics. In the proceedings of the conference Mathematical Modeling in the Undergraduate Curriculum, University of Wisconsin–La Crosse.

———. 1999b. Mathematics in action: Social and industrial problems. In the proceedings of the conference Mathematical Modeling in the Undergraduate Curriculum, University of Wisconsin–La Crosse.

———. 2000a. How to design and teach a project-based first-year finite mathematics course. *The UMAP Journal* 21.2 (June): 119–38.

———. 2000b. Modeling real-world projects in an interdisciplinary finite mathematics service course. In the proceedings of the Mathematical Modeling Symposium, University of Wisconsin–LaCrosse.

Linn, D., G. Skidd, and S. McVay. 2000. Less usual complex transition metal hydrides, $[MH6]^{4}$–: (M = Fe and Ru). Paper presented at the 219th American Chemical Society Meeting, March 28, San Francisco.

Maki, D. 2002. Mathematics everywhere. *Research & Creative Activity* 24 (3): 3–4. Indiana University Office of Research. See also www.indiana.edu/~rcapub/.

Pea, R. D. 1988. Distributed intelligence in learning and reasoning processes. Paper presented at the meeting of the Cognitive Science Society, Montreal, Canada.

Rintel, H., and M. Shearer. 2001. Mathematics & architecture. *Journal of Online Mathematics and its Applications* 1 (2): http://www.joma.org/offsite.html?page=http://www.joma.org/vol1-2/framecss/rintel/

Voakes, P. 1999. A course in mathematics and statistics for journalism students. Paper presented at the National Journalism Educators Meeting, June 3, St. Petersburg, Florida.

Wartell, R. 2001. Transforming Fourier series into Fourier transforms. Paper presented at the National Collegiate Honors Council Convention, Chicago, Illinois.

Appendix: MTC Courses and Instructors

Campus abbreviations:

IUB = Indiana University Bloomington
IUS = Indiana University Southeast
IUPUI = Indiana University Purdue University Indianapolis
IPFW = Indiana University—Purdue University Fort Wayne

IUSB = Indiana University South Bend
IUN = Indiana University Northwest
SUNY-B = University at Buffalo, State University of New York
F&M = Franklin & Marshall College

Analytical Decision Making. IUB. Wayne Winston (Business) and Daniel Maki (Mathematics).

Applications of Mathematics to Biological Problems. IUS. David Winship Taylor (Biology) and James J. Woeppel (Mathematics).

Applied Mathematics in Business. IUSE. Kathy Ernstberger (Business & Economics) and Chris Lang (Mathematics).

Biomechanics. IUB. Vassilios Vardaxis (Kinesiology) and Betty Haven (Kinesiology).

Calculus for Business. IUPUI. Bart Ng (Mathematical Sciences).

Catch the Waves to Calculus. IPFW. Peter Hamburger (Mathematical Sciences).

Concepts of Biology I: Plants. IUPUI. Robert Keck (Biology) and Richard Patterson (Mathematical Sciences).

Differential Equations & Chaotic Systems in Science. IUPUI. Raima Larter (Chemistry) and Wei-min Liu (Mathematics).

Finite Mathematics for Social Sciences. IUS. Mary Ann Baker (Social Sciences) and Dylan Shi (Mathematics).

Games and Decision Making. IUPUI. Subir K. Chakrabarti (Economics, IUPUI) and Charalambros D. Aliprantis (Management/Mathematics, Purdue).

Games for Business and Economics: How Strategy Matters. IUB. Roy Gardner (Economics) and Daniel Maki (Mathematics).

Mathematical Foundations for Speech & Hearing Sciences. IUB and SUNY-B. David A. Eddins (Speech & Hearing, SUNY-B) and Diane Kewley-Port (Speech & Hearing, IUB).

Mathematical Modeling of Physical Systems. IUPUI. Kashyap Vasavada (Physics) and Asok Sen (Mathematical Sciences).

Mathematics and Art. IUPUI, IUB and F&M. Annalisa Crannell (Mathematics, F&M), Marc Frantz and Ayelet Lindenstrauss (Mathematics, IUB).

Mathematics and Politics. IUN. Iztok Hozo (Mathematics).

Mathematics and Statistics for Journalism. IUB. Paul Voakes (Journalism) and Charles Livingston (Mathematics).

Mathematics for Environmental Change. IUB. John Odland (Geography) and Maynard Thompson (Mathematics).

Mathematics from Language. IUB. Hans-Jorg Tiede (Linguistics) and Larry Moss (Mathematics).

Mathematics in Action: Social and Industrial Problems. IUSB. Paul Kochanowski (Business & Economics) and Morteza Shafii-Mousavi (Mathematics).

The Mathematics of Finance. IUB. Victor Goodman and Joseph Stampfli (Mathematics).

A Statistical Study of History. IUPUI. Monroe Little (History) and Jyortimoy Sarkar (Mathematical Sciences).

Statistics for Business and Economics. IUB. William Becker (Economics).

Techniques of Data Analysis. (Criminal Justice and Mathematics). IUB. William Selke (Criminal Justice) and Steen Andersson (Mathematics).

Index

Page references in *italics* indicate
information contained in figures.